Pacific Worlds

Asia, the Pacific islands, and the coasts of the Americas have long been studied separately. This essential single-volume history of the Pacific traces the global interactions and remarkable peoples that have connected these regions with each other, and with Europe and the Indian Ocean, for millennia. From ancient canoe navigators, monumental civilizations, pirates, and seaborne empires, to the rise of nuclear testing and global warming, Matt Matsuda ranges across the frontiers of colonial history, anthropology, and Pacific Rim economics and politics, piecing together a history of the region. The book identifies and draws together the defining threads and extraordinary personal narratives which have contributed to this history, showing how localized contacts and contests have often blossomed into global struggles over colonialism, tourism, and the rise of Asian economies. Drawing on Asian, Oceanian, European, American, ancient and modern narratives, the author assembles a fascinating Pacific region from a truly global perspective.

Matt K. Matsuda is Professor of History at Rutgers University, where he teaches Modern European and Asia–Pacific comparative histories. His previous publications include *Empire of Love: Histories of France and the Pacific* (2003).

Pacific Worlds

A History of Seas, Peoples, and Cultures

Matt K. Matsuda

CAMBRIDGE
UNIVERSITY PRESS

CAMBRIDGE
UNIVERSITY PRESS

University Printing House, Cambridge CB2 8BS, United Kingdom

One Liberty Plaza, 20th Floor, New York, NY 10006, USA

477 Williamstown Road, Port Melbourne, VIC 3207, Australia

314-321, 3rd Floor, Plot 3, Splendor Forum, Jasola District Centre, New Delhi - 110025, India

79 Anson Road, #06-04/06, Singapore 079906

Cambridge University Press is part of the University of Cambridge.

It furthers the University's mission by disseminating knowledge in the pursuit of education, learning and research at the highest international levels of excellence.

www.cambridge.org
Information on this title: www.cambridge.org/9780521715669

First published 2012

A catalogue record for this publication is available from the British Library

Library of Congress Cataloging in Publication data
Matsuda, Matt K.
  Pacific worlds : a history of seas, peoples, and cultures / Matt K. Matsuda.
    p.   cm.
  ISBN 978-0-521-88763-2 (Hardback) – ISBN 978-0-521-71566-9 (Paperback)
  1. Pacific Area–Civilization.   2. Pacific Area–History.   I. Title.
  DU28.3.M34 2011
  995–dc23

2011025055

ISBN 978-0-521-88763-2 Hardback
ISBN 978-0-521-71566-9 Paperback

CONTENTS

ILLUSTRATIONS

MAPS

Maps by Michael Siegel, Rutgers Cartography.

ACKNOWLEDGMENTS

A work of this nature draws on generations of scholarship. For their oceanic global visions, I draw inspiration from Epeli Hauʻofa, David Chappell, Barbara Andaya, Greg Dening, Deryck Scarr, John Gillis, Jean Gelman Taylor, Leonard Blussé, Oskar Spate, Geoff White, and many others.

In particular sections, my colleagues will recognize their research and influences. To name but a few, thanks here to: Brij Lal, Donald Denoon, Margaret Jolly, Patrick Vinton Kirch, Paul D'Arcy, David Hanlon, Washima Che Dan, Noritah Omar, Leonard Andaya, Markus Vink, Sugata Bose, Carla Rahn Phillips, James Belich, Tonio Andrade, James Frances Warren, Vilsoni Hereniko, Eric Tagliacozzo, Vanessa Smith, David Igler, Dennis Flynn, Arturo Giráldez, J. Kehaulani Kauanui, Vince Diaz, Lamont Lindstrom, Ronald Takaki, Ian Campbell, Gary Okihiro, Evelyn Hu-Dehart, Keith Camacho, Teresia Teaiwa, Allan Punzalan Issac, Damon Salesa, Takashi Fujitani, Jack Tchen, David Robie, Kathleen Lopez, and Jerry Bentley.

For their support, good ideas, and tireless patience, thanks to Marjan Schwegman, Jaap Talsma, Peter Romijn, Frances Gouda, Michael Adas, Al Howard, Bonnie Smith, Mark Wasserman, Don Roden, Christine Skwiot, Kris Alexanderson, Jeffrey Guarneri, Robin Jones, David Meer, Henri Chambert Loir, Amanda Kluveld, Mike Siegel, Ann Fabian, and Remco Raben. Much gratitude to Michael Watson, Chloe Howell, and Sarah Turner at Cambridge University Press. As always, Lee Quinby. This book is for my students and my family, near and far.

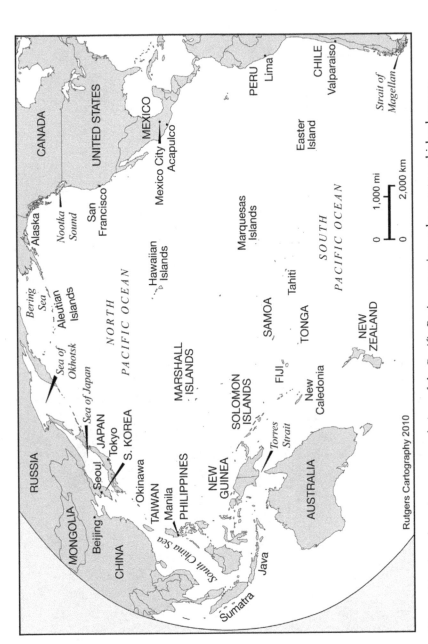

Map 1 Islands and continents: general view of the Pacific Basin, attention to key ports and island groups.

INTRODUCTION: ENCIRCLING THE OCEAN

What stories from Asia to Oceania to the Americas make up Pacific history?

Along the shores of Baja California, sixteenth-century porcelain from East Asia turns up in archeological digs, along with timbers and containers marking the resting place of great Spanish galleons that sailed with cargoes of treasure, silk, and slaves drawn from the Malabar coastline, Portuguese Macao, southern Japan, and the Philippines in transits from Manila across the Mariana Islands to the Americas.

Off the Malaysian and Indonesian coastlines stand *kelong*, fishermen's houses, raised on stilts of timber and lashed with rattan. They sit out in the waters, some within sight of the marketplace or the mosque, between land and sea on mud flats submerged by the tides, places for fishing and spawning cockles.

On the island of Tonga, a woman named Alisi contemplates her life. As a young girl, she dreamed of being a Catholic nun in her village. Instead, she met a man part Tongan, part Samoan, who had a wife and children living in Hawai'i. Alisi had two children with him and lived with her parents and endured the talk of the village, eventually emigrating to the United States and marrying an older man from Mexico with a residency card.

On June 30, 1997, the former British Empire sent Prime Minister Tony Blair with Prince Charles, representing the Queen of England, to Hong Kong, to sit on a stage with Jiang Zemin and Li Peng, the president and premier of the People's Republic of China. With great solemnity, the Prince of Wales read a speech and watched as the British and Hong Kong colonial flags were lowered. At midnight on July 1, the Chinese flag was raised.

In 2006, a new Auckland museum exhibition opened. Assembled by leading scholars, the interior space was a graceful dome that evoked the canopy of the skies and housed the museum's noted collection of Oceanian, especially Maori, cultural pieces in a technological environment: projections of waves for the visitors to experience, electronic winds and wayfinding programs against the carved prows of ancient canoes. The exhibition itself would also voyage, traveling to Japan, Taiwan, Australia, the Netherlands, and North America before returning.[1]

Imagining the history of Pacific worlds is not the same as locating the Pacific Ocean and then identifying the lands, littorals, and islands within its embrace. For Pacific worlds are not synonymous with just one declared and defined "Pacific," but with multiple seas, cultures, and peoples, and especially the overlapping transits between them.

This is a simple, but important point. The "Pacific" became a named feature encompassing one third of the globe after navigator Ferdinand de Magellan crossed the gigantic blue ocean in the sixteenth century as a legendary exploit of the European Age of Discovery. Yet, what if we do not first approach the Pacific in this way, as an immense space to cross? We might instead see it as a historical assemblage of smaller elements: interlocking navigations, migrations, and settlements within regions linked intermittently from the Philippines and the South China Sea, Sulawesi and the Sunda Islands, and the Banda and Tasman seas. The power of naming the "Pacific" imposed an encompassing European vision of endless water on the diverse particulars of Palauan atolls, the Eon Woerr (over the coral) of the Marshalls, the Japanese Nan'yo (South Seas), or the *moana* of the Maori and the Hawaiians.

The "Pacific" has been reimagined many times by historians, from tales of ancient voyagers, to Magellan's space of transit, to an Enlightenment theater of sensual paradise, to a strategic grid of labor movements and military "island hopping," to a capitalist basin, the key to a Pacific Century of emerging wealth and "globalization" at the end of the last millennium.[2] In a formidable multi-volume survey of a generation ago, the geographer and historian Oskar Spate suggested "there was not, and could not be, any concept 'Pacific' until the limits and lineaments of the Ocean were set: and this was undeniably the work of Europeans." This had been long true for conventions describing the peoples and boundaries of the great ocean.

In 1831, the French explorer Jules Dumont D'Urville suggested designating three regions of Pacific islands. One was the home of hundreds of distinct tribal societies and languages that flourished in jungles and mountain valleys, and across beaches from the Solomons, Vanuatu, and New Caledonia to Papua New Guinea. These he called Melanesia, for what he thought were the "dark" complexions of the inhabitants. Atoll and small island cultures in stunning multiplicity around the Marianas nearer Taiwan and the Philippines he called Micronesia. Islands from Tonga and Samoa to Hawai'i, Aotearoa New Zealand, and the impassive stone moai figures gazing out from Rapa Nui Easter Island became conventionally known as Polynesia, with related languages and aristocratic polities.

The names have stayed, been misused to collectively stereotype very dissimilar peoples, and have also been appropriated by those same peoples as parts of their own historical identities. *Melanesia* is a clearly racialized construct, yet it did not prevent the Kanak leader Jean-Marie Tjibaou in New Caledonia from organizing a "Melanesia 2000" cultural festival to assert the cultural pride of local islands. *Micronesia* may suggest "small," but numerous islands identify as the Federated States of Micronesia. Great canoe voyages from Hawai'i to Tahiti, the Marquesas, and New Zealand have been carried out by a Polynesian Voyaging Society to great acclaim.

Spate also readily extolled the achievements of Asia and the Americas, and civilizations from Aztec and Inca to Malay, Chinese, and Japanese upon the formation of Pacific histories, though maintaining that the great geopolitical space of islands and Pacific "rims" was "basically a Euro-American creation, though built on an indigenous substructure."[3] There is much truth to this. The Pacific as a named, comprehensive entity is historically European.

Still, there are other ways to talk about "the Pacific." If we begin not with the geopolitical "concept" of the sixteenth century, but instead with a multiplicity of locally connected histories, the picture can change. Such a new picture was most soundly articulated by anthropologist, writer, and scholar Epeli Hau'ofa, who envisioned the Pacific as a "Sea of Islands," reckoning not with a vast, empty expanse, nor a series of isolated worlds flung into a faraway ocean, but rather with a crowded world of transits, intersections, and transformed cultures.

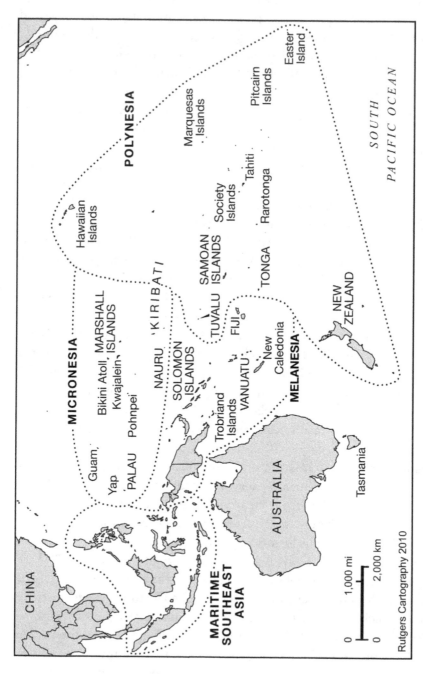

Map 2 Conventions and culture zones: Pacific states divided into Maritime Southeast Asia, Micronesia, Melanesia, and Polynesia.

He was speaking largely of the Oceanian – that is Polynesian, Melanesian, and Micronesian – domains. Scholars also continue to debate about whether such an entity as "Southeast Asia" exists. If we expand the Oceanian web of routes and voyages through time and space, we reconnect such histories with multiple ancient worlds that are in fact Irano-Arabic, Hindu, Buddhist, Malay, Indonesian, Chinese, and Makassan, joined by the mobility of people and practices, trade items, ideas, and beliefs.[4]

Here is an "Asian" Pacific constituted not at the moment of its naming, but as drawn together over millennia through local settlements, coastal waters, island provinces, and halting migrations as well as sweeping achievements on the open ocean. It begins at the Straits of Malacca in the way that a "European" Pacific does at the Straits of Magellan; eventually the both will overlap.

Such a Pacific is best understood in particularities, evoking the sea routes crossed by ancient Tongan exchange networks, the bustling port of Canton, or the factory ships of southern Japanese harbors searching fishing grounds around the Solomon Islands. Conceptually, such subjects can be studied as activities of a global trans-nationalism, maritime worlds defined by goods and peoples moving between islands and continents.

For our purposes here, however, "the Pacific" is better described as multiple sites of *trans-localism*, the specific linked places where direct engagements took place and were tied to histories dependent on the ocean. These are not sequential narratives of civilizations, countries, and nations. "China" with its millennia of dynasties, conquerors, and grandeur is not a subject, but the port of Canton with its customs agents organizing the trade of the world is. No pretense is made to tell the histories of "Australia" or "Vanuatu," but narratives instead mark the incarnated words of convict parties landing at Botany Bay or the shrewd negotiations of Melanesian headmen on the beach at Erromanga. The Pacific War is seen through the eyes of soldiers in Guadalcanal foxholes and islanders fleeing home villages, rather than dispatches of grand strategy from Tokyo or Washington.

This history is episodic, a collected set of characters and experiences that, taken together, define the Pacific. It is still, however, *trans-local*: the stories take on full meanings only when linked to other stories and places. Studies of "the Pacific" are usually divided by specialists of Southeast Asia, East Asia, Oceania and the Pacific islands, and North and South America. Yet these area studies say even more when they emphasize the interconnectedness of different worlds.[5]

The sixteenth-century pirate Lim Ah Hong is a colorful personage, but his exploits resonate globally because his marauding fleets tied the concerns of Chinese ports to settlements in the Northern Philippine islands and excited Spanish imperial dread. King Kalakaua of Hawai'i circled the globe, negotiated with European leaders, visited with the Meiji Emperor in Japan, and established ties with chiefs in the South Pacific for a federation of Polynesian states. The small phosphate island of Nauru became a protectorate of European empires in the nineteenth century, a Pacific War battleground, and then a detention facility for Asian and Middle Eastern refugees seeking asylum in Australia in 2001. The Pacific is startlingly crowded with such episodes, where local actors were pulled into overlapping circuits of struggle and ambition.

Such connectedness runs through Pacific histories. What oceanographers call the convergences of meanders, the current rings that form adjacent vortices and eddies, are constantly upwelling warm and cold waters from depths to surface. In 2007, ocean scientists in Australia confirmed evidence of an oceanographic phenomenon they called a Tasman Flow, a deep gyre that linked together the Pacific and Indian Oceans to the Atlantic across the lower southern hemisphere.[6]

Engaging such oceanographic thinking in history can be useful. Winds and waters are not mere analogies for historical movements: they have also been actors in the exploration, trade, marriages, alliances – and warfare – that have marked the peoples and civilizations of the Pacific, from monsoons and *voltas* powering ships, to fishing grounds and strategic harbors. The chapters that follow trace the tales of some of these peoples, from those who crossed straits and built cultures of taro, yams, and rice, surmounted by stone platforms, to those who came in ships to conquer with religion, trading goods, and mechanized armies.

The first chapters begin with an ancient Pacific, known through fragments, legends, and traces: the scholarly work of botanists, linguists, and marine archeologists, tracing Lapita pottery and seed crops. Ancient Austronesian migrations on lashed bamboo rafts transit islands and littorals that will become East Asia, Southeast Asia, and Oceania. Knowledge and trade from across the Indian Ocean bring Islamic, Hindu, and Buddhist traditions, establishing circuits of power among trading empires and coastal sultans.

Spreading outward, faiths and languages travel to the Philippines and east across New Guinea. In mid-Oceania, Tongan tribute systems of tapa barkcloth extend to Fiji and surrounding islands. To the north, similar voyages of trade and tribute pull island communities into the orbit of Oceanian rulers commanding volcanic highlands on Yap. To the south and around the coasts of maritime Asia come Chinese treasure fleets of staggering size, and then interlopers from Portugal and Spain.

In subsequent chapters, Iberians will assert claims with bases in Asia and with Manila galleons carrying cargoes from Canton and the Spice Islands, cresting the blue ocean by way of Guam all the way to Acapulco, tying New Spain to Seville, Mexico to Asia. Dutch East India Company traders arrayed with Bugis and Johore support will war and collaborate with Chinese pirate kings, and govern stockhouses from Batavia to Deshima, a miniature European outpost off the tip of the samurai world in Nagasaki, Japan.

In the middle chapters of the book, famed English navigators like James Cook sail with Polynesian erudites like Tupaia, and Samoan agents of Christianity debate the faith with Kanak elders in New Caledonia. From nineteenth-century New Zealand, Maori chiefs voyage on ships to London and Sydney, returning with new ideas of religion, agriculture, and stockloads of weapons. English and Irish convicts land in Port Jackson, Australia, and Makassan seafarers in the Northern Territories trade with Aboriginal clans. Colonial systems contract, coerce, and sometimes kidnap laborers from India, China, the New Hebrides, and Easter Island to work mines and plantations from Peru to Fiji.

In later chapters, coastal Indians in California struggle with Spanish missions and American settlers and gunboats look to Hawai'i and East Asia to fulfill a "manifest destiny." Korean dynasties and mestizo populations in the Philippines contemplate rising tides of nationalism, and traveling monarchs form Polynesian alliances.

In the twentieth century, a militaristic Japanese Empire drives deep into the Solomon Islands, New Guinea, Micronesia, and the Marshalls. Indonesian nationalists stake ancient Javan claims to contested Cold War territories, and anthropologists and anticolonial movements struggle over the meanings of "tradition." In the twenty-first century, political and diplomatic overtures over nuclear power, fishing resources, tourist economies, and political influence will shape the lives of women working in Fijian coastal towns, domestic laborers for wealthy families in Singapore, sovereignty activists, and the futures of entire island worlds.

From this confluence of narratives, Asian, Oceanian, European, American, ancient, and modern, a "Pacific" region is assembled, in parts and perspectives from multiple historical experiences. The connecting narratives are framed by histories of Southeast Asia, peninsular peoples of Malaysia and Indonesia, China, and Japan, and more are anchored in Australia, New Zealand, Polynesia, Micronesia, Melanesia, and Papua New Guinea, connected by movements of peoples and goods from the American coasts of North and South America. They move from tidal rings to deep gyres, across the deep historical currents of shifting Pacific worlds.

1 CIVILIZATION WITHOUT A CENTER

First they were sea peoples, they came in times that were legendary, passing along to the generations their tools, knowledge of islands, languages, and their tales. Many of these speak of ancestors. Keeping such histories is the work of their descendants. Some are inscribed in the Samoan poetry of Albert Wendt, tracing the bone flutes, the eel skins, and the sky-piercers of his voyaging grandfathers and -mothers. Others surface in archeological sites, where diggers of canoes and shell middens in the Solomon Islands or New Guinea unearth the remains of ancient settlements.[1]

More are pieced together in research laboratories tracing microscopic seed germs and separating out the codings of amino acids from bone marrow. Many are carried along in daily lives where children study the knowledge of wayfinders under palm thatch in Palau, and prayers to the Goddess of the Seas rise along with burning incense from cluttered shrines along the coasts of East Asia and the Indonesian islands around Java. Where do these many Oceanian worlds begin? Tales and traditions from some cultures trace origins to migrations from a legendary homeland; others say that they have always been where they are, having come from the earth itself. Remarkably, histories abound in the Pacific in which both are true about the same peoples.

Genealogies from the western Pacific from Fiji to New Caledonia tell which islanders are "people of the place," who first inhabited unknown landfalls. Fijians say they were shaped out of the moist damp earth and pulled up by a great fishhook. Tonga was populated by men

1 A time of gods and legends: A'a figure, Rurutu, Austral Islands.

tumbling from the sky and women rising from the underworld. Gods fished up the island of Tokelau, and then Tonga, where men brought women from out of the earth.[2]

Journeying among multitudes of islands large and small, and astonished by the presence of peoples everywhere, Europeans arriving in the sixteenth century puzzled over a water world of such remarkably diverse yet apparently related civilizations. Perhaps these were land dwellers now inhabiting islands that were in fact the mountain summits of lands that had sunk beneath the waves.

The tales of islands "fished up and thrown down" may not only be heroic mythologies. Some may be historical records of seismic uplift and the shifting of convergent plate boundaries in the Pacific, evidence for geological and oceanographic study. After generations of occupying stories of sunken civilizations, the volcanic instability of some islands can indeed have played roles in population movements, new settlements, and oral traditions of ancestors.

Mount Witori in the Bismarck Archipelago exploded with devastating force sometime in the second millennium BCE, blanketing a huge region with scalding volcanic ash and creating a distinctive stratigraphic layer over nearby islands. Archeologists learn how natural forces shape human populations by recording differences in land use based on evidence from obsidian tools and settlements after major cataclysms. Geohazard specialists calculate that in an archipelago like Vanuatu, particular islands may have disappeared three or four times in the last half-millennium. One called Mamata may have collapsed beneath the sea as recently as the late nineteenth century, forcing oceanic peoples with cultures, traits, and languages from different parts of the Pacific into refuge with each other. The tales of ancestors and material traces grow to validate each other.[3]

Both the earth and the sea have clues, and are actors in shaping histories and leaving legacies. Storms and seismic activity can pose devastating threats. In December 2004, an undersea earthquake and tsunami off Banda Aceh in Indonesia killed more than a quarter of a million people from islands, littorals, and low-lying coastal regions. A smaller tsunami off of the Solomon Islands in April 2007 washed away beach villages in Gizo, south of Honiara. Between 2010 and 2011, devastating earthquakes struck the Pacific nations of Chile, New Zealand, and Japan. A tsunami triggered by the latter sent surges across the entire ocean, and in northeast Japan itself claimed tens of thousands of victims in coastal regions. The nineteenth-century eruption of Krakatoa volcano in the Indonesian archipelago destroyed an entire island and created a tsunami of widespread destruction and legend, leaving tales in colonial registers and folklore in coastal villages. The ejected smoke and ash circled many times around the planet, altering the color of the sunsets in northern Europe, cooling the atmosphere, and changing the weather on Earth for many years.

Volcanic islands and subsidence also interested another Pacific voyager, the young English naturalist Charles Darwin, who formulated a theory of coral atolls and receding volcanic cones. He famously visited the craggy formation of the Galapagos Islands off of Ecuador, inspiring observations of diverse and differentiating fauna that would reshape theories of natural history. His work was part of a larger nineteenth-century European fascination with geology. Around the 1860s, British geologists studying sedimentary strata and fossil records claimed to find similarities between samples excavated from India and Africa to South America and Australia. Mammal-like therapsid reptiles and ancient seed plants recurred so widely that noted figures of the day, including evolutionary advocate Ernest Heinrich Haeckel, proposed a vanished world of submerged land bridges once linking the continents. He popularized the idea of Lemuria, a lost world of the Indian Ocean basin and the Malay Peninsula.[4]

Lemuria was discredited by later knowledge of plate tectonics, but submerged land bridges do form an integral chapter in Pacific histories. Darwin's contemporary Alfred Russel Wallace noted strong distinctions between large mammals like tigers and apes in the Indonesian islands and the very different marsupial and land bird species in Australia and New Guinea. He proposed that the distributions were shaped by historic changes in geography and environment. What is today known as the dryland shelf of Sunda encompassed Southeast Asia and the Indonesian islands, developing "Asian" forms of life, while the Sahul shelf encircled Australia, New Guinea, and Tasmania.

Wallace's widely accepted theory does not depend on legendary sunken continents. Rather, it came to correspond with a "Pleistocene sequence" of climatic cycles over millions of years. During the sequence, the earth would reach periods of "glacial maximum," when much of the world's ocean water was frozen in polar ice caps. As a result, sea levels were much lower, and greater surfaces of land exposed.

These fluctuations affected not only animal species, but human migrations. Some 60,000 to 40,000 years ago, human populations began to push south from mainland Sunda into Sahul, across partial land bridges now long disappeared. Still, despite the lower sea levels, much of this travel would have been by water across straits and between islands. Speculation suggests floating logs or rafts, and archeological evidence from islands not visible from Sunda indicates intentional drifting into the unknown. Tools, fishbones, and shellfish remains in rockshelters describe *homo sapiens* familiar with the sea establishing new settlements. Thermoluminescence dating techniques trace wandering bands to the Northern Territories of Australia, to become the ancestors of the Aborigines, and into New Guinea, where hundreds of local cultures and languages along river basins and in jungles and mountain valleys formed the basis for the Papuan-speaking world.

Ultimately, exposed dryland or littoral areas would once again disappear beneath the waves as sea levels rose with the melting of the polar ice caps. Sahul separated into New Guinea, Australia and Tasmania, each surrounded by deep seas. Set apart from Asia, Aborigines developed their distinctive hunting and foraging societies and the Papuans formed into clan cultures. These latter cultivated taro and root crops adapted to their islands, and are famed for evolving persuasive individual leaders that scholars have called "Big Men."[5]

Around the Pacific, waters rose. At Nanumaga in Tuvalu, local lore tells of a great house under the sea and divers map out submerged coral caverns with possible traces of carbon from cave fires, now lying hundreds of feet beneath the surface. Archeologists sample shell fragments and obsidian in the Sepik Valley, New Guinea, to read where mudflats, river valleys, and lowlands of cave dwellings have appeared and disappeared beneath coastal waters. In Northern Australia, Aboriginal stories tell of gods wreaking misfortune by walking through the lands of their enemies, saltwater flowing out of each footprint and laying the land barren.

Sea level changes across the Pacific brought challenges and adaptations. As cropping settlements were pushed back generation by generation, clans became more maritime, developing survival bases of fishing and scavenging the encroaching but richly diverse salt and mangrove marshes. Caves near the coast of Melanesian islands hold evidence of sorted catches in excavations of stone tools, and remnants of fish, turtle, and assorted bivalves and gastropods. Being pushed inland also, however, brought displaced clans into conflict with long-established peoples on the higher grounds.

The changes took place across generations and lifetimes beginning eight thousand years ago, but climatic shifts on such a scale are not consigned to distant epochs, nor are the impacts on human settlement unimaginable. In 2006, the peoples of the Lateu settlement and

Tegua island in Vanuatu were resettled with United Nations assistance as a warmer globe and rising sea levels made their traditional lands precarious, vulnerable to typhoons and flooding. On Tarawa atoll, families are increasingly pressed between a rising Pacific Ocean and central lagoon, to the extent that international projects bring sand in from Australia to prevent the beaches from eroding.

Tens of thousands of threatened islanders have begun requesting residency in larger Pacific states like New Zealand. The flats of Oceania may, within the lifetime of living generations, carry the marks of submerged homes for islanders in Vanuatu, the Marshall Islands, Tuvalu, Kiribati, and coastal island territories of Papua New Guinea.

Millennia ago, ancient peoples also followed the cycles of climate and population pressure to seek new homes, by choice or compulsion. While the humans who became ancestors of the Aborigines and Papuans headed south into Sahul, other groups from mainland East Asia continued to forage in river basins and alluvial plains. In regions like the Yellow River valley, camps grew into villages. Whether by the sprouting of discarded seeds or protection of food plants, early agricultural practices evolved. As populations and settlements developed and grew, animals like the wild pig were domesticated and millet, then rice, became staple cultivated grains.

By about 4000 BCE the ancestors of the Chinese expanded along the Yellow River to some one million inhabitants. Migrating groups also settled in the Korean peninsula and some pushed across the water to the Japanese island of Honshu. By the second millennium BCE the population around the Yellow River expanded fivefold and a dynasty of rulers known as the Shang kings recorded ceremonial and divination inscriptions on ox scapulae and tortoise shell known as oracle bones. The bones indicate that Chinese writing was already developed. Studies show that the Shang rulers established capital cities, and raised armies to expand into territories adjoining their own.

Perhaps driven by population pressures or political shifts, archeological records and intensive linguistic reconstructions indicate that another great wave of human migrations began about 3000 BCE. Raft crossings brought migratory waves of foraging, farming, and trapping cultures outward from today's China and Taiwan into island Southeast Asia and Oceania. Some transits involved migrations east toward the coral atoll and high island worlds of Micronesia: Palau, the Marianas and Caroline Islands. Around the Philippines, cave excavations turn up settlement evidence of similar stone adzes, shell ornaments, and shards of ceramic pottery. Venturing south, some of these parties divided into nearby islands. Across mudflats, swamps, and tropical forests, around littorals and coral reefs they built settlements, fished, and began to hollow out trees to shape canoes.

By their language and culture, they are collectively known as the Austronesians, and their global distribution is astounding. Domains of shared ancestry extend west from Southeast Asia across the Indian Ocean to Madagascar, and eastward across Oceania all the way to Easter Island, off of South America. A major crossroads of this east and west separation is the Malay world, especially today's Malaysia and Indonesia. From a period accountable only to oral traditions, linguistic and botanical tracings, and archeological reconstructions, villages built up sophisticated forest, jungle, and maritime cultures.

Lexical studies show that early Austronesians developed Indo-Pacific descriptions of the world around them, with words for coconut and breadfruit, and terms for the domesticated pig and stilt-dwellings raised on posts. Small bands in Indonesian islands hunted birds and fish, trapped turtles, harvested barks, and extracted resins from trees. The saps were useful as adhesives for binding tools, mending baskets, and making caulking and seals for canoes and rafts, along with medicinal and fumigant purposes.[6]

Notably, they were clearly seafarers, with elaborate vocabularies for the planks, carvings, masts, and sails of outrigger canoes. They also had ways to describe hooks, weirs, nets, rudders, steering, and drowning. Words were interwoven with cultures and traditions. Historians have noted that in a "water-connected" Southeast Asia, the words for boat and coffin are often interchangeable. Filipino chiefs were buried in *barangay* – a word indicating boat, yet also the smallest political unit of Tagalog society. In Makassarese poetry from the Indonesian islands, the sea defines men and women, and the union of husband and wife is "like two fishing boats / fishing together the big shiny fish."[7]

The lashed bamboo and stick rafts of early Austronesians gave way to the canoe, centerpiece of oceanic cultures as voyaging vessel, shelter, common space, and conveyance for spiritual journey and fishing. Trees for hollowing were cut under sacred observance and many cultures do not distinguish between trees and canoes in rites of respect. The one and the other signify the relationship of individuals and communities.[8]

As Austronesian-speaking peoples migrated south and eastward they crossed into the insular landmass and islands of New Guinea, encountering and mixing with the now indigenous Papuan cultures, some of which continued to evolve unique voyaging cultures. The descendants of the most famous today occupy the eastern tip of Papua New Guinea, Milne Bay and the islands of the Trobriands, Dobu, and the Solomons. In this circle of landfalls lies the famed Kula ring, a circuit of voyaging canoes sending shell arm bracelets and necklaces across hundreds of miles of sea among interdependent islands.

Part of this is trade, indicating local networks of commerce, as canoe parties move pigs, *pandanus*, pots, and reed baskets around the islands. But the Kula voyages regularly stand out in the exchange histories of Oceania precisely because they cannot be explained by economic motivations such as barter or profit. Rather, traded objects – of little value in themselves – acquire tremendous power by exchanging hands and passing from island to island, reinforcing political, kinship, and friendship ties.

The red shell disk necklaces and white shell armbands that make the circuit are male and female and move in opposite directions around the islands. Completed exchanges are regarded as marriage bonds. At designated islands, chiefs and Kula traders from across the regional archipelagos pull up their canoes on beaches and gather together to exchange tales, enhance the status of their valuables, and practice magical rites to ensure their success. Communities remain allied, individual leaders gain prestige, and traders employ supernatural invocations to define outrigger voyages that retrace the routes and draw on the powers of ancestral heroes and seafarers.[9]

As ancient Austronesian groups settled and pushed forward along the northern perimeters of New Guinea they also came into the Bismarck Archipelago. There, Austronesian and Papuan villages adopted, traded, and shared practices of seafaring, tree cropping, food preparation, and bodily ornamentation. In the region that would be later known as island Melanesia, biologies fused through intermarriage, and a "cultural complex" emerged that would become famous through a dentate-stamped style of ceramic known to the world as Lapita.

The history of Oceania in some ways depends upon Lapita – a ceramic pattern, but also an assemblage of theory, evidence, and inference, debated for decades and revised with every illuminating excavation. The storybook tale dates from 1909 when a priest, Father Otto Meyer, was establishing a mission station on Watom Island in an imperially colonized Bismarck Archipelago, Papua New Guinea. There, he uncovered some potsherds while building foundations for a church and wrote descriptions.

Over the next decades, archeological teams around the Pacific began to notice the similarities between numerous other pottery fragments that turned up at multiple sites, most notably in the Solomons, Vanuatu, New Caledonia, Fiji, Tonga, and Samoa, a remarkable sequence of islands from "near" to "remote" Oceania. The ceramic style was named Lapita after a major find in New Caledonia, but it did not remain just the name of a design. Rather it came to describe a seafaring, technology-producing Melanesian people with partial ancestors from the Austronesian migrations.

The Lapita people seem to have been coastal dwellers, occupying large villages of stilt houses along beach terraces or over lagoons. They cleared land for cropping, and brought with them domesticated animals, fishhooks, and stone adzes, using materials common from Borneo to Fiji. Their famous ceramics suggest extensive exchange with other islands for trade items or for ritual and ceremonial purposes.[10]

Some of the Lapita pieces appear to have human faces and figures impressed upon their surfaces. For contemporary islanders, Lapita can mean an incarnated connection to history through recognition and transmission. The Cook Islander writer and artist John Tunui reports being drawn to creating pots in a style that revealed "the faces of my ancestors . . . my memory of the bowls and the motifs goes back 3,000 years."[11]

Tracing the provenance of Lapita ancestors had long been the work of archeologists making studies of artifacts. In 1950, stunning news reached Pacific researchers that the chemist Willard Libby had determined the age of charcoal remains by measuring radioactivity. Carbon dating techniques revolutionized the science of archeological dating, confirming sequences of Lapita transmission across islands.

Later generations of researchers also learned to interpret clues in DNA sequences taken from rats and tusker pigs to study pasts and origins of Lapita cultures. Pigs are particularly valuable because they have been carried everywhere around the Pacific, serving as food, as prestigious markers of social and individual wealth, and in some cases as spiritual creatures with souls, critical to ritual exchanges and maintaining balance in the world.

2 Fragments of an oceanic past: Lapita pottery shards.

Molecular biologists in Vanuatu work with village chiefs, archeologists, and anthropologists to trace human and animal lineages at the core of Austronesian Lapita histories. DNA extracted from pig blood and hair samples is compared across a range of pigs from Hawaiʻi to Vanuatu, and wild boars from China to Vietnam. Working with chiefs and local cultural centers in Malo, Vanuatu, research teams construct a genetic corridor tracing the movements of pigs in parallel with Lapita evidence across the Pacific. Understanding the historical sites of pig domestication helps clarify the deep past of the Lapita people by reconnecting animal husbandry genealogies from coastal mainland Southeast Asia and the Pacific islands.[12]

What the Lapita story also confirms are the twin traditions of the ancient Pacific: that the peoples migrated from a distant homeland, and that they originated exactly where they are today. The Lapita were a voyaging people, but they appeared only when Austronesian migrations built new cultures with indigenous Melanesians in the western Pacific. This dynamic is especially true regarding the island societies that particularly amazed European explorers, spread across the central and eastern Pacific. They were the peoples who became known as the Polynesians.

Generations of scholars debated their origins, and proposed ancestral homes in Asia, the Americas, or Melanesia. Theories of diaspora and contact have been labeled "fast train," "slow boat," or "entangled bank," depending upon the likely trajectory of Polynesian ancestors across Asia and Oceania. The best evidence refines these views and their evidence to claim no singular origin. Though famed as navigators, the characteristic features of Polynesians were not necessarily carried from elsewhere, but may have evolved in island societies in the central Pacific itself. Lapita sites extend as far east as Tonga and Samoa, but at that point the transmission weakens, and instead new societies adapted over millennia entirely to an Oceanian world began to launch toward unexplored islands. More, original settlements may have been transformed by successive chains of migrations that continued to alter genetic markers now studied by DNA sampling.

What is clear is that once established in the central Pacific, Polynesians created a distinctive culture that extended by seafaring from New Zealand to Easter Island to Hawai'i, an immense triangle encompassing the northern and southern Pacific, from the equator to Antarctica to the near coast of South America. These new people carried the Lapita traditions drawn from Melanesia and Southeast Asia of fishing and root and tree cropping, but their pottery became simplified while other arts evolved distinctive decorative styles. Many tools and weapons were intricately inscribed to imbue them with spiritual power. These included the people's own bodies where sharp needle combs pierced the skin and dyed the marks with soot of burnt candlenut. This practice of tattooing, though ancient, became characteristically associated with the islands of Polynesia.[13]

Words like *ta'ata, tangata,* and *kanaka* for "man" across Tahitian, Maori, and Hawaiian languages indicated linguistically similar cultures, and the common training of *ariki*, or memory-men, to keep oral genealogies across generations developed as essential elements of spiritual and political life. A priestly order of teachers arose in Polynesian societies to

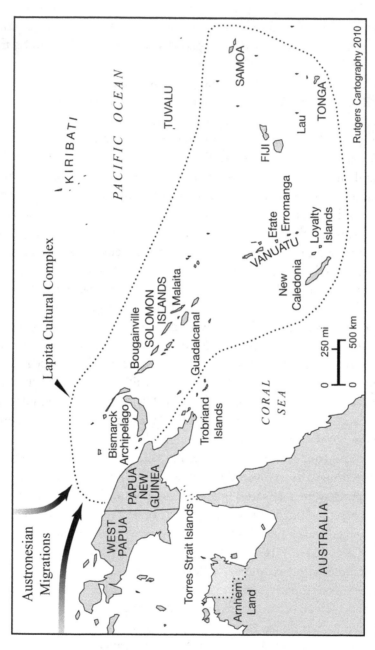

Map 3 Routes of ancestors: Austronesian migrations and the boundaries of the Lapita Cultural Complex.

assist rulers in negotiating the cosmic life-force known as *mana*, and the rules of sacred prohibition called *taboo*.[14]

Polynesian legends were filled with great ancestral heroes and gods inhabiting every feature of the known world. Melanesian practices of personalist leadership diminished in favor of hereditary aristocracies chosen by bloodline, and chiefly settlements ringed with wood and stone fortifications were organized around common ceremonial grounds. Most communities inhabited coastal margins where the sea was ever present. The ocean was not simply a blue expanse, and waters were distinguished between those inside and outside of reefs, and those that lay over coral formations, as the Thakau Lala empty reef of the Fijians. Different spirits or gods inhabited the depths and the sea creatures. Navigation and long-distance trading became highly developed for a completely ocean-dependent people.[15]

Polynesian Pacific histories are founded on an age of ancient navigators, long unknown outside the Oceanian world. When European voyagers came to explore the Pacific in the sixteenth century, they puzzled over and doubted the ability of any people, much less one without Renaissance sailing technology, to cross the open ocean and settle all the major archipelagos and littorals. Perhaps they were unintentional castaways, stranded by storms. What appeared not possible was that these voyagers may have navigated with purpose and by natural signs to create civilizations that would encompass entire ocean worlds.

Maori of Aotearoa New Zealand know that the sky father Ranginui and the earth mother Papatuanuku separated the worlds of light and darkness and that great fleets of voyaging canoes sailed from ancestral homelands to settle the islands they now call home. In the deepest part of the Maori ocean dwells Tangaroa, son of the creators, whose own sons breathe the rising and falling of the tides and whose waves can smash the canoes of men who do not bear offerings and tokens to appease the sea lords. Crossing unfathomable waters in the presence of shark gods and wind spirits, voyagers strain for navigational signs drawn from spiritual and natural worlds, "I will listen – to that long noise which rolls slowly landward ... we drift outward and back to the north; we saw the soot on the konant tree."[16]

Generations of speculation, and twentieth-century studies of current and wind patterns, voyaging routes, and computer models could not resolve the reality or not of the ancient navigators. It was artists, scholars, and cultural activists who saw there was only one way to offer demonstration of their voyages: build an outrigger canoe of the sort not seen in many lifetimes, and sail it with only the skills and navigational knowledge of the ancestors. So in 1976, somewhere out on dark swells, a canoe guided by the navigator Mau Piailug sailed by stars and a sea filled with signs and portents – colors, passing kelp, wave shapes – visible to his eye. He used a knowledge called *etak*, drawing forward his destination islands while standing still in an unmoving sea.

That sailing canoe was the *Hokule'a*, and as it sailed triumphantly from Hawai'i to Tahiti, a feat believed impossible without instruments, it recovered a legacy of voyaging that bound together distant islands. In subsequent voyages, the canoe also ventured far south to Aotearoa, east to Rapa Nui (Easter Island), north to the Canadian and American coastlines, and east to Micronesia and Asia in 2007, alighting in Satawal and in Japan to reinscribe a connected Pacific. These cultures had migrated and navigated for millennia, and had also always been the indigenous inhabitants of their Oceanian landfalls.[17]

2 TRADING RINGS AND TIDAL EMPIRES

That a reconstructed voyaging canoe from Polynesia should make a twenty-first-century journey to Micronesia to define the Pacific is historically fitting, for the water world of small islands and atolls had long played a key role in Oceanian histories. Archeologists have determined that Taiwan was a likely origin point for voyagers out towards the Marianas, and the indigenous language is a first-order branch of the Austronesian family that spread east. In addition, ceramics from the third millennium BCE seem to share common features with Marianas Red Ware and shell artifacts.[1]

Successive generations of voyaging settlers were original human colonizers. In the islands and atolls, Micronesian ancestors developed sophisticated trading and tribute systems and have been renowned across generations for their wayfinding genius. Navigator Mau Piailug himself hailed from Satawal and carried in him traditions of an epic heritage.

Micronesian heritage also encompasses the ancient authority of Yap, a high island surrounded by a ring of sand and coral communities. With low-lying atolls vulnerable to typhoon, famine, and drought, the Yapese rulers used high-ground political power and sorcery to invoke the power of gods and dominate an Oceanian trading and tribute network that some have called a maritime empire.

From the Caroline Islands, canoes came on a seasonal circuit. Many of the islands suffered from floods or months without rain, and entire clans migrated regularly in search of food and shelter, cutting *pandanus*, gathering bird and turtle eggs, and developing claims on reefs where fish schooled. Out of these foraging circuits developed trading rings, with island groups exchanging coconuts and woven goods and calling on each other to survive catastrophic storms or drought. Some traders offered valuables of beauty, red spondylus shell fashioned into exquisite adornments.

Following a circuit, these expeditions set sail from the eastern islands toward Ulithi and the ultimate destination, the chiefs of the Gagil district on Yap. As the expeditions moved from island to island, canoes and goods joined into flotillas of *pandanus* mats, coconut sweets, and sea shells. At Gagil, the chiefs surveyed the tribute of the Micronesian atolls and made gifts of their own: Yapese canoes, flint stone for igniting fires, and spices like turmeric.

As with Kula, the trading was attuned to material needs, but was much more a sophisticated reinforcement of political and spiritual alliance, an enactment of status and interdependence. The coral islanders brought their goods, and the chiefs of Gagil rewarded them, holding the connections together by invoking an authority to call ill-fortune and disaster on those islands forgetting to comply. On Yap, the chiefs used this power to create a ceremonial center, building up a compelling landscape of stone terraces and platforms for dwellings, orchard gardens, and fields for taro cultivation whose remains are still only being investigated.[2]

The island chains of Micronesia, famed for coral atolls and flat palm-fringed sandbars, seem scarcely locales for monumental ruins. Yet along the coast of Pohnpei, submerged around a lagoon, spreads megalithic Nan Madol, ceremonial and spiritual center, mortuary, and administrative city. Built from prismatic basalt with walls and huge stones quarried and floated into place, Nan Madol is hundreds of yards of seawalls, artificial islets, and passages built through lagoons. From here, according to histories shaded by legend, one thousand nobles of the Saudeleur Dynasty ruled.

Their influence extended out from the "other side of yesterday," likely the tenth century, when traditional tales say that two powerful holy men, Ohlosihpa and Ohlosohpa, had come from the west bearing sacred works and ceremonies. In the reefs off of coastal Pohnpei they and their party, assisted by island gods, built up more than ninety artificial islets of coral covering two hundred acres. The foundations of their city rested on columns of prismatic basalt, and unfolded into a priestly and administrative center, places for markets, and a vast set of enclosures around a tomb and funerary complex.

3 Histories in stone: the ruins of Nan Madol, island of Pohnpei.

Seawalls run across lagoons and canals crisscross the complex, with overwater and underwater passages. Later European travelers would declaim on archeological sights as stunning as the pyramids and as grand as an Oceanian Venice. To this day the ruins stretch across coastline and jungle, broken by the reefs and partially submerged by the tides, in striking interconnected districts visible on satellite maps.

As the Saudeleur amassed power, they came to dominate the entire island of Pohnpei, demanding tributes of fish and breadfruit, requisitioning labor to build their place of sacred power. Stories record the cruelty of the overlords and the suffering they inflicted. Local gods like Nahn Sapwe, who had made the heavens roll with thunder, were tormented and exiled by the foreign rulers. Fleeing to another island, Nahn Sapwe married a human woman who gave birth to a demigod, Isohkelekel, who vowed to return to Pohnpei with a war fleet to reclaim his birthright.

He kept his promise, but the Saudeleur proved a powerful foe with a well-trained army. Pushed to his doom on the beach, Isohkelekel found a champion with the arrival of the greatest of warriors,

Nahnesen, who speared his own foot to the ground, and refusing to move or let his troops retreat behind him, rallied them to victory. As the Saudeleur collapsed, one of Isohkelekel's priests cut a sacred tree that fell upward into the sky, returning as a floating canoe – the originary reference of many Pacific island cultures. In this canoe, gods and men communed to shape the new order of Pohnpei.[3]

The legendary history of Pohnpei broadly incorporates the foundational stories of strangers, gods, and heroes from beyond horizons, and the birth of a new Oceanian society. Some elements correlate with theories of Austronesian migrations from the west, multiple voyaging circuits across Asian and Pacific waters, and archeological evidence.

Much of Pohnpei's settlement history is known through a site called the Idhet Mound, where debris was recovered in support of traditional lore describing turtle sacrifice. The principle narratives, however, are embodied in oral histories, recounted and recorded by islander Luelen Bernart. Oral histories draw together variant traditions of tales and myths, weaving stories that not only relate the past but are themselves the very process of making histories. Their meanings connect the living and dead. The stories told by Luelen capture legendary ancestors becoming Pacific Islanders as they set out on their originary voyages.[4]

In Luelen's telling, a man, Japkini, builds a canoe for himself and many companions, a vessel with sails and a place for soil to plant food during a long sea journey. Reaching an island, the group establishes new lives but is also knowledgeable about exchange and return trips, sending the canoe with some of the party back to their homeland. Japkini and the others remain in the new world. Two women, Lioramanpuel and Lifaramanpuel, gather together stones and land to build over them, giving the island its name: Pohnpei – on a stone altar.

Great stones as markers of ancient civilizations emerge on other Pacific islands. Heading south into the Polynesian world, the trilithon at Tongatapu is an extraordinary sight, three forty-ton coralline megaliths built upon each other, an enduring tribute to monumentality. Raised sometime before the thirteenth century, and inevitably compared to Stonehenge, the actual meaning of the structure is not known. As portal to the kingdom it would have been the entrance to the royal gardens, a majestic extension of palm, hibiscus, and pandanus, enclosing the tombs of the kings. The megaliths are themselves carved with markings which the royal Tongan family has suggested are indicators of archeoastronomy, marking critical festivals, rites, or perhaps serving as practical orientations for a maritime polity.

Like Yap, the Tongan islands are famed for being the center of an "empire," or at least a powerful trading and tribute network across many island groups. Ancient Tonga was known for its complex family lineages and sophisticated political rule. The head of state was the Tu'i Tonga, who presided over a large royal court, numbering several hundred wives and concubines, brothers, sisters, children, and relatives who served as caretakers and food preparers. The court also had prescribed roles for *falefa*, ceremonial attendants, as well as war captives, family relations of low rank, and specialized craftsmen, including fisherman, carvers, and navigators.[5]

Among the principal activities of the court was to collect and distribute food and gifts, in consonance with the sophisticated obligations and duties of many Pacific societies. Chiefs held sway over *kainga* communities, whose members followed their directives to plant and cultivate crops from richly developed gardens for harvest and presentation to the Tu'i Tonga. The chiefs in turn were obliged to look after their people, and hear counsel from other men. Though perhaps resented or disrespected by some villagers, maintaining the status of a chief was essential, for the villagers' own lives were organized around it.

The more exalted the head, the more critical this could be. One of the early legends of the Tu'i Tonga relates a fishing journey taken by the sacred ruler. Coming ashore at a little island, he is recognized by an old couple who rush to prepare him a meal. He sits, however, under the leaves of a taro, the only food on the island, making it taboo. With nothing to offer, the old couple sacrifice their daughter and prepare her for the earth-oven. Upon learning this, the king departs the island in sorrow. Where the daughter's body is buried spring two plants – one kava root, the other sugar cane – which the couple present to the king. These become the bitter and sweet bonds that hold rulers and their people together through shared honor, sacrifice, and sympathy.[6]

The bonds remain sacred in life and death, evidenced by rituals concerning the decease of a leader, whose body would be washed in coconut oil and accompanied by ritual to burial mounds cut from gigantic coral blocks. Any attendant to the body would not be permitted to make use of his own hands for a period of ten lunar months, a practice that continued, if modified, following the decease of King Tupou in September of 2006.

The influence of ancient Tonga extended far beyond the immediate court of the Tu'i Tonga. In a great seafaring domain, called by some historians an empire, a formidable naval force of oceangoing canoes linked together Tonga with other archipelagos from the twelfth century. Trade was significant with Fiji and Samoa. With Samoa, the principal items were fine-woven mats, coveted by higher-ranking chiefs for their display prestige.

From the Fijian islands came woods harvested from the forests of the Viti Levu to build the enormous canoes bearing hundreds of warriors by which the Tongan navy connected the islands. At busy lagoons fronted by white coral terraces, the Tongan court monitored harbors with loading docks and canals that ran up and along the coastline. Relatives of the Tu'i Tonga met with crews floating koa and mulberry logs across the ocean to exchange for crafted articles of *tapa* barkcloth. Under the eye of the royal agents, traders presented incised Fijian pottery and clubs. Sandalwood cargoes were soaked and pulverized to create aromatic coconut oils, along with coconut-fiber cordage. Above all, stingray tails, whale teeth, and red birdfeathers were ransomed to decorate ceremonial spears and adornments of the royalty.

Whether an empire or not, the Tongan system of trade, tribute, and exchange worked like other Oceanian networks, intertwining trade with political alliances and kinship ties. The Tu'i Tonga sent lesser nobles to other islands where they intermarried into local dynasties. Some of the high-ranking Tongan women took Fijian husbands, and minor kings married high-ranking women from other islands, leading to the rise of legendary female rulers. The most noted is Salamasina, who united all of the Samoan islands under her sovereign rule later in the fifteenth century, and is revered for keeping peace for forty years. Her verifiable heritage was descent by marriage through the Tongan and Samoan aristocracies. Like many Pacific rulers, her legendary genealogy can be traced back to a goddess.[7]

The Central Pacific region encompassing Fiji, Tonga, and Samoa marks the general boundaries of the reputed Tongan maritime empire and also overlaps the easternmost sites where Lapita pottery has been found. One location, at the village of Nukuleka on the island of Tongatapu, has been claimed as the settlement site of Lapita ancestors who, over a millennium, would culturally develop Polynesian societies, including the dynasties that dominated the trade and tribute of the South Pacific.

Though uniquely evolved in Oceanian islands, Polynesians could still trace ancient kinship to peoples who dispersed and settled in island Southeast Asia. The Pacific is shaped by such overlapping histories. A reverse voyage from the Polynesian world traces Lapita culture back to island Melanesia, including the Solomons, and further back still to interactions between Austronesian and Papuan groups along the coasts of New Guinea and island Southeast Asia. In later centuries, European explorers like Abel Tasman sailed their ships exactly along these routes, from Polynesian Tonga to the Indonesian island of Java.

As Oceania evolved, so also did the Austronesian-speaking polities at the other end of the voyaging corridor. Migrating out of China, Taiwan, and south through the Philippines, the Austronesian ancestors developed deepwater craft and crossed south into Borneo and Sulawesi. Some headed east across New Guinea to form the taro, yam, and Lapita cultures in Melanesia with the indigenous Papuans. Some continued even further east to populate what became Polynesia. Others continued more directly south toward the islands of Sumatra, Java, and Bali. They settled among, and in some cases exterminated, the foraging tribal groups, bringing their larger village settlements, maritime technology, and their rice-based agriculture. Their overlays of culture, practice, and language have helped define an insular "Southeast Asia." In the Indonesian islands, these peoples became most broadly known as the Malay.[8]

The Malay world would be heavily impacted by distant contact with other great Asian civilizations of the time, especially in China and in India. After the fall of the Shang kings in the eleventh century, successive dynastic leaders called the Zhou controlled and warred over the Chinese domains for centuries. In this period iron and bronze technologies developed and the sixth century BCE saw the flourishing of classical Chinese philosophy, including the moral and humanistic teachings of Confucius.

By the fifth century, records called the "vintage texts" refer to the coastal Pacific outward from the China Sea as the Southern Ocean, and speak extensively of maritime trade, clearly with Persia and India, with some references to exchange toward the Indonesian islands in the south.

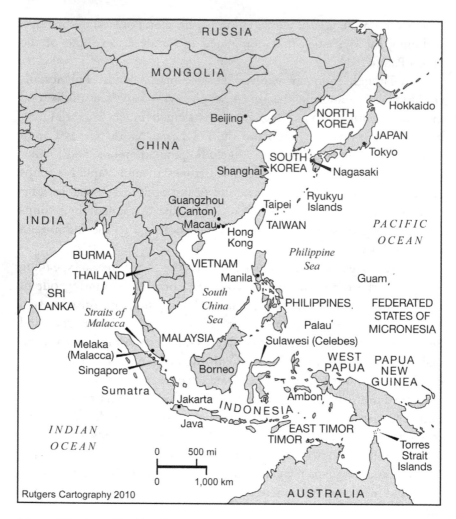

Map 4 The Asian Pacific: East Asia and Southeast Asia between the Pacific and Indian Oceans.

Strong rulers came to dominate. The King of Qin proclaimed himself China's First Emperor in 221 BCE and those who followed him, including Wu Di the "Martial Emperor" (141–87 BCE), raised armies to conquer or control frontiers from Korea and Central Asia to Vietnam in the south. This would be the era of the Han Empire, the historical core of Chinese identity. Wu Di is also noted for opening the Chinese end of the famed Silk Road that carried exotic wares across the steppes and deserts of Central Asia and the Middle East in caravans through trading outposts all the way to the Mediterranean and the Roman Empire.

On the Indian subcontinent, the early Indus River Valley world of the third millennium BCE was likewise evolving, here into an urban civilization with cities like Harappa, transformed by semi-nomadic Aryan warriors from the Afghanistan region. A complex caste system formed by about the seventh century BCE and the Hindu faith developed as a multiplicity of gods, rituals, and traditions. Hymns, praises, and philosophical and spiritual wisdom were collected as the *Vedas* and the *Upanishads*.

Around 563 BCE a northern Indian aristocrat, Siddhartha Guatama, was born and as a young man began to question the meaning of existence and suffering. His meditative practice and teachings gained wide followings and transformed him into the "enlightened one," the Buddha. His teachings quickly attracted converts, and the new Buddhists traveled widely, spreading their message and building monasteries and schools. The Buddhist teachings were carried by traders and monks into western China, and also traveled the Silk Road to the center of the Han Empire by the first century CE.

In the succeeding centuries, kingdoms were developing in Korea and Japan with royal courts strongly influenced by China, connected by tribute and trading missions. In the same epoch, commerce expanded in parallel along another long-distance trading corridor to the south. As coastal and littoral societies developed their maritime capacities, trade by water also connected the Arabian Peninsula with India and across Southeast Asia into the Indonesian archipelago.

This seagoing commerce flourished due to the wealth from extraordinary forests, where rare spices grew in the Indonesian islands – the only known such places in the world. Some of the cargoes were traded north to the Chinese Empire, but the circuits of the legendary spice routes were organized by Indian traders. One of the consequences was that Malay kingdoms developing in Sumatra, Java, and Bali were culturally shaped much more by exchanges with India than by emissaries from China.

The Indian give and take was felt particularly in political and religious organization. Millennia after the Austronesian migrations, Malay villages developed in clusters with thatched roofs and bamboo fencing, organized around terraced fields for rice planting and harvesting. Matted floors, utensils, and grinding stones surrounded daily lives of hunting, fishing, and drying rice in flat baskets.

Those by the sea often settled around inlets and mangrove strands where they would have access to turtles and seabirds and be protected from typhoons. Men out fishing or hunting meant village dependence on women foraging and gathering. Labor demands of planting and harvesting rice made all hands vital. Animal spirits, sexual signs, and fertility rituals charged the spiritual universe. Local village leaders had no dynastic claims, but were figures of unusual charisma and personal skill, able to gather followers and invoke supernatural powers to master rains, harvests, and natural threats. Personal status was all-important.

Some of these leaders took on roles as chiefs and began to dominate their neighbors. As the authority over larger populations consolidated into the hands of individuals with political talent, these nominal rulers – the heads of overlapping rings of allegiances – were interested in traders coming from the west in search of spices, bringing with them Indian textiles, gems, and pearls. More, the Indian scholars and preachers who sailed with the traders brought a written language, Sanskrit, and teachings from Hindu and Buddhist cosmologies that seemed to describe rulers endowed with sacred ritual authority, infused with divine presence.

Much of what India offered was appealing to local leaders, who exchanged and adopted some of the cultural practices into the Malay world. The new rulers patronized Buddhist and Hindu teachers, took up prayers and rituals, and called upon artisans to craft images of deities in bronze and gold. Statuary shows that some presented themselves as godlike bodhisattva, or commissioned images that united their own authority with that of the Buddha.[9]

In the later seventh century Yi Jing, a Chinese Buddhist monk, determined to make a pilgrimage from the Han Empire to India to study near the birthplace of the Buddha himself. Such pilgrimages were not unusual and Chinese monks were known for the decades they spent traveling to India, surviving travails and catastrophes, and inscribing and translating holy sutras. What was historically unique about Yi Jing's journey was that he did not travel overland following the general Silk Road terrains across northern China. Rather, like the spice routes, his was a maritime quest, launching on a Persian ship from the port of Canton, sailing south toward Sumatra, and continuing through the ocean lanes of Southeast Asia toward India. When he reached the Sumatran principality of Palembang, he described a world that is little known except for his chronicle and fragmentary evidence.

At Palembang, Yi Jing offers extraordinary details of a dynamic Buddhist center of learning that was part of an expansionist state whose existence was once legendary: the Srivijaya Empire. Here, the confluence of Buddhism and politics had strongly taken root. Yi Jing describes a fortified city, Bhoga, where more than a thousand monks studied ritual and holy scripture day and night, and he wrote in his diary, "Many of the kings and chieftains in the islands of the Southern Sea admire and believe in Buddhism." Those kings may have been wealthy as well as pious, profiting from their foreign contacts: the developing state of Srivijaya was not the classic Malay rice and village culture, but a maritime trading center.[10]

As it had absorbed trade and religion from India and attracted monks like Yi Jing from across the seas, so Srivijaya's growing authority rested upon control of coastal and inter-island networks spread around all of insular Southeast Asia. Founded about 683 and continuing to exert authority until the thirteenth century, Srivijaya grew from the Musi river basin in eastern Sumatra, where it regulated access to upstream trade in its own region, subordinating *datus*, or local chiefs, to a majarajah.

More critically, the Srivijaya rulers, notably the Sailendra family from Central Java, used their maritime power to control sea lanes around Sumatra, including the Straits of Malacca, effectively mastering ocean-going trade between India and China. By this they gained extraordinary tributes of ivory and gold, cloves and camphor, sandalwood and nutmeg. By the twelfth century, tributary principalities allied under Sailendra domination extended from the Indonesian islands to the Malay Peninsula, and north all the way to the Philippines.

Trade meant not only material wonders, but transfer of knowledge. As Buddhism flourished, both Chinese and Indian teachers brought their languages and literary epics to wider populations. Other traditions also gained new learning. The Taoist alchemist and philosopher Ho Kung remarked that Indonesian pine resin "cures ulcers and evil sores ... it clears up pus and removes wind," thus contributing to both bodily health and Taoist views of spiritual immortality.[11]

Still, Srivijaya's renown was its wealth. The riches of the polity at Palembang were such that the Arab geographer Ibn Khurdadhbih reported that the ruler would every day throw a gold bar into the sea. Perhaps this was a tribute to the maritime source of Srivijaya's wealth, and stories say that the treasure would be recovered and distributed to the royal family, military, and ordinary subjects upon the ruler's death. Some chronicles report that exotic rarities like plumes from the legendary bird of paradise also made their way to Srivijaya, acquired from hunters in New Guinea. The stunning feathers were given to Chinese emperors, and wrapped bodies with claws removed reportedly caused Europeans to later imagine that the birds floated throughout their lives, never touching the ground.

Though dominant across multiple trading regions, the Sailendra rulers of Srivijaya were nonetheless far from supreme, and maintaining authority over a maritime state required constant negotiation with parties that actually controlled the waters. Perhaps the best known of the majarajahs' allies were the *Orang Laut*, the sea peoples living in coastal or floating communities around the islands. Famous for their swift raiding boats, the Orang Laut accommodated local powers by patrolling waterways and collecting tribute – or protection fees – from ships, filling the roles of both police and pirates. Also valuable were direct alliances with regional chiefs holding strategic locations along estuaries or coral zones. According to chronicles, authority could be measured by the number of three-masted cruisers available to a local power; one region was credited with four hundred such ships.[12]

Sometime around the year 800, Sailendra commercial and political power was incarnated in spiritual form with the dynasty's own contribution to monumental architecture, later lost and recovered by colonial explorers. Famously, out on the plains of Central Java, they built a titanic unfolding Buddhist cosmology wrapped in stone.

At Borobudur, three extraordinary circular terraces sit atop six massive square foundations, all joined by gateways and some 1,500 carved relief panels. A pilgrimage site, the entire monument is meant to be circled level by level. Each step of the five kilometer cornered and concentric walkway is a passage through the life of the Buddha and the bodhisattvas. Galleries of bas-reliefs instruct and draw the pilgrim through joy, despair, and allegorical history, at the upper levels finally breaking free to a vista of perforated stupas contemplating the full measure of emptiness. Notably, the Sailendra did not forget the world that created them, for many of the Borobudur reliefs feature boats bearing the Buddha to his destinations, voyages of seaborne navigation and travel inseparable from journeys of enlightenment.[13]

4 Voyages of body and spirit: bas-relief from the temple of Borobudur, Java.

The Sailendra left their monument to eternity, but over the centuries rival powers from Java vied with Srivijaya for dominance in the Indian, Indonesian, and Chinese trade. A kingdom called the Singhasari militarily defeated Srivijaya and in 1293 attracted the attention of Kublai Khan, the emperor of the Mongol Yuan Dynasty in China. The Mongolian ruler had conquered the Han Chinese and is noted for his patronage of the Venetian traveler Marco Polo, who provided him with knowledge of Western states.

The Great Khan sent a huge invasion fleet to Java, but was denied conquest by the heroic prince Raden Wijaya, who founded his own dynasty called the Majapahit. Just decades earlier, in 1274 and 1281, the Great Khan had also tried to invade another troublesome archipelago – Japan. His plans had been wrecked by determined samurai warriors and fortuitous typhoons, which the Japanese called *kamikaze*, the divine winds. Naval power from China was not ready to dominate the western Pacific.

Elements of Srivijaya lingered but did not rule. Meanwhile, the Majapahit grew into a maritime empire throughout Southeast Asia, including the archipelagos and coastlines of Indonesia, Malaysia,

Brunei, parts of Thailand, the Philippines, and East Timor. By traditions of tribute from vassals spread across different islands, Majapahit chronicles also claimed rule over western Papua New Guinea.

Majapahit rule was strongest in the second half of the fourteenth century when Hayam Wuruk reigned, overseeing powerful trading and military alliances coalesced around the state, and a flourishing culture in epic literature, towering architecture, and gold and terracotta arts. This is the age which, centuries later, Indonesian nationalists would claim to define their glorious history and territorial boundaries.[14]

That history was marked by succession rivalries and conflicts across the fifteenth century, leading to political instability and declining authority. At the same time, new powers were emerging in the region. Some had been coming into the Indian Ocean as early as the seventh century: traditional traders, teachers, and navigators from the Arabian peninsula armed with a powerful new faith that challenged the Hindu and Buddhist traditions. Driven by sacred teachings, advanced scientific and mathematical knowledge, and especially by increasing control over the maritime silk and spice routes, bearers of Islam established themselves in entrepôts and trading ports across Asia.

By the tenth century, Arabic records spoke of the Indonesian islands. By the early fifteenth century, Malay rulers were hearing new teachers and gaining new trading possibilities, and Hindi princes were taking the title of Muslim sultans. To the north, new Chinese emperors, the Ming, were also finally ready to demonstrate that they could rule the seas.

3 STRAITS, SULTANS, AND TREASURE FLEETS

Iskandar Shah, the Sultan of Malacca, is today commemorated in a reconstructed royal palace with cast figures and courtiers attending him in royal splendor. He sits on a raised wooden platform surrounded by guards. The carved window frames and screens look out down a hillside where the hazy sea spreads away. That sea is narrow, a strait between the peninsula of modern-day Malaysia and the island of Sumatra. The Sultan's authority rests upon his control of a vital trading port, midway between the Indian Ocean with its domination by Indian and Arab traders, and the South China Sea and Pacific. The seas around Malacca are filled with merchants and tribute vessels, and by the Orang Laut sea people who serve as a patrol force, steering flotillas to shore for obligatory trade.

In its local history, Malacca (Melaka) is a powerful and wealthy city, spread across a river channel joined by a bridge. A palace rises on one side against the hills, while the opposite river bank is loud with activity from entrepôts, stockhouses, and trading companies. All year round, voices can be heard speaking in Malay, Chinese, Arabic, and Hindi. In its busiest years, more than eighty different languages and dialects from the Arab world to India and from Asia and Oceania will be heard in the streets and trading pavilions.

To the north, the Sultan knows, are his enemies: the Siamese Empire, ever struggling with him over trade and the control of the nearby seas. To the west, in the Indian Ocean, are the ports of Calicut, bringing magnificent textiles and woods. From the East, coming down around the peninsula, are his protectors the Ming emperors, bearing silks and porcelain. From them he receives seals to confirm his own ritual tribute to Nanjing, a tribute that keeps away the Siamese, who cannot risk open warfare with a vassal of the Chinese Empire.

At the Sultan's court in Malacca, the missions sit upon their knees on woven mats and carpets, resplendent in crimson threaded gowns. The Sultan dresses in white. He came years before, in 1400, as a young Srivijayan Hindu prince named Parameswara, struggling with the rulers of the Majapahit Empire and seeking to establish his own base of power. Parameswara and his followers attacked and overthrew the rulers of a Siamese vassal at Temasik – today Singapore – and ruled as pirate kings for five years. Siamese armies drove them out, and Parameswara fled to Johor, famous for its monitor lizards, where Chinese chronicles relate that he confronted fearsome, scaled dragons with crested backs, protruding teeth, and an appetite for men.

Fleeing both men and dragons, Parameswara's soldiers and retainers were driven to a coastal fishing village, a small cluster of sampans and dwellings pressed against the palm-covered hills. Here, as legend has it, a tiny mouse-deer challenged and scattered Parameswara's hunting dogs. Impressed by the audacious strength of the small creature, he founded a new city, naming his settlement Malacca, for the tree under which he sat. In this, he tied his destiny to the sea. Alluvial geography favored him: the straits channeled almost all maritime traffic between the Indian Ocean and the South China Sea within sight of his base. Control of this one waterway would give him power to rival, and then best, the Majapahit.[1]

As Malacca developed, the trading ships and cargoes commandeered by the Orang Laut carried more than the highly desired nutmeg, mace, and cloves from the Moluccas of Indonesia. Gold from Sumatra was also mined and traded along with pepper, as well as sandalwood from the island of Timor, famous silks and porcelain from China, and renowned textiles woven in Gujarat and Coromandel in India.

Down along the coast, among the mangrove roots and sandy shores, fishing villages sprouted with clusters of palm shacks, drying houses, and compounds of merchants in jackets of flowered cotton. Houses were built above the ground with pavilion roofs and floors of split coconut wood lashed with rattan. Here, among plank boats, Arab and Chinese traders waited, spreading out their mats and bedding, setting up cooking fires, looking towards the shifting of monsoon winds to bring in and ship out their foreign cargoes. Women and men offering services, companionship, or trade items could profit well from their goods, and also from their connections and personal alliances.

In the town itself, rambling street bazaars filled the eye with pearls and elegant textiles, rare woods, consignments of spices, and bird of paradise feathers. Wealth attracted Indian merchants, who brought teachers of Hindu theology, and Javanese artists labored to craft epics into shadow plays. Chinese traders brought the promises and conundrums of Buddhism, Confucianism, and Taoism, while teachers and storytellers regaled audiences with tales of legendary kings and near-mythical conquerors, like Alexander the Great. Gossip of court favorites and royal intrigues colored the atmosphere for the aristocracy and Malay commoners alike.[2]

One of the most pervasive and lasting impacts on Malacca would come from none of these sources. It had originated far off in the seventh century, when the Prophet Muhammad and his armies gained control of the Arabian peninsula. By controlling the ancient Roman and Central Asian trade routes with Arab caravans and armies, Muslim power spread east by trade and conquest, taking root in Central Asia, and coming to dominate South Asia under the Mughal Indian Empire by 1526.

The world of Arab trade was, of course, conducted both by land and sea. More than a millennium before Islam, about 500 BCE, early Arab mariners had already developed the shallow-draft, lateen-sailed dhow to ply the waters of the Arabian Gulf and the Indian Ocean. Voyaging that began at the Gulf of Hormuz also expanded to encompass the eastern coastline of Africa to Madagascar, and the Indian Ocean out to the Indonesian islands, the latter appearing in tenth-century texts by geographer Abu Zayd al-Hasan. Exchanges created very ancient knowledge corridors that extended from Tanzania to the Spice Islands, involving barkcloth, spices, linguistic patterns, and the elegant wind dynamic of the lateen sail.[3]

What brought oceanic voyagers into islands and the Arab and Indian Muslim traders into the straits and toward East Asia was strategic knowledge of nature. Prevailing eastward in the winter and westward in the summer, the timing of the monsoon cycle winds was the key to commercial power. Knowledge of the winds was apprehended in Roman Ptolemaic ports, but only exploited significantly by

5 For faith and commerce: Arab navigators depicted in thirteenth-century Hariri Manuscript.

Islamic merchants sailing in dhows along the coastline of East Africa out towards the Indian Ocean along spice routes for Southeast Asia. Muslim interest in spices was not merely for the wealth to be had from cinnamon and cloves. Aromatics like ginger and Sumatran aloeswood were also highly prized for their sensorial effects, to be used in ceremonies and religious observances.

Spices and other treasures, both earthly and divine, were collected in great entrepôts like Malacca. From the mariner's point of view, these were places of opportunity, and sometimes amazement. The epic seafaring tradition, built over centuries and thousands of maritime miles by Arab seamen, has been most singularly captured in the fame of Sindbad the Sailor, whose legendary adventures draw together heroic poetry, and Greek, Persian, and Indian epic traditions in cycles of stories from the eighth through tenth centuries. In seven voyages, the intrepid, often shipwrecked, Sindbad journeys out from Muslim Baghdad to encounter colossal whales like floating islands, landscapes of diamond and rivers of ambergris, and cannibal adventures.

Literary and historical reconstructions describe a far-ranging geography that encompasses the pearl beds of Serendib, the Kingdom of Mijraj, which may be Borneo, and cannibal islands resplendent with sandalwood, pepper, and coconut, indicating Timor, the Andamans, or Sumatra, where Sindbad is enslaved by an old man who rides on his shoulders, likely an orangutan. In different versions of the tales, Sindbad gives up travel, or is sent out by the Caliph of Baghdad, spiritual and temporal head of the Islamic world, on final voyages. In the end, Sindbad returns home to live out his days, wearied by the many journeys, but rich with tales of fantastic worlds, and wealthy with the treasure of his sojourns.[4]

Like Sindbad's multiple voyages, Islamic practice spread by trade, faith, and quests for new worlds to know. Guided by generations of seafarers who controlled the spice routes, Quranic teachers expanded the range of their teachings. The wealth, practicality, and the faith of the Muslims were adopted across the seas. The northern coastal states of Sumatra were strongly engaged with Muslim merchants from Gujarat, South India. More, the trading dependencies were reinforced by aristocratic and diplomatic marriage alliances. Fleets of small craft transferred cargoes and brides, and the two regions built closer ties.

The ruler of the Sumatran polity of Samudra accepted Islam in the late thirteenth century. He set the model by adopting an Arabic name and patronizing Arabic arts and learning, which were highly esteemed. He also took on the title of Sultan. The conversion was, however, less specifically Arabic than it was generally Islamic, embracing a faith that ran across merchants, traders, and teachers from multiple landfalls, ports, and coastal settlements.

Like other sultans, Parameswara married an Indonesian Muslim princess, took on the Islamic faith, and changed his name to Iskandar Shah. His title was now also Sultan, and he became the most notable head of a ring of Islamic ports and states that would be called the coastal Sultanates. His son also took on the Muslim faith under the name of Muhammad Shah. Coastal merchant princes followed the example. From Malacca, Islam spread through villages and towns all across the Malaysian islands.

Faith followed the trading routes so that not only commodities but ideas were exchanged. Imams and teachers professing the Qur'an grafted their teachings upon the ritualistic Buddhism or totemic plant and animal worship of coastal villages. New vocabularies and habits evolved. Settlements of Chinese traders and artisans were incorporated into service and provider work for a Muslim sea network. Except for the Hindu island-state of Bali, the main islands of the Indonesian archipelago were gradually linked together through Islamic villages, towns, and regions, to become the largest Muslim polity on the planet.

Like the adventuring Sindbad stories, Islamic teaching did not spread by scholarly erudition so much as by the preaching of charismatic teachers with glorious tales. Heroic Muslim holy men embarked on voyages in search of knowledge beyond the earthly, or were converted by miraculous encounters. Chronicles say that the ruler of Samudra, the first to take on the title Sultan, had been visited in a dream by The Prophet Muhammad himself, and upon waking found that he was circumcised, and could speak and read Arabic and interpret the Qur'an. The Sultan's astonished subjects also adopted the faith, with help from teachers sent by the Caliph. Holy men and scholars translated texts, built schools, and found alliances with traders, building a circuit of goods and spiritual literacy.[5]

This world of faith, exchange, adventure, and nobility was chronicled by one of the most famous voices in trans-oceanic world literature. Born into a Moroccan family of legal scholars and renowned as a traveler and chronicler, Ibn Battuta crossed much of the known African and Asian worlds in the fourteenth century, extending his sojourns all the way to Sumatra on his way to China. Traveling by sea and making frequent landfalls, he describes coastal tribes living in reed huts, women wearing "aprons of leaves," and entire regions with plentiful banana and betel trees but no religion.

He particularly highlighted where the riches of trade and Islam combined in the eminence of local sultans. Landing in Sumatra, he wrote of one ruler: "We sent him a present of pepper, ginger, cinnamon, (cured) fish from the Maldive islands, and some Bengali cloth ... this Sultan exacts from every ship that puts in at his land a slave girl, a white slave, enough cloth to cover an elephant, and ornaments of gold, which his wife wears on her girdle and her toes." The Sultan's capital was a wealthy city protected by wooden walls and towers.

Ibn Battuta also met another sultan who was a "lover of theologians," deeply committed to Muslim practice, and constantly raiding against non-believer enemies. But the ultimate goal beckoned. Catching a junk, Ibn Battuta sailed for weeks toward Quanzhou, Fujian province. Arriving in China, he was both impressed and dismayed. The Chinese arts and goods known to the world dazzled him, especially the silks – which seemed commonplace there – and the porcelain. The landscapes were beautiful and the cities compelling, but he reported that the world was alien and that he preferred the company of other Muslim traders and travelers. Notably, he recorded that the Chinese were infidels, whose temples and idols offended him. More, he did not accept that the Chinese "eat the flesh of swine and dogs, and sell it in their markets."[6]

As Ibn Battuta's chronicles indicate, Islam was a powerful linking faith from Arabia to Asia, but it was not based on an equality of beliefs, souls, or social standing. In fact, as it was adopted throughout insular Southeast Asia, the refined and higher status often ascribed to Muslims had significant appeal. Port residents who engaged in regular trade had significant exposure to teachers, literacy, and first access to imported goods.

As much as a faith, Islam came to denote prosperity and an urban life, distinct from the rural villages, rice paddies, and foraging. As trade expanded, agents, brokers, and keepers of accounts became new classes. The prestige of scholarly spiritual knowledge forged strong bonds with commercial growth and tribute.

These bonds extended to the very frontier of Asian and Oceanian contacts on the giant island of Papua New Guinea. The western half of the island faces the Indonesian archipelago, and Muslim sultans, especially at Tidore, claimed the Papuan world as part of their own. Some coastal island Papuans accepted the overlordship and were given honorific titles by the Sultan. In exchange for tributes, rituals involved the transfer of written letters from Tidore, whose inscribed words carried great material and even mystical power. The Papuan lords took on many Muslim dietary and prayer practices, but the adoptions were typically syncretic. They constructed local mosques, yet also often maintained many of their own customs and habits from the culture of the island interiors.[7]

As these overlapping worlds of homage and exchange developed across the southwestern Pacific world, key rulers like Sultan Iskandar Shah at Malacca were paying tribute to even greater powers. Much of what is known about Malacca in fact comes from Chinese chronicles and a visitor whose own name would become historic: the Muslim Chinese Admiral Zheng He. At the time Zheng He paid a call at Malacca in 1409, he was seeking tribute from local sultans and drawing together a series of maritime voyages that have continued to amaze the world.

In the southern outskirts of Nishou in Nanjing, China, the tomb of Zheng He (1371–1435) can be reached up twenty-eight stone steps that are divided into four sections with seven steps apiece. Each step represents one of Zheng He's voyages, staggering maritime enter-prises of trade and tribute that extended from China to Southeast Asia, across the Indian Ocean to Arabia and the coast of Africa. Zheng He's maritime exploits were not as a single explorer, but at the command of gigantic treasure ships and fleets of hundreds of vessels in veritable armadas that projected themselves thousands of miles across the known seas. From Malindi in Africa to Arabia, Java, and Quanzhou, he was in many ways the perfect expression of the multiple worlds intersecting. Over the top of his Chinese Ming tomb is the Arabic inscription, "Allah is Great," in consonance with his Muslim faith and background.

Born in an Islamic province under Chinese suzerainty, Zheng He's father and grandfather had both made pilgrimages to Mecca. Captured by raiders, the young boy was seized, castrated, and sent as a eunuch to serve the imperial court. At court, Zheng He acquired increasing influence within the inner circles. At this time, China was under the reign of the Ming Emperor Zhu Di, whose interests extended beyond securing the continental borders of the domain, warring with the Mongols, and exploiting revenues from farmers and peasants. Zhu Di also had global maritime ambitions.

Traders from China's ports had begun to assert themselves. For generations, under a politics of priority to land borders and invasions, China looked to supposedly tributary states to provide the maritime network for long-distance trade, as had happened in the Indonesian islands and the spice routes to India. But Chinese junks now began to carry their own cargoes. Maritime archeology uncovers the richness of the trade from wrecks across centuries. From reefs and shoals come bottles and inkwells, and bowls with pale green celadon glaze. Many objects can be traced to particular regions and kilns. Occasional underwater finds include kilograms of bracelets, ornamented jars from the kingdoms of Vietnam, bronze scales and gongs, crocodile teeth and tin ingots. Zhu Di knew from emissaries that such wealth and more could be acquired by trade and tribute exactions overseas, and he used his authority to build up a suitable naval force. For this, he engaged one of his most talented subjects – Zheng He – and made him admiral.

Zheng He was charged with the construction and command of treasure ships dwarfing any known craft of the time, and multiple missions between 1405 and 1433 to control the seas for Chinese trade and allies. Archeological pieces like rudder posts indicate that the greatest of the treasure ships stretched hundreds of feet long, had five, seven, or more sails, up to four decks, rows of individual cabins, watertight compartments, and could carry hundreds of passengers. The main ships were accompanied by a flotilla of warships, troop transports, supply boats, and special craft carrying horses, fresh water, and gardens. Navigators, doctors, cooks, and scholars were part of the crews, which numbered in the thousands. The fleet at sea was a veritable floating city.[8]

By sheer power, Zheng He was able to capture or destroy pirate and marauder fleets, and gained rich tributes, including rare glass and metals, sulphur, spices, perfumes, and cargoes of exotic hardwoods from as far as Mozambique and the Persian Gulf. He also was given a giraffe from East Africa, which he carried to the Ming court where it was revered as an auspicious *Quilin*, a legendary animal that had appeared at the birth of Confucius. Chinese maritime authority was recognized across the western Pacific, the South China Sea, and the Indian Ocean.

Zheng He visited, and as a result developed, major ports of tribute and exchange, including Ceylon in the Indian Ocean, the Indonesian archipelago, and the strategic straits of Malacca. Everywhere the treasure fleet appeared, the number of mariners, the scale of provisioning, and the flourishing of contacts meant new settlements, wells dug, fortifications built, and likely marriages

6 Masters of the Western Ocean: Zheng He's Chinese treasure fleets.

and new families with sailors. Some of the force would disappear at different ports; new suppliers and allies would become part of it. These places became the local sites of global oceanic and intercultural histories.

In Malacca, wells, temple grounds, and museums remember the treasure fleets with markers and statues. Malacca today is Melaka, a sweaty town of bridges and waterfront settlements crumbling against canals, mosques, temples, and churches adjoining each other on merchant streets. Rusted ferries and desultory harbors are circled by fishing launches within sight of glittering shopping malls and tea gardens. Street kitchens and stalls fill the air with the smoke of Chinese, Malay, and Baba Nyonya fish, rice, grilled meats, and simmered vegetables. Migrant workers and centuries of local generations occupy neighborhoods still infused with evening prayers, monumental architecture, and a collage of languages.[9]

A remarkable world was forged at Malacca. Iskandar Shah paid ritual obeisance to the Ming Emperor and exchanged gifts with Zheng He. The admiral's chroniclers report that the court closely followed Islamic rites and that the Sultan himself was splendidly arrayed in white cotton and green calico, textiles from local weavers and from India. He was carried about in a sedan chair through a handsome city framed by gates and drum towers, where sentinels watched over commerce – and threats – coming by sea. Iskandar Shah later traveled to China himself, engaging in lavish ceremonies and exchanges, and Zheng He's fleets made repeated voyages through the straits, bearing trade from near and far, leaving behind colonial settlements, and transforming world history.

The communities that grew from Chinese and local founders are in many ways the legacy of the treasure fleets. Trade with allies, control of pirates, and recognition of Chinese dominance through tribute were the principal goals of the voyages. In this the Emperor and the Admiral grandly succeeded, though their triumph was remarkably short-lived.

Political fortunes turned. Very much in contrast to the invasion flotillas assembled by Kublai Khan against Java and Japan, the Ming Emperor had little interest in overwhelming conquest, but he did demand subservience. Displeased with Vietnamese vassals, he sent occupying armies south, but was stymied and then driven out by the Le Dynasty. Along China's northern borders, Mongol power was also once again restive, calling attention to raids and skirmishes along the frontiers.

Maritime changes were coming into play. The Grand Canal, an astounding thousand-mile interior waterway stretching from below Shanghai all the way to Beijing in the north, was re-engineered at this time with new channels, reservoirs, and canal locks, thus reducing Chinese dependency on seaborne traffic. Most of all, Zheng He had exchanged sumptuous ritual tributes far and wide, but had not generated a trade economy focused on China that could support the expense of the treasure fleets.

All of these elements developed into locked battles between the eunuch household staff at court, identified with the Muslim Zheng He, and the Confucian mandarins who saw the voyages as wasteful distractions from the work of an agrarian peasantry, security at home, and moral rule by mandarins like themselves. Court officials believed that taxes should not go to pay for foreign adventures, and they placed little value on the offerings of barbarians from beyond China. The last mission of the fleets took place from 1430 to 1433. The Emperor Zhu Di had already died in 1424 before it even launched, and Zheng He passed away shortly after the last voyage. After that, the ships were brought to harbor and never sailed again. Some were broken up and others rotted at their moorings. Records are inconclusive; most were burned by Confucian officials wishing to erase the history of China's maritime moment.

That moment would be reconstructed five hundred years later by scholars, commercial interests, and government officials seeking to align China of the later twentieth century and a new millennium with a proud history of global trade, discovery, and cross-cultural connection.

That is one of Zheng He's legacies, for the Muslim Chinese admiral made a lifetime of crossing multiple oceanic worlds, carrying treasures and tributes, and leaving behind legends and temples. The Admiral's voyages also founded settlements that anchored generations of daily lives, joining the circuits of Arab, Indian, and Malay traders seeking China and reaching out to the Pacific.

4 CONQUERED COLONIES AND IBERIAN AMBITIONS

The Arab navigator Ahmad ibn Majid was a seasoned guide for bringing ships through the transits and ports that crossed the Indian Ocean from Africa to Asia. Born in Oman, he was a poet and scholar who wrote more than forty works, composed elegant verses, and compiled an extensive encyclopedia of navigational principles, star positions, accounts of seasonal winds, reckoning systems, and the traditional lore of sailors and other navigators, including members of his own revered family. He was a master of different rudder and sail designs and a student of compass bearings.

Maritime South Asia was a world he knew well. For centuries, Muslim trade had dominated, spreading faith and teaching along with cargoes of glass and perfumes, rivaling and bargaining with Chinese merchants, some in settlements and entrepôts left behind by Zheng He.

Ibn Majid's reputation as one of the great Arab navigators is unassailable, though he is often best known for something that he may – or may not – have done. On a particular voyage, Ibn Majid stood at the rail of a ship whose design marked it as distinctly not an Arab dhow, nor a Chinese junk. This boat had broad sails and a rounded hull, and he was pilot, by some accounts, for a captain he had recently met: Vasco da Gama. The Portuguese carracks, fitfully maneuvering the winds from the Atlantic and around the coastlines of the African continent, had come across the monsoons to the Indian Ocean on their way to Asia. Ibn Majid's actual role is unknown, but he seems to have met Da Gama in Malindi, on the east African coast, and he was recommended by the local ruler.[1]

Long active on the west coast of Africa, and spurred by the patronage of canonical figures like Prince Henry the Navigator, the Portuguese had slowly been making their way toward Asia by sea. The Indian Ocean world into which the Portuguese sailed in 1498 was unknown to them, but was ancient to the generations of regional navigators and trading powers who knew the routes. The new strangers seemed poor and out of sorts. They brought only some cloth, coral, hats, and brass vessels to trade for the fine textiles, spices, and precious decorative wares of Asia.

The furtive, first Portuguese parlay into Asia by sea would nonetheless open a new chapter in global history, for it not only heralded European expansion, but came at a time of parallel ebbs in Oceanian and Asian ambition. Along the Chinese coast, the Ming emperors turned inward to address continental challenges to their borders, burned the records of the treasure fleets, and ceded maritime mastery of the Asian seas to local traders and pirates. Around the fifteenth century, the Polynesian networks of expanding dependencies that had formed the Tongan seaborne "empire" became increasingly self-sufficient island clusters defining themselves with cultural and linguistic distinctions. The great transoceanic double-hulled canoes of the Tongans and Fijians pulled back.

After generations of voyaging, clans began to populate and grow dense within their own island territories, building insular dynasties. Marquesan groups evolved apart from Tahitian and Hawaiian. In Melanesia, local chieftain cultures evolved their "big man" practices of patronage and singular authority. In a century of monumental shift, the dominant Asian and Oceanian generations of expansion and navigation were occupied with local concerns just as European vessels and then fleets came to trade and conquer.

The new foreigners were centuries behind the great migrations and movements that had populated the territories and islands. From a European perspective, the wider Pacific was yet unknown, and journeys were organized around retracing or circumventing ancient patterns set down over millennia by Chinese, Indian, and Arab traders. The very mastery of the overland silk and spice routes dominated by Muslim powers across Central Asia was the challenge that drew the Iberians to launch into Asia by sea, hoping to secure claims to the cloves, pepper, mace, and nutmeg that were valued like silver in medieval Europe.

Da Gama's small force made it to India and bartered or extorted what it could in the name of "Christ and Spices," making little real impact, except to gain the pity and enmity of Hindu royalty. But Da Gama returned to Lisbon with stories – and evidence – of the wealth of the fabulous East. The Portuguese sent larger forces. On a second voyage, in 1502, Da Gama sailed again to India, this time with hundreds of men and more than a dozen ships, seizing vessels, burning local settlements, and murdering Muslim pilgrims and traders. He kidnapped local fishermen and butchered and dismembered captives. This time he returned to Lisbon with stores of silk and gold.

But India was only one goal, for the Portuguese were after the strategic port that would give them a stranglehold on all Asian and Indian Ocean trade. Following Da Gama's initial forays, Diogo Lopes de Sequeira sailed from Lisbon all the way to Malacca in 1509, seeking concessions for the Portuguese Crown. The harbor was filled with Muslim traders, many from bases on Java, and Chinese junks from the near coasts of Southeast Asia. The Sultan by that time, Iskandar Shah's descendant Mahmud Shah, was sympathetic to the threat and opportunities presented by the Portuguese.

A fabulously wealthy emporium, Malacca was properly speaking not a trading state itself. The Sultan commanded small patrols and cargo vessels, but did not have large draft vessels like warships. When Chinese naval power had dominated the region, the Sultan paid tribute. So the intrigues and stakes of dealing with the Portuguese were high. Aligning trade and power with the newcomers and their warships had attractions, but would involve conflict with the powerful Muslim merchants and trading houses.

Probable conflict was built into Portuguese designs. Malacca, as the Sultans had demonstrated, was ideally located to control trade between the Indian Ocean and the China Seas, fronting a narrow strait through which the commerce of the world had to pass, neatly resting at the geographical point where the monsoon winds alternated from west to east. The strategic value of such a port was unmistakable to the naval commander and governor of Portuguese India, Alfonso de Albuquerque, who saw little to be gained negotiating concessions if he could seize the entire settlement – and control of the waterway – by force.

War against a heavily defended kingdom was a tremendous risk, and the Portuguese awaited an opportunity. It came when the

7 The fabulous East: Flemish tapestry of Vasco da Gama in Calcutta.

Indian trader Nina Chatu saw the advantage of aligning his fortunes with the Portuguese. Working with sailors left behind from an earlier skirmish and expedition, Nina Chatu smuggled letters to Albuquerque detailing a scenario that led Sultan Mahmud Shah to execute his popular Prime Minister Tun Mutahir over an alleged plot to overthrow the Sultan. Though the plot was discovered to be false, the inadvisable executions of Mutahir's family – except for his daughter, the beautiful Tun Fatimah – split the subjects of the royal house.

With the court's loyalties divided, Albuquerque sailed on Malacca with heavily armed ships, threatened the Sultan with ultimatums, and launched his attack. The battle featured scores of troops, massive bombardments by both sides, and the Portuguese use of a tall-masted junk as a floating siege machine against the strategic bridge dividing the city. In the Melaka Museum, epic scenes of battle are captured in oil paintings as the Sultan's troops charge the Portuguese with war elephants at the palace. Portuguese prints in tandem show a resplendent Albuquerque in armor, leading troops over bodies and crumbling bulwarks.

Ravaging fires were set to the towns on both banks, and the fractured alliance within the Sultan's family emboldened non-Muslim traders who began to see their fortunes tied to Portuguese success. The brutal siege brought Albuquerque victory. His army plundered extraordinary wealth, tearing open storehouses of gold dust, silks, sandalwood, caches of aromatic resins, spices, porcelain, and bronze cast statues.

To mark the victory and protect his position, Albuquerque built the A Famosa gate and stone castle on a commanding hillside, and the Portuguese managed to retain control over Malacca for 150 years. From here, they established a network of trade, exchange, and influence, with ships and entrepôts stretched across Africa and the Indian Ocean, all the way to Western Europe and east to China and Japan.

Regional traders began to take interest. The Portuguese now controlled major stores of gold and precious cargoes, but Portuguese captains also became notable for trading technologies like the flintlock arquebus, and military commanders across Asia became keen on the advanced cannon and artillery of the Europeans. Craftsmen and local aristocracies also took interest in intricate mechanical clocks and timepieces, as well as mirrors and other instruments. Scholars responded to new and often unfamiliar treatises concerning government, architecture, and science. Books and documents meant access to a written culture to compare, perhaps favorably, with Islam or with Classical Chinese, and a sacred scripture based on texts.[2]

Even as Portuguese material technology, governing ideas, and Catholic influences spread, the base at Malacca remained insecure. Muslim Aceh launched repeated attacks, laying siege and even recapturing the city briefly in 1628. These struggles continued in concert or in alternation with battles led by the coastal sultans, armies from Johor, and the flotilla of the Javanese warrior Patih Unus. As they warred and skirmished, the Portuguese held their positions but also looked further east. They did not intend to remain only in their fortress city on the straits, for their aim lay somewhere beyond: to capture the legendary Spice Islands.

Spices had circulated from the Banda Islands through Chinese traders to Asia and had been carried to Europe since the time of the Roman Empire. The rise of Islam had seen the trade dominated by Muslim merchants, and the city state of Venice monopolized those connections by controlling maritime traffic in the Mediterranean. The Portuguese ambition was to circumvent that monopoly and establish another by sailing around Africa to Asia and launching directly into the tiny islands that commanded the attention of the world.

Those islands lay somewhere beyond the straits, past the trading ports of Sumatra and Java. The Portuguese dreamed of entire islands covered with trees that sprouted wealth. Those visions came closer to being realized when in 1512 the captain Francisco Serrão followed fragmentary information and took on Malay pilots to steer a ship from Malacca into the Indonesian islands. In Java he married a local woman, and turned north, reaching the Banda Islands, the first known European to find the long-sought route.

Surviving shipwreck, sailing on Chinese junks, and employing Indies crews, he became known and even respected in the region, trading locally and jousting with island warriors. Serrão ultimately signed on as a mercenary for the Sultan of Ternate. There, he became a trusted advisor and never returned to Malacca, one of the intriguing individuals who would abandon his former life to live and die where Asian, Islamic, and European worlds were becoming joined.

Malacca and known sea routes to the Banda Islands gave the Portuguese Crown the guaranteed passages it wanted for the maritime

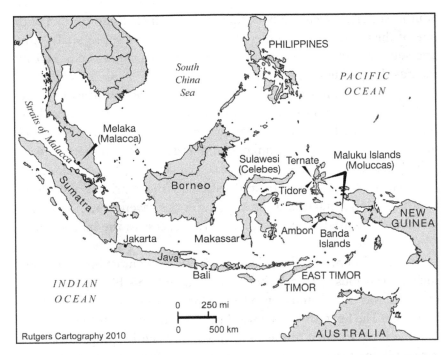

Map 5 Islands of Southeast Asia: attention to the Indonesian archipelago including the famed Spice Islands.

control of Asian spice and silk trades. More, those passages were nominally guaranteed by the 1494 Treaty of Tordesillas, by which the Pope had divided the world into Portuguese and Spanish claims with a north and south meridian through the Atlantic Ocean. In strategic terms, this meant that the Portuguese had rights over territorial claims realized by voyaging east following Da Gama's routes, and the Spanish by traveling west, following Columbus.

Ambitious Portuguese mariners wanted to reinforce Lisbon's claims to Asia by also mapping out a western route to the Spice Islands. One of these was a bold captain named Ferdinand de Magellan. Enshrined over the centuries as the man who named the Pacific, and the first to circumnavigate the globe, Magellan is an epochal hero in narratives of European global expansion, forming a trinity with Vasco da Gama and Christopher Columbus as navigators and "discoverers" of uncommon ambition and ability.

His exploits are well known. In April 1521, he alighted in the islands today called the Philippines, the first European to transverse the entire Pacific from the Antarctic tip of South America to the islands of

Southeast Asia. Welcomed by local chieftains, he fell into conflict with one of them and was slaughtered. A decimated crew, originally some 270 souls, returned to Europe months later with a cargo of cloves from the East Indies but only sixteen survivors.

What shapes these singular feats are the centuries of trade and slaving, cultural exchange and political conflict that marked the Asian Pacific. Magellan was not just a European with a bold idea to explore. He was a colonial commander who had served with Albuquerque at the conquest of Malacca. Having fought alongside his cousin Francisco Serrão and sailed in the maritime worlds of Southeast Asia, India, and the sultanates for seven years, he understood the potential of securing an untried access to the Indies from a westward route.

In Lisbon, Magellan vied with rivals to promote his project but such a hazardous approach, both untested and possibly a provocation to Spain, was of little interest to King Manuel. Magellan took his plans to Seville. The Spanish Crown was keen on having access to the Indies, and the Privy Council of the King was impressed by Magellan's navigational knowledge, and his presentation of a Sumatran woman and a Malayan slave named Enrique de Malacca.

Magellan had purchased Enrique, who was possibly a captive of the Malaccan conquest, during his service in the East Indies, and given him the Christian name by which he is historically known. For over a decade, Enrique was Magellan's servant in postings along the coasts of India and Africa. In a 1519 will Magellan decreed that upon his death, "my captured slave Enrique, mulatto, native of the city of Malacca, of the age of twenty-six years more or less, shall be free and manumitted, and quit, exempt, and relieved of every obligation of slavery."[3]

Magellan and Enrique were companions on the oceanic journey that went forward under the banners of the Spanish Crown. The ships under Magellan's command were beset by mutiny, shipwreck, disease, and near starvation. Upon navigating the storm-wracked tip of South America through the strait now bearing Magellan's name, the remaining ships came into an ocean so blue and calm that the captain called it the Pacific. But it was also immense, and for more than three months the ships sailed without provisions, so that the voyage's chronicler Antonio Pigafetta famously recorded, "we ate biscuit, and when there was no more of that we ate the crumbs which were full of maggots and smelled strongly of mouse urine."[4]

In March, 1521 the expedition was saved by sightings of the Ladrones – today Guam – and the archipelago of Saint Lazarus, renamed the Philippines. At every island group, the Spaniards called upon Enrique to translate but the Oceanian languages were unfamiliar. Then, upon reaching Samar and Cebu in the Philippines, all were astonished that Enrique and the islanders shared a tongue.

Generations of historians and storytellers have speculated that Enrique may have had origins in Cebu. Sold as a slave in Malacca, it is not impossible that he could have been from a Cebu village and been taken as a captive by marauders who terrorized coastal villages in the Sulawesi Sea. Raiders in prahu boats were known to sell hostages for servants and laborers in Southeast Asian kingdoms, and the networks of traders in spices and human cargoes were well established.

The evidence also has other explanations. The dense networks of trade and political tribute radiating across maritime Southeast Asia reasonably insured that Malay speech and customs would have wide currency among the rulers of the western Pacific. As Magellan's ships crossed into Asian waters, the peoples of the outlying islands did not comprehend Enrique's Malay greetings, but he was logically understood nearing Cebu, one of the dominant trading kingdoms of the Philippines. The port of Sugbu, where the Spanish came ashore, was a coastal emporium where Chinese, Annamese, Cambodian, and Arab traders bargained for gold and finely spun Lumpot cotton in exchange for silks, spices, and possibly slaves.

Rajah Humabon was the King of Cebu, with a Visayan title indicating lineages to the Hindu and Muslim empires to the south. He received the Spaniards in robes of purple silk, adorned by gold bracelets, seated within a wooden pavilion guarded by heavily tattooed sentries, the Pintados. Speaking with and through Enrique, he served his guests from bowls of Chinese porcelain, and entertained them with Malay dancers and drums and gongs cast from bronze.

Humabon and his wives listened to Magellan's exhortations of the Christian faith and converted to Catholicism along with eight hundred others. Magellan erected a giant cross. This marked the advent of Christianity in the Pacific and shapes Philippine society to the present day. The moment of conversion, however, involves a complex of motives. The generous reception Humabon showed his guests included blood compacts, and Humabon was quick to request

Magellan's help in subduing a rival chieftain, Lapu Lapu in nearby Mactan. The Spanish party could not refuse.

Humabon encouraged Magellan's overconfident plan to land in boats and battle Lapu Lapu with a small force of soldiers. Slowed by the tides and their own armor, the Spanish were massacred by 1,500 warriors on Mactan beach. Magellan himself was speared and killed. Lapu Lapu in the Philippines would by the nineteenth century become enshrined as a national hero, the first warrior to resist European imperialists in the islands. In the southern islands he is recognized as a Moro or Muslim hero, a figure of Islamic resistance to the Catholic Spanish.

Enrique's fate remains mysterious. After the massacre, he invited the remaining officers to a tribute dinner with Humabon, and all were murdered. The surviving sailors fled in panic and report seeing Magellan's cross being torn down. Enrique disappeared from the historical record; after years of servitude, traveling in royal courts and colonial outposts around the world, he may have found common cause with the Malay world from which he had come.

The Spanish did not return to the Philippines for fifty years, but when they did under Miguel Lopez de Legazpi, they stayed for three hundred and fifty. Ordered by the King of Spain, Philip II, to secure positions in the Pacific and find anew the route to the Spice Islands, Legazpi set sail from New Spain, today Jalisco, Mexico. Following Magellan's course and landing in Cebu, he advanced slowly north toward the island of Luzon in search of a developed Muslim port to conquer.

On an alluvial shore ringed by peninsulas and lagoons, Rajah Soliman built up a fortress of coconut trunks, anchored in mud walls enclosing *nipa* huts and the frame structure that was his palace. Like many island rajahs, he lived well with collections of porcelain and textiles, and maintained a forge for fashioning copper and iron. Seated in an area that had been the center of the ancient Indianized kingdom of Tondo, an archaic ally of Ming China, the population surrounding the rajah numbered some four thousand fishermen, merchants, traders, and cultivators clearing swamps and harvesting rice and tropical fruits, mostly Tagalog-speaking people. The Tagalog reference to a common regional plant reportedly gave the area the name "Maynilad."

In 1570, Rajah Soliman received word of strangers coming north from Cebu with a reputation for conquest. Marshall Martin de Goiti

8 Circling the globe? The Ortelius map of the Pacific, with Magellan's flagship.

arrived under Legazpi's authority with orders to have Soliman and Maynilad submit to Spanish authority. The rajah declined, and Goiti built up his forces while gaining the alliance of Soliman's rivals in the region.

Goiti attacked the city and Legazpi himself arrived to proclaim the Spanish city of Manila, in islands named after Philip II. Demonstrating authority, Legazpi made common cause with other local rulers like Matanda, who was buried a Christian at the Manila Cathedral, and Lakandula, who helped arm Legazpi's forces and gained favor as a district headman, collecting tributes and taxes. Soliman was defeated.[5]

Away from the chronicles of battle and intrigue, the world of the Philippines was very much that of the *barangay*. *Barangay* were settlements, usually along a river, littoral, or coastline, with dwellings spread against the banks, set upon posts, and thatched with palm or banana. Many place names were derived from terms meaning "where the water flows." In the *barangay*, cultivation and fishing shaped all life, but individuals also worked pottery or were called upon for spirit knowledge and midwifery. Basic foods came from wet-rice planting, fishing with rattan baskets, and harvesting of bananas. Fermented coconut sap for a drink called *tuba* was widely known and would become famous when introduced later in Mexico.[6]

Ships from the Arab, Chinese, and Malay worlds came through the island water worlds of the *barangay* seeking spices and gold, more often finding pearls, yellow wax, and hardwoods. The traders launched from Sumatra and Java, bringing Hinduism, Buddhism, and Islam, marking the islands with different faiths and traditions, built around temples and mosques, rajahs and *datus*.

Upon this, the Spanish imposed yet another culture, with settlements organized around plazas and cathedrals. Most were fortified by masonry walls and divided into designated quarters for different social ranks, ethnicities, and religious faiths. In design they incarnated the Spanish bureaucracy that ruled through a distant viceroy with parallel orders for civil officials and clergy. As they were incorporated under the authority of a Spanish friar, the *barangays* became pueblos and barrios, jurisdictions to organize colonial demands for goods and services. The Catholic missions filled the Philippines with missions, first Augustinians, then Francisans, Jesuits, and Dominicans.

Not all of the inhabitants of Manila could be so readily incorporated. Organized, and frustrated by Spanish impositions on trade, traditional Chinese trading communities rebelled against the new overlords. A first revolt came in 1574 in alliance with the pirate Lim Ah Hong and a flotilla of warships but was put down, with the consequence of the Chinese communities being relocated from the city to the Parian de Alcaceria district where they were concentrated and could be guarded by Spanish fortifications. Major violence also broke out about every twenty years after 1600, colored by conspiracy claims, and followed by brutal reprisals and expulsions.

During peaceful interludes Manila earned its reputation as the "Pearl of the Orient." Spanish domination spread over the archipelago through parishes and military commands, but the Asian character continued to assert itself through the constant interplay between the Malay, Muslim, and Chinese cultures, preserved by customs and advanced by commercial interests. The Chinese, most originally from Fujian and Canton, set up neighborhoods and markets with plastered stalls hung with fruit and dried fish, bolts of cloth, and jars of rice and oils. Some had access to the silk and spices coveted by Europeans. Porters and merchants with the familiar men's braided queue bore satchels and calculated accounts at writing desks. Gradually, mutual aid groups built school houses and rudimentary hospitals, and donated altar pieces for temples and also churches.

Immigrant Chinese men married Malay or Tagalog women, and some adopted Christian teachings, raising mestizo children who collaborated in business and politics with the Spanish. The native-born Spanish continued by legal and historical privilege to dominate colonial administrative offices and high positions in the Church. In an evolving society, the Asian and mestizo communities built the commercial economy and changed the cultural face of the Philippines.[7]

Political and religious dominance was by no means secure. Just as they reeled from Chinese challenges and struggled to accommodate mixed cultures and faiths, so the Spanish also faced continuing resistance to their empire from the south. As Augustinian friars set up missionary bases in the Lake Lanano region in 1639, fortified villages were considered essential to succeed in the "stronghold of heathenism." The conflict they anticipated would be with Muslim populations, established over generations by Arab and Malay seafarers, traders, and teachers.

By the seventeenth century, the best-known leader, defender of territory, culture, and faith, was the formidable Sultan Kudarat, a direct descendant of the religious teacher Sharif Muhammad Kabungsuwan, who had married into local royalty and established Islam in the Philippines a century earlier.

Kudarat watched as European settlements expanded into Muslim territories and Spanish power was demonstrable. In Kudarat's own region, fifty villages were reduced to tributary status and compelled to build churches. Kudarat was adamantly against submitting to the Spaniards, and Jesuits wrote of his scorn: "Look at the Tagalogs, the Visyans ... do you not see how any Spaniard tramples them underfoot? ... will you suffer just anybody with some Spanish blood to trash you, or that he seize the fruit of your sweat and labor?" Thousands of Muslim warriors rallied behind Kudarat's leadership and cut off the missions in Lake Lanano. The Spaniards raised the siege with reinforcements, but, overmatched, retired from the Lake Lanano region and would not return until the nineteenth century.

The battles, however, had just begun. In the 1640s a volcano erupted on the Davao Peninsula near Jolo and a terrifying typhoon struck Luzon. Following these portents, Muslim raiding fleets attacked Spanish positions, gaining some assistance from Dutch interlopers. Kudarat opened full-scale war in 1655 until 1668, with fierce attacks "so shameless that ruin was seen almost at the very gates of Manila." Monuments portray Kudarat as a determined, muscular warrior in flowing, Malay-style warrior dress, firmly grasping his double-pointed *kampilan* sword. Spanish forts withdrew their soldiers, pueblos were overrun, churches destroyed.

Some of the Muslim principalities consolidated their territories and political hegemony. Spanish authority in the south remained tenuous before expanding again. Kudarat's enemies had to wait a long time; he did not die until 1671, at the age of ninety. Even the friars who hated him could not help but admire him as a heroic figure, a fighter of higher purpose, as they wrote in letters: "He was a Moro of great courage, intelligence, and sagacity, besides being exceedingly zealous for his accursed sect ..."[8]

The evolving struggles for faith, community, and influence mark the history of the Philippines from the early *barangay*, Asian networks, and Muslim domains to the Chinese communities, and mixed populations that were reshaped under the Spanish imperium. Clergy and noble officials were rewarded with tax concessions and land grants in exchange for maintaining administrative order and providing religious indoctrination. Villages were enclosed into pueblos and land-lords rented to small farmers for cash crops.

What most specifically ties the islands to Spain, however, was the eternal pursuit of mercantile wealth built on long-distance trade. What draws Manila back into the broader history of the Pacific is less the transit that brought Magellan and then Legazpi to Asian shores, than the return voyage made by Andrés de Urdaneta, which brought him in a wide arc of Pacific gyre winds called a "volta" from the Philippines and across the ocean to Mexico in 1565. Conquistadors had already claimed much of North and South America. It was along the west coast of these continents that the Spanish staked their Pacific claim.

5 ISLAND ENCOUNTERS AND THE SPANISH LAKE

From palm-thatched settlements and sandbars along the Peruvian and Ecuadorian coasts, fishermen followed and revered the winds and currents. The ocean of the Incas was the home of Mama Cocha, protector of seafarers and source of the sardines, mackerel, and anchovies dragged by woven nets into reed boats. Whales were worshiped. Kon was the master of the rain and winds, and could be gentle or tempestuous, capable of rolling waves at sea or inundating the land with storms.

The sea and sky were places of the visible and invisible, and apprehending them meant life or death. From the sixteenth century, fishermen reported unusual winter seasons when fish disappeared and fierce storms battered the South American coast. At the same time, across the Pacific, rains disappeared and lands as far as Indonesia and India parched and burned under severe drought. In the twentieth century, researchers described a phenomenon in which irregular cycles in the winds and currents pulled warm water from the tropics to the eastern Pacific, diminishing the deep, cold, waters filled with plankton and algae that attracted fish to the region. As the fish migrated away, larger sea animals and human populations starved. More, the rising sea temperatures charged winter storms and unleashed devastating torrents and flooding. The phenomenon was called El Niño, for the birth of the Christ Child.

The inscription of Catholic faith upon the weather had a logic from the sixteenth century, for the Spaniards were developing a Pacific empire dependent upon oceanic crossing. That history would be impossible without strong knowledge of natural and environmental signs, corridors and channels of winds and currents. These included marking the doldrums, the terrifying places of nothingness where ships sat still as their crews perished in the sun, and a mastery of the wind cycles in which hot, high-pressure regions pushed increasingly moisture-laden air to convergence zones at the equator and back around to the higher latitudes.[1]

Calculated knowledge of these phenomena allowed Spanish navigator Andrés de Urdaneta to sail from the Philippines to the coast of the Americas by setting out from Manila and sailing north to capture the prevailing winds. His feat was not so much to make the crossing, but to demonstrate that a regular cycle of departure and return across the great ocean was possible, giving the Spanish Crown an inestimable imperial claim on what would be called "the Spanish Lake."

Urdaneta's voyage historically marks the beginning of the fabled Manila galleon trade that annually sent heavily laden treasure ships from Asia to the Americas and back around Urdaneta's "volta" of the winds. The aims of the Portuguese and Spanish were targeted on the riches of the spice trade and the wealth of China. By the Treaty of Tordesillas, however, the Portuguese already had claims to the favored Indian Ocean routes to the East staked out by Vasco da Gama. Finding another way to Asia had been the ambition of Magellan, and the Spanish followed that vision; their empire in the Pacific would be built by launching missions from colonies in Latin America.[2]

Key among these was the Spanish Empire of the south, especially in Peru, with its staggering silver lodes mined by Indio slave labor. When the conquistador Francisco Pizarro claimed Los Reyes – the city that would become Lima – as his capital in 1532, he was fully aware that just downriver was a superb natural port that would become the center of the silver trade. The harbor was protected by an extended peninsula occupied by an indigenous fishing community known as the Pitipiti. Renamed Callao, a settlement was built around a fortress and became a favorite berthing place for traders, maritime merchants, and pirates.

Callao is also tied to Pacific histories of even more ancient provenance. In 1947, the Swedish scholar and adventurer Thor Heyerdahl launched a raft from the port made of forty-foot balsa logs lashed with bamboo, following designs known from early coastal traders. Sailing with the currents and provisioning from squid, bonito, and other fish of South American waters, he and his crew made landfall on Rairoa reef in French Polynesia.

Heyerdahl had studied Oceanian settlement patterns and meant to demonstrate that ancestors of the Polynesians came from South America, and he underscored linguistic, archeological, and botanic parallels between the culture of islanders and those of the Inca, including the staple sweet potato and mythical traditions. The *Kon-Tiki* name of the raft in fact recognized the pre-Inca sun and creator god who disappeared from the world by walking out across the Pacific, never to return. Heyerdahl's work indicated that sailing and cultural exchange likely occurred between Polynesians and civilizations such as the Inca, though greater bodies of cultural and scientific evidence confirm originary migrations from Asia with the Austronesian expansion.[3]

From sixteenth-century colonial Callao, the Pacific was still widely unknown to Europeans. Despite Magellan's crossing and the Manila–Acapulco volta of the galleons, only general sailing patterns and predictable corridors were followed by most European mariners. Trade was known to the Spice Islands, China, and the Philippines, but what lay to the south and west across the ocean?

Scriptural traditions and legends decreed that the wealth of King Solomon was hidden, perhaps on undiscovered islands. Maybe Pacific landfalls were themselves only outliers of undiscovered countries with incredible wealth and legendary rulers. Key to these visions was the search for a Great Southern Continent – a huge domain at the bottom of the world with treasures to capture and souls to save. Finding that continent obsessed European explorers for centuries.

The conquistador legacies of Hernán Cortés and Francisco Pizarro fired these ambitions. The Spanish had, after all, overthrown the Aztec and Inca rulers in the Americas and captured their cities of gold and silver. In doing so they excited visions of wealth and glory, and also controlled the territories in Mexico and Peru that would be the key launching points for Spanish expansion in the Pacific.

In 1567, two ships set sail from Callao under the sponsorship of Governor Garcia de Castro with a mission to find and claim rich islands for the Crown. Chosen to head the mission was Alvaro de Mendaña y Nera, the governor's nephew, a young man of strong Catholic fervor and little command experience. The ships began in the wake of Magellan's famous trajectory, but then steered due west instead of north. As with the earlier navigator, Mendaña's ships managed to miss encountering numerous landfalls until sighting what is likely Tuvalu, and after three months sailing came ashore in a place he called Santa Ysabel.

Spanish rumors said the Inca Tupac Yupanki had known of island worlds populated by black people and filled with gold. The people of Santa Ysabel were dark but the villages were organized around root cropping, lagoon fishing, and pig rearing. They were hospitable, but had limited resources, and Mendaña's party, wasted from hunger and exhaustion, made severe demands on provisions and raised tensions. The mission had crossed an enormous expanse of water from the South American coast and was already deep in the Melanesian islands.[4]

Driven by phantasms of glory, and some trace gold from the Mataniko River, Mendaña built a small boat and explored the surrounding islands for months, naming them after King Solomon, but discovered no treasures and did not establish a colony. The name alone remained. After disputes with his crew and local skirmishes, he sailed north and back along the winds toward the California coast, making port in Callao two years after departing.

Excitement over the encounter with the Solomon Islands was marginal and it was almost another thirty years before Mendaña convinced Spanish authorities to let him make a return voyage. In 1595 he finally sailed with a small fleet of four ships and chief pilot Pedro Fernandez de Quiros. Within a month his ships came upon three dramatic islands rising out of the sea that he named Las Islas de Marquesas de Mendoza, after the Spanish viceroy of Peru. As one historian has described them, "Their shores fall to the sea in giant cliffs which are broken by the deep rifts of valleys . . . a man standing against the sky is always startling."[5]

Around the bluffs, canoes and boats quickly appeared and disappeared. Men fished in the bays and women pulled shellfish from rocks and tidal pools. Remarkably, accounts of Mendaña's trip to the Solomons and now the encounter with the Marquesas are among the first written records of Oceanian peoples – in both Melanesia and Polynesia – since their ancient dispersion dating from the Austronesian migrations.

Quiros' journal shows admiration for the warriors and the beauty of their fine bodies, and the islanders were likely equally astonished by the strangers. Hundreds swarmed the ships in curiosity, and then took whatever they could, leading to the Spanish drawing their weapons and firing guns. The islanders responded with spears and stones and an estimated two hundred island lives were lost.

Each party tried to make sense of the other. For the Spanish, the Marquesan peoples might have been lost tribes of a biblical race, or the primitive survivors of an ancient sunken continent. For the islanders, they themselves were the *Enata*, "the men" of the land, and the strangers might have been enemies from other islands, or returning ancestors bearing gifts. To be sure, the worlds did not yet overlap. The Spaniards came with the institutional fervor of Catholicism, and the avarice of zealous empire builders. The Enata lived in a universe of sacred power. Plants and animals had dozens of names and uses. The world itself was built of stone and earth, shell, wood, and plant fiber, coral, bone, and bird feathers.

For the Enata, complex *tapus* or taboos ruled over bonito, squid, or turtle for food; leaves that shaded men's heads should not be touched; the person of a *hakaʻiki* lord was inviolable. Power came from ancestral lines and the ability to recite the names of all those who had come before directly back to the gods. For the Spaniards, it was a savage and innocent world, ripe for Christian conversion. Quiros openly lamented that the "fair creatures" he saw would be "left to go to perdition."

Beyond such chronicles, what can be known of the Enata comes through material histories and studies and archeological sites, a record of a dynamic political and spiritual sophistication. Houses were raised on stone platforms along waterlines or near groves of breadfruit and paper mulberry trees. Ranks and wealth were indicated by access to sleeping houses and cooking shelters, and materialized in the colors and textures of building materials. Power was shared by the hakaʻiki chiefs, priests, and warriors adorned with ear plugs and hair spools.

Basalt adzes from neighboring island groups indicate ocean voyage exchanges of tools and weapons that begin to fall away in the fifteenth century. Bone heaps indicate diminishing bird and sea mammal prey across generations and the gradual domestication of agriculture and wild pigs. When Quiros and Mendaña crossed their waters, Eastern Polynesian societies were becoming strongly hierarchical and centrally organized.

9 Strangers and sacred power: tattooed man in the Marquesas Islands.

Quiros may have seen a savage world in need of salvation, yet for the Enata it was a time of monumental building, growing populations, and competition between the hereditary elites, priests, and warriors for distinction. The mountainscapes were marked by ridgetop fortifications, dance and feast structures, and leveled terraces for ceremonial centers. These indicated a world of local strife and territorial aggression, but also a classical flourishing of stone architecture and craft specialization, particularly anthropomorphic statues.[6]

Of this, Mendaña and Quiros knew little, continuing their western passage from the Marquesas until sighting and landing on Santa Cruz island, having sailed once again to Melanesia. Epidemiology plays a role here, for within a month, almost fifty of Mendaña's crew died of tropical fevers, probably malaria, and Mendaña himself shortly also succumbed.

Quiros took over command of the expedition, made notes on islanders, their canoes, and ceremonial stone platforms, then made sail again, recording and naming local landfalls, until making shore in May 1606 at a place he called Espiritu Santo. He was in islands later called the New Hebrides, now comprising the nation of Vanuatu.

Looking out across the beach, Quiros' ships came creaking from a world of monotheistic fervor, elevated by royal patronage and exalted by the Holy Spirit. Conquest of both territories and souls was Quiros' calling. He had been born in 1565 in Evora and schooled in Lisbon. The territory of his family was the Piedro, an outer hinterland known for Extremadura peasants and rude, pagan savages. Radical Franciscans were filled with millenarian fervor and Quiros carried his chivalric code and pious determination with him to the Pacific, leading him to declare Vanuatu the New Jerusalem under the Order of the Holy Cross.

The New Jerusalem Quiros dreamed of was to be a grand city with doors carved from marble and plazas outlining the shape of the cross. He had read Sir Thomas More's *Utopia* and entertained grandiose visions, though his critics would later liken him more to an Oceanian Don Quixote, vaguely delusional.

The New Jerusalem of Quiros may in fact have had some elements of an earthly paradise. Archeological evidence suggests that early settlers arrived in canoes bearing pigs, and found shelter along rock outcroppings and in caves. Clans survived on root crops and shellfish harvested from the ocean and rivers. They may have been pushed by clan expansions and quests for fishing territories, or drawn by trade, as Lapita pottery was part of their culture. In the centuries before European contact, oral traditions also tell of volcanoes that shattered local islands, and more canoe voyages. It was a constantly evolving society marked by secondary waves of migration defining Melanesian cultural traits from Vanuatu to Fiji.

Across the Vanuatu chain, groups developed sophisticated rites and practices, and men gained status by slaughtering pigs. Women on some islands pounded bark cloth, and dyed mats or painted their faces. Quiros described Espiritu Santo as a land populated by rival, suspicious tribes, and was impatient with attempts to prevent him from claiming what he considered a part of the Great Southern Continent. Pitched battles with Vanuatuan warriors led to bloodshed and wrecked his hopes of conversion, though later missionaries from an array of competing churches would make Vanuatu one of the most Christian societies in the Pacific.

Still, Quiros claimed the lands for Spain and appointed officials to govern his unbuilt New Jerusalem. He also established his baroque Order of the Holy Ghost by issuing crosses and decorations to soldiers, clergy, and servants alike. An aged Fray Martin commented on the "diversity of knights ... negro-knights and Indian-knights and knights who were knight-knights." On making little headway establishing the colony, Quiros abandoned the islands and European contact fell away for another 168 years. What the party had sought was not there, and Vanuatu was not the Great Southern Continent.[7]

Quiros followed the winds and returned to Spanish authority in the Mexican port of Acapulco. His second-in-command, Luis Váez de Torres, captained a second ship that separated from Quiros and ended up sailing between Australia and New Guinea through a strait that now bears his name. He ended up in Manila; they were at the two Pacific ends of the transoceanic Spanish galleon trade. Quiros never got another mission.

The Quiros story illustrates the minds and motives of the Spanish explorers coming into contact with Polynesia and Melanesia. Islander societies are largely known through archeological study and oral traditions. The burial site of Roy Mata, a legendary ruler on Retoka Island near Efate, gives insight into a coeval Vanuatuan world. By custom, laborers working on Retoka Island will not sleep there after darkness falls, and tradition says that Roy Mata was laid to rest along with many kin and clan members who were buried alive.

Historically, he is known as an Efate chief who used his personal power to end a brutal conflict known as the Takarua War, sometime around four hundred years ago. In a series of ceremonial rituals, he compelled warring peoples to lay down arms, meet in peace, and exchange symbols that allowed holders safe passage and protection even in the territory of enemies. For this, Roy Mata gained a mythical reputation. He was, however, undone by his own jealous brother, who struck him with a poison dart. In death, he was reportedly borne by a great party of mourners through coral lava tunnels to the underworld and, following legendary practice, interred along with living men and women.

In 1967 the French archeologist José Garanger secured permission from local chiefs to search for Roy Mata's burial place and try to confirm oral traditions. Piecing together stories and traces, his teams mapped out a site and began to dig. They uncovered skeletal remains ornamented with pig tusk bracelets, and shell bands and beads. Some were men and some were women. They also found a remarkable key figure adorned with high-status ovula and spondylus bracelets.

The chiefly body was surrounded by other bodies and all were laid out over a large area of hard-packed earth that had been buried along with dance ornaments. The entire tableau seemed to be like a feast or celebration in which the participants had fallen or been cast down. Some bodies were alone, others in couples. Almost fifty were uncovered, many in positions indicative of being buried alive. Piles of bones and limbs were strewn about.[8]

Whether this was Roy Mata remains inconclusive, but the evidence of oral traditions and archeology outline a history of legendary rule, sacred power, and ritual death in the 1600s. These give one reconstruction of a Vanuatuan island society in the epoch that Spanish chronicles relate Quiros' visit to Espiritu Santo. As around Oceania, political organization was becoming complex and often localized. Groups communicated and paid tribute across archipelagos, but major migrations diminished. At the same time, long-distance voyages were increasingly taken up by crews of Europeans.

The general contours of the Pacific were becoming known to Europeans, as Asian islands and archipelagos had been known to Chinese, Arab, and Malay navigators radiating out from wealthy trading harbors and brackish mangrove littorals. Seafarers flying many colors regularly circulated between the domains of coastal sultans,

Portuguese and Spanish entrepôts, Chinese tributary markets, and on from the Spice Islands to Manila for the galleon trade to the Americas. Spanish visionaries made their fitful meanderings with Mendaña and Quiros to the Solomons, Vanuatu, and the Marquesas.

Yet Hawai'i was not known to these newer voyagers, and the Maori of Aotearoa New Zealand had not yet encountered European strangers. Most of middle Oceania, from Fiji and Tonga, to Samoa and Tahiti were not recorded on paper maps and charts. The southern and western coasts of Australia were mysteries to Europe, perhaps still holding the promise of the Great Southern Continent.

For generations, this did not change. Decisively, new energies developed instead in Asia from struggles taking place within Europe. In 1580 the King of Portugal died and the Spanish Crown claimed a united rule over the Iberian peninsula. The Lisbon East Indies trade was cut off for Dutch traders, who exploded into rebellion. In 1588, the Dutch and English were at war with Spain, and the Spanish Armada disaster off the English coast marked the decline of Spanish influence and the Spanish Lake.

In 1595 the Dutch captain Cornelis de Houtman was already sailing toward the Indies around the cape of Africa and across the Indian Ocean. He was not trying to rival or outwit the Portuguese and Spanish, but to directly replace them. For it was the Protestant Dutch, launching a seaborne empire from Amsterdam, Rotterdam, and the river and port cities of the Netherlands, who would lastingly reconfigure Iberian rule along the silk and spice routes. The Dutch presence brought a new dynamic to negotiations and displays of force with heavily armed warships and an enmity toward the Catholic states. The Portuguese were already overextended and wracked by political conflict. Malacca was bombarded and surrendered in 1641.

The collapse came from within, but also from a historic shift, for the Dutch had something that made them more powerful than raiding parties and gunboat conquest. They organized under trading charters for well-armed and provisioned ships supplied by the great commercial interests of the Netherlands. When, in 1602, these contractors were combined, they became what was arguably the world's first multi-national corporation, and a government unto itself: the Dutch East India Company.

6 SEA CHANGES AND SPICE ISLANDS

The most famous tree in the Maluku Islands of Indonesia stands off a little road that turns up the flank of the Gamalama Volcano, rising high in a hot, humid, and aromatic wood of clove and nutmeg. Amidst the other greenery that blankets the island of Ternate, this giant clove, knotted and gnarled, is famous for sprouting hundreds of kilos of fragrant leaves and fruit, as it has done for nearly four hundred years.

The tree has a local and personal name, Afo, simply understood as "the giant." It is famed not only for its size and generous productivity, but because it is a living sign of survival and defiance: a tree that at one time would have been cut down and burned if its existence had been known. Afo stands over a history that took the lives of many islanders – and other trees – across the centuries.[1]

The Portuguese had sailed in 1512 into the Banda Sea region, lured by remarkable and legendary islands, the only known places in the world where spices – cloves, mace, and cinnamon – grew miraculously from trees, and pepper could be cultivated away from dominant suppliers on the Malabar coast of India.

Errant sailing took the Portuguese into the hands of the Sultans of Ternate, controlling the greatest of the clove islands, and the newcomers began to build entrepôts and forts to protect their access. Tensions ran across the region. The Sultans of Ternate and nearby Tidore were ferocious rivals, locked in battles across generations for paramount control of the spice trade, often aided by small pockets of foreign traders and advisors, including Spanish adventurers. Their palaces were adorned with tributes of Chinese porcelain and Venetian glass.

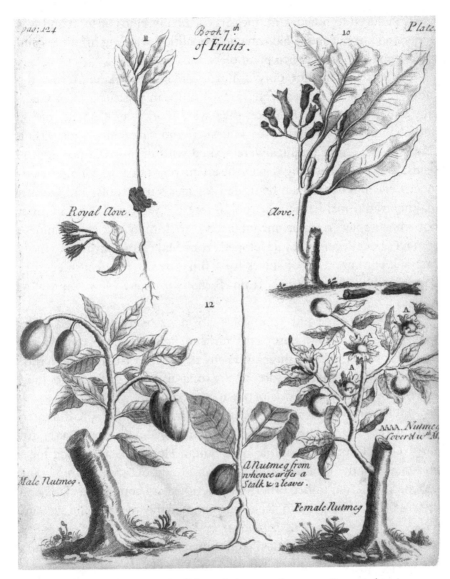

10 Seeds of empire: botanical studies of cloves and nutmeg. Image of antique engraving courtesy of www.FineRarePrints.com

Cloves, aromatic, pungent, and slightly sweet, had been used in Chinese and Indian Ayurvedic medicine for centuries to treat digestive and fungal ailments. Ground, they were sifted together with other spices in curries and pickling. The familiar nail-like buds are actually dried tropical flowers, used to infuse stocks and wild game. The nutmeg is part of a mottled fruit and has a bright covering, inside of which rests the seed itself. Reduced to powder, nutmeg flavors many kinds of food and was understood in Europe to have magical qualities, warding off illness and misfortune by being carried in amulets and charms.

Spices were not only a European luxury trade. Across the Indonesian islands spices were, as in European ports, parts of medicine and religious belief. More, they were workaday elements of life and change for the Banda Sea and surrounding archipelagos. Using simple tools, entire families were tasked with drying and peeling the seeds, and spice exchanges were used to pay taxes to village headmen. Revenues could then be traded for men's iron tools, and women making traditional barkcloths took interest in imported cotton fabric. For elites, spice revenue meant access to Indian silk and Chinese coinage. Local economies developed from Malay and Javanese sailors carrying consignments of spices for China; by the fourteenth century Banda sailors were trading from Ternate to West New Guinea to Malacca.[2]

This oceanic and Asian spice world was well established in the sixteenth century, but Europeans radically reshaped the multivalent trade, for their goal was singular. From 1536 the Portuguese Governor Galvão used his military forces to strong-arm the sultans and their successors; his objective was his own monopoly.

Portuguese tactics to master the trade in the 1570s created strife with Sultan Hairun on Ternate, and his son Sultan Baab. An anti-Islamic Captain Mesquita lured Sultan Hairun to a meeting for a presumed goodwill mission, then captured and decapitated him. The treacherous action rallied otherwise fractious and competing clans and sultans behind Sultan Baab, who soon claimed the loyalties and warrior forces of more than seventy islands from Makassar and the Celebes Sea to New Guinea. Baab even called on and had support from Ternate's ancient rivals, the sultans of Tidore.

Together, they lay siege to the Portuguese fortifications; by 1575, the starving Portuguese survivors were forced to surrender. Baab did not waste the opportunity. Commanding a fleet of impressive war vessels, he sailed like a head of state to the far islands of the alliance, building up a seaborne network of trade and loyalty with displays of power and tribute exactions. With the Portuguese routed, the sultans returned to their own affairs.[3]

Still, European stations continued to develop. The Spanish established claims and English traders like Henry Middleton landed ships in 1604–6. But the greatest presence would be the Dutch, who spread out from a base to the west. The Dutch ships first sailed into the Java of today's Indonesia in 1596, loading the holds of their ships with forest woods, coffee, and indigo and planning to project their influence into the nearby Spice Islands.

At first contact, the Dutch were just one more seafaring people with trade ambitions, making the island circuit, bargaining and trading consignments. In Banten on Java, local Muslim women would have been more occupied in their street markets, selling melons, beans, and textiles they wove themselves from customary tubular baskets. Turbaned men unrolled packages of fish and butchered animal parts, as well as pots of sugar and honey. Indian traders with weavings hailed from Gujerat and Bengal, and Chinese had small goods emporia. The Dutch were marginal and unprotected. The captain Frederik de Houtman was imprisoned for more than a year after disputing with Muslim authorities and refusing to convert to Islam. The Sultan eventually made use of his European knowledge regarding trade cargoes and political affairs.[4]

Initially, Dutch interests were represented by a number of firms and alliances, competing for contracts and cargoes. But powerful stakeholders in Amsterdam consolidated the Dutch claims in a joint-stock organization under a board of directors known as the Seventeen Gentlemen. Together they forged a 1602 agreement with the royal government to create a trading monopoly, the Dutch East India Company.

No mere business corporation, the Company, or VOC by its Dutch initials (Vereenigde Oost-Indische Compagnie), was given exclusive rights to exploit trade in maritime Asia, to raise and provision merchant fleets, and to recruit and supply necessary warships and mercenary armies to protect the trade. It would become a commercial, political, and military power unto itself, with bases, storage entrepôts, and fortifications from the Spice Islands to the Straits of Malacca to the Cape of South Africa.

The authority of the Dutch East India Company was consolidated in the hands of its governor, a severe and ruthless former bookkeeper, Jan Pieterszoon Coen. Key among his aims was establishing a permanent Dutch presence in the Indies at which to set up a headquarters and dispatch trading and military parties across Asia. His ambitions came up against the interests of Matram, a Javanese kingdom led by the charismatic Sultan Agung, and warfare marked the encroaching Dutch presence. In 1619 Coen landed forces in western Java at Sunda Kelapa, a place where rivers ran to the sea and multiple trading communities had built villages ringed by rice paddies and sugar cane. Coen attracted the interest of the Indian and Chinese traders and declared the founding of a Dutch-dominated trading center, Batavia, today's Jakarta.

Batavia would become the wealthy center of a global trading network, but in the early seventeenth century immediate riches were still to the east, in the Spice Islands. To control the spice trade, Jan Pieterzoon Coen pursued the VOC's monopolistic imperial vision. He made little distinction between trade and military operations, raising mercenary fleets to attack the outposts of sultans and European rivals alike, force treaties, and control the waterways around growing Company territories.

In a global maneuver that would have lasting resonance, the Company sought to control a British emplacement on Ran Island in the Moluccas (Maluku Islands), with close access to the spice routes. But the British were not willing to concede their position so a deal was struck. The Dutch took their prize by trading away claims to another territory on the other side of the world: Manhattan Island on the eastern seaboard of North America.

By 1611, Dutch traders and colonists built up a Fort Belgica to thwart the presence of other spice traders in the region. The commercial logic was compelling: a cargo loaded in the islands could be sold in Holland for more than three hundred times the original investment, a staggering profit that fueled both commercial interest and murder. In 1621, Coen landed soldiers throughout the Banda Islands and forced the local cultivators off of their customary land. Resistance was met with violence and nearly 15,000 islanders were massacred by troops to prepare for the Dutch takeover.

Those who survived were subject to punitive Dutch authority and forced to cut down their own staple sago palms in order to grow more spice trees. Sago is a starch extracted from the pith of the palm trunk. The starch is crushed, kneaded, and strained, then fashioned into flours and flat cakes. Though slight in nutritional value, it is a substantial food source when rendered into steamed puddings, noodles, breads, and combined with fish and other protein. But the palms did not contribute to Dutch export revenues. As the spice plantations grew, local villages starved to death.

Clove harvesting disappeared from Ternate and Tidore. To gain the long-desired monopoly, clove growing was prohibited beyond the island of Ambon. In 1650, the Dutch systematically uprooted, cut down, and burned all other trees in the region; anyone attempting to plant, nurture, or sell cloves was ordered to be executed. Nutmeg trees were also destroyed or consolidated into plantations under strict VOC control. Attempting the biological and botanical control of a global market by dominating a local place, Dutch agents drenched all nutmeg shipments with lime so that no fertile seeds could be used to germinate plants anywhere else.[5]

The strategy partly succeeded. But with such high profits at stake, rivals risked their lives to steal and smuggle the seeds, such as a Frenchman, Pierre Poivre, who would become governor over the island of Mauritius in the Indian Ocean. More, sea birds and even typhoon winds carried some of the seeds aloft and renegade trees sprouted on volcanic slopes around the region, perhaps tended, perhaps by chance.

By the 1800s, the Dutch monopoly ended. Despite the severe measures, surveillance, and lives lost, cloves grew in Java, Sumatra, the West Indies, and East Africa from smuggled or naturally carried seedlings. One clove tree – "Afo" – miraculously survived in Ternate, and is today four hundred years old. For centuries it grew as witness and survivor, escapee from the VOC's attempt to monopolize and exterminate both peoples and trees, the tragic legacy of the global wars for spice.

Though the spice monopoly did not survive, the Company was still the major power in the Indonesian archipelago. Batavia grew from a settlement into a crossroads for Asia, Southeast Asia, the Pacific, and the Indian Ocean. Holding off Sultan Agung and making alliances with other more accommodating sultans, the VOC put extensive lands and plantations under cultivation and monopolized exclusive trading agreements for Dutch carriers.

Chinese junks and a burgeoning Chinese merchant and labor population expanded regional exchange and helped to build canals, neighborhoods, and fortifications for the settlement. Slowly, villages of bamboo and palm thatch gave way to wood-frame houses reinforced by quarried stone chiseled into bricks, tiles, and pavements. Personnel working for the VOC lived inside the Batavia city walls, accompanied by family members and servants. In nearby neighborhoods, the *mardijkers* established themselves: general Dutch townsmen, mixed-race mestizos, and Christian Asian communities. The Chinese of Batavia first lived inside and then were forced out of the walled city by ethnic violence, building up a Chinatown in the adjacent district of Glodok, which flourishes today as a commercial hub of restaurants, markets, and shopping centers.

As in Spanish Manila, the population was a shifting blend of communities and cultures, with Dutch and Chinese urban concentrations woven into Javanese landscapes and incorporated villages. The faces, customs, and languages were equally mixed, with Eurasian families issuing from Dutch and Javanese marriages in which Christian conversions, polyglot tongues, and local adaptations to food and fashion styles were pronounced.

Batavia became noted for Dutch-Asian women with colorful and elegant colonial manners and styles, very unlike their somber and severe European counterparts. Attended by slaves from other regions or islands, the women perpetuated their social standing by astutely managing inheritances and trading fortunes, promoting their sons for administrative posts, and marrying their daughters into aristocratic circles. Some of these intercultural women are known to us through painstaking historical reconstruction. Cornelia van Nijenroode was the daughter of a Dutch VOC merchant, born in Japan to a Japanese concubine, but raised in Batavia. She married a Dutch company official and, widowed, later remarried – to her regret – an avaricious lawyer named Johan Bitter, who used legal procedure to seize her wealth. Her Batavian life encompassed ties back to Japan, as well as petitions and lawsuits in the Netherlands, another figure of intersecting worlds.[6]

Batavia became the center for a sophisticated Eurasian population, yet its fortunes ultimately still depended on what happened at sea. Trade was the city's lifeblood and control of commerce the true VOC imperative. As long as Southeast Asian junks, European merchantmen, and small craft on long and short hauls could make port wherever they liked around the archipelago, the Dutch position would be insecure. The VOC demanded agreements with the coastal sultans to divert all maritime traffic to Batavia, and established patrol inspections and customs outposts.

Harbormaster records detail the loads carried by traders, and cargoes of small, local boats are windows into the material priorities of everyday life and struggle. One trader, Bappa Dagang from the island of Madure, carried coconuts, tamarind, tobacco, sacks of fish, and

11 Canals and commerce: the Dutch and Asian world of Batavia, East Indies.

small weapons including light cannon and gunpowder. A Chinese trader named Tan Biko registered weights of salt, rice, opium, *pinang* nuts for betel chewing, and a load of Javanese cloth.[7]

Such shipments were taxed, but actual restrictions were reserved for products that the VOC deemed critical for global trade and political power, particularly plantation crops from spices to sugar cane and coffee, the latter synonymous with its origin, Java. Around these the VOC enacted strong regulations, built up controlled labor forces, and maintained a willingness to act with force against rivals.

Even so, the VOC's clear dominance did not go uncontested. At times, it was thwarted by charismatic leaders like Prince Nuku of Tidore, whose rebellion against the Dutch monopolies drew on alliances of discontented island rulers, in a move reminiscent of Sultan Baab's coalition against the Portuguese. In 1780, when the Company forced a treaty upon local sultans, politically reducing their authority, Nuku declared his own sovereignty over adjacent island groups.

Nuku demonstrated a talent for understanding the grievances of wide-ranging groups united in their dislike of the Dutch. From Papua, raiders who had thrived on the slave and ransom trade for generations joined Nuku to protest the Dutch control of slaving markets for their own colonial benefit. In Seram, military leaders sought redress for the scorched earth destruction by the VOC of traditional spice growing and trading networks. Alliances with Nuku also served the grander scheme of reuniting a confederation of local powers to free the islands from foreign interlopers. All parties sought their share of the enormous revenues extracted from the wealth of the Indies.

Not all VOC rivals were canny sultans or Asian potentates. Some challenges were coming from the Netherlands itself: Dutch competitors looking to break into the Company's monopoly. One of the few ways to do this would be to find an undiscovered, alternative route into the Indies, thereby circumventing the Company's chartered control of access to the East. In 1616, Willem Schouten and Jacob LeMaire sailed from the Netherlands around southernmost South America, looping below, and not entering, the Strait of Magellan. Coming into the South Pacific, they claimed to have bypassed the sea lanes over which the VOC had exclusive rights.

Their voyage is notable for the case against monopoly, but also because they revived the South American approach, the trajectories of the Spaniard Quiros, and demonstrated interest in the continuing quest of centuries: the search for the Great Southern Continent. More, however, Schouten and LeMaire provided points of contact with a South Pacific largely unknown to Europeans. At each encounter, records appear of a Pacific where millennia earlier Austronesian Lapita peoples had established villages and migrated into separate island societies.

In the Tuamotus, local clan leaders guardedly watched the strangers from forest positions, and showed interest in iron nails in the ship's framework, bearing slings and spears crafted from the sea and swordfish points. The Dutch reported that herbs and plants seemed to have medicinal value against maladies like scurvy, and crabs, shellfish, and "snails of very good flavour" made for a routine of marine harvest among the locals. In Tongan waters, canoes patrolled and confronted the Dutch ship. Some were blasted by the ship's guns, and after wary bartering, cordial exchanges developed. Women and men had black hair and gave woven mats and coconuts for beads and knives.[8]

The Dutchmen had crossed over into the trade, kinship, and expansionist circuits of the reputed Tongan maritime empire. A powerful aristocracy dominated the islands, and Schouten and LeMaire received shipboard visits from the rulers of Tafahi and Niuatoputapu, who approached them in impressive voyaging canoes accompanied by scores of other craft filled with warriors and retainers.

The canoes were parts of the Tongan naval presence throughout the local islands, and centerpieces of myths, legends, and oral traditions that recounted the exploits of skilled seafarers and maritime conquests. One of the greatest of Tongan epics recounts the odyssey of Kau'ulufouna, whose father was assassinated by political rivals. Vowing revenge, he pursued his enemies by canoe across all of the major Tongan islands and then also to Samoa, Fiji, Futuna, and Uvea before finally finding and killing them. Kau'ulufouna became the supreme Tu'i Tonga. The very hierarchical nature of such political rule itself also encouraged constant expansion. With limited possibilities to rise in power, young chiefs were directed to conquer new territories and form alliances across expanding circuits of islands.

One of those, Futuna, was also a landfall for LeMaire and Schouten. There, they noted impressive circular and tapered huts, kept language notes, and offered knives, nails, and blue beads that would later resurface in nineteenth-century Samoa, presumably transferred by traders. They were also honored with the binding community practice of kava drinking. The local King's men masticated the herb and covered it with water. The Dutchmen declined to partake, whether from personal revulsion or fear of poisoning.

In this they missed an opportunity. Throughout the Pacific islands the *Piper methysticum* has been long revered for its mildly narcotic qualities and central role in group cameraderie. The root itself, chewed, spit out, and drunk from a common wooden bowl, is bitter and aromatic. Oceanian legends of its origins differ across islands, though the most exalted tales come from Samoa, where kava was first given as a great gift of spiritual and natural power to a high chief, Tagaloa Ui, the offspring of the Sun God and a young virgin, Fituita.[9]

Schouten and LeMaire continued to sail along the northern coast of New Guinea before entering the sea lanes where the Pacific overlaps Indonesian waters. They harbored at the spice island of Ternate, and finally made port in Batavia. Governor Coen was not amused by what he regarded an infringement of the VOC monopoly and had

Schouten and LeMaire jailed, their ship and cargo seized. He did not believe their claim of a new route. They fought legal battles for years, but the Company was not willing to brook competition, and spread the word that the expedition had discovered nothing important in the Pacific. Exchanging trinkets and customs with islanders meant little to governors fixated on spices and silk. This narrative of insignificance would do much to keep Oceania and Asia separate.

Still, all explorations of Oceania were not quite finished for the seventeenth century. Another governor, Anthony Van Diemen, recognized that the question of the Great Southern Continent had still not been resolved. Perhaps profit still beckoned. This ambition inspired a voyage between 1642 and 1644 under the navigator and explorer Abel Janszoon Tasman, commissioned to survey the unexplored coastlines of New Holland (Australia) and out to the Solomons.

Tasman's course took him southeast below the Australian continent where he encountered an extended coastline he called Van Diemen's Land after his patron, renamed Tasmania by his own admirers. He did not ascertain that it was an island. Instead, he continued due east and after about a week sighted a large, high land. His ships dropped anchor off the coast of Taitapu Bay, looking for a place to put ashore for provisions and fresh water. As night fell, the crew could see fires along the shore.

From the littoral, and around the fires, the Ngati Tumata watched the ships. They were a community, an *iwi*, that had settled in generations earlier, migrating and integrating with other clans. All *iwi* recognized some common great ancestors, such as the mythical Polynesian navigator Kupe, who was judged by later scholars to have arrived in the early tenth century. By a debated tradition calculating historic generations, a Great Fleet of voyaging canoes reached the land sometime around 1350. They came from an ancient homeland somewhere in Eastern Polynesia, becoming the people known as the Maori on new islands they called Aotearoa, later New Zealand.

These early settlers at first clustered around the coastlines and river basins, introducing farming and new animals such as the dog. They also took to hunting the astonishing new creatures they encountered, including the moa, a flightless giant bird up to nine feet tall, weighing hundreds of pounds. Archeological surveys show remains of earth ovens and base camps where the enormous carcasses were butchered and roasted. Evidence also indicates clans organized around seasonal trapping and provisioning cycles, and the use of whale, moa, and other animal bone tools.[10]

Other food sources included the cultivated *kumara,* a tropical sweet potato, with multiple species introduced into the islands over centuries. Food was precious and surpluses were stored in *pataka* houses mounted on piles situated in common village areas, decorated by master carvers with spiritual designs indicating sacred abundance. Maori clans were highly stratified with strong political and religious leaders. Gods, heroes, and ancestors infused the experience of everyday life. As groups evolved, or contested neighbors for resources and authority, many built fortified settlements, with wooden palisades and protective embankments. Others moved outward, settling into villages ringed by trees, or set against sheltering mountains and open to bays.

The latter was the territory of the Ngati Tumata. Their lands encompassed the nearby plains used as trading routes, and the estuary where they now observed the strangers and their ships. The mudflats were rich with oysters, mussels, snails, and fish. Local plants were stripped into fibers and woven into snares and traps for seabirds and eel. Legends recorded that much of the landscape was created by ancestors who leveled the plains and dug out the lakes.[11]

The representatives of the Dutch East India Company came upon a complex society, bold and wary of outsiders. As the Dutch watched, two canoes with strong men appeared from the shore, calling out and blowing on giant shell trumpets. If the display was intended to frighten off the strangers – who may have been uninvited spirits or ancestors – it did not work. Instead, the Dutch responded to the calls, asking the Ngati Tumata to come aboard, but perhaps confirming an apparent challenge to the warriors. Meanwhile, a Dutch boat took to the water to carry a message between the VOC ships. It was rammed by one of the canoes; four sailors were massacred and the body of one was dragged away. The Dutch fired with muskets and guns, but after collecting survivors, Tasman weighed anchor. No other European contacts took place for another 127 years. When Europeans did return, they came to stay.

By navigational reckoning, Tasman's voyage was extraordinary. He had entered the Pacific along the Australian coastline, mapped the southern contours of Tasmania, and been the first European to encounter the Maori peoples of New Zealand. On his return circuit, he confirmed the sea routes through the middle Tongan islands.

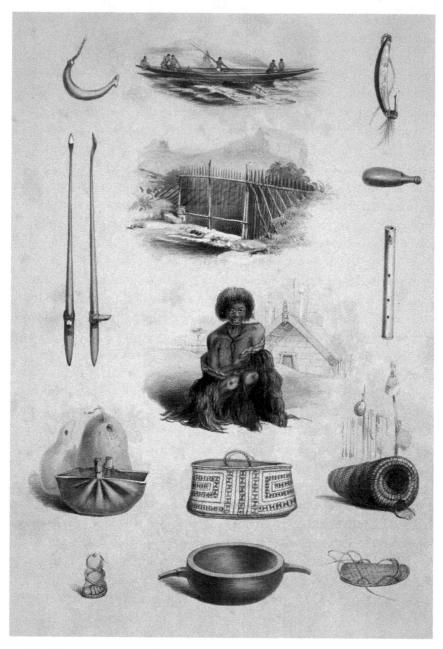

12 Traditional terrains: artifacts and practices of early Maori culture, Aotearoa/
New Zealand.

Still, the VOC was disappointed. There were atolls, islands, and curiosities, but no rich entrepôts like Asia, and most significantly, still no confirmation of the Great Southern Continent. As Tasman pursued his missions across the South Seas, the VOC governor also decided to push north, sending fleets to gain information about another fabled land that had excited the interest of Europeans for centuries: the place that Christopher Columbus had called Cipangu – Japan.

7 SAMURAI, PRIESTS, AND POTENTATES

The southern Japanese island of Kyushu is famed for its maritime celebrations. The festival of Kunchi in Nagasaki annually draws huge crowds to riotously decorated boats borne about the streets that evoke the trading ships of China and Portugal, and of the Dutch. As processions make their way to the Suwa Shrine down the clamorous side streets and through the neighborhoods and districts, the city is alive with the spectacle of dazzling lacquered and gilded boats carried on undulating seas of shoulders and cries, sailing across the boulevards.

Rites and rituals crowd the streets and are a colorful spectacle of lavishly staged and costumed dance troupes working on a seven-year cycle of neighborhoods, accompanied by fireworks, prayers, chants and songs, lanterns and drums. The ceremonial boats frame dances by golden dragons, and pantomimes of collared Europeans in face paint, jousting amidst stylized sail imprints of the Dutch East India Company, billowing with authority.

As the voyages of Schouten and LeMaire and Tasman encountered seafaring societies from Tonga to Aotearoa but found no evident commercial potentials, VOC interest in Oceania waned. Instead, the Dutch remained keyed on the water world of the East Indies and, following the rival Portuguese to the coasts of Asia, the millennial dream of Imperial China and the little-known archipelago of the Japanese islands.

The Kunchi festival was launched in 1634 and visually captures the civic pride of an international maritime city, a centuries-old crossing point for trade and exchange between Japan, East and Southeast

Asia, and European interlopers from the sixteenth and seventeenth centuries. Yet the festival is more than the spectacle of colorful, cross-cultural trade and communities. For Kunchi is a festival marking an extraordinary and critical juncture. It captures the assertion of "native Japanese" interests under the patronage of an imperial and military state challenged by both Asian neighbors and European rivals in a new age of foreign contacts.

For a key century, from about 1540 to 1640, histories were made and unmade in the seas around Japan, drawing together and bringing into collision Portuguese traders at Macao, Jesuit priests from Goa, Dutch merchants from Batavia, Chinese and Vietnamese cargoes, tributes from the kingdom of the Ryukyus, conflicts with Korea, and the forays of the Spanish in the Philippines. All were histories of challenge and exchange, and the infusions and melding of cultures.[1]

The Kunchi festival tells a series of tales. Some are frankly romantic, and underscore alliances of affinity and commerce. One boat carries a child, the offspring of a Japanese trader and a Vietnamese princess. This is the story of Araki Sotaro, a Kumamoto samurai who moved to Nagasaki in 1588. He was noted for his seafaring ways, traveling to Vietnam, Thailand, and Cambodia for trade, and returning with Wakaku, an adopted daughter of the Vietnamese King, in 1619, honored as Ani-o-san. Together, they built a trading emporium in Nagasaki, symbolic of a Japan defined by Asian-wide commercial interests and cultural engagement.

The boat also marks chronicles of Vietnamese history, for centuries shifting between tribute and conflict with powerful China, and falling under Ming occupation in 1407. This was before the legendary Le Dynasty forced the Chinese to retreat and began annexing territories to the south, leading to an extended period of political instability and feudal warfare across the territories that would become Vietnam.[2]

Across the rival domains, politics were divided between two regimes, the Trinh in the north and the Nguyen in the south until the seventeenth century, when Jesuits began to establish themselves, bringing Latin and Vietnamese catechisms and Catholic European influences. At the Kunchi festival, many floats underscore a similar tumultuous period when Nagasaki also became an entry point for early Portuguese traders, leading to the establishment of a Christian principality run by Jesuits with the support of the local Japanese lord.

The arrival of the Portuguese was tied to Japanese tensions with China. Since the eighth-century Tang dynasty, China's merchant boats had traced out a commercial network from Japan to Champa and Java. Four centuries later, Japanese ships launched toward China for regular trade. During the Ming dynasty in the sixteenth century, however, Japanese pirates increasingly attacked traders and harbors along the coastlines of China and Korea. In 1547, the Ming government responded by closing off all direct trade with Japan. This shift favored maritime agents, who could serve as intermediaries.

The opportunity was taken up by what the East Asians called the seaborne "southern barbarians." After conquering Malacca in 1511 for the Portuguese Crown, Alfonso de Albuquerque now controlled one of the key waterways between Asia and the Indian Ocean. He and the Portuguese King sent diplomatic missions to Canton which gained some off and on favors from the Chinese emperors, but relations remained fragile until the 1540s, when the Portuguese were able to offer something the Celestial Empire actually valued: assistance in combating the pirates.

With their war vessels chasing marauders and guarding passages, the Portuguese were invited in the 1550s to conduct trade missions from Shangchuan Island near the Pearl River Delta and to put up storage and warehouse facilities to protect and dry out cargoes brought in by sea. Portuguese governors slowly built up settlements and a walled village. Woodcuts and prints show irregularly clustered residences and stockhouses marked by churches, overseen by fortifications and jetties. In the town, Iberian arches and colors marked roadways and muddy landings.

In 1557, the Ming court gave official consent for a permanent base. Merchants from across Asia made port, seeking the profits of trade now under joint Chinese and Portuguese protection. Trading junks soon carried cargoes to Malacca and on across the Indian Ocean to Europe. Another circuit headed south toward the Philippines, unloading in Manila for restocking aboard the great Spanish galleons headed across the Pacific to Acapulco in Mexico. The early base would grow from a modest outpost of Asian and European commerce into the twenty-first-century glittering port of Macao (Macau). Casinos, gardens, and world heritage sites today adorn a small island of Catholic churches and plazas, crowded night markets and Chinese temples.[3]

Despite Macao's global reach, one of the most lucrative and quickest profits in the sixteenth century was to be had very close by.

With Chinese merchants forbidden to trade directly with Japan, the Portuguese were given a remarkable monopoly: the right to carry commercial goods between Macao and Nagasaki in an annual great ship of a thousand tons, the carrack. What the Portuguese brought would write an entire chapter in Japan's history.

The first Portuguese traders had arrived in Japan in 1543, a small party on a Chinese junk, blown off course by storms. Landing at Tanegashima island off of Japan's southern coast, they were met by a priest and a Ryukyu woman who interpreted in Chinese and Portuguese. The local authority was the fifteen-year-old Lord Tokita, who found the European barbarians interesting, and was particularly impressed by their arquebus firearms, called *teppo* in Japanese.

Tokita gave one to his blacksmith, who created a copy within a few months. Legend has it that the blacksmith, Yaita Kinbee Kiyosada, learned the techniques of the weapon by offering his 16-year-old daughter Wakasa to be the wife of one of the Portuguese. Wakasa became a heroine of filial piety, leaving her own family for the sake of Japan's future. A park today bears her name and a statue shows her with a *teppo* cradled in her arms.[4]

Wakasa's image insinuates her legend in the late medieval history of Japan known as the Sengoku Period – an era of epochal civil war. From the early thirteenth century, military rulers known as the Ashikaga Shogunate began to lose the loyalty of powerful samurai warrior lords, the *daimyo*. Trade with China and agricultural developments promoting greater expansion of a commercial economy challenged Japan's traditional feudal system. By the fifteenth century, retainers and farmers alike rebelled against impositions, exacerbated by famines and natural disasters.

Assaults on the central ruling authority of the Shoguns in the capital of Kyoto led to a complete breakdown in social order and civil war spread throughout Japan as rival lords took to the field. Japanese painted screens, such as those of the battles of Kawanakajima, show swarming foot soldiers and cavalry, imperious samurai in lamellar armor wielding swords, lances, and clan banners. The *daimyo* were interested in the Portuguese guns. Chinese gunpowder and cannons had been known for centuries, but the arquebus was light, reasonably accurate, and easy to train with. Proud samurai scorned its use, but commanders recognized the military advantages. Japan's great warlords employed them effectively in gaining territories and influence.

13 Alliances of interest: the Portuguese arrive in Japan.

The impact of the arquebus was not as a firearm alone. Its decisive power grew in tandem with another Portuguese import: the political alliance of Christianity and Jesuit organization. This development is again traceable to a Pacific story of voyaging and cultural exchange. An opportunistic but tormented Japanese named Yajiro one day killed a man where he worked in the port town of Kagoshima. At first hiding in sanctuary in a Buddhist monastery, Yajiro took passage on a Portuguese ship and fled to Macao, where a captain advised him to seek redemption through the Jesuit priest Francis Xavier.

Xavier was a man to reckon with. His work ministering to and saving lost souls was appreciated back in Lisbon, and his renown was spread across Asia by followers from a base in Goa, India. Xavier was a priest of miracles and remarkable acts, and he spent much time at sea, tracing out a religious network between ports and islands. According to chroniclers, in 1546 a crucifix lost overboard during a storm in the Moluccan Islands was brought back to him by a crab. While becalmed on the way to China, he saved his shipmates from dying of thirst by blessing salt water and rendering it fresh. His prayers calmed raging storms and turned away pirates, and his chroniclers reported that he called back life to a drowned Indian child. He reportedly restored the sight of the blind, and cured others of demonic possessions. In Malacca, Yajiro sought out Xavier, followed his teachings, and became Anjiro, the first Japanese convert to Catholicism. Encouraged by Anjiro, Xavier decided to spread his mission to Japan.[5]

The priest and his successors met with initial success. Samurai found the teachings of the militant Jesuits not unfamiliar to aspects of their *bushido* warrior code. The greatest impact, however, was on the *daimyo*. By allowing the Jesuits the freedom to preach and establish small churches, local lords gained weapons and substantial profits from Portuguese trading ships. Not surprisingly, competition among the warring lords was soon fierce for this privilege. Samurai adopted the Catholic faith and poor farmers and fishermen were pressed to convert in order to increase Portuguese visits.

Jesuits preached, "it is of absolute necessity that a Christian cast away his life than worship Buddha or gods." Local farmers and villagers in any case often welcomed the message of salvation; for many commoners, the Buddhist monasteries were despised protectors of wealth and privilege. Christian samurai armies were happy to oblige by destroying and looting Buddhist temples.[6]

Omura Sumitada was a man who understood this well. A minor Kyushu *daimyo*, in illustrations with a wide forehead and sober and serious countenance, he was assailed by stronger clans on his borders. As he watched the Jesuits moving their bases around southern Japan, he was keen to offer them a mutually supporting arrangement in the small fishing village of Nagasaki. Sumitada's domains, difficult to access and mountainous, had not been favored places of settlement. But for an alliance with foreigners coming from the sea, the enclosed harbor was suddenly advantageous.

Threatened by the rival warlords, and facing succession struggles, Sumitada turned to the only party that seemed capable of providing him with support. In 1562, he invited Jesuit teachers and Portuguese traders into his domains, and the following year became the first Christian *daimyo*. Rival lords led coalitions against him, but with Portuguese warships and weapons backing him, Sumitada kept his enemies away for almost two decades. His strategy had worked.

In 1580, however, came a threat from Lord Ryuzoji Takanobu, too powerful to counter. Concerned that Takanobu would drive out the foreigners, Sumitada took a remarkable gamble: he officially "gave" Nagasaki to the Jesuits, maintaining for himself the rights to collect duty tariffs. Sumitada calculated that Takanobu would not dare attack a territory directly belonging to the Jesuits protected by the Portuguese. He was right, and the Jesuits found themselves in the extraordinary situation of being Christian rulers in Japan. They were also patronized by other *daimyo* such as Arima Harunobu, who built up his own defensive alliances with the Portuguese, hiring Jesuit advisers and endowing Catholic schools.[7]

Yet this extraordinary "Christian Century" of exchanges and accommodations from 1540 to 1640 was under challenge. The instability of the Warring States period was drawing to a close as the first of three great warlord unifiers, Oda Nobunaga (1534–82), moved to eliminate independent religious establishments that had become centers of political power. Nobunaga was not immediately concerned with the Catholics, but with the powerful Buddhist monasteries and strongholds. In Central Japan, samurai forces were challenged by armies of commoners led by warrior-monks of the *Jodo Shinshu* True Pure Land Buddhist sect, battling in robes with their famous *naginata* bladed spears.

Nobunaga never got south to Kyushu, but his successor Toyotomi Hideyoshi shared an intolerance for any type of "Church domain" that could rival his authority. In Nagasaki, he watched warily as the Jesuits gained tens of thousands of converts. In 1587, Hideyoshi suddenly issued edicts banning the teaching and practice of Catholicism; the Jesuits were taken by surprise, but the apparently capricious move had a historical logic. Like the merchants at Macao who carried China's trade with Japan, the Jesuits had established themselves as local power brokers in Japan's warlord struggles with their faith and weapons.

With centralized authority reasserting itself in Japan, alliances between *daimyo* and the outsider Portuguese were unacceptable. The Catholic world of southern Japan was a threat to a reunified Shogun state, and barbarians who could land troops from heavily armed warships coming from Macao or Manila were dangerous. More critical was the internal danger of hundreds of thousands of Japanese rebels following a "foreign" faith. Hideyoshi meant to demonstrate what his limits would be.[8]

The very unification of the Japanese warring states also meant that Portuguese trade was less important. A centrally organized militaristic Japan would deal with China and the rest of Asia directly. This meant not only commerce, but seaborne conquest; Hideyoshi's ambitions turned toward Korea. Since 918 a dynasty called the Koryo had come to dominate the major East Asian peninsula and became known in the West as "Korea." From the thirteenth century, Korea struggled like China with Mongol invasion threats, yet also developed a refined Buddhist culture that was noted for extensive textual works printed with moveable wooden blocks.

Studies of Confucianism became state ideology within a civil service examination adopted from China, and Arab traders introduced their astronomy, mathematics, and agricultural technologies. In 1392, the Choson Dynasty took power, building a new capital at Seoul, with massive walls and administrative buildings. The Choson further elaborated Confucian education and social ranks, establishing schools, emphasizing filial piety, and defining ranks of the bureaucracy.

In 1446, King Sejong convened scholars to create a unique Korean alphabet, the *Hangul*, though privileged factions at court opposed its general dissemination. Impressive pagodas and pavilions were built, and green celadon pottery evolved into white porcelain, both highly prized and rivaling Chinese wares in popularity. Meteorological and technological sciences flourished. Highly developed agriculture produced great wealth for the privileged orders holding land grants.[9]

Hideyoshi knew of all this, and from 1592 to 1598 his armies took to ships and made their first strikes against the Asian mainland, invading the Korean peninsula. With forces of more than 100,000 warriors, the Japanese intended to replace Chinese Ming influence in the region and distribute spoils to samurai armies.

Korean and Chinese troops were pushed back, but the decisive battles turned out to be at sea. While successful on land, Hideyoshi's forces were repeatedly defeated by the naval genius Admiral Yi Sun-shin, who attacked in elegant, entrapping formations, and cut off Japanese supply lines. The Korean navy also employed its famed turtle-boats, armored troop ships that employed rams and cannon to destroy Japanese craft still relying on a hand-to-hand style of combat. The Japanese withdrew.

Interrupted by a brief "peace" or cease-fire, the invasion of Korea, or Imjin Wars, characterized a militaristic and expansionist Japan, quite at odds with the "isolationist" Japan just a generation later. The significance of the Imjin Wars for the greater Pacific lies partly in this shift: the failure of Hideyoshi to dominate East Asia and its seas left behind a legacy of grievance between Japan and its neighbors. Hideyoshi's death curtailed immediate future invasion plans, and Japanese shoguns retreated behind their coastlines to consolidate power in their own islands.

The Imjin Wars are also called by some the Pottery Wars. It was one of the enduring legacies of the violence that entire populations of artisans were displaced to develop a new ceramic art in Japan that would be demanded by, studied, and then imitated in Europe. All across Korea, Japanese armies left devastation, starvation, and atrocities. As invasion forces withdrew from the Korean town of Namwon, they took with them the potters and ceramicists of nearly two dozen different artisan families.

The Koreans were taken across the sea and set up as foreign prisoners in Kyushu, Japan, where they attempted to rebuild their kilns and craft. Eventually, the Korean population was granted a "Koryo Town," where they constructed Korean houses and worshiped at altars and shrines to ancestors now lost across the waves. Men wore horse-hair hats and gowns, and, as potters, crafted tea bowls famed for their restraint and favored by Japanese Zen tea-masters.

Among the most famous of the Korean potters was Yi Sam-pyong, who found and exploited kaolin-rich clay for porcelain of rare quality and beauty. His kilns produced cobalt blue and enamel glazeware favored in Japan, but also highly valued by the VOC maritime empire. Dutch ships packed and carried the pottery from the seaport of Imari around the globe, connecting the world to Korean histories of war, exile, and art through cargoes of cups and dishes. In aristocratic households across Europe, expensive Asian ceramic ware, much of it Korean or Japanese, became known generically as fine china.[10]

Korea was not the only site of maritime challenge and exchange in the early modern Asian Pacific. Hideyoshi's Shogunate also raised alarms in the Spanish Philippines. Here again, Japanese politics were entangled with Christian designs. A Japanese merchant named Harada had become a Catholic convert of the Portuguese Jesuits. As a determined rival of the Spanish, now named Faranda, he used connections at court to encourage Hideyoshi's interests in capturing the rich Manila trade from Asia to the Americas.

Faranda operated as a seaborne ambassador, carrying letters from Hideyoshi to the Philippines governor, Gomez Perez Dasmariñas, threatening invasion and demanding tribute and influence. The governor in turn dispatched ships with Dominican and Franciscan Spanish friars to Japan. They negotiated for peace, delayed any action, and preached and spread as much Spanish influence as possible. Meanwhile, the governor contemplated how to defend a highly vulnerable Manila against an overpowering Japanese military strike. As one letter to the Spanish Council of the Indies noted already years before, "The Japanese are those who are more feared in the islands than all the neighboring nations, for they are very courageous and arrogant."[11]

Missions and attempts to gain favor crossed the seas as Japan and the Philippines negotiated emigration policy and trade. Positions hardened when a Spanish galleon launched from Manila was wrecked on Japanese shores in 1596 with Franciscan teachers aboard. Hideyoshi's men looted the cargo, and in attempts to impress the Shogun, a foolish member of the Spanish party boasted to Hideyoshi that after priests converted much of the population, military invasion by the great Spanish King would follow.

The Shogun ordered twenty-six Christians to be crucified in Nagasaki – including some Portuguese Jesuits – in a place still commemorated as a site of martyrdom. The Manila governor later sent another mission, drawing on his trade contacts to include the gift of a

Siamese elephant in hopes of maintaining good relations. The invasion of the Philippines never took place, thanks to active Spanish diplomacy, and in large part because of Japanese withdrawal after Hideyoshi's failure in the seas off Korea.

An assertive Japan did, however, see its designs realized in another part of the Pacific. In 1609, the island kingdom of the Ryukyus fell under Japanese domination; it was renamed and later incorporated into Japan itself as Okinawa.

Sixth- and seventh-century Chinese chronicles had long reported tales of smoke or mist rising out of the sea from a place many days distant by sail. The islands that became known as the Ryukyus were full of caves and protected by fences, with palaces decorated with animal inscriptions. Over a millennium, trade and tribute began with the Chinese Ming court in sulphur and horses, Chinese porcelain, and silks. By the sixteenth century, sugar cane, sweet potatoes, and tropical fruits brought traders to and from China, Korea, and Japan, as well as Java, the coast of Vietnam, and Malacca. Chinese-influenced castles rose under a succession of kingdoms, centered by grand halls and tiled roofs built within walled compounds.[12]

During the Warring States period in Japan, traders from Ryukyu were especially active supplying the *daimyo* of Japan's southern islands and carrying cargoes in the seas between Japan and Korea. The Japanese language and court practices became familiar in the Ryukyus.

But the alliance of trade, profit, and cultural sharing would soon become one of dominance. After Oda and Hideyoshi, the third and last of Japan's unifiers came to power – Tokugawa Ieyasu. Like the Portuguese traders and Jesuits, the Ryukyuans may not have appreciated how much the consolidation of Japanese political power would drastically alter their status and value. A newly centralized state under Ieyasu demanded respect and tribute from vassals large and small, and as Hideyoshi's earlier foreign adventures showed, had a willingness to use force. Unmarked by the violence in the Japanese islands, the Ryukyu kingdom did not understand the significance of the transformations taking place.

In 1609, a force set sail with three thousand men from the Japanese province of Kagoshima. For centuries, the Ryukyus had been a major entrepôt, protected by the common interests of East and Southeast Asian traders. They had little effective ability to resist a major invasion. Rather than shed blood, King Sho Nei surrendered and was taken away, and for almost three centuries the Kingdom of the Ryukyus would be controlled by the Satsuma Clan of Japan. Certain formalities were preserved, such as tributary status to China, which allowed the Japanese to use the islands as their own intermediary for trade with the rest of East Asia.

In 1879, the state was annexed and the Ryukyu government was abolished, becoming the Japanese province of Okinawa. Japanese education and institutions incorporated residents into a national identity. Still, some Okinawans today resist a Japanese identity and promote Ryukyuan culture and independence, based on an ancient island heritage.

The circuits of maritime challenge, conquest, and collaboration were especially complex at the beginning of the seventeenth century, when trade and politics brought even newer "barbarians" to Japan. The Catholic Portuguese and Spanish had reason to be hostile to the encroaching presence of their familiar rivals: the Dutch. In 1600, an English navigator, William Adams, brought the first Dutch ship, the *Liefde*, crashing ashore. The Dutch added Protestantism to the struggles between the Jesuits and the Franciscans, but their approach intrigued the Shogun, who recognized the Dutch indifference to preaching and faith. Interested almost exclusively in trade, the VOC provided an effective counterweight to the Catholics, developing profitable commercial exchange without dangerous conversions, followers, and adherence to a new religion. The Dutch factory at Hirado quickly rivaled the Portuguese and Spanish presence.

Meanwhile, the anti-Christian tide that had risen under Hideyoshi now fully crested under his successor, Ieyasu. In 1614, the Shogun began official repression of Christian practice, leading to the expulsion of many teachers, and forcing worship underground. Furtive congregations, hidden prayer books, encrypted messages, and cabinets with secret compartments for icons and elements of the Host became markers of the time. Within a few years, campaigns of torture and execution became widespread. A score of Europeans and some two thousand Japanese Christians were martyred, and a hundred times as many were beaten, burned, or hung upside down in excrement until they renounced their beliefs.[13]

Between 1633 and 1639 came the edicts for which Japan would be known for centuries: the *sakoku* closing of the country. Not only were foreigners ordered out, but orders of execution awaited any Japanese attempting to return from overseas, or trying to leave the islands. For generations, Nagasaki had been a Jesuit domain, the center of Catholic Southern Japan, marked by Christian rites like the Easter procession. Now the Shoguns took control, mandating public Shinto activities tied to the town's Suwa Shrine. This was the Kunchi festival, launched in 1634, a celebration of local merchants, farmers, traders, and harvests on Tokugawa "Japanese" terms.

Still-necessary trading partners like the Chinese and Dutch were placed in the roles of guests and observers under the eye of the Shogun. In fact, the most notable aspect of the *sakoku* was that foreign commerce was not so much banned as resettled. The Dutch, in particular, were pushed offshore, committed to a tiny artificial island called Deshima, built by the Shogun in Nagasaki harbor. This followed what would be the last major reaction of the Christian-built domains in Japan: the bloodshed of the Shimabara Rebellion.

Amakusa Shiro was a young Christian, only fifteen years old, when he became the leader of tens of thousands of impassioned warriors against the authority of the Shogun. The former apprentice of a great samurai, he reportedly had mastered Confucian literature while very young, and Christian tradition foretold that the Savior could come in the person of a child. Amakusa Shiro's story was full of miracles, and he preached a philosophy of human equality and dignity. Villagers recounted stories of a dove that laid an egg in the palm of his hand; upon hatching, the egg revealed a picture of Jesus Christ and a small scroll of divine scripture. In Shimabara today, his statue overlooks the hills and fields where his followers gathered.

Peasants and wandering samurai from Shimabara and the nearby Amakusa Islands had desperately sought a leader as they rose in December of 1637 against feudal taxation, famine sickness, and persecutions suffered by many as Japanese Christians. Some 20,000 rebels rallied to the battle, routing local lords and samurai and burning towns. Following the merciless line taken against the Buddhists, the Tokugawa Shogun amassed over a hundred thousand troops against the rebel stronghold, Hara castle.

Seeking anti-Catholic allies, the Shogun also requested aid from the Dutch. Nicolas Koekebakker headed the Dutch Hirado station and obligingly ordered the twenty guns of his ship to bombard the castle. The artillery had little actual effect, but the Shogun took note of the Dutch willingness to attack other Christians as his samurai troops besieged and massacred the rebels. Amakusa Shiro died with them. As Europeans were expelled from Japanese territory, an exception was made for the Protestant Dutch, who were allowed to continue to trade with Japan.[14]

The nature of that trade, however, was carefully controlled. All foreigners were obliged to live on tiny Deshima island, built in the shape of the Shogun's fan, clearly symbolic of the absolute Japanese authority over the barbarians who were so powerful in other parts of the Pacific. As Japan closed itself off to the outside world, the Dutch stayed on in their little compound for two hundred and fifty years, an island within the harbor of an island.

The Dutch were a favorite subject of Japanese sketches and prints, figures of intense curiosity regarding their clothes, manners, servants, big noses, and reddish hair. Illustrations fixed on their drinking, carousing, and promenades. One agent wrote in his diary, "Several students and senior servants of the Nagasaki governor and other officials came to satisfy their curiosity and have a look at me." Prints portray the gangly foreigners in spaces redolent of the overlapping worlds, pine rooms with woven *tatami* mats and *shoji* paper doors filled with chairs, wooden settees, and billiard tables.

The Dutch presence was numerically small, but significant, for Deshima became Japan's most significant "window" during the *sakoku*, and attracted not only traders and gawkers, but scholars seeking exchange of ideas and new forms of knowledge. It was through Deshima that "Dutch learning" spread, especially European geography, navigational science, and cartography, but also developments in mathematics, astronomy, botany, medicine, and hydrology. A Dutch agent wrote, "the governor asked me for a pocket spyglass for his own use and a collection of nautical charts . . . the governor asked me for an explanation of a diving-bell and if one could be had in Batavia." Studies of new plant and animal species, languages, theories of blood circulation and celestial mechanics gained attention among Japanese scholars.

The centuries of daily routine, captured in registers, rosters, and illustrations, are full of cultural fascination and the tedium of everyday life in this tiny world of global exchanges. Some news followed the continuing religious struggles: "in the city, all the Japanese, women and children included, have had to perform the ceremony of trampling upon the images of the Roman Catholic and Portuguese faith." Others followed the rituals of cultural exchange through gift-giving: "On behalf of the Company, we have presented the hassaku to the authorities of Nagasaki ... camphor has been weighed and the silk gowns, which are destined for the fatherland, have been packed ... I have been given sake and dried fish as a present."[15]

The miniature world of Deshima represented the changes of the early seventeenth century. The era of the Japanese Catholic empire was lost. The Portuguese withdrew to their base at Macao, the Spanish to Manila. Exchanges with China continued through Nagasaki and the Ryukyus were a colony. Korea, a tribute kingdom to China, continued to look down on Japan even as Korean communities took root there. The powerful Dutch gained profits in Japanese silver, but were a tiny presence in an East Asian world.

The maritime festivals of southern Japan celebrate those histories. In Nagasaki, in colorful itineraries, the teams and their lacquer boats make their way through the city, ringed by Catholic churches, monuments to Christian martyrs, the Glover mansion, and, not too far off, Huis Ten Bosch, a reconstructed Dutch town and tourist park. Along the coast of Kyushu, Hirado is a peaceful castle town facing the straits. It is also a port town where, along with Nagasaki, foreign trade with the Portuguese, Dutch, and British had flourished during the sixteenth and seventeenth centuries.

The port had also been the home of *wako*, the infamous and loathed Japanese pirates. Nearby island festivals feature lantern floats such as "The Boat of the Envoys to Tang China" and "Japanese Pirates' Ship." These boats represent other histories of collusion and struggle in Asian waters, particularly the tales of plunder that had given the Portuguese and Dutch footholds in Asian circuits as seaborne intermediaries. Those footholds had been direct results of another storied maritime circuit: the Pacific world of pirates.

8 PIRATES AND RAIDERS OF THE EASTERN SEAS

Scrolls and paintings from the sixteenth century show them coming. Along the China coast, the seaborne gangs were marauders, murderers, kidnappers, and extortionists, terrorizing villages, stealing children and women. Accounts indicate that they arrived in swarms of boats as raiding parties numbering hundreds as they struck along coastal settlements, burning and pillaging. Storehouses were looted, farmers murdered, graves robbed. Victims were tortured, scalded, and disemboweled, sometimes for entertainment. Chinese troops serving provincial authorities were helplessly overmatched and fled; official residences were ransacked and burned, boats and ships confiscated.

The marauders, called *kaizoku* or *wako*, were societies unto themselves, often bound by loose feudal codes and chiefs, occupying coastal settlements beyond the reach of imperial or prefectural authority. Some established formidable outposts on small islands and ruled as local lords; many lived around inlets and mazes of sandbars under no political control. Originally Japanese from coastal provinces under the nominal authority of reckless *daimyo*, they preyed on Korean and Chinese merchants. Historically, they were in fact from no single country. Dominant Japanese clans would gradually be organized by Chinese raiders, with crew from across East and Southeast Asia.

Generations later, in the early nineteenth century, one English captain wrote of visiting a rajah on the island of Borneo when pirates swept up the river in raiding canoes, "one following the other, decorated with flags and streamers, and firing both cannon and musketry ... the Iranuns are fine athletic men; their bearing was haughty and reserved, and they seemed quite ready to be friends or foes, as best suited their purpose." Rowing through the fleet the captain noted that the men were notorious slavers: "Every boat they take furnishes its quota, and when they have a full cargo, they quit that coast and visit another in order to dispose of their human spoil to the best advantage."[1]

The force the captain described was in Borneo, but it may well have been in the Sulu Sea, the Straits of Malacca, or along the coasts of China and Japan. As chronicles across centuries demonstrated, piracy marked, and indeed shaped, practices and policies of maritime kingdoms and nations. Whether the "robber dwarfs" that caused the Chinese emperor to close off trade against Japan, or the Iranun and Maluku of local waters, pirates came with generations of legends carried down from villages and families, of terror, brutality, and rampage.

Since the days of Zheng He, the end of the treasure fleets and the withdrawal of Chinese naval patrols from the seas had opened spaces for smugglers, criminal bands, and impoverished fishing settlements to survive through extortion and violence. Unable to reassert authority, the great Ming Emperors instead pulled back further, banning citizens from trading abroad, especially to Japan after 1547.

The famed *wako* were only the most visible and loathed of marauders from the Asian coastlines. It was because of them that China formed intermediary alliances with European barbarian maritime powers. In the sixteenth and seventeenth centuries, Dutch and Portuguese ships eager to secure Chinese trade wrestled with these international "villains," at times seaborne armies intent on plunder and pillage, at times small bands on the margins of a black-market maritime economy.

The pirate experience was shaped by land and seascapes, growing out of coastlines and inshore islands, shallow saltwater passages, and sheltered bays with hidden coves. Chinese maritime tradition recognizes multiple adjacent and overlapping water worlds – an inner sea, a South China Sea, a Southern Ocean. The historic Southern Ocean, or Nan-yang, encompassed offshore islands and coral reefs defining the boundaries of Vietnam, Cambodia, Thailand (Siam), Sumatra, western Java, and parts of coastal Borneo. The Vietnamese territories of Tonkin and Annam especially harbored fresh and saltwater deltas where villagers traded and contested with

Chinese partners and rivals. Coastal trading junks called at ports carrying and transferring cargoes of lumber, charcoal, and roofing tiles, cooking oil, rice, chickens, pigs, ducks, and textiles from cotton to silk. At times, they also took on passengers seeking new lives up and down the coast.

Trading ports were also often pirate centers. Population distress was a common factor. Whether by famine, epidemic, or war, major calamities brought refugees and outlaws into close contact at the waterline. Where crops failed or violence succeeded, displaced clans were pushed from mountains and valleys to seek a living from the sea, living in clusters of veritable floating villages along shorelines. Local denizens met with roving sailor bands. Where even the sea itself was not support enough, some harvesters and fishermen turned to piracy. Pirates generally developed as small gangs, with laborers, peddlers, and impoverished merchants filling out the ranks. Many were by then already marginally associated with gambling, prostitution, or smuggling, and combined their hopes for income with their knowledge of coastlines and hiding places.

Leaders emerged from among the most ambitious, often those who also had strong networks of family members and like-minded friends. 1795 records show that one man, A-yang, learned of piracy from his cousin, who regaled him with tales of attacking seaborne junks and confiscating shares of the cargo. A-yang joined the gang, and he in turn called on friends and associates in town to join him, forming a group that assailed vessels carrying rice shipments.[2]

In Japan, many pirates began as *kaizoku* – inland sea marauders – and were organized maritime bands, not unlike the raiders dominating Japan's Warring States era. Losing their lords or fortunes, many eventually turned to outlaw activities. One of the best known was not Japanese at all, Wang Zhi, a sixteenth-century Chinese pirate-trader and a feared *wako* leader. In the 1540s and 1550s, he organized armed fleets to protect his lucrative network of trading junks. Like many "pirates" of the time, he was a political and military authority unto himself, yet also allied with government forces when it suited his commercial interests. When Chinese rules began to interdict his operations after 1551, Wang turned his forces against district fortifications and treasure houses, raiding and sacking granaries and provincial outposts, and forcing villagers to flee their homes.

Over the next years, Wang's ships attacked with increasing boldness, landing garrisons and building fortifications and bases from which to launch attacks against towns along the Yangtze River Delta, including Nanjing. The number of pirates raiding from such bases was estimated in the thousands. The Chinese authorities in turn called for assistance from commanders raised in and knowledgeable about coastal territories, like Yu Dayou. Backed by armies of conscript farmers and professional soldiers, Yu attacked *wako* camps in coastal islands, turning the littorals into battle zones of burned ships and constant pursuits.

Pressed by such Chinese authority, and in search of less hazardous plunder, some pirate leaders struck out for other parts of the Asian Pacific. Local lore in Barrio Estanza, Lingayen, the Philippines, recounts a twentieth-century tenant farmer digging a well and striking a porcelain jar "filled with gold pieces and old Chinese coins." The treasure was attributed to the settlement created by the fabled Lim Ah Hong centuries earlier.[3]

Lim Ah Hong was a legendary pirate, a seaborne warlord who established a reputation as an outlaw of the imperial system, and also as a would-be colonist with the political power to rival provincial monarchs. Lim Ah Hong is remembered today by a channel near Manila Bay, reportedly excavated in the sixteenth century by his fleet of Chinese and Malay pirates. Partly commanded by a former Japanese samurai, his force attempted to create a colony in the Philippine islands by overthrowing the Spanish. Apocryphally – somewhat like Parameswara in Malacca – Lim Ah Hong was a son of royal Chinese descent who broke with his dynasty, choosing exile from his homeland and seeking to create his own alternative state.

Sailing south and away from China in 1573, Lim Ah Hong began his quest with a force of more than three thousand and hundreds of craft to raid, steal, and establish an island base to control the wealth of Spanish shipping. As was widely known, the Manila Acapulco trade brought in riches from the Spice Islands, and lacquerware and silks from China to be shipped across the Pacific to the Spanish Viceroy in Mexico. Lim Ah Hong's target was thus the Philippines.

As the Spanish were displacing Rajah Soliman around Manila, they tried to crowd out the Chinese merchants and traders who had long dominated the economy. Unsurprisingly, the Chinese were angered by new commercial restrictions and laws forcing them to pay tribute to Spain. Skirmishes and then major rebellions broke out.

In 1574, Lim Ah Hong arrived to besiege Manila with more than sixty Chinese warships, and Spanish authorities claimed a conspiracy between him and the local trading community. The attacks were repelled by Spanish defenses, however, and Lim Ah Hong and his band were forced to retreat. They remained in the Philippines, raiding and skirmishing, building fortifications and a base at Barrio Estanza, along with the canal – an escape route to the sea – that bears the pirate's name. Spanish and Chinese relations in Manila remained tense. Some accounts say Lim Ah Hong was captured; some say he sailed away and was never seen again.

Not all pirates were at crossed swords with Asian and European states. In some cases, they were also collaborators of the empires themselves. In these instances, royal houses or trading companies had their own pirates, and used them to war against their rivals. The visibility and impact of piracy increased as maritime commerce expanded and governors themselves employed "pirates" in the archipelagos, straits, and waterways.

Among the places most contested were the seas and islands near the China coast that were not actually "Chinese." A particular center was the island of Taiwan, called Formosa by Spanish and Portuguese claimants, a notorious locale of overlapping transits for pirate smugglers and oceanic traders from China, Japan, and Europe.

Because of early Austronesian migrations from Taiwan east and south, the island has long been critical to the history of the Pacific. Indigenous groups bridged the Asian and Oceanian worlds, transmitting language and culture. Knowledge of the Taiwanese Austronesian aborigines comes from later Chinese and Dutch reports. In 1603, the Chinese scholar Chen Di described a brave people that "like to fight." Women were active cultivators, using slash and burn techniques, and men lived in special houses, stalking deer with spears and traps, constantly training for lives of hunting and war. Dutch accounts also noted the warrior culture on the island, the sparring exercises, and the men's houses bearing "a great number of heads of their enemies."[4]

In 1624, the Dutch began establishing fortifications and a trading post on the island, incurring attack from clans wary of the political shifts that intruders would bring to the balance of power. Through the 1630s, the Dutch East India Company negotiated with village leaders for trade and peace agreements, exchanging goods while building up wooden and bamboo fortifications called Fort Zeelandia. Meanwhile, Chinese mullet fishermen worked in seasonal camps along the coastlines, setting out fishing nets and carrying away venison and deerskins.

The presence of all of these interests had been hastened since the Ming court had broken off trade with Japan. With direct commerce prohibited, Taiwan became a well-located base for gaining valuable trade items from the aborigines, as well as an offshore entrepôt for Japanese merchants and Chinese peddlers and sellers. The waters around Taiwan and the China Sea, predictably, attracted not only maritime commercial interests, but smugglers and then pirates.

Such was the case of Zheng Zhilong, who harried both Chinese and Dutch trading in the waters around Taiwan. Chinese sources of almost folkloric quality relate how Zheng came to leadership of a powerful clan formerly led by the half-legendary Yan Siqi and Li Dan. Yan had reportedly been a humble tailor who joined forces with the likes of fighters Deep Mountain Monkey, Iron Zhanghong, and other colorful characters to become leader of an outlaw band. Li Dan, his tenuous associate from Fujian, was a ruthless trader who had acquired both titles and wealth in the Philippines and Japan before becoming prominent smuggling deerskins and venison. Clever strategists, the men asked the Dutch for ships and support to help in raiding against Chinese merchant junks. The Dutch East India Company was happy to oblige, and the clan profited when both sides offered gifts and protections to defend their interests against the other.[5]

Other local pirates were also engaged in such protection and insurance. Chinese fishermen regularly paid part of their catch for guarantees of safety in local waters. In efforts to assert their own authority, Dutch officials began actively patrolling the straits and issuing licenses for legitimate trade. But the trader-pirate clans were already too strong. After Zheng Zhilong came to power, open contests developed.

As a young man of talent and reported good looks, Zheng sought his fortune in Macao, learning the ways of Europeans and Christianity, and becoming a translator for the Dutch East India Company. At the same time, he secretly joined the Yan Siqi pirate gang. After 1625, he became head of the gang, manipulating his ties with the Dutch for commissions to raid Chinese shipping while financing his own operations. Zheng attacked merchant and government forces and avoided pillaging villages to build up an image as a "rob the rich, feed the poor" bandit; his popularity gained him support in many regions, as well as thousands of recruits. Chinese officials now called on their Dutch rivals to demand an alliance against Zheng, but could not come up with a successful strategy against the wily pirate.

Unable to defeat Zheng, in 1628 the Chinese instead appointed him to an imperial position, naming him "Patrolling Admiral" with a commission to rid China's seas of pirates. This suited Zheng well, and he systematically destroyed his pirate competitors. The Dutch also benefited by contracting with Zheng for silks and other trade goods at fixed rates of silver. Zheng's power grew, especially around bases in Taiwan. By 1637, his cargo ships and war fleets had crushed all rivals and connected trade from the Chinese coast on up to Japan and all the way down to the Straits of Malacca. Traders in East and Southeast Asian seas sought his support and paid him for protection. No mere renegade, he controlled a far-flung maritime network, built a luxurious castle residence, and continued to mount challenges to the Dutch in Taiwan, helping finance a rival Chinese colony.[6]

When Zheng Zhilong died, his son Zheng Chenggong, known in the West as Koxinga, inherited the network. Koxinga was another oceanic, Asia-wide figure. Born to a Japanese mother in the trading port Hirado, he contested the authority of the Dutch East India Company, like his father, and also engaged in attacking the rulers of China. In 1644, the last of the once great Ming emperors was overthrown by rival powers out of Manchuria, to the north. As the Manchu lords conquered China, they proclaimed a new dynasty, the Qing.

Some Chinese, Ming loyalists, never accepted the rule of the Manchu Qing. In 1662, Koxinga attacked the Dutch colony at Taiwan, forcing the governor to surrender his fort. In claiming the island, however, he also challenged the reigning Qing Empire on the mainland by calling for a return to the previous Ming dynasty, and over the years continued to harass and raid against Qing authority.

Like many Pacific figures from multiple worlds, Koxinga leaves a complicated legacy. In China, he is revered for having expelled the Dutch from Taiwan and making the island into a "Chinese" territory. In Japan, he is noted for his half-Japanese parentage, while Taiwanese supporters underscore his campaigns as evidence of early Taiwanese independence and autonomy. "Pirates" were shapers of worlds and histories.

14 Villains and victims: pirate challenges to Asia and Europe.

Some pirates were truly remarkable characters. Among the best known would be Cheng I Sao, perhaps the greatest pirate leader among women. Known by different names, including Ching Shih and Lady Ch'ing, she came out of the familiar Canton coastal world of villages and junks, where marginal families lived from the sea, maritime trading, and smuggling. A former prostitute married to a sea robber, she and her husband organized gangs in the nineteenth century to attack ships, ransom crews, and force local settlements to pay for protection.

Cheng I Sao became head of a considerable pirate confederation when her husband died in 1807. She took her husband's adopted son as a lover and together they commanded a formidable alliance of raiding fleets. She is perhaps best known for establishing a rigorous code that set forth the percentage shares of each pirate in plunder, and elaborated a code of conduct-defining punishments for deserters and thieves. She also decreed execution for illicit affairs with captives, and decreed beheading and drowning for men and women who violated her rules.[7]

She was known for meticulous organization and ruthless energy, building up warehouses of ready stores, supplies, and weapons for her raiding campaigns and brutally torturing and butchering opponents. Chinese imperial fleets were overmatched by her firepower, and some officers and even an admiral reportedly committed suicide rather than be captured. Unlike the earlier Zheng Zhilong, Cheng I Sao cultivated no popular favor. Villages that resisted were systematically destroyed, the men beheaded and the women and children enslaved or held for ransom.

Always a step ahead, Cheng I Sao did not wait for the Chinese imperial government to gather the forces to crush her. When a serious alliance of Chinese and European navies threatened, she moved decisively, agreeing to withdraw and negotiating her own amnesty in 1810. Thousands of pirates, seeing the end of their livelihoods, turned over their weapons. Some were tried for crimes, but many kept their plunder and profits and some took up commissions in the Chinese military, including command positions with patrolling junks.

Cheng I Sao retired still enormously wealthy and powerful, but no longer a state enemy. Chronicles suggest she courted smugglers and gamblers, built up new businesses, and quietly passed away in 1844. In the end, she returned to her Canton home world, within reach of the sea, the marginal lives, and the harsh ambitions that had shaped her life and made her the most inspiring, feared, and reviled pirate of her day.

Not all of the best-known Pacific pirates bedeviled the Chinese Empire. Living in mangrove inlets and small islands protected by bays, sea raiders also regularly attacked local settlements as well as Spanish and Dutch traders connecting Batavia, Manila, and Malacca. Chronicles report that "In 1792 a fleet of raiders consisting of thirteen *prahu* and three smaller vessels hove in sight at Ratu Jaya in the Puti region, robbed the people of the newly harvested rice, destroyed the whole area by setting fire to it, and kidnapped three women and one man."[8]

Entire populations lived anxiously. Around the Indonesian islands, the revered and feared Jagos were men outside the law noted for their banditry, terror, and raiding, who reputedly gained followers by the powerful attraction of their spiritual or mystical authority. Legendary strongmen like Trunajaya were part of this tradition, and came from a historic line that extended also to the Malay *Orang Laut* and sea peoples of the Sulawesi archipelago, marauding for profit and in service of the local sultans.

These sea raiders were known to be organized and well-provisioned, maintaining stockhouses and arsenals and building redoubts. As the Dominican Francisco Gainza wrote in the 1840s from Southern Mindanao, Iranun communities were loosely allied confederations of fierce, well-armed criminals, building palisades and maintaining their "bellicose spirit by continuously engaging in robbery and theft. Through piracy they strike to gather slaves for aggrandizement and to provide their subsistence."[9]

Some of this was not so much piracy as privateering sanctioned by regional rulers. Such was the case in the armed rivalries between the Dutch East India Company and Sultan Mahmud of Johor, who sponsored trade out of his domain, Riau. As monopolists, the Dutch in Batavia and Malacca were threatened by the growth of ports that rivaled their own trading networks. More, the Dutch complained that the Sultan allowed such ports to be safe waters for Bugis parties raiding Dutch shipping.

In 1784, the Dutch subjugated the region with a naval attack, but three years later the Sultan called on an alliance of Iranun war vessels to expel the Europeans. Juragan Urip, a Bantanese trader, witnessed another three hundred Malay, Chinese, and Bugis raiders arriving to plunder coastal settlements and mass against Dutch shipping.

Unwittingly or not, it was the mercantile logic of the new empires that created many conditions for these conflicts. Battles with pirate confederations were strategic contests over the new colonial wealth of the Europeans and struggles for lost livelihoods. As Thomas Stamford Raffles, the founder of Singapore, observed, "A maritime and commercial people, suddenly deprived of all honest employment or the means of respectable subsistence, either sank into apathy and indolence or expended its natural energies in piratical attempts to recover, by force and plunder, what it had been deprived of by policy and fraud."[10]

The history of piracy, populated with colorful individual personalities, was a phenomenon of global political economy by the eighteenth century. For opportunistic villagers and small-time criminals alike it meant exclusion from traditional livelihoods, and a new status as outlaws – as defined by imperial powers. Spanish authorities called attackers rats for defying Spanish monopolies on trade. For the Dutch at Batavia, it meant extra customs duties paid by vessels to finance anti-pirate forces and patrol boats. The patrols may have noticed that the sea robber and slaving networks expanded in tandem with global trade. The growing popularity of tea meant increasing demand for sugar, which required plantation slaves supplied by increasingly active Iranun raiders in the Sulu Sea and Mindanao regions.

Accusations of violence and terror spread by marauders and pirates were accurate enough, and fearful traditions of unknown boats and sails are recorded in generations of tragic tales and oral accounts across archipelagos and coastlines. But imputations of savagery understand only part of the story. Piracy was a malleable evil, responding to naval patrols and military challenges, seeking profitable trades, and challenging the intrusion of empires into local seas. Pirates confederated, struck deals with governments, and changed businesses when they could no longer benefit from illegitimate commerce due to powerful opponents or declining profits.

Nor were Pacific pirates only in Asian waters, issued from coastal villages and mangrove deltas. It was Europeans themselves, particularly the privateers of increasingly powerful maritime states like England, who truly began to challenge the Dutch and Spanish at the other far end of the Pacific that broke upon the beaches and coastlines of the Americas.

9 ASIA, AMERICA, AND THE AGE OF THE GALLEONS

On November 3, 1579 a ship dropped anchor at Ternate, the Spice Islands, guided by fishermen in canoes off the island of Siau, north of Celebes. Onboard, its captain was one of the best-known pirates of his generation, and he had just sailed across the ocean from the coast of South America. The Chinese Lim Ah Hong had just a few years before vanished from historical records. Here was a pirate from another line, that of the Anglo-Saxons: Francis Drake. At Ternate, Drake met with Sultan Baab, himself recently victorious at having ousted the Portuguese, and they regaled each other with tales and traded for spices.

Drake avoided the nearby island of Tidore, where a Spanish position would easily have recognized him. Drake was emblematic of a new presence in the Pacific, coming not across the Indian Ocean, but across the Pacific by the Straits of Magellan. This presence was Dutch and British, arriving for exploration, but more, for the specific purpose of preying upon the empire of the powerful Spanish Crown by capturing its treasure ships, the fabulous Spanish galleons.

In 1577, Drake had sailed from Plymouth, England with a small fleet including his flagship, the *Pelican*. After more than two weeks in the Straits of Magellan his force entered the Pacific and he began to attack Spanish settlements along the coast, seize ship cargoes, and terrorize population centers like Valparaiso in Chile. He carried off so much treasure and ransom that he renamed his ship the *Golden Hind*, and drew the wrath of Spanish war vessels. While they waited for him to return to the Atlantic along the South American coast, he headed west for the open ocean instead, crossing the Pacific and provisioning in the East Indies.

The career and notoriety of Drake remain inextricable from the ambition that sent him into the Pacific: the plunder of Iberian shipping. Like Thomas Cavendish, who would later capture the galleon *Santa Ana*, Drake was one of a handful of captains who were hated as pirates by the Spanish, but operated under nominal agreements with European royalty, commissioned as privateers to attack and confiscate the wealth of rivals. By the late eighteenth century, such attacks were carried out directly by Royal Navy commanders acting with the full authority of the Crown.

The Spanish galleons were extraordinary prizes to have, as rich as rumor had them. Of the *Santa Ana*, Cavendish wrote of his staggering conquest, "to wit, an hundredth and 22 thousand pezos of golde; and the rest of the riches that the ship was laden with, was in silkes, sattens, damasks, with muske & divers other merchandise." Upon the successful transit and merchandizing of galleon treasures depended the fortunes of entire colonial settlements, and a global economy built on the east and west transfer of Asian wares and Spanish silver. More, the galleons were mobile worlds of transoceanic culture and exchange, migration, and slavery, connected to the founding of new communities in North and South America, islands like Guam, and in the Pearl of the Orient, the Philippines.[1]

For generations between 1565 and 1815, the galleons circled the Pacific at a rate of two or three per year, protected by armed escort. They were behemoths of the early modern maritime world, with three or four masts, carrying thousands of tons of cargo, on a scale unknown since the days of Zheng He's treasure fleets.

The trade had begun almost immediately upon the formal colonization of the Philippines under Miguel Lopez de Legazpi. Returning from the islands in 1565, Andrés de Urdaneta divided his fleet, seeking the most favorable winds to the Americas and coming upon his famous "volta" to the north. In the eighteenth century, galleons and other ships from Manila were still sailing with these winds to North America, crossing the breadth of the Pacific, though keeping a distance from the unknown California coast, famous for its fog, treacherous currents, and shipwrecks.

In time, provisioning stations were established in locales like Monterey on the way to Acapulco in Mexico. Much of the knowledge about the ships has been gained by maritime archeological digs, teams of field workers uncovering Chinese porcelain on the beaches of Baja California, or locating sources of Philippines' candle beeswax used in the Americas. Historians have tied sites and artifacts to registers of lost cargoes. Some forty galleons are known to have vanished or been wrecked, capturing the imagination of generations of treasure seekers.

The galleons were widely known to carry not only porcelain and wax, but ivory, lacquerware, and silk from Asia. In exchange, the Spanish paid in precious metals from Mexico and from Peru, where enslaved *Indio* populations worked the mines. Some of the cargoes traveled overland from the Pacific to the Gulf of Mexico, where they were shipped on to Spain across the Caribbean. The Manila–Acapulco circuit defines the galleons, but the global importance of the trade was that it connected Europe and the Americas to the real provider of treasure: China. Far from a colorful maritime episode of Latin American history, the galleon trade was actually the heart of the global economy beginning in the sixteenth century, an economy centered in the Pacific and anchored by Chinese goods and the circulation of Spanish silver.[2]

Above all, however, the impact of the galleon trade was that it carried not only treasure, but voyagers and cultures, and that it centered the interests of builders, traders, governors, merchants, and suppliers, as well as free laborers and unwilling slaves. Entire economies were built around the galleons. For two and a half centuries, hulls, planking, and masts came out of Pangasinan, Albay, Mindoro, Marinduque and Iloilo in the Philippines. Gangs of men in the thousands, called *cagayan* by the Spanish, were organized for hard and dangerous toil cutting trees and hauling heavy loads to shipyards. Filipinos faced labor exactions and brutal conditions, but were reportedly proud of the remarkable ships they built from hardwoods impervious to cannonballs.

At the other end of the circuit, some Filipino shipwrights made the Pacific crossing and developed lordly reputations in Mexico. Gaspar Molina settled into the coastal region of Sinaloa, married a local woman, and received a commission from the Spanish viceroy in Mexico City for a Jesuit ship to be built in Baja California. The ship, *Nuestra Señora de Loreto*, was launched in 1760. So pleased were the authorities that Molina was charged with a second ship, four years later.

For centuries, the great ships from the Philippines were delivered to syndicates in Manila. In 1750, Manila was a densely populated urban center, connected to adjacent pueblos teeming with workers in diverse trades: tailors, barbers, and leather and woodworkers set up shop. Boat builders, pilots, and metalsmiths found work for their talents, and printers produced documents and illustrations. Villagers from local provinces around Luzon crowded Manila neighborhoods, and sellers from the Visayas brought their produce. Many individuals were escapees from pueblos, seeking small jobs in colonial service, shipyards, and as laborers, fleeing customary tributes and mandated church services, sermons, and confessions.

They milled around in poor quarters and passed by large Spanish masonry houses with stables and carriages, in the shadows of palaces and cathedrals. City walls were guarded by bastions and gates, with guns trained upon the provinces and sea. Work was done by the provincial Filipinos, and by Chinese and mestizos. Spaniards worked in bureaucracy for titles and stipends and many looked to galleon trading for riches.[3]

Trading season in Manila brought Chinese junks, Malay merchants, and especially the galleons themselves, with their lucrative cargoes. Agents sold space and shares of precious stones from India and Ceylon, pepper from Sumatra, cloves from the Moluccas, carpets and damasks from Central Asia and the Mediterranean, and always, silk and porcelain from China. Travelers willing to risk the crossing from either side of the Pacific included convicts, Spanish women, friars, officials, clerks, and requisitions of servants and slaves captured from raiding or piracy.

Despite the lore of wealth and prestige of the galleons, travel on them was far from luxurious cruising. Cases like those of the *Santisima Trinidad* in 1755 are notable in their exemplary record of life and death. Journeys took months, and on this one both commoners and nobility suffered. Leaving Manila in July, the ship was still at sea in the early months of the following year. An ex-Spanish governor died on board, two women gave birth, some committed suicide, and more than two hundred were sick, had no food and were consumed by a "universal raging itch."

The slow transits threaded the ships through islands around the Philippines as well as the breakers and bays of the Americas. They also made passage among the Micronesian worlds of the Pacific. In this, over generations, the Spanish route transformed cultures across oceans, islands, and continents. Contacts, especially with the Mariana Islands and with Guam, leave insights into island life in the sixteenth, seventeenth, and eighteenth centuries.

Guam, Magellan's first Pacific landfall, is today a place of multiple histories: ancient sites, American military bases and shopping malls, Japanese and Spanish relics, golf courses, beaches, dive shops, and sport fishing centers. The archeological evidence suggests an early island people, the Chamorros, clustered in matrilineal oceanfront villages.[4] Traditionally, Chamorro authority was linked to beliefs in ancestral spirits such as the Taotaoomo'na, "people of before," and other spirits that inhabited plants, rocks, and bodies of water. Such spirit ancestors were challenged in 1668 when the Jesuit missionary, Padre Diego Luis de San Vitores, arrived to establish a colonial settlement. It started well. San Vitores was welcomed by the chief Kepuha, who provided land for a mission and was himself baptized, thus setting the foundations for a Spanish port of call in the Marianas.

But dissatisfaction would increase with the abandonment of Chamorro cultural practices and impositions by the Spanish. Strife developed. When a boy collecting wood for crosses was killed, Spanish soldiers retaliated. Chamorro leader Magalahi Hurao in turn led thousands of supporters against the Spanish, aided by a Chinese Buddhist named Choco Sangley. Skirmishing continued over the next year, with the chiefs battling, regrouping, and bargaining.[5]

In April 1672, Padre San Vitores and an aide from the Philippines were killed by Chief Mata'pang, whose child had been baptized without the Chief's consent. San Vitores' death brought violent reprisals and the Marianas mission was consumed by a generation of warfare. Chamorros were isolated into five villages by Spanish forces, and put under regimes of daily mass and surveillance by priests supported by soldiers. Most of the Chamorros of the northern Mariana Islands were forcibly relocated to Guam.

Local faiths and traditions struggled over generations. The cultural skill of ocean navigation weakened as outrigger voyages circulating between the Marianas and Carolines disappeared with islanders dispersed from warfare, depopulation, and cultural erosion. Legacies of the early Chamorro culture and celestial knowledge were secreted away in drawings in grottos and caverns known as the Star Caves, waiting to be rediscovered in a distant future.[6]

The traditions, knowledge, and narratives of oceanic voyagers were subsumed by the Spanish and their galleons. The crews and passengers that sailed with goods to and from the Americas did not, however, leave only a Spanish legacy, but chains of uniquely hybrid immigrant and cross-cultural communities across the Pacific. Perhaps one in five crew members was a native Filipino, though on many ships the number may have been more than half. Mexicans and Portuguese were also regular sailors, along with the Spaniards; some took on the services of East Asians, Chinese or Japanese.

The earliest Asians crossing the Pacific to the New World appear to have been Filipinos, often generically denominated as *Chinos*, sailing with the galleons from the sixteenth century. Men from Cebu crewed the *San Pablo* in 1565, and Portuguese pilot Pedro de Unamuno records a 1587 reconnaissance landing in Morro Bay, California, where Filipino crew members "armed with shields and spears" fought with attacking Indian parties, losing both Spanish and Filipino shipmates. In other incidents, shipwrecked crews were assisted by local Indians, who helped build rafts and engaged in provisioning and trading with the strangers.[7]

What is known of California Indian cultures is reconstructed from archeological traces and later ethnological studies of living communities like the Ohlone, Costanoan, Esselen, and Salinan. Ancestors had likely come across a semi-frozen Bering Strait as Siberian hunters more than ten thousand years earlier, much as migrations were pulled from Sunda to Sahul in Southeast Asia at the last glacial maximum. Foraging and pursuing prey southward, they dispersed and settled into hundreds of local cultures and languages.

In northern and central California, coastal groups found rich territories and created communities. Many are famed for their black obsidian arrowheads used for game hunting, and their dwellings built on spruce and pine frames, lined with hanging storage baskets woven from willow and twining. Staple diets were founded on acorn mush and cakes, with ground kernels leached to remove bitter acids. In river deltas and along the ocean, fishing was a key element of everyday life. Societies taking root on littorals and around bays were regarded for their elegant canoes.

Spanish navigators noted furtive contacts and then moved on; they would return in the eighteenth century in force with armed parties, establishing naval bases to protect trade, provide supplies, and make colonial claims. With these came a mission system of churches built first from timber, and then from adobe brick and stone up and down the California coast.

15 Spanish and Indian worlds: Junipero Serra holds mass in Monterey, California.

Under Franciscan leaders like Junipero Serra, the missions developed as outposts for Catholic administration and the indoctrination of local populations, with worship halls, regular rites of baptism, and an expansion of livestock and plowed-field agriculture tended by Indian labor. This would be a time of radiant Spanish power in California with widely travelling priests, converted settlements under the authority of a Father, and regular prayers before dazzling altarpieces surmounted by the crucifix. It would also be a time of uncertainty for many local Indian cultures, some warring against the intruders, some collapsing from disease and expropriation, others searching for adaptation to a new colonial world.[8]

Mixed colonial societies grew from the earliest contacts up and down the west coast of the Americas, drawn together by the ships and crews of the Spanish Pacific circuits. Heading south, traces of Manila in Mexico are regularly identified by chroniclers in cultural borrowings. The fermented coconut drink *tuba fresca* is generally attributed to members of the galleon *Espiritu Santo*, who abandoned ship in 1618 and passed on their knowledge to locals. In addition, food preparation, such as ceviche and shellfish broiling, are also claimed as transplants to Mexico from the Philippines, along with mangoes, the *palmera* coconut tree, and the *rambutan*, introduced by botanist Juan de Cuellar.

Tracing Filipino histories through individual lives is challenging since the common use of the designation "Filipino" did not develop until the end of the nineteenth century. Most records and oral traditions would refer imprecisely to "Chinos" or "Manila Men." Researchers tracing family lineages often seek out heritage in Mexican coastal communities and villages, though as one in tropical Espinalillo, Coyuca confessed, "racial identity has become dissipated through intermarriages with other races. Mexico racial mixing is a very rich brew. One has only to look at its people today to reach this conclusion."[9]

Still, such pursuits at times turn up common family names and stories that recount grandparents of grandparents sailing from the Philippines to Mexico. Estimates suggest that tens of thousands of Filipinos made the galleon crossings across the centuries, and that the great majority were native laborers, with a representation of merchants and officials, often Spanish and Filipino mestizos of mixed heritage.

The transits flowed both ways across the Pacific. Linguists in Manila have traced the Mexican Nahuatl origin of numerous Philippine Tagalog words, from avocado and balsa to chocolate and *zapote*. Some historians argue that the Spanish Empire in Mexico should, in fact, be regarded as more Mexican and less Spanish. Legazpi, the conqueror of Manila, was himself from northern Spain, but had been decades in Mexico City when he set out for the Philippines from the Americas. His grandson Juan de Salcedo, who battled Lim Ah Hong the pirate, was a Spaniard born and raised in Mexico City. In the later seventeenth century, colonists, military recruits, and servants settling around the Philippines in Cebu and Panay were partly European Spaniards heavily mixed with creoles, mestizos, and, according to some reports, Aztec *Indios*.

Along with the galleon trade also evolved a system of financial support to the Philippines known as the *situado*. Manila had to schedule wages for military personnel, compensation for clerks and officials, donations to hospitals, widows' pensions, and other administrative costs. Tributes and taxes were levied and regularly increased in the islands but were never nearly enough.

The ultimate dependence of the Philippines on the Mexican treasury to continue functioning has led some historians to suggest that Manila was legally a subject of Spain, but properly a colony of the Viceroy of Mexico. A 1566 letter from Seville noted that the galleon route was a source of tremendous esteem for colonial subjects: "those of Mexico are mighty proud of their discovery, which gives them to believe that they will be the heart of the world."[10]

Taxes, revenues, and payments from Mexico City could, however, only partly support Manila. Great profits still depended on the success of the galleon trade, whose final destination from Asia was Acapulco, a great port sheltered by an inner bay with a deep anchorage. Many navigators considered it perhaps the finest along the North American coastline, protected by peninsulas and mountains. In the galleon era, ports like Acapulco and also San Blas were active maintaining the galleons. Both men and skilled women from the Philippines worked as sailmakers, shipwrights, and carpenters.

Though ideal for maritime trade, ports like Acapulco were not otherwise notably hospitable colonial settlements: Spanish officials called Acapulco a "hot and sickly land" within a burned and tormented landscape. The population remained at a few thousand Indians, mestizos, Chinese, and Filipinos, laboring in extreme heat with few provisions. In the early sixteenth century, visitors would have seen cluttered houses of mud, straw, and wood, rounded off by a convent and parish church. Acapulco was something of an impoverished fishing village, meaningful only in that it connected the Hispanic world to China.

But that connection was all-powerful. In Mexico, the galleons were critical to supplying the viceregal capital of the Spanish Empire with goods and generating revenues in sales and taxes. Cottons and silks from Asia dominated the tastes and cultural status of the well-to-do, and provided the basic stuffs of everyday garments. Cargoes unloaded in Acapulco were shipped overland to the Gulf Coast. In early eighteenth-century Vera Cruz, the luxury trade was on full display following the afternoon traffic on the Alameda, with thousands of coaches rolling along the roads, and streets reportedly "full of Gallants, Ladies, and Citizens, to see and to be seen, to court and to be courted." Exclusive shops sported coveted Chinese porcelain and textiles. The trade of galleon goods was closely regulated by municipal authorities, and challenged with equal energy by smugglers who paid bribes and made threats to gain control of cargoes.[11]

16 Traders of wealth and cultures: Mexican marketplace of the Manila–Acapulco galleons.

Some of those cargoes were human beings, for the galleons also brought thousands of slaves from Mindanao and Indonesia and from the Indian Ocean. Some were carried to become laborers as Mexican Indian populations were decimated by epidemics and abuse. Many were enslaved domestic help, requested by officials of New Spain. One of the women who traveled on the galleons became globally famous within the Manila and Acapulco transit worlds. In the city of Puebla at the Church of Compania, a tombstone is built into the wall: it marks the resting place of Catarina de San Juan.

A saint of the Catholic Church, Catarina's history, in part apocryphal, is both remarkable and ordinary. Chroniclers say she was born a princess named Mirnha in western India to a Mongolian line fleeing from Turkish invasion. Her family settled along the Indian coast where it happened that Portuguese slavers were active. According to popular accounts, Mirnha was distinguished, with dark hair and eyes. While walking on the beach with her brother, she was set upon and carried off as a prisoner to Cochin, and then on to Manila. She became another transoceanic soul pulled into the global Pacific circuit.

Mirnha's circuit saw her placed on a galleon around 1620 and carried as a slave to Mexico, arriving in Acapulco to be the property of a Captain Miguel de Sosa and his wife Margarita de Chavez in Puebla. Mirnha was striking and exotic in Mexico, known for her long braids, and colorful embroidered garments. Her appearance was initially read as Chinese and she was called the *China Poblana*; yet in a world impacted by the galleons, her look ceased to be foreign and was adopted in full skirts, shawls, and swept-back hair by other women. By way of Pacific crossing, the Indian slave became a "Chinese" progenitor of the archetypical young Mexican woman celebrated in fashion, art, cultural heritage, and by nationalist folklore.

But Mirnha's influence went beyond her appearance. She was baptized in Mexico as Catarina and sent for a Catholic education. As a domestic, she was treated as a member of the household and married Domingo Suarez, a Chinese slave, though she refused to cohabit with her husband. Entering a convent, Catarina would gain the pious reputation of a saint, attracting generations of chroniclers. Many emphasized the inherent worthiness of her supposedly noble birth, and praised her for embracing Catholicism, demonstrating humility and practicing virtue.[12]

More, admirers reported on her mystical levitations, her night battles against demons, and her powerful visions of global politics.

She became, intentionally or not, a revered figure not only of faith, but of struggles for empire. In 1678 she reputedly joined the Virgin Mary to save Spanish fleets in hurricanes and provided spiritual strength to armies combating French forces. Perhaps unsurprisingly, she was noted for her prayerful assistance of Spanish commanders against English and French pirates. She also told of night voyages filled with comets and journeys across China, Japan, and the Philippines. The Pacific world had shaped her life and inhabited her dreams.

Catarina's visions might have given comfort and inspiration to Spanish rulers, but imperial struggles in the Pacific were actually heralding an end to the very galleon circuit that had brought her from Asia to the Americas.

The eighteenth century saw significant shifts in global maritime power and during the Seven Years' War (1756–63) the British seized control of Manila for two years. This was to secure British dominance along strategic trading routes and protect colonial India. It was also a concerted effort to outwit France and to break the historic monopolies of other states on trade and territory in the Pacific. For Britain to flourish, the Spanish Lake had to come to an end. The seventeenth-century legal theorist Hugo Grotius had famously argued for a *liberum mare*: a free or open sea; this meant global trading and competitive access to a Pacific that was defined continuously with the Indian Ocean and the South China Sea.[13]

When Britain launched a force from Madras and occupied Manila in 1762, the city was sacked, the galleon trade interrupted and looted, and the Spanish governors began to recognize the vulnerability of an economy founded on the success of the galleon transits. The galleon merchant monopoly came to an end and the Royal Philippines Company was chartered in 1785 to become a direct investor in tobacco, coffee, sugar, and pepper, seeking to compete on global markets with the other European powers, relying much less on the luxury trade out of Asia.

But investments came from many national sectors and, by the nineteenth century, American and British trading companies began to dominate in the Philippines economy. Notably, many of these focused on cash crops grown by wealthy Chinese mestizo families employing tenant laborers. These regional wealthy families formed a highly cultured society, sending their children for Spanish and European education in Manila and around the world.

Those children, aware of their privilege, but also of their inferior status as colonial subjects, were influenced by liberal ideas and began to agitate for greater legal rights equivalent to those of Spaniards and to separate the authority of the Church from politics. Some like the young erudite José Rizal would become known as *Illustrados*, and would shape an identity not as Indios or Chinos, but as Filipinos.

By the time agitation for Filipino independence exploded in the late nineteenth century, the galleon trade was already extinct. It had expired along with the profound economic and political upheavals shaping Latin America. Beginning in 1802, the Acapulco trade fell into decline as three galleons were returned to Manila with unsold cargoes, an almost unthinkable loss a few generations earlier. The arrival of European and American interests into Mexico's marketplaces, along with the founding of the Royal Philippine Company, had been encouraging direct shipping between the Iberian peninsula and Southeast Asia, cutting the monopolistic advantages so long held by the galleons.[14]

The revolutionary changes of modern Latin America then cast an inescapable shadow upon the galleons, hastening their demise. Mexico's independence in 1810 was framed by battles, sieges, and trade disruptions including port closures that prevented galleons from landing. One, the *San Carlos*, was re-routed to San Blas and unloaded its wares at an enormous loss. Authorities in Manila, meanwhile, had only fragmentary news about the situation in Mexico, and sent the *Magallanes* across the ocean to Acapulco. It was held in the harbor for four years, ultimately one of the very last galleons to make the transit.

Political ferment was everywhere along the Pacific. In 1819 Monterey, California was attacked by South American adventurers from Argentina allied with Filipino seamen recruited by the Frenchman Hyppolite Bouchard, who commanded a patrolling warship along the American coastlines. Halfway across the Pacific in Honolulu, Bouchard negotiated with Hawaiian King Kamehameha for the *Santa Rosa*, a ship tied up by the monarch over compensation for cargoes of sandalwood.[15]

Manila continued to send ships – sometimes frigates – to Acapulco, but with military clashes disrupting entire regions, trade and profits fell off. In 1821, the city finally proclaimed itself free. By 1825, the last ships sailed the treasure routes between Manila and Acapulco; the famed galleon trade that had defined the European Pacific world for centuries in lives and treasure, had finally come to an end. The fragments washed up as archeological treasures along the coasts of the great ocean.

10 NAVIGATORS OF POLYNESIA AND PARADISE

For two and a half centuries the Spanish galleons and their attendant marauders and rivals crossed the Pacific from Manila to Acapulco. Still, the great volta of Spanish transit was almost as remarkable for what it did not do. As Magellan had crossed from South America to Guam without making landfall, so the galleons followed winds and sailing routes that allowed them to never sight Hawai'i, in the middle of the Pacific Ocean. Despite speculation that galleons of Juan Gaytan in 1542 might have stopped in the islands, no definitive case has been made that the voyagers of the Spanish Lake ever did more than pass by hundreds of miles to the north and south.[1]

Separated from European contact and drawing on a voyaging heritage of Polynesian ancestors, Hawaiians developed richly complex cultures and political organizations. A number of small kingdoms dominated the islands, each led by a ruler assisted by chief ministers. Ranked below them were *ali'i*, or chiefs, whose power depended upon their ancestral genealogies and personal *mana*. The famous *kahuna* were priests also skilled in traditional arts, building, and medicine.

Most of the work – fishing, farming, making *tapa* cloth, harvesting – was performed by commoners. They paid taxes in food and cloth and were bound by the sacred *kapu*, or taboo, system, which organized the society according to right behaviors in correspondence with the Hawaiian spiritual cosmos. A commoner was never to let his shadow touch a high chief. Particular foods, practices, and parts of islands were prohibited to all but a few sacred persons. Spirituality infused everyday life, from canoe building to planting in muddy taro patches. The remains of Hawaiian stone temples, honored by offerings of fruit and flowers, to this day attest to the lingering power of ancient gods like Ku, Kanaloa, Lono, and Kane.

Far south in the Pacific, valley and river cultures in New Guinea also developed from ancient migrations and customary exchange networks distinct from European contact. As across much of the western Pacific, archeological digs indicate early migrations from Southeast Asia by way of then-existing sea and land passages, and the development of both coastal and forest cultures with sago cropping and shellfish gathering. The Papuans were later joined by Austronesian migrations and the spread of Oceanian peoples along the island that would be called Papua New Guinea.

The first European sightings came early in the exploration of the Pacific. In 1526–7, Don Jorge de Meneses called the principal island "Papua," after a Malay term describing the texture of Melanesian hair. "New Guinea" was subsequently applied in 1545 by the Spanish navigator Íñigo Ortiz de Retes, who thought the local peoples similar to those of the Guinea Coast on the African continent.[2]

European navigators continued to cross local waters and explore the coastlines of the islands for generations, yet detailed knowledge was remarkably sparse. Chinese and Makassan traders navigated the western half, and Dutch captains of the VOC had some arrangements for procuring Papuan slaves and aromatic *massoi* bark in the seventeenth century at Onin Island, which was under the authority of the Sultan of Tidore. In general, Western navigators charted coastlines and trading stations, but for almost four centuries, no expeditions journeyed far up the great Sepik river basin, or knew of the mosquito bags in which the river dwellers spent the night. Skirmishes and trade between clans marked encounters from estuaries and basins up into dense forests.

In the highlands were the Sky People, connected to their descendants the Enga by fourteen generations of genealogies and legendary tales. In valleys, cultivators turned soil for yam harvesting and ritual adornments of tusks drawn from pig-rearing and the spirits of ancestors. But little of this was known.[3]

For generations, parallel Pacific worlds developed; islanders held counsel in pantheons of gods, highland tribal organizations, and traditions of canoe fleets and long migrations with little concern for the

17 Overlapping seas: Malay, Papuan, and European coastal encounters.

"rim" that dominated the seventeenth-century Pacific of galleons and the Spanish Lake. Conversely, European knowledge of Oceanian cultures and islanders remained scarce. The Portuguese and Dutch were still contesting the South China Sea and the East Indies. The Dutch maintained their window on Japan from Deshima in Nagasaki harbor. The Portuguese continued at Macao, and the Malacca to Goa routes carried the trade of China and India. New interlopers, such as the French and English, arrived in Asia.

Some emblematic figures captured such continuities and changes as they took place in the Pacific between the sixteenth and eighteenth centuries. One set of figures was a remarkable pair, William Dampier and Jeoly, the "Painted Prince." Dampier, whose National Gallery portrait in London identifies him as a pirate, explorer, and scientist, was like Francis Drake notorious for his raiding on Spanish shipping. His self-reported adventures of sea battles and pillage are, however, matched by a broad eye for natural history and ethnography. His accounts look back to buccaneer romanticism, and also forward to the exploitation of technical and cultural knowledge that would mark British naval mastery after navigators like Captain James Cook.

In a career of intrigue, Dampier raided Spanish colonies in the Caribbean, Panama, Peru, and Mexico in the early 1680s, and by mid-decade turned toward the Pacific, attacking shipping around Guam and Mindanao, making port in Manila, China, and even along the coastline of Australia. Yet he also wrote journals of the Galapagos Islands, where Charles Darwin would much later follow, commenting on the "varieties of woods, manatees, iguanas, land tortoises and sea turtles," and he studied meteorological conditions and volcanic, coastal, and savannah landscapes.

In Mindanao, Dampier first met Jeoly, a chiefly man from the Miangas atoll, who had been wrecked in the Philippines with his mother. Kidnapped and robbed by fishermen, the castaways were sold as slaves to the Sultan. Later, they reappeared on the slave market in Madras, India, where they were bought by an English trader. At this point Dampier purchased half ownership and in 1691 sailed to London to exhibit Jeoly, calling him "the Painted Prince" because of his extraordinary tattoos.

By accounts, Jeoly was an earnest captive determined to get home, regaling Dampier with tales of rich islands and women, proposing voyages, and inconsolable about the untimely death of his mother. Dampier made use of English curiosity and had Jeoly display his tattoos as living art. Whereas medieval Europeans had regarded curiosity as a suspect quality contrary to faith, by the seventeenth century "imported objects and local artefacts" from an expanding world were sources of fascination, passed along maritime trading routes and tied to ideas of pursuing useful knowledge.[4]

These intellectual currents shaped new encounters with the Pacific. Just as Dampier stood between the Renaissance pirate and the English navigator, so did Jeoly have a marking role as a trophy exhibited for his tattoos. His world was the Pacific of the East Indies with its generations-old struggles and collaborations between sultans, seaborne empires, and Chinese and Indian traders. Yet Jeoly was also an ethnographic symbol, one of a series of tattooed visitors making the Pacific circuit who by the next century would be celebrated in European capitals as exemplars of primary and uncorrupted nature.

Great currents of wealth, promise, and misery ran to Europe and the Americas through the Pacific of the spice, galleon, and Asian slaving trades. Yet in the early eighteenth century, only occasional forays intersected the Polynesian and Oceanian worlds. Such was the case for the island people of Rapa Nui. From their place in the eastern Pacific, some two thousand miles from the next nearest landfall, unknown sails on the horizon would have been an extraordinary sight; especially if none had appeared for more than a millennium.

The ancient Rapa Nui most likely migrated from the Marquesas Islands or from Mangareva, perhaps around 400–600 CE. They brought food, and plants and animals. Obsidian was available for tools, and volcanic craters held drinking water. The Rapa Nui built dwellings and ceremonial sites, and carved enormous statues called *moai* that would become the most famous archeological remains in the Pacific, commanding the attention of the world.

A 1722 encounter was with a Dutch ship commanded by Jacob Roggeveen; he renamed his landfall for the day of its sighting: Easter Island. Roggeveen, like many contemporaries, was on a mission to find the Great Southern Continent. He was astonished by the Rapa Nui peoples, who were excellent swimmers, but whose own terrains seemed sparse and canoes too flimsy for ocean-going travel. How had they arrived and built up the extraordinary statues in such a barren place?

The world of the early Rapa Nui must have been very different from that encountered by Roggeveen. Oral tales buttressed by archeology of bone collections and waste heaps, pollen analysis, and paleontology tell a story. Thirty thousand years before human arrival until the dawn of Polynesian settlement, the island was a subtropical forest of towering trees, ferns, and grasses. Birds nested and marine mammals flourished in its waters. But as Rapa Nui established themselves across generations, growing populations harvested the forests for canoes, dwellings, for firewood, and for moving the huge statues. Research also shows the destruction of seeds and plants by rats. Seabird colonies and small animals disappeared, and without trees, large canoes became impossible. After 1500, bone heaps show no more porpoises or deep-ocean food sources.

Without these reliable surpluses, the complex political and spiritual organization of a Polynesian society was no longer possible. Islanders described to their European visitors warriors taking over from hereditary chiefs and fragmenting into battling clans. Settlements were abandoned for caves, and in the eighteenth century rivals toppled the statues of their enemies.[5]

Roggeveen's ships made contact at this critical juncture, seeing a society whose growth and ingenious culture had outstripped its resources, leading to political upheaval. It was a scenario that had likely been played out many times before across Oceania for unknown generations as Polynesian navigators set sail for new islands drawn by adventure, but also pressed by growing populations, resource competitions, and political challenges. Easter Island was simply a smaller, more precarious example.

In this, Roggeveen saw parts of an evolving Oceanian past little known to others and, if he had wanted, a cautionary tale. Subsequent Pacific histories would also have to account for the impact that Europeans themselves made in the transformations of island societies, as worlds separated for centuries now drew together.

The Central Pacific was where new encounters and possibilities would be most dramatically realized. In multiple Polynesian kingdoms, European ships came upon complex political states with expanding populations and ambitious rulers. Many were at critical junctures as clans evolved into powerful kin-based alliances led by families such as the Pomares in the Society Islands and the Kamehamehas in the Hawaiian Islands. Rivalries between regions and chiefs generated internal tensions, creating special opportunities for outlanders who could trade and exchange prestige goods, weapons, and new forms of spiritual authority.

In the Society Islands, political and spiritual power had long been aligned. The Leeward Island of Raiatea is little known compared to the fame of its neighbor Tahiti, yet it plays a key role in Polynesian history, for it was a center of religion and knowledge. There, in houses of learning, men studied genealogies and heraldry, and elders taught astronomy and navigation. This scholarly culture was radiated outward by voyagers and colonizers west toward Aotearoa New Zealand, east to Rapa Nui, and north to Hawai'i. On Raiatea is a sacred stone platform; according to custom, every such platform built by Polynesians across the Pacific must have a stone from the original.

As a sacred site of learning, Raiatea became the center for a powerful and demanding god, Oro, associated with war. From around 1600, the eminence of Oro was incarnated in his closest worshipers, a legendary core of elite young islanders who were raised apart from their families and reputed to have supernormal abilities acquired from their teachers, the priestly Tohunga. Chosen for their beauty, physical prowess, and mastery of traditional knowledge, this *Arioi* elite of Oro were taken in secret initiations and famed for their special tattoos, rituals, and open sexuality.[6]

Charismatic, striking, and superbly organized, the Oro cult was favored by important chiefs who built up ties as means to enhance their own political authority. Whether by persuasion or violent conquest, the power of Oro spread. Some chroniclers have argued that Oro was the center of an Oceanian alliance of islands and chiefdoms, meeting at Taputapuatea in regal processions of canoes for political and religious convocations, making ritual sacrifices of shark, turtle, and human enemies.

Whatever such alliance developed would ultimately collapse as priests and chiefs from different islands fell into violence. Traditions maintain that the last canoe to leave the sacred meeting place marked it with a taboo. Descendants of islanders from all around the Pacific returned centuries later in 1992 to Raiatea to rebuild their spiritual heritage and to finally lift the taboo.[7]

In the eighteenth century, European history began to coincide with the legacies of Oro and Polynesian politics. Oro had become the foundation for the authority of families like the Pomare line, with kin and marriage alliances on Tahiti, Moorea, and Raiatea. But Oro was not the only god; rival clans adhered to the deity Tane and contested their enemies' claims to power. Into these struggles for *mana* and authority came strangers from Europe.

Most of these encounters are well known as European narratives, marked by the names of eighteenth-century explorers: Samuel Wallis and Philip Carteret sailing for England, Jean-François de Galaup de Lapérouse and Louis Antoine de Bougainville exploring Tahiti, Samoa, New Guinea, and the Solomon Islands under French royal colors. The French and British were not interested merely in "discoveries." They meant to map out trading and strategic routes that would give them commercial and naval advantages, and significant political prestige. Remarkably, their early journals and logs instead created an indelible vision of Pacific islands as places to ponder paradises and lost elysian worlds.[8]

The Tahiti landing of English Captain Samuel Wallis in 1767 set a familiar template. Arriving in Matavai Bay, his ship was enveloped in fog. As it lifted, Wallis found to his astonishment that he was surrounded by hundreds of small canoes and over eight hundred Tahitians, waving plantain branches. A few days later over two thousand men attempted to claim his ship and bombarded it with rocks. Wallis used his English cannon, shot some of the warriors, and destroyed their beached canoes. The Tahitians decided to accommodate the outlanders.

Wallis rhapsodized about the woman who had paramount authority in the region, Purea (also Obrera), whom he called the queen. She was, in fact, a chieftain and wife of the leader of the Teva tribe. She dined aboard ship, ordered him a *lome-lome* massage, and worked with the ship's surgeon on herbal and medicinal balms for injuries. Wallis reports that she seemed inconsolable at his departure, a flattering thought, though not unmerited. He had demonstrated the efficacy of firepower and trade gifts, and though Wallis did not emphasize it, she was locked into political struggle with rivals.

So much depended upon accidents of landing, as the French would also find, arriving just months later. Bougainville elaborated Wallis' stories, observing a natural timelessness which he himself invented. The Tahitians had learned from Wallis, and there were no violent incidents; hogs, fruit, and water were exchanged, and islanders and sailors entertained each other both shipboard and in the villages. Sailors' small valuables and tools disappeared, but no major confrontations developed.

Bougainville had discovered what he believed was "the true youth of the world," and reconfigured "the Pacific" from a place of Asiatic trading, slaves, and treasure to that of an unspoiled natural paradise overgrown with wild ginger, tree ferns, and tropical flowers. Matavai Bay, a small place, had a stupendous impact on Europe. Bougainville's tales suited the reigning sentimentalist tendencies in Continental literature of the era, and seemed to validate the popularity of the philosopher Jean-Jacques Rousseau and the idea of the "noble savage," inspiring writers like Denis Diderot to pen imaginary tales of graceful Tahitian lives. Even theft seemed a sign of innocence in a world where all things were shared, including personal possessions and even amorous affections. As chronicler Commerson would enthuse, "They know no other god than Love."[9]

Wallis had begun this narrative, as island women seemed so willing to freely consort with his men, officers and sailors alike. Behind the sensuous bodies desired by haggard seamen, little was understood about the women's political roles, sent forth by chiefs and clans wary of European weapons, or at times themselves desirous of the status and gifts they could acquire, especially pieces of iron, an unknown technology. Parts of Wallis' ship, the *Dolphin*, were in fact famously made almost unworkable by sailors wrenching out spikes and nails to exchange for favors.

For the Tahitians, this meant access to a remarkable new material for fashioning into tools and weapons. For the sailors it meant a world of bodies and pleasures. For both it was an exchange of resources, natural and industrial, utilitarian and abundant. The French mission, so closely following Wallis', embellished this world, reading an erotic poetry into Tahitian curiosity, hospitality, and struggle for dominance among intricate rival family clans.[10]

The European vision of idyll would immediately dominate Pacific representations and never lose its power: images of sensuality and complaisant nature founded scores of stories, reports, and pictures. Later, these images developed into dominant representations for a global tourist industry. At first contact, however, it was not only adventurous Europeans alighting on stranded isles who were touring distant worlds. Pacific peoples were also making the global circuit.

If Jeoly with William Dampier and Melanesians taken to Peru earlier by Quiros had been little more than curiosities and candidates for servitude, unique individuals met by European ships in the eighteenth century were soon celebrated world travelers. As he sailed from Tahiti, Bougainville took onboard an enthusiastic brother and son of chiefs, Ahutoru, whom he hoped to use as an interpreter. Ahutoru was personally eager to exchange cultures and curious about the world of the white strangers. He was noted for his strong memory and cultural knowledge, providing the French party with details on natural history and edible plants taken aboard ship. He also offered knowledge of star navigation to the Leeward Islands, and collaborated on a basic Tahitian vocabulary.

In France he was a celebrity, the right man at the right time to embody Rousseau's ideas of natural goodness and noble savages. Ahutoru seemed to enjoy the attention, and was presented in aristocratic circles by Bougainville to great acclaim. He was fascinated by the city of Paris, loved to explore, shop, and took great pleasure in dance and visiting the opera. He seemed to incorporate what his hosts expected: strong enthusiasms and curiosity, a shrewd common sense, and an attachment to his patrons. The most notable was the Duchess of Choiseul, and between them a strong bond developed, marked by gifts, praises, exchanges, and lingering visits.

Still, Paris was not Tahiti, and Ahutoru longed for home. Despite their affection, Ahutoru's patrons also believed that a noble savage must return to his own world. Bougainville and the Duchess gained him passage on a ship, along with significant stocks of seeds, plants, livestock, and tools as return gifts. He sailed to Mauritius in the Indian Ocean where he contacted governor Pierre Poivre, who had made an earlier name smuggling spice out from the Dutch East Indies, and a naval office named Marion Du Fresne, who was keen to explore the Pacific islands. Unfortunately, a smallpox epidemic soon claimed Ahutoru on a transit to Madagascar. It was a terrible loss as the charming enthusiast wasted away at a French colonial outpost. Du Fresne continued on his exploratory mission without Ahutoru, and would become famous for being killed and eaten by the Maori in New Zealand for breaking a taboo.[11]

Back in Tahiti, the paradisical world of Bougainville was already not as he had imagined. When another voyager arrived a year after him to Matavai Bay, populations were declining, diseases like syphilis were widespread, and Purea, though still a commanding presence, was besieged. She had tried to gain authority for her sons by moving one of Oro's sacred feather girdles into a *marae* controlled by her clan, and the conflict had been devastating. Long skirmishing had left animals slaughtered and crops decimated.

The new visitor who witnessed all of this, Captain James Cook, declined to become directly involved in the internecine warfare of Polynesia. With a temperament more ethnographic and technical than philosophical, he is famed as being the first of the great modern European navigators, uninterested in the privateering bravado of Drake, and targeted instead on missions of exploration, mapping, natural history, and navigational knowledge. Whereas the Dutch had turned back when no obvious commercial profit was to be had from their Oceanian ventures, Cook carried his sponsor with him: Joseph Banks, a botanist commanding a team of naturalists and artists to record the views, with a keen interest in theorizing settlement, migration, and culture patterns.

All of this would serve the British Admiralty well, of course, and Cook provided invaluable strategic knowledge to the navy. He became especially noted for preventing scurvy among his sailors, which earned him a humanitarian legacy, but he was still a taskmaster, imposing severe discipline and flogging on his sailors, and he made good use of cannon, punitive raiding, and burning of island villages and canoes to attain his ends. What remains indisputable is that he was the most extraordinary navigator of his time.

Cook's fame rests upon three multi-year missions; simply listing the passages and Pacific locales he mapped for European knowledge is a staggering task. The first voyage, following the stage set by Wallis and Bougainville, was nominally scientific, landing in Tahiti to observe the transit of the planet Venus across the sun. From there, he continued on to map New Zealand and the unknown west coast of Australia including the landings for Botany Bay and Port Jackson, later Sydney. Connecting Oceania and Asia, he looped through the Torres Strait and passed Timor and Dutch Batavia before returning to Europe across the Indian Ocean.[12]

One of the resonant legacies of this voyage was not only Cook's storied navigational precision, but his talent for incorporating local learning into his own. Much of the expedition's cartographic, cultural, and historical knowledge was developed in collaboration with a highly skilled and noted navigator-priest named Tupaia, who had been driven out of Raiatea to Tahiti by Boraborans.

Joseph Banks was impressed by Tupaia's knowledge of islands, winds, currents, arts, and language and had Cook take him onboard. Tupaia helped guide the ship from Borabora to the Australs, and notably parlayed and translated for the English in their encounters with the Maori in New Zealand. Famously, he inscribed a chart that located the major Society Islands, and also an expanded network of trade and voyaging atolls and archipelagos including the Marquesas, Tuamotus, Australs, and Cooks. He also showed possible knowledge of Samoa and Tonga far to the west. All of these Cook noted and used to refine his British naval charts.

From Tupaia also came explanations of seasonal westerly wind shifts. The wind cycle had long confounded Europeans, unable to understand how voyage by sail to and from the western Pacific could be possible given the prevailing breezes. Understanding the seasonal reversal was as significant as the ancient knowledge of the monsoon winds of the Indian Ocean in grasping Polynesian migrations and settlement of islands. Tupaia proved to be an extraordinary resource for Cook, and himself gained unimaginable new knowledge of the Pacific by going ashore in Australia and Southeast Asia. He unfortunately did not return to Tahiti with his knowledge of the Aboriginal peoples or the sultans and rajahs of the Indies. As had been the case with Ahutoru, he contracted virulent fevers, and died in Batavia, the center of the colonial Dutch spice monopoly.[13]

In ways not really matched since the great Polynesian migrations centuries before, Cook's expeditions were voyages of not just exploration, but return. Emboldened by success, the Admiralty sent Cook back to the Pacific for a second voyage to concentrate on an age-old quest: to find the Great Southern Continent. Sailing into the ice of the farthest southern latitudes, he verified the frozen world of Antarctica, but disproved the legendary Continent once and for all. The return trip brought his crews through New Zealand, the New Hebrides (Vanuatu), Tahiti, Tonga, and the heretofore unknown home of the Kanak, New Caledonia.

As on the first voyage, Cook took on another Raiatean exile, Omai, who proved not to be as impressive as Tupaia in knowledge or status – he was a commoner – but was inquisitive, gracious, and had the distinction of dazzling English society and living to tell the tale when he returned to the Society Islands years later. In London, following the model established by Ahutoru, Omai was brought before the Admiralty, hosted by Joseph Banks, and had an early audience with King George, whose approval quickly made Omai the "Lion of London."

He was a favorite of drawing rooms and polite society, was famously painted by the most sought-after portraitist of the day, Joshua Reynolds, learned to dress in English style, ride horses, and appreciated gifts of globes, musical instruments, medieval armor suits, and ceremonial weapons. He studied English animal husbandry, arts, and technology. He possessed a grace and kindness taken for natural simplicity, and was remarked upon for his openhearted ways and strong sentiments. As in France, dramatists and satirists made him the centerpiece of philosophical and political debates about nature and civilization.

Omai's return to the Pacific was aligned with a third voyage of Cook, ordered for 1776 that was dedicated to yet another unresolved question: the existence of a Northwest Passage, presumed to allow a transit from the Atlantic to the Pacific above the Americas. Crossing the Indian Ocean, Cook's ships made port in Tasmania and New Zealand. Omai was granted permission to take two young Maori boys on the continuing voyage, and he served as interpreter in the Cook Islands, Tonga, and Tahiti.

Omai disembarked in the Society Islands, settled in at Huahine, built a house, and shared, lost, or traded most of his possessions. He talked about the ice he had touched in Antarctica, which few believed, and about the islands he had visited and the world of the Europeans. His experience became part of the local knowledge, while his homeland remained embroiled in dynastic alliances and struggles between the priests and warriors.[14]

Cook, meanwhile, was heading north into the fabled and secretly guarded sailing lanes of the Spanish galleons. His course, however, crossed their routes instead of following their windward circuit, and he came upon an "unknown" archipelago: the Hawaiian Islands. In 1778 at the island of Kaua'i, he anchored for provisioning and received a friendly welcome. Exploring the islands, however, would have to wait. His mission was to reach the Northwestern coast of Alaska, Canada, and the American territories in search of a northern waterway to Europe.

The north Pacific had long been as mysterious as the south and what European knowledge existed had developed from Russia. From the seventeenth century, Cossack bands moved into Siberia, pursuing the fur trade. One of them, led by Vladmir Atlasov, pushed to the extremity of Russian territory and then south into what is now known as the Kamchatka Peninsula, battling with the Koriak peoples, known for their small band societies organized around fishing, foraging, and the reindeer – a staple for flesh, organs, milk, and hides for garments. Atlasov also met a prisoner of the Koriaks, a man named Dembei. He had been shipwrecked on the peninsula for years after hitting a typhoon along the coast of islands to the south. Taken to St Petersburg in 1701 to meet the Tsar, the Russians learned he was from Osaka, and began to understand how close they were to Japan, secluded for a century by the Tokugawa shogunate.[15]

Seeking further knowledge of Siberia and Kamchatka, the Tsar sent a Danish captain, Vitus Bering, on a mission to chart the remaining unknown coastline. In 1738, Bering crossed through the strait between Asia and North America that bears his name. Importantly, his ships also later explored the Aleutian Islands, and so reconnoitered the littorals of the Alaskan coast. Within a generation, Cossack and Aleut parties were hunting for sea otters in Alaskan waters.

Cook also headed into the Alaskan currents, passing through the Bering Strait and reaching the ice of the Arctic. After navigating the cold, and seven months of hard mapping, trading, and bargaining for goods and information with trappers and local peoples, he headed south for winter layover, raising again the Hawaiian Islands, passing Maui and finding anchorage at Kealakekua Bay off the big island of Hawai'i.

The welcome was warm, but this time also uncommonly reverential. Even Cook was surprised by the reception, a ceremony that covered him in red *tapa* cloth and provided the ships with hogs and provisions. His party was brought to the local *heiau*, a place of sacred practice. The crews were fed, attended, and islanders prostrated themselves before Cook's presence. King Kalaniopu'u sailed into the bay in a party of three magnificent canoes attended by chiefs in red and yellow feather cloaks and moored next to Cook's ships. Cook was presented with his own extraordinary feather cloaks and helmet, and reported that he was treated not unlike a god.

That would be a fateful observation, for Cook had landed in the islands in coincidence with the important festival of *makahiki* season – a time of spiritual activities and games, when conflict and struggle were to be put aside, and reverence paid to Lono, god of the harvest, of fertility, and growth. Tradition recorded that Lono would return in the season on a floating island or great ship. To say Cook was regarded as a deity is an unlikely claim; what is clear is that his landfall coincided with the sacred observances, and his treatment fortuitously gave practical shape to the celebrations, as well as the authority of the chiefs and the *kahunas*.[16]

At the same time, an extended presence required provisioning by many villages, and even bountiful stores were not unlimited. Weeks passed and some of the chiefs grew restive, indicating a strain on local resources and attention. But even Kalaniopu'u could not simply break the practices of ceremony and *kapu* that surrounded the tributes. When Cook finally departed on February 4, he and his crews were presented with generous provisions of hogs, yams, and vegetables. The chiefs and villagers had carried out the proper order of tribute, yet having given much, were undoubtedly relieved to see him go.

But, just a week out, a gale ripped the sails and the foremast of the *Resolution* and Cook was forced to return to Hawai'i – choosing to anchor again at Kealakekua Bay. This time, there was no grand welcome, and in fact Cook was treated with a general silence, perplexity, and resentment. The *kahuna* maintained ritual politeness, but scuffles and theft began, and Kalaniopu'u, who had already departed, was compelled to return. The *Resolution*'s landing boat was stolen. After all the generosity shown to the visitors, it appeared, they had returned for more – and the *makahiki* season had closed.

Cook unwisely decided to take Kalaniopu'u aboard ship until the cutter was returned. What before might have been a ceremony of honor was now a hostage question, and the Hawaiian chiefs would have none of it, brandishing weapons and crowding Cook's party on the beach. The English opened fire with birdshot and muskets, and Cook, at water's edge, was clubbed and stabbed to death as he signaled to his ships.

His body was dismembered and distributed among the chiefs, with a small section returned to the remaining crew. All parties regretted the killing, and through European channels Cook was elevated to the status of legend. Scores of publications and popular tragic dramas ran on London stages, and great painters recreated, in classical and romantic flourishes, both the visionary captain and the final death scene of the "great navigator." His image became iconic, and was revered not only in Europe, but by some islanders who knew him and almost all colonials in Tahiti, New Zealand, Tonga, and Australia.

The myth and the debate about Cook's deification, apotheosis, or final tragedy is in many ways his legacy. In the wake of his death, global interest accelerated in the Pacific, as the Edenic image was replaced by one of corrupted innocence, savagery – and opportunity. Islands were marked for ports of call, stations, and commercial ventures from copra to sandalwood. The seas themselves promised profits from whale hunting to sealing, and Cook's crews had seen for themselves the lucrative fur trade of the Pacific Northwest.

Even larger imperial issues loomed as Oceanian landfalls were pulled into the designs of distant European powers. One of the most resonant examples was Britain's 1787 decision to dispatch the royal ship *Bounty* on a mission to recover breadfruit trees from Tahiti and have them transplanted in the Caribbean. Under the command of William Bligh, who had served with Cook, the mission originated from an idea by Cook's companion Joseph Banks, and fit the Admiralty's imperial vision. Breadfruit, a nourishing starchy staple in Polynesia, would be grown to feed African slaves in the Caribbean, where British colonists had established a profitable sugar cane plantation system. Knowledge from the Pacific would support

18 Legendary in life and death: James Cook killed in the Hawaiian Islands.

slavery on the other side of the world. The keys for colonial expansion would be a ship, a crew, and a botanist.

The *Bounty* was fifteen months at sea and in Tahiti. On the return voyage the crew mutinied. Some said Bligh was a tyrannical taskmaster who abused his crewmen. But many tales arose that the men – who had all volunteered for the voyage – had been seduced by the sensual pleasures of Tahiti and rebelled against returning to their lives of harsh discipline. Visions of paradise had debased them. Bligh and his officers were set adrift in a small boat and remarkably navigated themselves to the Dutch East Indies. Some of the mutineers unwisely returned to Tahiti and were arrested by pursuing British authorities.

The mutiny leaders, including the commander Fletcher Christian, took the *Bounty* in search of an island to settle where the British navy would never find them, and vanished. Their complete disappearance became part of the legend; despite Cook's achievements, the Pacific was still a place where the unknown beckoned.[17]

Almost twenty years later, the American ship *Topaz* alighted on the tiny island of Pitcairn in the Eastern Pacific and was greeted by islanders who, amazingly, spoke English and had unusual features. They were the children of the original *Bounty* mutineers. The fugitive party had included the Europeans and a number of Tahitian men and women taken as servants or looking for new lives. After some seasons, the men apparently fought and killed each other off, except for one, who was left with some of the women and children. The dream of a new island home was once again a European Paradise Lost.

The biblical splendor of this tale, evolving out of the new Pacific of European interest and opportunism, would be perhaps best exemplified by the arrival of groups of spiritual warriors in the years to come. The sons and daughters of Oro and the *kahunas* of Lono were to meet the brothers and sisters of Jehovah.

11 GODS AND SKY PIERCERS

Maretu, from the village of Ngatangiʻia, island of Rarotonga, was a man of power. As a boy he ate defeated enemies from his father's cannibal oven, and once angered his elders when he stole a victim's head to have for himself. In 1823, he met a Tahitian named Papeiha, who told him of an omnipotent god and, suitably impressed, himself became a preacher for the new religion. Stories about Maretu accumulated. A man who insisted on seeing Maretu's hand, scarred in an accident, was told he would die, and collapsed the next day. Villagers assisting Maretu wade across a lagoon feared the spiny creatures on the bottom and found that they moved apart to create a clear footway.

At Manihiki, where Maretu himself was preaching the new faith, he introduced the technique of igniting lime by burning coral rocks. As his memoirs record, he called "heathen" islanders around him in the night. One said to him, "I suppose the fire of the god of darkness down below is something like this," to which Maretu replied, "tomorrow this fire will die, but the one you speak of will never die. It burns forever ..." The heathen asked what kind of firewood it was that burned forever, to which Maretu replied, "Those who refuse to believe in Jesus are the firewood." "And what's the fire?" "That's the anger of God ... if all the people believe in Jesus Christ, then the fire will die." All of the listeners decided to become Christian.[1]

Maretu was an outstanding example of what the London Missionary Society (LMS) would call men of "native agency." These were Polynesians instructed in basic Christian doctrine and sent out to teach in villages and on beaches from the Society and Cook Islands all the way to the New Hebrides and New Guinea. The members of this "native agency" were an advance guard, spreading and mediating the new faith before English missionaries were dispatched to settle and build up permanent churches. In practice, they often worked quite independently. The Tahitian, Papeiha, whom Maretu refers to often in his manuscript, was one of the earliest products of this native agency, and had taught next to the LMS leader John Williams. Both Papeiha and another teacher, Vahapata, were from Raiatea. They introduced Christianity into Aitutaki in the Cook Islands in 1821, wrote autobiographies and preached virtually on their own until 1827.[2]

The Word in the Pacific was not completely unprecedented. A Franciscan padre had tried raising the Cross in Guam in 1596, and Padre Diego Luis de San Vitores landed to establish his mission in 1668. In 1774, learning of the English in Tahiti, a Catholic mission had tried to stake a claim, but the priests were illiberal, quarrelsome, and alone in dealing with the familiar "gawking, prodding, noise, chatter, exuberance." Too many bodily displays and too much theft caused them to abandon their stations.

The new missions of the eighteenth century differed from those of previous generations, sailing not in the company of the Christ and Spices of the Iberians, nor the relative agnosticism of Dutch traders or Enlightenment explorers, but with an evangelical fervor, a martyr's view into a world of both savagery and salvation. The end of the eighteenth century saw the rise of energetic religious societies and challenges to the "dull respectability" of the Church of England. In 1795, the London Missionary Society formed around public meetings with a vision to "spread knowledge of Christ among heathen and unenlightened nations."[3]

Part of this was inspired by new knowledge of the Pacific itself. Since Cook's voyages, new territories were known for such projects, and since the great navigator's brutal death, the Eden ideal had worn off; the benevolent state of nature was now a fallen paradise. Here is where accounts of South Sea islanders became crucial: church groups eagerly read shocking tales of island immorality and lack of stable governments. The London Missionary Society chartered quick passage on the *Duff* to the epicenter of intrigue: Tahiti. Of the thirty original missionaries, four were ordained, and the others were what the LMS called "godly mechanics," carpenters, weavers, bricklayers, shoemakers, and craftsmen, all embodying ideals of Faith as an integration of virtue and hard work. The group was split up: eighteen men and women married each other and all chose to work in Tahiti; ten went on to Tongatapu; two to the Marquesas.

Progress was slow, even retrograde. The missionaries were enthusiastic, but had little preparation beyond having read Cook and Wallis. None had any competence in the Tahitian language, relying on a *Bounty* mutineer lexicon, and little to offer the ruling Pomare family. Infanticide and cohabitation continued as ritual practices among the chiefs and the missions found that their clothing, tools, and other possessions were considered common property. Two men renounced the gospel and married Tahitian women, and the Marquesas station, with only one missionary, William Crook, was abandoned. In Tonga, three missionaries were massacred, others fled on a whaling ship, and one decided to "go native."

This last, George Vason, is famed for undergoing a conversion, in reverse. He was one of a category of white strangers who became known as beachcombers: exiles, escapees, and sometimes eccentrics who found themselves somewhere between cultures, neither European nor local, useful and amusing outsiders trying to live inside, usually under the patronage of a local ruler. Sent to preach the word, Vason instead was attracted to becoming himself as Tongan as possible, indicating both the possibilities and limitations of crossing cultures and beliefs.

A powerful chief, Mulikiha'amea, took an interest in Vason. Beachcombers could be useful: they had knowledge of European ways and languages, skill with tools and possibly weapons. Vason was granted his own fifteen-acre domain, exemption from tributes, and a woman companion. Vason renounced his mission, declaring that he would forget "that I was once called a Christian, and left a Christian land to evangelize the heathen." Instead, he spent his time learning the Tongan language, developed cropping methods for his land, had himself tattooed, practiced fishing with nets and canoes, and forthrightly thought little about religion for four years.[4]

Vason became embroiled in island politics when his patron conspired to take over as paramount leader, but in the ensuing battles Mulikiha'amea was killed and another chief, 'Ulukalala rose to power. Though still protected, Vason had made enemies in the struggles and was targeted for murder when he decided to flee on a passing European ship – by chance, a supply vessel for his former fellow-missionaries still in Tahiti.

The new ship reached Tahiti – four years after the initial mission – with not only supplies but also nine new helpers, and the LMS mission's fortunes began to change. Education and training began to pay off. Henry Nott preached the first sermon in Tahitian in February 1802. King Pomare I died, and Pomare II was interested in Christianity and in learning to write, an enormous skill associated with power. Nott began to expand to the islands of Huahine, Raiatea, and Bora Bora. But the cycle turned yet again with civil war: Pomare II was defeated and forced to retreat to Moorea where, disappointed by his fortune, and perhaps the old gods, began to listen more carefully to the missionaries. By this time, scattered servants of the mission were holding prayer meetings in a banana grove, but with Nott's support they expanded to hundreds and planned a reconquest of Tahiti.

In 1815 Pomare's army crossed from Moorea to Tahiti. The missionaries were by now very useful, able to communicate and coordinate in both English and Tahitian, and able to draw on European weapons. Pomare conquered in the name of his new war god – Jehovah. His enemies, the supporters of Oro, had meanwhile been losing popularity. Important Oro chiefs were killed in battle. Priests burned their idols, *marae* were torn down, prominent chiefs violated taboos. In this collapse of traditional beliefs, Pomare supported the building of churches and the enforcement of missionary law codes that enumerated new rules of behavior and obedience for a King of Tahiti who would rule over all subjects in the name of the True God.[5]

As authority and collaboration of such missionary kingdoms consolidated, a second generation of preachers sought to spread the word across Oceania. The ambitious and tireless John Williams established himself in Moorea in 1817, but within a year left for Raiatea, the sacred center of the former Oro imperium. At first stymied for an audience, Williams profited by helping a canoe-load of castaways from the Austral Islands in 1821, and put his "native agency" approach to work, teaching basic Christianity accompanied by two Tahitian deacons, and with a purchased schooner, setting out for the Cook Islands with the talented Papeiha.

There, the missionaries encountered Maretu, who would be devout and strong-willed in building churches and congregations. Maretu and other missionaries were treated as a special kind of chief, with a unique status and authority, and access to goods as well as education. As a preacher he could claim a "tribe" identified with the congregations of churches on many islands, and he could speak knowledgeably to villagers about the challenges in their own lives, the values and advantages of Christian teaching, and his role as a voyaging man of the world.[6]

Maretu was devout, yet he also knew how to use fear, desire, and intimidation to build his followings. Understanding village life, he argued how acceptance of a Christian god would lead to a plentiful supply of food, and rejection would lead to punishment and misfortune. Maretu himself did not seem obliged, in his own writings, to disguise the rough and tumble quality of his campaigns and his pious work made use of talents he gained as the son of a chief. "Two missionaries and the students climbed the mountains and ambushed the heathens and threw them into a stream ... everything was plundered and taken by the Christian party." Captives were bound and carried to Christian villages where many ultimately converted.[7]

Sometimes the messages were genuinely attractive and say less about Christian preaching than about reception. This was particularly true where teachers were few and individuals constructed their own doctrines. In the middle 1820s a young Samoan, Siovili, crewed on a whaling ship to Tonga and Tahiti and possibly Australia. He returned to Samoa a prophet and captured a large following. Samoa was part of an ancient network of trade and voyaging between Tonga and Fiji, but was little known by outsiders; Roggeveen and Bougainville had passed by, and European contact remained limited until traders and some beachcombers appeared in the early nineteenth century. Traditional Samoan villages were organized around family networks with elected heads and gifted kin who communicated with ancestral spirits. No organized priesthood or single worship had ever developed.

Siovili had a great knowledge of the outside world, but also a message which he spread from village to village about the God of Heaven and his son, Sisu Alaisa. Listeners might have thought of Jesus Christ, but there had never been any Christian teachers in Samoa. The movement Siovili created, which eventually numbered some five thousand adherents and lasted almost forty years, was a bridge between ancient Samoan practice and the coming missions. Siovili's church met once a month, on Saturdays, was characterized by music, songs, and dancing, and featured healing by miraculous touch. Old women with gifts of healing and prophecy were the chief priests, in conjunction with Siovili's direct messages from God.

This may have all been unorthodox to John Williams, who arrived in 1830, but it was powerful and popular. In fact, the coming of the missions only confirmed the elements of Siovili's teaching by displaying the relative material wealth of those who had books, clothes, and their own ships. The chief, Fauea, made clear his understanding of Christianity as a belief in prosperity: "I conclude that the God who has given to his white worshippers these valuable things must be wiser than our gods, for they have not given the like to us." The highest ranked chiefs, like Malietoa, understood that the new faith, especially if one kept teachers nearby, enhanced both prestige and wealth.

Alliances and fractures grew between the Siovili followers, congregations of the London Missionary Society, and Wesleyans who had carried their doctrine from Tonga. Some of Siovili's members were mediums for ancestor spirits and prophesied the coming of Sisu and the end of the world, or cataclysm by fire. Followers cleaned graves, and left their fields and animals, but after nothing happened, eventually drifted back, giving an ear to other churches, or becoming even more determined in their waiting.[8]

In some cases terrifying, epic disasters did occur, notably virulent epidemics. Most came with traders and sailors, but some diseases were probably introduced inadvertently by missionaries themselves. Sometimes this made teaching easier, as one report notes: "one thousand people were buried at Rangititi and six hundred at Araugaunga ... The people were frightened ... and it was for this reason that they decided to join the classes and the Eklesia."[9]

Yet missionizing this way was always fraught, for the dread terror could cut both ways. The preacher Ta'unga, who like Maretu hailed from Rarotonga, appreciated that Christian teachers were always targets for local rulers in new locales. As he related in his chronicles in New Caledonia: "When the people realized that a disease had become widespread they would fetch the priests and ask them, 'Where does this sickness come from?' If all the priests said that a particular priest had caused the disease, the people would kill him ... many epidemics occurred while we were there and we were blamed for them."[10]

Preachers were, after all, outlanders. They were highly mobile Pacific peoples, but they also had their own cultural gaps to bridge, for Rarotongan and Samoan teachers from the Polynesian Pacific were not familiar to, or with, locals as they entered the Melanesian islands to the west. The local nature of clan and kin organization meant no paramount leaders, certainly no kings or queens to convert, but instead rival tribal groups and multiple languages and customs. Both Polynesian preachers and Europeans considered Melanesia to be "the dark islands," not only for what they saw as the black skin and woolly hair of the inhabitants – which became synonyms for savagery – but because of the difficulties and confrontations faced by their own mission frontiers.

Estimates suggest that nearly nine hundred native agents took up stations in Papua New Guinea, the Solomons, and Vanuatu, as well as Kiribati and Tuvalu. In this Pacific-wide web of missions, stations, and teachers, New Caledonia was at the far reaches of the Rarotongan mission. Ta'unga reported conversations with a Kanak chief who asked him, "Is it a day's journey from here to Rarotonga?" Ta'unga replied, "It was four months after we left Rarotonga that we reached these islands ... If one went direct here without calling anywhere, perhaps one could get here within two months because it is far away." Ta'unga further noted, "He and the chief of Lifu were amazed at this and they laughed."[11]

New Caledonia was indeed a distant world, but also a familiar story. Archeological evidence suggests Austronesian Lapita cultures dating back more than three millennia, following even more ancient migrations through Southeast Asia and Australia. The Kanak peoples who developed formed multiple clan-based societies around fishing and agriculture, along coasts and in mountain valleys, first known to Europeans after James Cook made a brief landfall in 1774. Subsequent visits were largely limited to small supply and shore contacts.

A mission ship from Apia, Samoa in 1840 with Christian teachers was one of the first substantial contacts, reaching the Isle of Pines in the New Caledonian archipelago. There, Samoans matched wits with the ruler, Touru, who was displeased with their refusal to kowtow to him, and enraged by their unwise suggestions that diseases were God's punishment for his refusal to convert, his many wives, and his interest in trade goods rather than salvation. Touru was already worldly: savvy about European sandalwood traders, he had attacked at least one ship, and he drove away the missions.

Polynesian and Melanesian worlds did not readily comprehend each other. On the main island of New Caledonia itself, Ta'unga wrote of the Kanak, "we found no great evil in the land, war was abandoned, but the people still had the appearance of savages." Appreciative of the kindness of the local chiefs, Ta'unga began his work as cultural interpreter, learning the local tongue, yet commented, "it is a strange language, it sounds like the noise made by turkeys." Similarly, in descriptions of the people of Tanna in Vanuatu, Ta'unga noted, "they are black and quite small ... have a wild appearance and evil-looking faces."[12]

Some of the Melanesian islands themselves were actually not new frontiers. The New Hebrides and the Solomons had, after all, been among the first encountered by the Spaniards Mendaña and Quiros, almost two centuries before European knowledge of Tahiti. But, except for the aborted New Jerusalem of Quiros' Espiritu Santo in the New Hebrides, contact had been glancing, and the complex histories of local island peoples, beliefs, and practices remained mysterious to outsiders.

For some, the very edge of apparent savagery was all the attraction, and this included, most famously, John Williams himself, who insisted on landing on the island of Erromanga with companions. The locals were not interested in his gifts or message and he unfortunately arrived after skirmishes with sandalwood traders. His brief visit ended with his preferred martyr's death. A famous print extolling his falling in the surf captures his imagined beatific grace in the moment before he was pulverized by clubs and spears.

Other missions, such as the Anglicans that followed, were more sober about their campaigns. George Selwyn, the first bishop of the diocese of New Zealand, reversed the practice of sending teachers into the field and instead sent vessels to bring potential students to Auckland for religious instruction. In due course Polynesians and Melanesians would be preaching to each other, taking passage on ships and establishing facilities, including the Melanesian Mission training school operating from New Zealand.

John Williams' protégés, like Ta'unga, found that in cases where the Christian community was better entrenched, a European brought status; partly because an ordained minister actually had solid scriptural instruction, and also because heads of mission usually had impressive houses, churches, trade items, and the protection of chiefs to their credit. In his later missions back to Samoa, Ta'unga found that the islanders wanted a white father, not another islander, to teach them.

Still, native agents benefited greatly from their connection to the missions. Elekana, a Rarotongan in Tuvalu, made excellent use of his

literacy. "Day after day old and young men, and women came, requesting me to spell and read to them, and begging for part of my book ..."
The Christian message that salvation was revealed in sacred, written
texts and publically worshiped as a community gave significant standing
to the preachers. Well taught, it provided understandable lessons in good
and evil, sin and virtue, love and forgiveness for all.[13]

Maretu baptized children and gave them biblical names, a popular practice that created bonds of commitment, much as the Polynesian
ritual exchange of names. The Word was never simply a European
message. Not schooled in the fine points of European theology and
history, the teachers transmitted their own cultural heritages, metaphors,
and stories in words and analogies that interwove foreign messages and
island beliefs.

Many preachers also made ethnographies of other island
peoples and their distinctive customs. Though his own islands were
considered cannibal territory, Fijian evangelist Poate Ratu distinguished the Papuans by observing, "they cut up their victims like one
does fish ... so if you hear of one of us being killed, you would know
that we were not baked in an oven, and roasted, but that we were
grilled in small pieces over a fire." His Fijian perspective focused less on
moral condemnation of cannibalism than on bemused curiosity about
reputations and practices in other islands.[14]

Papua was a frontier even for other Melanesians, for little
would be known to the outside world until the later nineteenth century.
Knowledge of New Guinea was largely restricted to the western region,
with its Malay-facing contact zones. By the nineteenth century, interest
was coming from the opposite direction, across the Pacific islands, and
eastern New Guinea was imagined by traders and missions as part of
the Oceanian world. In fact, New Guinea remains one of the places
where the "lines" between Asia and Oceania are indistinct and
overlapping.

Despite centuries of coastal contacts, little was known of the
inland inhabitants by outlanders, except that the tribes relied on bone,
wood, and stone tools, were scattered in numerous valleys, and had a
productive agricultural system. Ethnographic works suggest that the
forest and jungle societies were marked by fertility and ancestor cults,
and organized around collective rituals guarding sacred knowledge.[15]

Each clan had its own recognized deities, and communicated
with local spirits and kin ancestors. The famous art from this part of

the world developed from the carving of embodied spirits, of real and legendary worlds only vaguely apprehended by the senses. Many of the meanings are known fully only to the initiated.

As everywhere across the Pacific, inward worlds did not mean isolation. Coastal groups traded with canoes from the Solomon Islands, the Moluccas, and the Celebes Sea. Forest barks and resins made their way to water's edge, and shell ornaments circulated back up river basins and along mountain ridges, to decorate people who had themselves never seen the ocean. Despite such trails and trading routes, the terrain and climate were formidable, and mission work in Papua New Guinea proceeded slowly. Polynesian teachers had no more resistance to fevers and diseases than Europeans, and faced high mortality rates in their efforts to spread the faith.

In Papua New Guinea, terrain was not the only challenge. The local Melanesian clan and kin structure also made the political dissemination of the faith difficult. Traveling teachers, both islander and European, were more accustomed to the structured, central chiefdoms and single languages of Polynesian island groups, rather than the multiplicity of cultures they encountered.[16]

It was, in fact, in the Polynesian world that perhaps the greatest initial impacts of Christianity took place. The success of the London Missionary Society's expansion from Tahiti across the South Pacific inspired Boston-based evangelists to launch their own mission initiative in 1810. An American Board of Commissioners for Foreign Missions declared a plan to set up a base in the Hawaiian Islands, and to move mission activities west toward Micronesia. A young Hawaiian named Obookiah inspired the establishment of a school in Connecticut to train missionaries, and two students at Andover Theological Seminar, Hiram Bingham and Asa Thurston, were inspired to lead a group with conservative Congregational beliefs – original sin, strict moral codes, hard work and education, industrious lives – to the islands.

As with the timing of earlier European forays into the Pacific under the Portuguese and Dutch, the missionaries were extraordinarily fortunate in their moment, for Hawaiian society was undergoing a revolutionary change just upon their arrival. Knowledge of the Hawaiian Islands – a large archipelago in the almost exact center of the Northern Pacific – was quickly noted by the European and emerging American powers from the missions of James Cook. Already, traders and merchants, and warships from Britain, France, and New England were mooring.

The legacies of the Cook visit also impacted Hawaiian royalty. A young chief, Kamehameha, had been impressed by the English visitors and their resources as he planned for his struggles against other chiefs for rule of the islands. Kamehameha rapidly mastered the exploitation of trade, and another resource carried by foreign ships to his shores: beachcombers.

The best known in Hawai'i were Isaac David and John Young, captured and detained from trading vessels by Kamehameha, and skilled enough with cannon and muskets to be offered wives and land by the great chief, whom they served throughout his military campaigns. They provided artillery support against the powerful Kahekili, ruler over Maui, Kaho'olawe, Lanai, Molokai, and Oahu, and then against Kahekili's sons, who would jealously turn on each other and their own allies, allowing Kamehameha political and tactical advantages. By 1810, all opposition was defeated or forced into tributary status.

Unlike some disinterested tribal groups or suspicious Asian rulers, Kamehameha favored trade. During his reign, Hawaiian ports became critical to the development of the global trade in sandalwood and otter fur. The tropical fruit synonymous with Hawaiian agriculture, the pineapple, was imported for growing in 1813, and five years later, coffee acreage was cultivated. Whalers especially had a significant impact in places like Lahaina and Honolulu. Favored by those pursuing the Japan and Arctic whaling grounds, American whalers came to the islands simultaneously with Hiram Bingham's missionaries, and so contributed to the changes and upheavals taking place in Hawaiian society.[17]

Monarchical interests in foreign trade made Hawai'i open to rapid developments in the building of wharves and shipyards. Boarding-houses, saloons, and brothels clustered along waterfronts and livestock and produce were carted from inland to harbors, creating a cash economy tying villages to semi-permanent whaling settlements. Young men and women were curious about the activity on the coasts, and some of the men shipped out with whalers and traders, bringing back sights and stories from other islands, Asia, and the Americas. Commoners at home were increasingly burdened by exactions to pay foreign debt, while struggling under customary law.

When he died in 1819, Kamehameha left behind a changed archipelago: a unified political state, active commerce, and increasing interactions with other worlds. One thing that had not changed for most

Hawaiians was the traditional *kapu* system, also called *tabu*, or taboo. *Kapu* defined behaviors and privileges for royalty and commoners alike, but more, it acted as a form of law structured on a cosmic order in which gods and men cooperated. To violate *kapu* would be to challenge the very nature of order and existence.

In spite of all the changes in Hawai'i, *kapu* continued to rule daily life and especially the activities and behaviors of women, who were not allowed to eat with men, fish in salt water, or taste bananas, red meat, or pig. Use of canoes was restricted, and menstruating women had to keep away from their husbands. To break the *kapu* system was not something that interested Kamehameha, for he and his priestly *kahunas* knew that it would not only change local customs, but potentially unravel the entire social order.

This did not deter the remarkable Queen Ka'ahumanu, daughter of nobility and favorite wife of the King, from advancing the transformation of Hawaiian society where Kamehameha stopped. Noted for her intelligence, audacity, and beauty, Ka'ahumanu took up the King's own cloak and spear upon his death and confirmed her status as *Kuhina nui* – a co-ruler – to the royal heir, Liholiho, soon crowned as Kamehameha II. If there had been questions about the future of the realm after the great King, they were soon gone. No one dared oppose her.

Where Kamehameha had remained resolute on the ancient law and religion, Ka'ahumanu set out to demolish the *kapu* that kept her apart from the world of men. She and the new King's mother worked on the young Liholiho, finally convincing him to do something simple, yet earth-shattering: to eat in public with her. The occasion came at a banquet notably given in honor of foreigners. In the midst of festivities, while Liholiho joined his guests to feast on roast pig, Ka'ahumanu took a place beside him and also began to eat. Hawaiians looked on in shock, but nothing happened. The priestly *kahuna* appeared powerless in this affront to their sacred authority. Social distinctions and cosmological beliefs held in place by *kapu* began to disintegrate.[18]

This turmoil within Hawaiian society framed the 1820 arrival of Christian missionaries. Their timing gave them extraordinary advantages in preaching a new faith, and their knowledge could be captivating. Hawaiian chiefs found parts of the new faith attractive. There was power in learning to read and write in Hawaiian and English. Chiefs

19 Power and purpose: portrait of Queen Ka'ahumanu of Hawai'i.

close to the missions gained trade goods and *mana* from new uses of their own language, quickly producing declarations, promulgations, and newspapers for their subjects. With a mission printing press and teachers, Hawaiian society soon became one of the most literate in the world.

Along with this came a framework of moral codes and rules that the monarchy adapted from the biblical teachings. More, the presence of trading ships and the missionaries themselves spread virulent diseases like smallpox and measles unfamiliar in the islands. As elsewhere around the Pacific, scores of villages collapsed in agony, and uncertainty and terror reigned. With the *kapu* system gone, the missionaries developed a legal code based on the Ten Commandments. A devout power broker, Ka'ahumanu allied with the missionaries and destroyed carvings of the former gods. Where the old gods were broken and chiefs converted to the new faith, entire villages and districts regularly followed.

But not everywhere. The people of the Puna and Ka'u districts on the Big Island of Hawai'i lived in the literal shadow of Pele, the most tempestuous and feared of the goddesses, who rained down fire from the crater of Kilauea volcano. When the ardent Puna Chiefess Kapiolani converted to Christianity, her people did not follow.

In 1824, Kapiolani decided to assert her authority by traveling to Kilauea volcano on a mission to confront Pele directly. Her family and retinue pleaded for her to reconsider, but she would not be swayed. She said, "If I am destroyed by Pele, you may worship her. If I am not, you must turn to the only true God." Accounts say that she was challenged by Pele's priestesses as she descended into the crater to read scripture aloud. She picked up and cast stones into the volcano's fires and ate sacred berries, calling out "I do not fear Pele." Nothing happened.[19]

Such support was critical for the success of the missions, and the missionaries in turn exerted tremendous influence upon government and society. They served as advisors to the royal family, establishing schools and churches, which the nobility patronized and supported. Missions also monumentally colluded with business interests to force the monarchy to register, divide, and break up Hawaiian communal lands in favor of private property, large tracts of which they purchased for their own accounts. Even in dispossessing common people of land and traditions, missionaries were generally tolerated by the monarchy, for they served as counterweights to traders – the often lawless, debauched, arrogant, and unscrupulous whalers and merchants whose goods and business the chiefs wanted, but whose behavior could be dangerous. Piety, power, and the struggles of a rapidly changing society grew entwined.

This was particularly true in port towns like Lahaina. Though arriving in the islands about the same time, missionaries and whalers conflicted, the one preaching against the vice, rum, and disorderly saloons, brawls, and vulgarity of the other. Whalers were loathed and feared for their drunkenness, violence, and diseases, both venereal and epidemic. Mission leaders worked with monarchs to promulgate laws controlling sailors and keep Hawaiian women off of visiting ships. Whalers retaliated with threats and violence: in 1825, the Reverend William Richards of Lahaina and his family were saved from an armed mob of angry sailors only by an equally determined crowd of native parishioners. Over the years, other mobs would overpower local police, burn buildings, and – if armed with cannon – threaten to bombard the towns to protest vice laws.[20]

Such conflicts and cooperation between rulers, missions, and ship crews grew in whaling centers all across the Pacific, from Kosrae and Pohnpei in Micronesia to Papeete, Tahiti. The Bay of Islands,

New Zealand, was another favored port, rich with rivers and timber, and politically dominated by local chiefs who were happy to trade with whalers and expert at tracking down and hauling back sailors who tried to desert their ships. As elsewhere, liquor and firearms were major demands of the chiefs, but so also were metal tools and cotton goods in exchange for sweet potatoes, pork, temporary wives, and servants. European captains reportedly acquired occasional tattooed heads as souvenirs, at times procured from secretive missionaries.[21]

Common interests allied most mission leaders with chiefs and rulers, though some were more profound than mere expedience and mutual exploitation. This would clearly be the case with Ruatara, a young chief from the Bay of Islands. Ruatara was neither a simple credulous villager nor a cynical chief. Like other young Maori men at the beginning of the nineteenth century, Ruatara served on a number of ships in South Pacific waters, and spent almost four years from 1805 to 1809 sailing for transports and sealers, being treated sometimes fairly but often starved, cheated of pay and promises by the captains. During his travels he befriended Samuel Marsden, the chaplain in the Australian colony of New South Wales.

Marsden, by all accounts, was a thoughtful man. He had known Ruatara's elder Chief, Te Pahi, and went to Britain to petition for the establishment of a New Zealand school where intellectually engaging men like Te Pahi could send students for church instruction. Te Pahi, unfortunately, was murdered by a whaling crew in mistaken retribution for the massacre of the crew of a cargo ship, the *Boyd*, by a rival Maori chief. In 1809, on his way back to Australia, Marsden was surprised to discover Ruatara on board the same vessel. Ruatara had worked a voyage to England on a cruel promise he would meet King George III. Ill and vomiting blood from beatings he had received, he returned with Marsden to Parramatta in Australia to recover, learning a great deal about farm tools, seed, and techniques.

Ruatara returned to the Bay of Islands, assumed Te Pahi's leadership, and ambitiously tried to implement some of his agricultural plans. To the envy of his rivals, he also made good on an opportunity to offer protection for a church in his territories, along with all the trade, Western education, and Australian contacts that would follow.

In late 1814, Ruatara brought a missionary party led by his friend Marsden to the Bay of Islands, and made preparations for the

20 The Word and the warriors: Samuel Marsden meets with Maori chiefs.

first service on New Zealand soil, on Christmas Day, 1814. Fencing in half an acre of land, Ruatara set up a pulpit and seats made from old canoes. At ten o'clock, he called the whole village and Marsden began his preaching. It is a local tradition that an elder asked Ruatara, "What is the meaning of the pakeha's words?" Ruatara replied, "You do not understand what he is saying now, but you will by and by."[22]

It would be a comment to ponder. Ruatara had, after all, become chief upon the decease of Te Pahi, who had also been Marsden's friend, and had traveled more than once to Australia to learn of the colony. Te Pahi had been impressed by English technology and settlements, but also appalled by the penal system and the poor estate of the indigenous clans, whom he considered wretched.

Indeed, a quarter century after Marsden, the principal settlement of Kororareka in the Bay of Islands would be still only a ramshackle settlement of badly made houses, tents, and a floating population of drifters, sailors, vagabonds, and laborers. John Brown Williams, an American consul to the islands, estimated that despite the opportunities of exchange, the settlements seriously weakened the Maori communities, calling visiting ships "floating castles of prostitution," and guessing that "from 1818 to 1839 . . . more than one half of some tribes have died of disease."[23]

Ruatara, before himself dying, was enthusiastic and ambitious for English ideas and was protective of Marsden and his teachers. But he was not without his doubts, as he told Marsden, of rumors he had heard in Port Jackson that the missionaries would simply be the first of many Europeans who would eventually reduce the Maori to the same state as the Australian Aborigines.

12 EXTREMITIES OF THE GREAT SOUTHERN CONTINENT

In 1995, a five-million-dollar replica of James Cook's *Endeavour* – the famed navigator's flagship – left its moorings and sea trials in Fremantle, Australia and sailed for Sydney. An armada of small boats accompanied the ship sailing into the harbor, and a thousand spectators watched from the parapets around the opera house. As the ship docked at Man O'War Steps, the curious and enthusiastic joined the welcoming celebration.[1]

The *Endeavour* replica had been commissioned in January of 1988 as a bicentenary gift to the people of Australia to celebrate the navigational feats of Captain Cook, who charted the eastern Australian seaboard for the British navy in 1770. The *Endeavour* gave a heroic preface to European knowledge of and interest in the island continent, leading to the first colonial settlement, epitomized by Captain Arthur Philip raising the British flag, first at Botany Bay, and shortly at Port Jackson, and claiming possession of the eastern Australian seaboard on January 26, 1788, with eleven ships and 1,350 passengers – half of them convicts – of the First Fleet. The date would come to mark Australia Day. The rest of the Fleet was mainly convicts and guards, sent now to the South Pacific after the 1776 American Revolution made the British practice of exiling prisoners across the Atlantic no longer tenable.

At Port Jackson, where the Fleet began to build its prison colony, poor agricultural conditions, would-be farmers with no farming experience, lack of familiar basic tools and seed, epidemic illness, and harsh conditions led to starvation and near decimation of the prisoners. Only subsequent provisions and transported prisoner colonists sent from Britain saved the settlement, which two hundred years later would be celebrated as the metropolis of Sydney.

Also present that day, behind nearby barricades, indigenous groups raised the red, yellow, and black Aboriginal flag and banners reading "Don't forget White Australia has a Black History," and "Isn't Once Enough?" Transiting to New Zealand, the crew of the *Endeavour* replica were well-received in Auckland harbor, but hours later received word from Te Runanga O Turanganui a Kiwa, the tribal council at Gisborne, that the ship was not welcome in Poverty Bay. Protesters boarded the ship at Auckland, resulting in a police presence and a tense six weeks of sailing around the North Island. Tribal groups welcomed the ship without incident at every other port, many with canoe meetings and respectful ceremony, but the ritual *haka* challenges they danced for the visitors were also taken as serious declarations.[2]

As the bicentennial celebrated the hardscrabble heritage of transported prisoners and a pioneer immigrant population, Sydney newspapers also reported on Koori activists in England planning to claim the British Isles in the name of the Aboriginal flag. Protest marches around Australia also made headlines. None of this was new. Indigenous protests had accompanied the sesquicentenary in 1938, and the bicentenary of Cook's landing at Kurnell on April 29, 1970 had been marked by the Federal Council for the Advancement of Aborigines and Torres Strait Islanders declaring a day of mourning under the leadership of Kath Walker. In Melbourne, a sizeable crowd rallied at Captain Cook's Cottage in the Treasury gardens, condemning the navigator and demanding action to restore Aboriginal land rights.[3]

Restoring history and redressing those rights came in a celebrated legal case not from Melbourne or Sydney, but from islands to the far north in the waterway between Australia and New Guinea. In 1992, Torres Straits Islander Eddie Mabo won a High Court ruling concerning tribal and customary lands that overturned the fiction of *terra nullius* throughout all of Australia – the legal principle that British possession had taken place upon an empty continent and that indigenous peoples had no native title to territory.

That the continent was not empty, nor even isolated, is evident from the more than four hundred different linguistic and cultural groups collectively called "Aborigines," regionally and tribally self-defined in particular territories, such as Koori in New South Wales and Victoria, and Yolngu in the northeastern Arnhem Land. The

Yolngu communities are particularly rich in oral histories, legends, and myths, which relate tales of spirits and ancestors tied anthropologically to Austronesian migrations of scattered clans transiting the islands and partial land bridges of Sunda and Sahul, down through New Guinea, across the islands of the Torres Straits, and throughout the continent.

Tales of human arrival are engaged by archeological testing and can be traced through charcoal and evidence of fire used by Aboriginal groups to clear forest or drive game animals. Archeological and anthropological studies indicate settlements reaching an ecological stability within their environments, and then also developing into large-scale hunting. Records indicate mass extinctions of large, flightless birds, giant tortoises, and aquatic mammals that in addition to environmental changes are likely linked to some form of human predation.

Over millennia, the ancestral groups spread south as far as Tasmania. The Australian landscape itself was crossed over and again by hunter-gatherers more than forty thousand years ago. As the Pleistocene glaciers began to melt and sea levels once again rose, plains and flats between New Guinea and Australia and, far to the south, Australia and Tasmania, were covered by ocean. Coastal and island communities were pushed back, and Aboriginal legends relate phenomena of fish falling from the sky and great waves that inundated and drowned the land.

Such tales are key in Aboriginal histories, for the depth of indigenous cultures is most famously known not through materials, monuments, or archeological settlements and trading patterns, but through songlines that trace out the contours and spiritual meanings of the continent. In the nineteenth century Australian researchers began detailed studies of Aboriginal ancestry and cosmology, focusing on Arunta terms like *Alcheringa* that became generally translated and expressed as an experience known as the Dreaming or the Dreamtime.[4]

From a distant historical epoch, the great southern land of Bandaiyan – Australia – finds its originary stories not in a First Fleet, but as a topography crossed by the First Peoples, legendary ancestors naming and singing the world into being, creating the elements, land, plants, and animals as they traveled. The Dreaming encompasses this ancient time of creation and also the spiritual and material reality of the present against which the transitory events and passages of everyday lives unfold.

21 Dreams and histories: Aboriginal journey of the soul between worlds.

In traditional stories, the Rainbow Serpent rises from her slumber under the earth to carve out the features of the landscape with her body, and the lakes and rivers are filled with waters from the mouths of frogs who are spirit ancestors. Aboriginal communities are the immanent inheritors and performers of the Dreaming, maintaining relationships with spirit deities through dance, stories, and "ownership" of experiences.

Some living humans can pass between the Dreaming and the physical world, inhabiting a continuous and simultaneous past, present, and future. Among the northern coastal Aboriginal peoples, the sea is an inseparable part of cosmology in life and death. Along the Kimberly coast, a woman becomes pregnant when a spirit child from reefs and rocks enters her body. Among the Yolngu people of Arnhem Land, designated submerged rocks are birthplaces for spirits and serve as "reservoirs of souls." Such entities can be incarnated in dugongs and fish like the shark and rock cod. Everyday experience is composed of multiple realities and beings.[5]

For European explorers, Australia was a blank. Aboriginal cultures were deemed "remarkably unchanged" over tens of thousands of years. In a noted tome *The Tyranny of Distance* the historian Blainey wrote, "In the eighteenth century the world was becoming one world but Australia was still a world of its own ... It was more isolated than the Himalayas or the heart of Siberia."[6]

The Down Under narrative began with this vision of isolation. In March 1606, Dutch explorer Willem Janszoon (1571–1638) was the first European to sight Queensland, and later that year, the Spanish explorer Luis Vaez de Torres navigated his ship through the strait that divides northern Australia from Papua New Guinea. The coastal outline of the continent known at the time as New Holland was slowly charted across generations by Abel Tasman and other European navigators, but detailed knowledge remained sparse.

In 1688, William Dampier brought his ship to the northwest coast of Australia, the earliest British explorer to do so, and mappings and soundings were taken also by a host of French contacts. The east coast, however, remained largely unknown to Europeans until James Cook charted and claimed it for Britain in 1770.

With the independence of the United States, Britain moved to claim new overseas territories to serve exiled prisoner populations. British Australia developed as a penal colony, with close to 160,000 men and women forcibly transported there as convicts between 1788 and 1868. Free immigrants also formed part of the population from the 1790s. Most convicts were minor criminals with no knowledge of farming or homesteading. Some were women, usually in their twenties. From Ireland or England, they tended to be single and literate enough to read, though not write. Most were convicted for stealing, some for prostitution, and condemned to seven years' transportation.

Early convict life was harsh and deadly. Men and women were thrown together and violence, riots, and executions were common. Many convicts were urban dwellers with no knowledge of farming, so crops died and starvation reigned. Sheep and cattle that wandered away from settlements into the bush would later be found to have done much better without human efforts to raise them.[7]

Convicts married, and as documented in archival registers, had many sons and daughters; initially, however, no real provisions for education or religious instruction for children were made. England sent only more convicts. With cause, the prisoners complained that governors were not developing a colony with free settlement and pioneering, but maintaining a cheap convict labor force under military rule.

Land was given to some soldiers, but governors also profiteered supplies and hijacked the liquor traffic. Struggles over military authority led to the arrest of the third governor of the colony, William Bligh, who had found his new position after the *Bounty* incident. Markers in national Australian history from the Rum Rebellion (1808) to the populist resistance of the Eureka Stockade (1854) define a temperament which champions the energy and grievances of local settlers, and heaps scorn and derision on a tyrannical British imperial government.

Many convicts meanwhile died of scurvy, cholera, and other diseases, and the earliest years were characterized by servitude, illness, hunger, and grinding poverty. The colony was known for its runaways. One such was Mary Bryant. In 1786 she was twenty-one years old, arrested for thievery and sentenced to death. Her sentence was commuted to the standard punishment of the day: seven years' transportation to the Australian penal colony.

Shipboard, she became pregnant with fellow convict William Bryant. Mary and William had a son together, Emmanuel, but a few months after reaching the colony all were starving. Desperate, they stole a tiny boat and sailed north in the direction of Timor, the site of many Dutch settlements. Coming ashore, they told the local governor they had survived a shipwreck, a believable tale in that part of the world, but once authorities learned the truth, all were locked up and sent to disease-ridden Batavia. Mary alone lived to return to England, pardoned in 1793; her life has been made into numerous novels and film stories, and is a favorite of writers for young adults.

For those who could not flee, everyday life was harsh. Their lot as convicts was to serve out sentences as unpaid workers for others, laboring at farming, building, cleaning, and washing. After 1804, convict women were largely routed to confinement within the Parramatta Female Factory, where they were tasked with sewing and spinning, or agricultural labor. Factories for women were also built in Brisbane and Tasmania. Some of these facilities were designated for convict women who were pregnant. They also served as nurseries for babies; older children, however, were sent to orphanages unless their mothers could demonstrate means to support them, or were already finishing their sentences.

A few women prospered by ably working the strategies of the day – marrying well, using smart business sense, and persevering. The Australian $20 note commemorates a young English orphan, Mary Reibey, who stole a horse and was sentenced to transportation for seven years; her prison-ship docked in New South Wales in October 1792. After two years she met and married a man with his own oceanic connections: Thomas Reibey, a former employee of the English East India Company in Asia. The couple obtained a land grant north of

Sydney and established a homestead. Mary built up a farm and Thomas, with business partner Edward Wills, prospered with a wine and spirits business.

Reibey and Wills were maritime traders, owning three ships and earning admirable profits with a Sydney import business. In 1811 both Thomas and Edward Wills died and Mary was suddenly a widow with seven children. She skillfully managed her business and accounts and went on to acquire larger property tracts in Tasmania as well, and around the growing town of Sydney. Today she is recognized as a philanthropist and school founder.[8]

Such stories recognize the aspirations and tough sense of the convicts, making lives in a hard new world. Many worked through and served out their sentences. The archives of transportation from England to New South Wales are well studied and the penal documents offer glimpses of their hard and unsavory lives, but also the foundations of a British Australia more than the general characterization of "a lazy, insubordinate, disorderly, drunken lot of ruffians."[9]

Henry Kable was sentenced to death at Thetford, Norfolk in 1783 with his father for theft; the father was hanged and Kable's sentence commuted to seven years. He met Susannah Holmes in prison and the two had a son. In the colony, Kable worked as a night watchman and was granted thirty acres of land from which he developed a small business and by 1799 got himself appointed Chief Constable. Seven years later, he built up an estate of more than two hundred acres from trading in sealskin, rum, iron, and timber with part ownership of a cargo sloop.

John Randall was tried in 1785 for stealing a silver watch chain, and was sentenced to seven years' transportation. He married twice and received a land grant which he sold to another man who described him as a "well made black about six feet, played the flute and tambour well." By 1810, he was a Sydney Town Constable and later moved on to official positions in Tasmania.

Edward Pugh was convicted in 1784 of stealing a coat, and was transported to New South Wales as a carpenter. When his sentence expired, he was granted seventy acres of land west of Parramatta. One military officer noted that Pugh's land was not promising: water was scarce, settlers were regularly robbed by bushrangers – fugitive convicts and outlaws – and "few of the farmers showed determination to

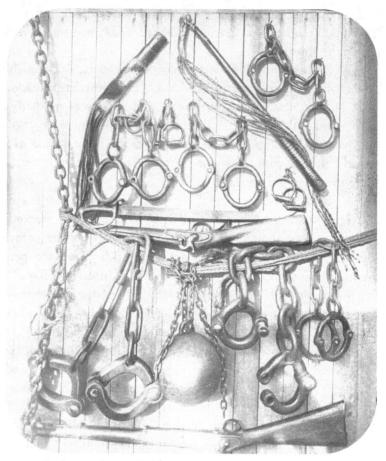

22 Relics of a convict past: whips, leg irons, and British penal discipline.

persevere, being most disconsolate and dispirited." Yet Edward Pugh
seems to have prospered. Records show that by 1802 he was given a
land grant of a hundred acres near a lagoon which was later named
"Pugh's Lagoon."[10]

All of these narratives illustrate, and in some cases celebrate,
the hard-won lives of the convict-colonists who shaped British Australia, pulled into a Pacific circuit. Behind many of these "success" stories
lay a common interest that joined freed convicts and the government:
grants of land to expand the Australian settlement. But it also meant
conflict, for despite the doctrine of *terra nullius*, colonists were moving
not into empty lands, but into regions occupied for thousands of years
by Aboriginal peoples.

The Port Jackson area was heavily populated by local Aborigines, and early contacts with surveyors, work parties, and small traders were managed with curiosity and uncertainty. British Governor Philip attempted dialogue, and tried trading bread and rice for fish, and metal tools for weapons, but cultural and linguistic knowledge were fragmentary and impatient settlers were pressing for large land claims. As early as May 1788, two convicts, gathering rushes for thatch, stole a canoe at a fishing place and were killed. Continuing skirmishes raised tensions.

The following year a smallpox epidemic led to the shocking decimation of local Aboriginal clans, with bodies of the sick, dead, and abandoned lying across the beaches and in the brush. One colonist noted, "At that time a native was living with us; and on our taking him down to the harbour to look for his former companions, those who witnessed his expression and agony can never forget either ... not a living person was any where to be met with."

As settlers took and enclosed land, Aboriginal hunting and foraging grounds were cut off. Aboriginal groups became increasingly dependent upon smaller terrains, water sources, game, and fishing areas. Groups fought, crops were stolen, lost convicts speared, and Aborigines shot. Settlers organized their own bands to hunt down and kill. In a notorious 1838 incident at Myall Creek, settler men from cattle stations murdered twenty-eight men, women, and children; they were hanged even while claiming it was not a violation of the law to kill blacks. Indigenous Australians were displaced and dispossessed. The worlds of the Dreaming were posted and fenced off by miners and rangers, and the European colony grew under legal codes that made all untitled lands part of the British Crown: everyone else was a trespasser.[11]

Free settlers increasingly came to Australian shores as immigrants, drawn especially by promises of livelihoods in sheep and wool, and imagined riches in the 1850s triggered by gold rushes. These included thousands of Europeans who made passage to raise sheep and cattle and stake mineral claims, and tens of thousands of Chinese immigrants who worked marginal mining territories, leaving legacies of occasional success and constant tension with Europeans. Historical records report anti-Chinese riots and gangs, and also capture pictures of camps with board shacks, storefronts, and the lacquered posts of small temples and joss houses.

Out of this, the Australian past developed as a story of vast landscapes and hard beginnings, but also opportunity and new wealth from trade, natural resources, and strong laboring traditions on farms, ranches, and in mines. The Commonwealth of Australia was formed in 1901, as six states were politically federated under a unifying constitution. Anti-immigration acts simultaneously excluded Asian immigration in favor of an official "White Australia" platform. Pacific Islanders were deported. At the turn of the century, the colonial and settler population was estimated at close to four million.

Meanwhile, the indigenous population figured less than a hundred thousand. According to government policy, the many clans would inexorably become extinct, and children were separated from their families as a "stolen generation" to be raised in state and church compounds with the thought to prepare them for lives upon the disappearance of their own people. Administrators did not see Aboriginal culture developing in familiar ways, as in Europe or Java, Bali or Polynesia. Australian clans had no kings, built no temples, had no great gardens and farming communities. The government view seemed not to differ from Dampier's infamous assertion more than a century earlier, that Aboriginal peoples were primitive, stone-age, without clothes or constructed shelters, and as Dampier put it famously, "the miserablist people in the world."[12]

Yet Aboriginal cultures continued to evolve, especially where they were not strongly in contact with the expanding European colony. The bicentennial celebrations at Botany Bay or Port Jackson in 1988 were complemented by celebrations in northern Australia as an ancient *prahu* from the Indonesian islands of Makassar made port. The arrival of the *Hati Marege* was celebrated in Arnhem Land as a historical reunion. Yolngu elders embraced Makassans, as an act of resuming a forgotten past.

Australian history is necessarily oceanic: though steeped in an imaginary of the desert outback and the bush, it is first a story of coasts and bays: the littoral of Port Jackson as it evolved into Sydney and spread in ranching, settlements, and farms toward the Blue Mountains.

It is also a history from the north. The north is the place of prehistoric migrations of Austronesian ancestors, linking the continent by ancient and submerged land bridges to Southeast Asia. Populations in the Torres Straits developed sophisticated cultures in taro and yams, as well as techniques in farming and harvesting shellfish and eels that were adopted in coastal enclaves across the continent. Domesticated animals like the dingo were human companions from Southeast Asia. Tools, new vocabulary, weapons like spears, seeds for planting, and captured game or crops were part of trade and adoption of new crafts and tool-making practices.

Prior to and coincident with European arrival, the records of northern shores also enmesh trading networks that connected the continent to China and the Malay world in the centuries before the British arrival. Australian history is continuous with earlier worlds of Arab, Indian, and Chinese commerce, interacting with Aboriginal cultures. Evidence litters the landscape, and is captured in archeology and popular tales. Near Cairns, Queensland, a coin of the Egyptian ruler Ptolemy IV was unearthed in 1909. Near Darwin, a Taoist soapstone figurine is dug out of the roots of a banyan tree. Fifteenth-century Ming Chinese porcelain turns up in the Gulf of Carpenteria.[13]

For the British at New South Wales, the northern history of Australia was one of extremity and isolation. As the colony at Port Jackson expanded, the governors needed more detailed mapping – searching for new settlements and trade opportunities. More, they knew that French navigators under Nicholas Baudin were looking to stake claims and a strategic race was on to chart and claim other coastlines and territories of the vast, and to them unknown, continent.

The first maritime tales of northerly exploration, colonization, and settlement were marked by the Dutchman Janszoon, who charted the west coast of the Cape York Peninsula, and Torres, who navigated the strait and islands that bear his name. On a commission from the governor at Port Jackson, Captain Matthew Flinders was charged with making the first circumnavigation of the continent (1801–3) and his crew explored the Gulf of Carpenteria and the north for many months.

On sandy islands the men were astonished to find "clearly foreign objects that they had seen elsewhere – broken earthern jars, a wooden anchor, three boats' rudders, remnants of bamboo lattice work, a Chinese-style hat of palm leaves sewn with cotton thread, a remnant of blue cotton trousers." They also found forty small stone enclosures of unknown purpose on the beach.[14]

Flinders was puzzled, but the mystery was solved by the appearance of six Makassan vessels. First expecting pirates, Flinders soon realized that the *prahus* were harvesters from the Indonesian

23 From distant waters: Makassan fishermen harvesting sea cucumber in Northern Australia.

island of Sulawesi. He invited the six captains aboard his own ship and had his Malay cook interpret. The captains were all Muslim traders and their chief was a stocky man named Pobassoo. His squadron was part of a great fleet owing loyalty to the Rajah of Bone, and had sailed with the monsoon winds to harvest trepang – sea cucumbers – from Australian waters, a practice generations old. The stone enclosures seen on the beach became clear. They were not foundations for boat building, but fire pits for boiling and processing the trepang.

Resting at anchor in the Gulf, another trans-local Pacific place, British Australia came into contact with a Malay Muslim world, planning to sell marine creatures to Chinese merchants and Dutch traders of the East India Company. From Australian waters, *prahus* laden with a season's trepang navigated back to the island of Sulawesi. Old illustrations show the port, merchants and laborers casting shadows along covered landings and sea walls, the stone wells and elevated thatch houses under palms, crowded along muddy roads. The trepang crews were from the Makassar region, but also the more northern Bugis domains, carrying divers and laborers from New Guinea, Java, and Ceram. In port, the fishermen and their agents bargained and closed out their agreements, and the trepang were bailed and loaded onto Chinese junks.[15]

Such evidence of regular contact worried Flinders. If Pobassoo's trading stories were accurate, Flinders' own surveys could be challenged by prior Chinese, Dutch, and Malay claims to "Australia." Pobassoo indicated no interest in such contests, though both he and his son were intrigued to learn about Port Jackson; they had never heard of a European settlement on the continent.

The encounter with Flinders was momentary, but the maritime world shared between Australia and Southeast Asia was the site of long histories between Makassan and Aboriginal peoples. The visits are parts of local chronicles, transmitted by bark paintings, rock etchings, and in verse and dance. Material traces also carry these histories in records of trading goods, including tobacco, rice, and textiles. Practices of cooperative fishing are also parts of these stories.

Some cultures of Arnhem Land, particularly the Yolngu, became sea-based when introduced to Makassan canoes, fishing for large animals like turtle and dugong. Laborers and adventurers from both sides crossed between straits and seas. A Makassan pidgin was adopted as a common language, creating shared vocabularies between coastal Aborigines and Makassans, but also between networks of Aboriginal groups. *Balanda* became the word for a white person, adopted from the Dutch *Hollander*.

The Dutch knew the other end of the Makassar circuit that connected to Australia. Makassar brought in slaves to Batavia, and 1685 delivery records show two hundred laborers supplied to wealthy colonial widows, and Malay and Chinese contractors. Harbormaster records from the early eighteenth century also describe the fishing hauls of Bajau "sea nomads," and credit bills show Chinese traders placing requests for turtle shell and trepang from the far-off but lucrative Australian waters.[16]

When Dutch ships later came directly into Northern Australian bays they found Aboriginal groups wise in the ways of bargaining from Makassan traders. Exchanges based upon what Europeans called "trinkets" soon evolved into specific demands. One captain reported trading one man's carrying load of trepang for "two Javanese dresses, two pieces of lining chintz, two red karwasses, two parangs or chopping-knives, two bush-knives, two plates, two combs, two handkerchiefs for the head, and two catties ... of copper wire."[17]

The British colony at Port Jackson became interested in this trade. Following Flinders' report and continuing political struggles with the Dutch and French, the Admiralty proposed trying to control the north, perhaps as an alternative to the rival port and trading colony of Singapore, established by Thomas Raffles. Trading stations and fortifications were built up and, increasingly, the trepang trade was interdicted by customs, taxation, and seizure of cargoes. In 1883, the South Australian Government forced Makassans to pay for licenses to fish and imposed a duty on goods used to trade with Aborigines. Europeans began trepanging directly in the late nineteenth century.

Finally, in July 1906, *prahus* were officially prohibited from coming to Australian shores. A Government Resident's report argued in favor of protecting European colonial interests: "Now that the local boats are exploring the coast, there can be no valid reason for continuing the issue of licences to Malays." The report was written when anti-Asian feeling was running high in Australia. The Commonwealth Government had formulated the Immigration Restriction Act and White Australia Policy. A 1902 Pacific Island Laborers Act had also led to the deportation and exclusion of thousands of islander workers. In these years, many of the older *prahu* captains retired from the sea. By the early twentieth century, the Makassan heritage disappeared from the national history of Australia.[18]

On January 1, 1988, the bicentenary began with national television programming and more than seventy satellite link-ups across the country. The organizing committee had labored long over how to showcase competing groups, including "the cattlemen who complained that an early publicity exercise showed too many sheep," and representations of singing and dancing in front of famous natural wonders like Uluru. Scores of publications recounted Australia's history of frontier settlement, and recognized Pacific contacts from an early colonial pork trade with Tahiti to Melanesian labor convoys to Queensland plantations near the end of the nineteenth century.

On January 26, two million people gathered on the shores of Sydney harbor with ten thousand boats for official speeches, music, balloons, an aerial show, and fireworks, and a tall ships parade of two hundred sailing vessels from around the world. A privately funded First Fleet re-enactment spearheaded by a descendant of one of the early governors of New South Wales also received cheers from well-wishers and historians who argued it would teach Australians about their British heritage.[19] Aboriginal groups staged their counter commemorations.

Far to the north, the arrival of the *Hati Marege* in 1988 commemorated and renewed another connection for the bicentennial of Australia's other history – not only British, convict, immigrant, and Aborigine, but Asian and oceanic. The landing honored Husein Daeng Ranka, the last of all the Makassan captains to visit the Yolngu. He arrived for a final season in 1906 to say farewell to his Aboriginal family, convey a letter from the Makassan merchants, and to bring sarongs as tokens of friendship.

Observers of the commemoration were taken to a banyan tree believed to be the home of a spirit and a Makassan grave. In traditional tellings, "whenever it sees a prahu sail into the bay it goes to a rock in the sea and cries for it, and when the prahu leaves, it cries for it again and returns to the tree." One participant remarked, "They knew straightaway this country, like this is my place. Their culture, like our culture. Similar dreamings."[20]

13 THE WORLD THAT CANTON MADE

Off the coasts of Vanua Levu, Fiji, during the reign of Naulivou, voyaging chiefs from the Bau region one day regarded a strange vessel from beyond the coastal arrowroot and tobacco weeds. The outlanders made shore and offered iron hoop, knives, and hatchets, and unknown animals like geese, a monkey, and a cat. The chiefs had long traded canoes, woven mats, and spears with Tongans, but the outsiders wanted only croppings of heavy trees with rough, mottled bark, unsuitable for canoes, which they cut, scored, and loaded into their vessel. The boat would be only one of many to follow, and in a few years, the chiefs were not only trading, but negotiating contracts for their forests and the work gangs to cut and haul them.[1]

Many of the ships then made port in a place largely unknown to the chiefs of Bau. In April 1805, the governor of New South Wales wrote from Sydney, relating "the circumstances of a small Vessel belonging to an Individual being sent in quest of the Bêche-de-Mer. That Vessel is returned, and altho' they failed in that Object, yet they acquired another of not less Value, namely, Sandalwood." It had been long known, according to the Governor, that the aromatic wood "was a production of some of the Feejee Islands, which are a Group hitherto not much known." He induced an expedition to survey, barter, and harvest some tons of the wood, pleased that "it may hereafter be an advantageous Object of Commerce with China."[2]

Ship crews putting in at Sydney made port and provision, but it was not their final destination, for Australian sailors and merchants had little local market for joss sticks, incense, and fragrant furniture: the cargoes continued on to their final destination: the South China coast and the famed Pearl River. Upriver from the Delta lay the entrepôt of Pacific trade for generations: Guangzhou, the port of Canton.

Sailing the channels and the wide river delta in the eighteenth and nineteenth centuries, here were waters plowed by hundreds of craft, sails and rigging billowing in the winds, that tied together colonies, chiefdoms, Europeans, islanders, and Asians. Tea, silk, spices, had long moved out into the China Sea and up from the delta from around Southeast Asia and the Indian Ocean. Now, a newer island trade began, bringing goods and also islanders and Europeans in Oceania directly into renewed contact on boats and in foreign trading colonies.

The port was like nowhere else. Guided upriver, captains could observe the shoals, treacherous for craft of large draft, and the sampans following ships offering rice, fish, and vegetables. Other traders moved along the banks unloading heavy cargoes of wood, calicos and silver, trepang and manufactures, chasing downriver pilots, laborers, or supply boats among the junks and the dhows. The river front was covered with warehouses and stations – the famous factories of the foreign merchants – flying international flags and surrounded by storage yards. Around them were the competing companies and the palatial gardens of the agents, Chinese managers, and stock account intermediaries for Asian, American, and European trading companies.

The crossing of worlds was nothing new here. Foreign merchants had traded in the region for a millennium, and Arab connections were reported from the Tang Dynasty. Centuries later, as Ming traders expanded throughout island Southeast Asia, a thriving junk trade carried the commerce of foreigners into Chinese waters. Zheng He's great treasure fleets also patrolled these sea lanes. The Portuguese were the first Europeans to arrive by sea, establishing tight control over external commerce, but they were expelled from the mainland and finally settled around Macao in 1557. They were largely unrivaled as masters of foreign trade, challenged only when Dutch carriers began to appear in the seventeenth century.

Foreign trade also expanded after Taiwan came under Chinese authority in 1683 and Qing rulers encouraged commercial exchanges. Along with the Portuguese, the port of Canton centered the Spanish trade out of Manila, Muslim merchants from India, and the ships of the French and English East Indian Companies. Dutch, Swedish, and Danish traders also set up factories, along with Prussians, and, by the 1780s, Americans and Australians. The port was a raucous world of Portuguese, Spanish, Mandarin, Cantonese, pidgin English, Malay, and Indian languages, peppered with words from all of Europe and Oceania.

The Spanish connection is particularly notable, for the fabled galleons that dominated Pacific-wide crossings for centuries were largely transshipments. Some goods originated in the Philippines or came from the Spice Islands, but detailed ship manifests show that the Manila-Acapulco cargoes of silk and porcelain were heavily requisitioned in China. Indeed, traders of the time often called the Spanish galleons *naos de China* – China Ships – because of the textiles, glazed pottery, gold, jade, and other riches of the Celestial Empire that made the cargoes so valuable.

The silver coins that poured into Canton from Peruvian and Mexican mines were standard currency of trade, and the port grew into a global marketplace. The Dutch, Portuguese, and Spanish brought the wealth of the Indies and the Americas. In the late eighteenth century, English, French, and American ships explored the routes established by Captain Cook and connected the northwest coast of the Canadian and Oregon territories to the Hawaiian Islands on a fur trading circuit. In Polynesian ports, merchant ships anchored beside whalers, sandalwood boats, trepang sellers, and tea-traders that had looped through Papeete or the Bay of Islands, New Zealand, or Queensland, Australia with cargoes for China.

The empire was accessible only through the intricate formalities and administration of the "Canton system." Concerned about foreign expansion, the Qing emperor had issued a 1757 decree explicitly limiting foreign commerce to Guangzhou – Canton – at the head of the Pearl River estuary where it meets the South China Sea. There, foreigners were restricted to a special zone outside of the main city walls built on a riverbank and crowded with warehouses or "factories." A trading season from October to March guided their lives with con-tracts and deals, and summer months meant obligatory withdrawal to the European colony at Macao.

In high season, Canton could be an extraordinary experience, a world of global, trans-local exchanges. Hundreds of foreign ships, their masts extending for miles downriver, crowded the outer port and the

24 Crossroads of the world: traders and merchants in Canton, China.

available landings. With them came the thousands of local suppliers and workers who built their livelihoods around the ships and crews, brandishing baskets of fish and fruit, offering labor for repairs, hawking small trade items to captains and sailors. As ships made their way upriver, sampans and launches crowded with chickens, vegetables, grains, cloth, and people covered the water as floating marketplaces.

Ashore, foreign crews were hustled along waterfront lanes to tea houses and sellers of rice wine. On the western side of the Factory district, shopkeepers with storehouses of writing desks, lacquered chests, elegant carvings, and artworks bargained with captains. Some of the neighborhoods were well known, such as around Thirteen Factory Street, where lay "a maze of narrow, winding streets crowded with sightseers, peddlers, and porters ... each street with one trade, dried foodstuffs, edible bird's nests and trepang, cloth, silk, painted glass, herbal medicine." In these neighborhoods, traders and visitors from all over the world made deals, passed along tips, and exchanged fragments of languages and tall tales. Both Chinese and foreign agents wrote up signs and newsletters in major languages, publishing recommendations and stories, and offering advice and services.[3]

Out on the water, exchange and negotiation also defined everything from hiring helmsmen to simple provisioning. Foreign ships needed pilots to navigate the shoals and sandbars of the Pearl River, and linguists to translate documents, confirm cargoes, and arrange meetings with inspectors. Purchasers and agents oversaw the ships and crews coming and going and the provisions necessary for crews – cattle, fowl, wine, also timber and tar, and cordage for repairs. Laborers called tidewater men waited at the docks for the loading and unloading. Ships had papers checked by the Chinese officials and could proceed only if they were carrying cargo – silver alone or empty holds were signs of likely smuggling. Political and profit disagreements were enacted daily along moorings or in the holds of covered boats loaded with contraband merchandise.

Foreign ships anchored in the port called Macao Roads and were required to hire a pilot for passage to a customs house at Boca Tigris, the mouth of the river. At Boca Tigris, ships were inspected by Chinese officials and allowed to proceed to Whampoa Roads, upriver. From there, ships had to be measured to determine port fees and all cargoes unloaded onto Chinese sampans called "chop boats," then transported through tollhouses and customs points to Canton and the Factories.

Surveying all this was the powerful customs superintendent known as the "Hoppo." He sailed in among the traders on a regal junk, accompanied by a small fleet of forty or fifty other vessels. Adorned in dignified formal costume, the Hoppo determined what government levies ships would pay to trade and invited captains to offer gifts to the Emperor. Foreigners saluted him, and he responded by sounding a large gong mounted on his deck.

As his officials took to the task of measuring ships and assessing fees, the Hoppo made speeches and shared ritual toasts of wine and dishes of candied fruit and sweetmeats with ships' officers. Chinese musicians played fanfares along with sailor bands, and the crews sometimes performed plays. The official port linguists would translate both conversations and documents. After signing a bond for fees, duties, and guarantees of conduct, the Hoppo often received mechanical clocks or music boxes to be turned over to his own Qing superiors in the imperial bureaucracy.[4]

The Hoppo was not the only authority to reckon with as trade expanded. During the long period from 1757 to 1842, all official commercial activities had to go through Chinese houses licensed to trade with Westerners. These were supervised by the Hoppo and known as the Hong merchants. In the eighteenth century, the merchants formed a cartel which foreigners called the Co-Hong, and fixed monopolistic prices for cargoes in and out of Canton; with trade increasing, the imperial court, the Co-Hong merchants, and the traders all competed for rising revenues. In the mid-eighteenth century, tea replaced silk as the most significant export, along with items carried from Madras, Calcutta, and Malacca. In the nineteenth century, cotton and opium began to dominate, raising new opportunities and challenges.

Some of the powerful Hong merchants amassed stupendous fortunes to their firms and trading accounts. Stories tell of fires at their warehouses that melted down precious metals stocks into rivers of silver that ran through city streets. Better verified are accounts of the opulent banquets of bird's nest soup with trepang and shark fins they held for each other, attended by innumerable servants and accompanied by performances of Chinese opera. Sandalwood furniture and fans perfumed the air. Their residences were staggering compounds of carved and tiled interlocking pavilions built around terraced gardens and private canals serviced by boatmen in decorated gondolas.[5]

Of the Co-Hong merchants, one in particular had a clipper ship christened in his name: this was Wu Bingjian, known to Westerners as "Howqua." The ship featured a figurehead and a design "as sharp as a pair of Chinese shoes." Portraits show his long, thin face, slight moustache, and courtly demeanor, "dressed luxuriously in a dragon robe and an expensive fur-lined overrobe with insignia badges and long beads."

Both officials and merchants derided him as "The Timid Old Lady" for his willingness to pay ransoms and extortions to mandarins and, later, British gunboats, but it was all the cost of doing business. And he could easily afford it. The richest and most powerful of the Co-Hong merchants, Wu Bingjian was the third son in a family company. A shrewd businessman, he was heavily engaged in tea and silk, supplying both the British East India Company and American firms in Boston.

He was also a leader in credit ventures, advancing capital to weak merchants for considerable interest, and single-handedly paying off debts – including that of the Chinese government – in impressive displays of patronage. His wealth, invested in trading and banking concerns around the world, was many times that of the Rothschild family dynasty, his contemporaries in commerce and finance. In particular, he is noted for advancing American interests, creating a partnership with Russell & Company, the major American tea and silk trader, and donating buildings for missionaries and hospitals. Chinese newspapers in San Francisco (1855) reported on Howqua as a "master of international trade," and some historians claim that he was a major stockholder in American railroad companies, the great intercontinental transport lines built with so much immigrant Chinese labor.[6]

In Canton itself, such global connections would be most regularly incarnated in the single figure of the *comprador*. The *compradors* were merchant house agents charged with contracting stewards, suppliers, cooks, cleaners, and laborers, and with ferrying sampans laden with pigs, cattle, grains, fruit, cloth, wild ducks, and chickens to anchored traders. From the eighteenth century, they were one of many port functionaries, but when the Co-Hong system declined in the 1840s, the *comprador* became the key Chinese collaborator of foreign merchants.

Chinese stewards had long run the daily maintenance of offices and living quarters – hiring servants and purveyors, renting and repairing properties, purchasing land. The *comprador* increasingly also took on the role of a business manager, drafting and confirming bank orders, maintaining a firm's treasury, examining coinage, and being informed about shipping schedules, local business deals, and future prices on everything from rice to wood oil. He also guaranteed loans and credit for business partners and arranged entertainments and dinners for Chinese officials. In many cases, the *compradors* would be charged with large sums for inland journeys, where foreigners were not permitted, to make purchases of tea and silk.

Trading on their own accounts, some *compradors* built up small fortunes. Somewhat like the Hong merchants, but in the service of foreign firms, they were products of a multicultural, international world, envied for their privileges, reviled for serving the interests of Western companies. Many were necessarily cosmopolitan. The *compradors* moved in family circles of Confucian and Buddhist practice and morals, while sending their own children to instruction in church schools, using Western education in grammar, geography, and mathematics to maintain political and social status at the intersection of worlds.

One Wang I-t'ing was a classical Chinese calligrapher and painter while serving a foreign firm; another *comprador* spent his fortune spiritually situating his ancestors' tombs. Others adopted hybrid identities in names like "Robert" Ho Tung. As a profession, the *compradors* managed and promoted schools and new businesses, headed district relief campaigns, worked with regional governors on political and policing questions, and created for themselves unique and profitable roles at the meeting of Sino-Occidental culture.[7]

Such overlapping of commercial pursuit with foreigners and adherence to Chinese practices was present from the beginning of the Canton system. In fact, visitors often reported business practices that were also commentaries on culture: customs, manners, and new knowledge gained in Canton. The world of Chinese *compradors*, merchants, and officials created a dense network of exchanges, and in some cases, those at the center were not Europeans but Pacific Islanders voyaging into unknown worlds along with the Westerners.

From the late eighteenth century, one was Lee Boo, from Micronesia. He crossed from Oceanian to Asian worlds with Captain Henry Wilson of the East India Company, whose merchant ship had been wrecked off Palau, and whose crew was stranded while rebuilding a schooner to reach Canton. Wilson became a friend of King Abba

Thulle, who was impressed by the captain's technology, knowledge, and descriptions of England, and requested that his son, Lee Boo, be taken on the continuing voyage.

The young prince impressed the foreign traders with his manners and disposition, and demonstrated his skill at spear-throwing. In turn, he learned about tea, European women, and the Chinese marketplace, and was fascinated by the high-rising houses and streetlife in Canton. In 1784, Lee Boo arrived in Portsmouth, met with the directors of the East India Company, and was an object of curiosity and admiration before succumbing to smallpox after just five months. His patrons penned him an epitaph, and his story of noble and simple generosity entered into English schoolbooks.

The Chief Ka'iana, younger brother of the king of Kauai, Hawai'i, did not leave a sentimental legacy, but he certainly made a strong impression in Canton. Traveling with Captain John Meares, a fur trader crossing from the Pacific Northwest to China, Ka'iana was by all accounts an imposing presence – tall, muscular, proud, "handsome and haughty," with a feathered cape, helmet, and *toa* wood spear. Crowds gathered around and shrank from his presence. Over several months in Macao and Canton he demonstrated contempt for the Chinese, whom he regarded as small and servile, and the merchants in turn scorned him for being unable to make use of coins, instead trying to barter with iron nails.

In Macao he followed the rituals of the Catholic mass with great interest, and was moved by the plight of beggars in sampans; impressed by the ships and ports, he could not comprehend the spectacle of poverty and daily hunger that he witnessed. He eventually returned to Hawai'i bearing a cache of weapons and, finding the islands at war, became a strong ally of Kamehameha.[8]

By the first decades of the nineteenth century, such ennobled visitors to Canton were but single faces in an increasing population of largely anonymous islanders, not guests under the patronage of captains, but common labor *kanakas*, joining the lascars, the Kru-men, and the Manila men in a Pacific circuit of ships and trade cargoes.

The clamor of markets at Canton reverberated in Pacific worlds thousands of miles from China's shores. Small groups and individual islanders joined whaling and sealing crews and signed on for fur trapping, voyaging from their homes to the Americas, around the north and south Pacific, and across the ocean in search of goods for the South China Sea. For them, life onboard ships was an adventure and a brutal servitude, circumscribed by the strict hierarchies and rites of life at sea, beatings, abuse, insults, and the tensions of different groups working, earning, and often dying together.[9]

Whaling was the most famous, notorious, and romanticized of the trades. The first ship sailed from London in 1787, but the majority of the business would quickly belong to Americans out of New Bedford and Nantucket. By the 1840s, some 675 American whaling ships were hunting the north and south Pacific, chasing prey and provisioning in an Oceanian circuit from the Solomon Islands across the Central Pacific, where the cachalot – the sperm whale – crushed giant squid in its jaws and moved in great migrating pods from the waters of Micronesia and Japan and north to the Arctic.

In all these environments, whaling ships sailed with white crews mixed with, and sometimes specifically manned by, islanders, the latter especially noted for their swimming, rowing, and spear-throwing talents. Generically called Kanaka, islander whalemen suffered wasting diseases and climates, brutal work, and regular dangers to life and limb. In this, they fared not much differently than other crewmen. Ship's records of passage preserve the not quite anonymous Kanakas, with islands of origin and English names given by captains to a Joe Bal and Jack Ena, a John Jovel and a Sam How.[10]

At the same time, passage on whalers meant unusual opportunities to travel the oceans, often in the track of gods and ancestors, to trade and learn new languages and customs. While learning the ways of shipboard life, including rites of passage and sea-stories, islanders like Hawaiians brought their own ancient chants and tales. Oral traditions across Polynesia spoke of whales carrying humans on spiritual journeys to become religious leaders or priests. Only high chiefs and chiefesses wore sacred whale-tooth necklaces. These legends and practices became part of maritime lore, exchanged across Oceanian circuits.

The business itself could be thrilling, and was always dangerous and dirty. The Reverend Henry Cheever recorded a kill: "the huge creature rose hard by the captain's boat, and all the harpooner in the bow had to do was to plunge his two keen cold irons, which are always secured to one tow-line, into the monster's blubber-sides. This he did so well as to hit the 'fish's life' at once, and make him spout blood forthwith." Boats were spun, tossed, and often overturned.

25 Chasing the leviathan: global crews and whalers at sea.

A successful hunt concluded with an exhausted whale, bleeding and wrapped in lines, struck at close range. Towed by the whaleboats and secured to the ships, the great carcasses were stripped of blubber and rendered in flaming, smoky pots while the crew butchered the flesh on decks running with oil and blood.[11]

This world was canonized by the sailor, adventurer, customs agent, and writer Herman Melville, whose tales of South Sea island encounters like *Typee*, and his classic *Moby Dick*, were inspired by his own voyaging and a historical case of a ship rammed by a whale in the South Seas. From this, Melville fashioned a genuinely international literature populated by characters from a Yankee seafaring world like Captain Ahab and Ishmael seeking prey and serving destiny along with multi-ethnic crews.

Such literature not only recorded in exquisite nineteenth-century detail the toils of an encroaching American commercial presence in Pacific waters, but shaped a greater vision of the global novel, characters like the harpooner Queequeg transiting and making port with crews from Africa, the West Indies, Oceania, and the Americas around Atlantic and Pacific worlds, held in shipboard hierarchies dominated by maritime authority.[12]

Less immortalized than whaling, but critical to the initial connections between North America, the Hawaiian Islands, and Canton, was the fur trade. The sea otter is a large cousin to the terrestrial weasel or badger, but itself a fully marine mammal like the whale. Inhabiting the coastal North Pacific Ocean in kelp beds and feeding on urchins and clams, its fabulous pelt made it in turn prey to the interests of English, American, Spanish, Russian, and islander traders who descended especially on the Nootka Sound, vying to gain cargoes for sale in Macao and Canton.

From the seventeenth century, Russian traders had come from Kamchatka to establish camps across the Aleutian Islands and Alaska for the trade, meeting now and again, as they headed south, with Spanish captains who considered the coastline to be part of their domain. In 1769, the Spanish sent expeditions and set up a colonial administration in Monterey over a new colonial province they called Alta California. The bay of San Francisco was its border. There was little they could do, however, about the increasing presence of European intrusions further north or, after 1776, interest from the Americans.

After James Cook's exploration of the region and the recognized Hawaiian transit to and from Asia, commercial ships began to arrive in numbers to the Pacific Northwest. The first, which gained a stupendous cargo of nearly six hundred pelts, was launched from Canton by an English businessman, John Henry Cox, in 1785. The tremendous profit ensured more would follow, often flying false colors to evade the monopolies of the mercantile trading companies.

The primary anchorage in the 1780s and 1790s was in the territory of the Nuu-chah-nulth people of the Nootka Sound, Canada, a "local" place with global resonance. Different villages vied for advantage, but one, Yuquot, became dominant under the powerful chief Maquinna. He himself wore otter fur dress under a conical, feathered hat, and led settlements of sturdy wooden houses, canoe fleets, and a thriving population fed by salmon and herring. As the British established their presence in his territory, the Spanish Crown quickly sent ships and soldiers to map territorial claims and establish a fortress. The British entrepreneur-seaman John Meares established his own trading post, and conflicts led to possible war between Britain and Spain, a showdown known in European history as the Nootka crisis.

Maquinna and his people were forced to move their village because of the incursions, but the chief did not allow himself to be sidelined: he played an important role engaging both the Spanish envoy Juan Francisco de la Bodega y Quadra, and the British representative, Captain George Vancouver. Maquinna also translated their episodes into histories of his own, mimicking the Europeans with plays and dialogues using imagined or invented versions of their languages and actions, rendered in the theatrical potlatch style of the Northwest Coast.

He was also a shrewd warrior and saw the utility of some white prisoners, notably holding blacksmith John Jewitt as a well-treated slave for three years after massacring the crew of the vessel *Boston* in reprisal for conflicts with Spanish and American parties. Maquinna weighed his allies and enemies, carefully distributing the valuable fur that his trappers hunted down from the powerful otters, some as big as men.[13]

Meanwhile, in Canton, traders continued to conspire for the profits. Among the British, the monopoly exercised by the East India and South Sea Companies was resented, even by some of their employees. Charles Barkley, an East India Company naval captain, resigned his position and ran up Austrian colours for an illegal Canton factory, hoping to earn a personal fortune. His wife Frances sailed with him, and during a Hawaiian stopover, employed Winee, a Hawaiian woman, as her maid. In June 1787 they became the first European and Island women to follow the trade at the Nootka Sound. In November of the same year they discharged almost nine hundred pelts in Macao.[14]

Just months earlier, the tireless John Meares had also returned to the South China Sea. In Canton, he hired carpenters and outfitted a new trip and sailed again for the Northwest, this time carrying the Hawaiian warrior Ka'iana, whom he was returning to Kauai. He also picked up Winee from the Barkleys' ship and a man named Comekela, who was going home. He was the brother of Maquinna and had left Nootka Sound on his own voyage to Canton the previous year. He had reasons to see for himself the distant place where all the otter of his seas were being taken and traded.

Indeed, the chiefs of the Northwest Coast, like those in Hawai'i where the trade ships laid over, were always curious about the handling and profits of the cargoes that passed from and by them on the way to China. In some cases they took control directly. In Hawai'i, Kamehameha notably bargained with *haole* – white – traders, made deals, and also assembled his own fleets. Upon unifying all of the islands under his rule, Kamehameha created a monarchy resembling a feudal state, granting lands and tying chiefs to him by common interest. One great priority for Kamehameha was increasing foreign trade, and he had a royal monopoly on an important resource: Hawaiian sandalwood.

For each major cargo or contract he exacted a brig or schooner to build up his navy, adding half a dozen vessels along with European and American wares like silverware and crystal, wardrobes of jackets, carriages, and Canton export china. He assembled workteams of carpenters to build him dozens of sloops, and hired foreigners and lower-ranked chiefs with language skills to aid him as business agents and negotiators, setting taxes and duties on a developing Pacific entrepôt.[15]

But Hawaiian sandalwood was a limited resource and by the death of Kamehameha in 1819 it was dwindling and soon gone. A decade later in 1829, Captain Samuel P. Henry pulled together a work crew of Tongans and landed in Erromanga, the New Hebrides, to explore a more recently discovered source. News of the developments reignited Hawaiian Pacific-wide ambitions.

The governor of Oahu, Boki, had just a few years earlier sent his aide Manui'a to Manila and Canton from Honolulu with sealskins and sandalwood to pay off royal debts to traders. Now, he had grander designs, commanding two vessels with four hundred Hawaiians and one hundred Rotumans to sail south not only to cut and ship the wood to China, but to fight the Erromangans and annex "Certain Islands in the South Seas which are now in an Uncultivated State." Boki's ship was lost at sea, and most of the remaining crew were killed by disease and warfare with the Erromangans.[16]

Fijian chiefs also benefited from these decades of sandalwood trade, which developed and declined in their islands much as in Hawai'i. By the 1820s, the accessible stands were gone from their shores, but the Canton connection was not played out. In about 1828 a ship from Salem came into the Fijian islands looking for any undiscovered sandalwood, and instead found an astonishing abundance of *holothuria* – the trepang that Matthew Flinders had learned about from Pobassoo in northern Australian waters. As it happened, the captain had just been cruising the Moluccas where he learned the techniques of harvesting and curing from Malay fishermen.

As practiced for centuries by the Makassan traders and Australian Aborigines, the trepang enterprise was a delicate operation requiring sometimes hazardous collections from coastal ebb tides and by diving, followed by saltwater cleaning and removal of slime, repeated parboiling, and lengthy drying and smoking. The last necessitated on-site construction of enormous drying sheds, watertight and up to a hundred feet long, with clay embankments, wooden racks, and reed filters upon which the trepang were arranged for slow, smoky curing from constant smoldering fires. Errors or bad luck meant the fish would turn into gelatinous masses, become rotten from exposure, or be simply lost when the tinderbox sheds would occasionally catch sparks and go up in flames.

As with sandalwood, to produce a cargo for market of any value required enormous amounts of labor, for the fishing and preparation, for timber cutting to provide construction materials and smoking wood, and for security – operations were highly vulnerable to raiding parties. This created alliances between the Canton traders and Fijian chiefs, particularly the long-standing rival clan regions of Bau and Rewa.[17]

Out of the conflict between these two chiefdoms rose the dominant political figure of the mid-nineteenth century, paramount leader Ratu Seru Cakobau. The chiefs of Fiji had, from the sandalwood days, a loose system of trade and tribute to deal with strangers, traders, and other useful interlopers. There was no such thing as a European presence at the time; there were only the occasional ships in search of wood, copra, and seals. The chiefs closely guarded their prerogatives and, as around other Pacific islands, constantly struggled against each other.

Now Cakobau learned that the white strangers wanted the *dri* – the sea cucumber that luxuriated in Fijian waters. The Canton connection was not Cakobau's concern, but the European and American captains were willing to bargain for what he wanted, paying out exchanges of woolens, metal, and cargoes of muskets and powder. Over the years, the number of firearms in the Fijian islands would be estimated at nearly five thousand, and would tip the balance of power between the warring chiefs. In exchange, Cakobau used his authority and conscripted entire villages to work the reefs and gather the creatures for the traders.

Captains were pleased; their attempts to entice islanders directly with small trade items had been rebuffed. Cakobau, however, had the authority to command entire clans to the tidal waters for the difficult collections and processing labor. He used his revenue to buy trade articles and build a small war fleet. Over the decades, as marine stocks were depleted and harvests declined, Cakobau famously sent out his entire army to scour the waters. In 1852, his forces employed more than a hundred canoes to drag in a catch for Cakobau to sell in exchange for two American ships, part of his continuing attempts to build a navy.[18]

It was American ships, in fact, though not under Cakobau's control, that would reshape Fijian history. Having no central government, the dominant chiefs struck their own land deals with European and American settlers. In 1846, John Brown Williams, lately of the Bay of Islands, became American commercial agent in Fiji and belligerently held Cakobau responsible for the personal loss of his residence, which he himself had accidentally burned down during a July 4 celebration. American warships backed Williams' claims. At the same time, Cakobau was facing pressures from rival chiefs in northern Fiji, and by 1858 he began to propose cession of the islands to Britain as a means to maintain his authority.

Such maneuverings over commercial and strategic alliances rippled across the Pacific around the mid-nineteenth century. The British declared sovereignty over New Zealand in 1840. That same year Tahitian Queen Pomare Vahine faced bombardment by the French Admiral Abel Dupetit-Thouars over the establishment of a French protectorate. Cakobau looked to a deal with Britain to save his kingdom from the Americans. In dealing with foreigners, monarchs no longer negotiated with supplicant parties, but faced the increasing strategic and military power of Western naval forces, backed by nation states. Nowhere did this become more resonant than back at the port of Canton itself.

Though extremely lucrative, the sandalwood, fur, and trepang trades of the Pacific were small fare compared to the great addictions that would drive the British and Chinese into conflict: tea and opium. Whereas the luxury trade could make fortunes for savvy traders, the tea and opium trades changed the chemical habits of millions and threatened to bankrupt the treasuries of empires.

Already, from the early eighteenth century, the English had embraced tea as a therapeutic drink, then as a social and cultural tradition, thanks to royal patronage and the initiative of tea-sellers like Thomas Twining and his family. In Australia the anthem

Waltzing Matilda would describe a colony embracing tea not only as a popular drink, but as an essential daily ration for convicts and settlers alike.

Yet tea was not easily cultivated, and Chinese growers were secretive about their processes. Harvested by pickers in season, especially in Fujian and Guangdong, the rough *camellia sinensis* leaves were rolled in bamboo containers to release their oil and fired in iron woks to halt their oxidation. Storehouses dried the leaves and infused other scents such as pine, while batches were sent to tasters, blended, and stamped into the wooden chests known to clipper captains. One of the earliest samples, about two pounds, had left China for Britain in 1664. By the 1830s, it was 30 million pounds a year. The trade imbalance was of mortal concern.[19]

Neither England nor Australia, however, had substantial products to sell to China in return. They made accounts with woolens, some crops, manufactures and devices spawned by the Industrial Revolution, calico from India, and the wood, furs, and marine products of the Pacific. But most payment was silver. When Lord Macartney arrived in Beijing in 1793 to expand trading opportunities, the Qing Emperor famously responded, "We possess all things. I see no value on objects strange or ingenious, and have no use for your country's manufactures." Subsequent missions did not change this view.

The imperial court regarded other countries and rulers as tributary vassals. Visitors were expected to kowtow by prostrating themselves three times before the Emperor; there were no such things as diplomatic negotiations or trade agreements. Strangers were welcome to be awestruck by the Celestial Empire and engage in commerce through the Hoppo and the Co-Hong, but for the imperial household a top British envoy was no more than "The English barbarian chieftain."[20]

The tea addiction drained the royal exchequer in London of silver. English traders began to counter with rival tea growing in India and Ceylon, but developing exports would take decades. To pay for Chinese tea, they turned to another trade product from their Indian colony that the Chinese would buy when all else had failed: opium.

Though the East India Company knew opium trading was restricted in China, the non-company traders, operating unofficially, pursued a lucrative contraband and smuggling trade. Opium had been known in the empire since it began to arrive with Arab traders in the seventh century. By the seventeenth and eighteenth centuries, along with tobacco, it was diluted, combined, and smoked as a stimulant, and for treating some cases of malaria and dysentery. It was widely recognized as a medicinal painkiller, but also by Confucian officials as a moral poison and was interdicted in the 1720s.

By the 1790s, as smoking opium became habitual across a broad population, new rules in China banned trading and growing completely, calling the drug "a destructive and ensnaring vice." Officials closed down some operations, but traders and merchants continued to collude and profit. In 1811, Americans began to ship in opium from Turkey, and by the 1820s European companies openly maintained huge funds to pay bribes to officials and publish market prices for arriving shipments.

The stakes rose higher. By 1830, the fiscal position of British India was dependent on selling opium in China, and in England manufacturers and private traders agitated against the East India Company monopoly and adopted the motto "freedom of commerce." With support from some Members of Parliament, the Company monopoly was broken and powerful private merchants, industrialists, and speculators crowded into the China trade, lobbying for aggressive reform of taxes, duties, and, indeed, all commercial codes and practices they deemed unfair.

The British sent an envoy to pressure the Chinese trade officials, but they responded by shutting down all Canton trade, forcing him to retreat. It was traditional Chinese policy: tame the foreigners. As the Governor politely yet contemptuously informed the English traders, "It is unnecessary again to appoint a barbarian headman, thereby causing friction and trouble."[21]

These episodes were closely watched by Commissioner Lin Zexu, a brilliant and strict administrator. Methodical, organized, and willing to take strong action, Lin was chosen by the Qing Emperor in 1839 to take direct control of the opium trade in Canton. He was the paragon of a virtuous Confucian official. With a long, white beard and serious gaze, he traveled soberly in a sedan chair, paid his own expenses, and maintained only a small retinue. He ordered and studied tomes on English law and culture, reading for insights, and paid a visit to Macao to see the workings of the foreign – barbarian – communities and firms there. He had his subordinates buy a British armed merchantman so he could understand the strangers' maritime technology.

He then enforced the law, quickly. Within weeks, smokers and suspect Chinese merchants groveled before him, and thousands of pipes were taken and storehouses raided. The British traders, however, refused to comply, so Lin cut them off in their compounds until Superintendent Charles Elliot himself demanded the stocks be surrendered. It was a financial loss worth an entire year's trade, and to mollify the traders he implicitly promised that the British Crown would compensate for the seizures, making the government in London both responsible and liable for the trade. Lin had his agents dig a special canal, contaminated the opium with salt and lye, and washed or dumped the remains into the sea.

Lin also wrote an extraordinary letter directly to Queen Victoria in a high Confucian moral register, asking "Let us suppose that foreigners came from another country and brought opium into England, and seduced the people of your country to smoke it. Would you not, the sovereign of said country, look upon such a procedure with anger?" The letter was likely never delivered and the government could not respond to its implication, instead accusing Lin of property destruction and interference in open trade.[22]

Despite Lin's careful preparations, his actions had devastating consequences. The barbarian traders and missions had always backed down before; this time they sent a British Indian army from their crown colony and huge, mobile warships. From 1840, they launched the Opium Wars. Heavy gun platforms devastated Chinese coastal defenses and well-armed and drilled troops landed and overtook the positions of Qing forces.

The British soon controlled Canton, and continued the battle up the Yangtze River, seizing tax barges and forcing the Qing to sue for peace in the Treaty of Nanjing, negotiated in 1842. China was obliged to pay an indemnity, open more coastal ports to foreign traders, and cede the island of Hong Kong as British territory. Shortly, the Qing rulers also had to concede the unthinkable: recognition of Britain as an equal, with extraterritorial rights in all treaty ports.

The results were momentous. Other Western nations, particularly France and the United States, also demanded and gained similar concessions. The new treaty ports like Hong Kong and Shanghai became permanent bases for settlements, foreign offices, and missionary establishments. *Compradors* took over the business

26 Power and profit: the Opium Wars.

rule of the abolished Co-Hong. Thousands of Chinese migrated out from coastal cities on overseas labor contracts in mines and plantations in Indonesia, Malaysia, Australia, and out toward Hawai'i and California.

The incursions, upheavals, and demonstrated incapacity of the government stirred unrest against foreigners and especially against the ethnically Manchu Qing dynasty itself. Demands for social reform were accelerated by peasant rebellion and attacks on Qing authorities. These found a charismatic voice in Hong Xiuquan, a student of missionaries who had failed the traditional state examination system, and claimed to be the brother of Jesus Christ. He led the messianic movement known as the Taiping Rebellion against the government from 1850 to 1864 as China plunged into a titanic civil war. In the middle of those years, continuing conflicts over trade and sovereignty also led to a Second Opium War, which resulted in the British sailing on Beijing and gaining even greater concessions from a weakened and fragmenting Chinese state.[23]

Lin had not stopped the opium trade. He had prepared well, but never saw the Europeans as more than barbarians, nor comprehended the growing scope of their national and global colonial powers. A furious Qing Emperor blamed him for the humiliating results, and sent him off to provincial exile. Generations later, however, Lin would be lauded as a national anticolonial hero and commemorated as a patriot, wise and decisive – if overmatched, of Chinese grandeur and virtues at the beginning of an encroaching age of global European empire.

14 FLAGS, TREATIES, AND GUNBOATS

In 1812, Tengku Hussein, heir to the Sultan of Johor on the Malay peninsula, was in Pahang getting married when his father died. As he waited for monsoon winds to return to Johor he received word that his younger brother had become the new Sultan. It was a contested claim, but Hussein remained in exile.

Seven years later, Hussein and Thomas Stamford Raffles, British lieutenant governor of the British colony of Bencoolen on western Sumatra, landed at a small Malay settlement near ancient Temasik, where Srivijaya had once ruled and Parameswara came as a pirate king before moving to Malacca. The area had a superb natural harbor, timber strands, and fresh water spreading out from the mouth of a river. Here, at Singapore, Raffles came with an ambition. He wanted the British to establish a port to overcome Dutch dominance in the region, a goal underscored by the critical importance of China routes for the British India trade, and growing interests in the opium market. The Dutch had been resisting the British with high tariffs and port restrictions.

The current Sultan of the Singapore region, Tengku Abdul Rahman, was, however, already allied with Dutch interests; a British base was not possible. So Raffles and the local governor instead brought older brother Tengku Hussein back from exile with a plan: Raffles would recognize Hussein as the legitimate Sultan of Johor in exchange for rights to a British trading post. Museums and dioramas portray them signing their agreements in gold silk gown, head wrap, and scarlet British officer's uniform. Both Hussein and the governor accepted annual stipends, and the younger brother conceded. Hussein established himself in royal fashion under British protection.[1]

In the nineteenth century, Asian and Oceanian peoples saw new colors flying from the mastheads of ships that crossed the circuits of Spanish, Portuguese, and Dutch authority they had known for generations: the British and the French were arriving in force. From East and Southeast Asia to Melanesia and Polynesia, British claims developed from invasion at Canton, patronage deals at Singapore, and adventurism in Sarawak, Borneo. New Zealand was different yet again, part warfare, part treaty arrangement.

The French brought gunboats to the Marquesas and Tahiti, built up a complex colonial society in Vietnam, and founded a penal colony in New Caledonia. There was no singular model for what happened between local peoples and the new interlopers, but all territories would soon become places on maps that European states would claim as possessions of empire, often pressing upon or pushing out former empires to do so. Earlier generations of trade, beachcombers, and dominant chiefs and island rulers were increasingly replaced by unequal contracts and European strategic dominance.

As Raffles and Hussein demonstrated, clever deal-making was one route to power. Singapore was a modest base, but also a major challenge to the Dutch and sultans in the region, indicative of a once-again shifting course of empire. As had been the case from Srivijaya to the Majapahit, from the Portuguese to the Dutch, a new system and new players were coming to the fore. Raffles gave settlement command to Major William Farquhar and a small Indian military regiment, along with a mandate to establish a free trading port without duties. The strategy proved effective, as traders looking to avoid Dutch control and taxes began to unload goods carried from Chinese, Bugis, and Arab trade routes. Population and revenues in Singapore soared.

Expectedly, the Dutch protested. In the seventeenth century, after torturing and massacring rival traders at Ambon, they had rather easily forced the English to all but abandon the archipelago. But a markedly different situation faced them in the nineteenth century. By this time, the great Dutch East India Company was gone and Britain was the rising power. The VOC had built its power on clove and cinnamon monopolies, but global products of the nineteenth century like tea, coffee, and pepper could not be controlled in the same way.

For tea, Chinese plantations were the key source of supply. Where the Dutch built up wealth in pepper, the British set up a factory at Bencoolen and traded directly for pepper from carriers in the Sunda Strait, including pirates, who bargained for arms and supplies. Overseas Chinese also established rival plantations, using their own circuits from Brunei to the Malaysian peninsula to find buyers in Canton or among the British. Batavia was marginalized. Dutch losses became unrecoverable, exacerbated by corruption, lack of investment, and crushing bureaucratic expenses.

Back in the Netherlands, internal revolutionary struggles and war in the Atlantic and Caribbean with England made all VOC ships targets. With the French Revolution collapse was foretold, as Dutch territories were invaded and annexed by Napoleon. The VOC, already in decline, reached a breaking point and was declared bankrupt in 1799. The once formidable power of the Company languished as the British moved to control Dutch colonial territories, including the island of Java itself, by 1811. At the end of the Napoleonic wars in Europe, the British withdrew and Dutch colonial rule, minus the VOC, returned to the archipelago.

From the early days, a Dutch force could still easily have conquered the small, rival Singapore settlement. But after Anglo-Dutch wars across the eighteenth century, both sides were willing to be circumspect, and Singapore trade and settlements continued to grow. By 1823, Raffles negotiated a new treaty with the Sultan that gave the British authority not only over the trading port, but over most of the island. Chinese populations rapidly expanded. These included Peranakans who traced their ancestral lines to early traders and settlers, and common laborers escaping from hardship in southern China. Malays also built lives in fishing and wage labor, building up traditional timber and thatched stilt houses, the *kampungs*. Raffles organized the sectors of the colony into ethnic and trade neighborhoods.

Raffles' impact was also felt in the Dutch territories. During the brief British occupation of Java, he had instituted a new land-tenure system that diminished the customary, feudal services owed by villages to rulers. When the Dutch returned, elites were short of revenue and farmers were left trying to satisfy changing administrations and the exactions of their traditional rulers. The discontent awaited a spark to ignite major unrest.

In 1825, Pangeran Dipanagara, the first son of the Yogyakarta Sultan, protested a Dutch road-building project, which would cross his domain at the site of a sacred tomb. Inspired by a vision of the Goddess of the Southern Ocean promising he would be a king, Dipanagara rose in defiance, rallying a popular force against the Dutch.

He cut a striking figure with his white turban and ceremonial *kris* dagger tucked into an embroidered sash. As an aristocrat he appealed to an embittered elite; raised in a rural village in traditional Islamic schools by his grandmother, he spoke well to common villagers and farmers, as well as religious mystics who followed his vision. The grievances fueled a deep-seated conflict that went on for five years, leading to the deaths of up to 200,000 Javanese. The Dutch established fortresses and eventually defeated Dipanagara, who was exiled to Makassar. Yogyakarta was reduced and his compound today, with a broken wall where the Dutch reportedly made siege, is a place of reflection.

Dipanagara would later be commemorated as an anticolonial hero, though his goals were not for a revolutionary society, but traditional rule without the Dutch. After the Java War, however, it was the colonial system that was returned to its old ways, with Javanese regents administering districts backed up by Dutch officials.[2]

In 1830, the policies known as the Cultivation System also began. In an effort to be profitable where the VOC had failed, the Cultivation System mandated export cropping, particularly coffee, tea, sugar, indigo, spices, tobacco, cotton, and cochineal. These were sold to the government at fixed prices, and a balance was supposed to be struck with rice production for local consumption. The actual practice was foreseeable. The export trade was extremely lucrative for the regents, officials, and Chinese traders, and so export growing became an obligation. As profits increased, so did district taxes and forced labor. Without support for local rice growing, shortages, famines, and epidemics spread among farmers and villagers in the 1840s. Officials and Javanese regents continued to prosper.[3]

Not all parts of the Indonesian territories were under such strict colonial rule as on Java. Around Borneo, Dutch policy was desultory in general, held together by customary treaties with sultans, and small garrisons guarding coastlines and waterways, negotiating with Chinese settlements and watching out for Iranun pirates. The northwestern regions under the domain of the Sultan of Brunei were independent of European control.

Such places attracted East India company employee James Brooke, who was inspired by Raffles, a man he took to be an adventurous empire builder. With a family inheritance, Brooke purchased a schooner and set out for Kalimantan, the island of Borneo. In 1839, as the Opium Wars were breaking out in China, and the Cultivation System pushed villages to famine, Brooke sailed his schooner up the Sarawak River, a world of mangrove, nepa palm, creepers, frigate birds, and crocodiles.

Rajah Mudah Hassim of Sarawak received Brooke with offerings of tea and tobacco, surrounded by officials in velvet jackets and red sarongs. Knowing of Brooke's schooner, the Rajah was looking for someone to intimidate members of a "rebellion" against his authority in the interior, and was interested in whether the English would come to his aid if the Dutch tried to take over his domains.

With indirect assurances made, Brooke sailed upriver, meeting with Bidayuh Dayak chief Sejugah, making notes on spirits, Allah, courtship, and head-hunting, and staying in a customary longhouse some six hundred feet long. The longhouse was an entire elevated village built on piles under one roof, with common livestock areas, cots formed from hollowed trees, bamboo balconies, and partitioned quarters like apartments for the married. Brooke took an interest in Sejugah's world of ritual harvests, in which rice was the embodied spirit of ancestors, and interiors of river systems defined the regions where Dayak and Malay intermarried in systems of alliances, friendships, and tributary regard.[4]

Finally meeting up with armed raiders and their stockade, Brooke used artillery to support a clamorous party of Malay, Dayak, and Chinese warriors and routed the Rajah's rivals. Mudah Hassim made offers to continue the alliance, but Brooke was not content to be the advisor or protector of the local aristocracy, and in fact described himself as a champion of the "wretchedly oppressed" hill Dayaks. He threatened sympathies with the Rajah's dissatisfied subjects unless given real authority. "I explained to the Raja that several chiefs and a large body of Siniawan Dayaks were ready to assist me, and that the only course left to prevent bloodshed was immediately to proclaim me governor." In September 1841, Brooke became the White Rajah of Sarawak.[5]

The Sultan of Brunei recognized that Brooke might help contain the expansion of Dutch influence, and confirmed his rajah status. Brooke found himself with authority over a land that he believed might be very rich in mining and trade concessions for the Singapore market. As his seizure of power indicated, however, his regime depended upon the support of chiefs and Dayak leaders. He created councils, and adopted local knowledge of *semargat* – a quality of power with analogies to *mana* in Oceania – by exploiting his title for wealth and patronage, creating circles of loyalty around his person.

His subjects helped him establish trading posts, courts, and codes, and schools for religious instruction, taking advantage of opportunities in education and foreign contacts. The Bidayuh Dayaks, not quite as helpless as he made them seem, supported Brooke's state but also resisted his inevitable taxes and labor exactions. Malay elites instigated plots to overthrow him, and Chinese miners, never impressed with his title or power, forced him to flee his capital in 1857, regarding him as little more than another barbarian.

Brooke's position was commanding, but tenuous. As a private citizen, his rulership caused friction with the British Foreign Office. Political enemies disliked his adventuring and the British government refused to recognize his claims until 1863. After family struggles, Brooke left Sarawak rule to his nephew, and the Brooke name continued on for two more generations. Brooke remains the romantic paragon of the colonial adventurer, establishing empire as the charismatic white leader of a private kingdom. Certainly, he presented himself as one who could, after all, just sail away, at one early frustrated point claiming, "In that case I will collect the remnants of the money I have laid out, and cry, 'Hey, for O-Tahiti,' or New Zealand."[6]

Had Brooke, in fact, sailed to New Zealand in 1840 rather than stay in Sarawak, he would have come upon British Empire once more: here, claiming sovereignty over the islands with the signing of the Treaty of Waitangi. In New Zealand, empire was not the tale of a single adventurer, but an intricate drama of common and competing interests among traders, land speculators, rival chiefs, missionaries, and colonial governors.

Depictions of the treaty signing show a vast and fascinating gathering of Maori chiefs from around the North Island, and the officials of a British party led by Lieutenant Governor William Hobson and Resident James Busby in ceremonial costume under strings of colorful banners. The treaty is one of the most studied documents in Pacific history, for it stipulates that the Maori signatories cede all of their lands to the Queen of England, while at once confirming that the Queen guarantees full Maori possession of their own lands and homes.

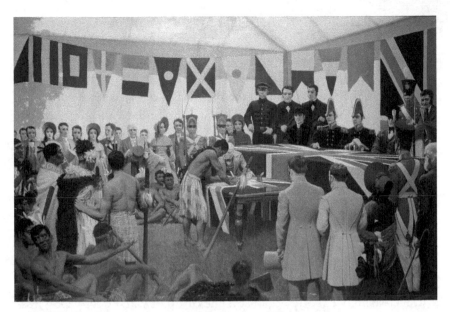

27 Documented dispute: signing of the Treaty of Waitangi.

The Queen enjoys the privilege of selling land between consenting parties, and also grants protection to the Maori and the rights of British subjects. In fact, there was not actually a single document, but parallel Maori and English language versions. "Sovereignty" in the English version was translated *kawanatanga*, or "governance," in Maori by missionary Henry Williams, and along with many other terms, left plenty of room for interpretation.[7]

The chiefs signed the Maori version, led by Hone Heke, who would take it upon himself to embody all of the treaty's promises and limitations. He was already heir to the generation of contact and conflict that had led to the meeting at Waitangi. The first port for most Europeans in New Zealand had long been the Bay of Islands, controlled by the Nga Phui people. Ruatara, the friend of missionary Samuel Marsden, had been chief there. When Ruatara died, the mission feared the consequences, but the chief's nephew, Hongi Hika, took over and continued to protect the mission and its connections to Australia, where he voyaged to study the Europeans, returning with tools and plants to grow potatoes for trade.

He never thought much of Christianity as a faith, but did look after the missionary Thomas Kendall, who abandoned the Church and took Maori wives. In 1820, Hongi Hika voyaged to England on a whaling ship and spent almost half a year in London and Cambridge, where he had an audience with King George IV and helped Professor Samuel Lee assemble a Maori and English dictionary.

Hongi Hika returned to the Bay of Islands by way of Australia, where he sold off all of the gifts showered on him by admirers, except for a suit of armor given him by King George. He purchased hundreds of muskets and other weapons, more than had ever been seen in New Zealand, and upon returning proceeded to slaughter his enemies and rivals. His infamous Tamaki raid killed an estimated two thousand men, women, and children. Subsequent "musket wars" over the next eight years devastated entire communities and led to mass retreats and relocations. The wars led to unsolvable disputes about territorial boundaries and traditional land ownership.

Meanwhile, the majority *pakeha* – white – settlements were also increasingly chaotic. Against a backdrop of war, effective lawlessness, disease, and crime were on the rise and missions were overwhelmed. Transient populations of whalers and traders came through the Bay of Islands, joined by a good percentage of former and escaped convicts from Australia who had gotten passage on ships. With them came land speculators, especially Edward Gibbon and William Wakefield, who rapidly built up enormous claims on Maori land with suspect trades of guns and ammunition, tools, tobacco, and liquor.[8]

In 1840, when the Treaty of Waitangi was presented, land tenure and political rule were insecure in many regions. The British sought order and land for a settler colony. The Maori chiefs had different aspirations. The smart and ruthless Hongi Hika had already died, famously inviting supporters to listen to the wind whistle through a bullet hole in his chest. The first Maori signature on the Treaty was his nephew, Hone Heke.

Heke had good reasons to favor the Treaty. It seemed to promise the protection of a powerful ally, hinted at lucrative land and trade deals, and the mere signing of a ceremonial document in the presence of so many chiefs and dignitaries gave him tremendous *mana*. He was very favorable to the Christian missionaries from whom he had received a good education. Heke is most remembered, however, for soon becoming the most vocal critic of the British failure to carry through on the promises and protections of the treaty. He was a warrior, and had a tactical genius for knowing how to make his point and rattle the empire: destroy its flag.

Heke was not anti-*pakeha*; in fact, his first complaint was for the revenues he lost from whaling ships that no longer stopped at the Bay of Islands and instead berthed at the colonial capital, Auckland. In many ways, he wanted more interaction with whites, not less. But the trade and land deals he expected to fill his coffers were instead diverted to government commissions.

In 1844, two American whalers were fined for smuggling, and their angry representative let out a tirade against the British, telling Heke that the flagstaff overlooking the town of Kororareka was the means by which the Queen had taken over the Maori lands. In July 1844, Heke and his men marched up the hill and cut it down. Some chiefs objected, but others, sharing Heke's indignant sense of grievance, began to plunder settlers. Heke felt in his rights, as he wrote to the governor: "Let your soldiers remain beyond the sea and at Auckland. Do not send them here. The pole that was cut down belonged to me. I made it for the native flag, and it was never paid for by the Europeans."[9]

The British, though, replaced the flagstaff and the following year Heke once again cut it down. The Colonial Secretary and members of the Waka Nene clan, who feuded with Heke, vowed to stop him. But ten days after a new flagstaff went up, Heke walked through the Nene guards, daring them to lay a hand on him. The flagstaff fell again. Now the symbolics of empire escalated as the government immediately raised a new flagstaff, this time protected by two blockhouses and artillery, and a combined force of 140 soldiers, sailors, and marines.

The morning of March 11, 1845, Kororareka awoke to shots and chaos as Maori raiding parties descended into the streets. Surprised troops pulled back, and panicked residents evacuated to ships. Reports dispatched to Auckland indicated a general Maori uprising against Europeans and a British sloop bombarded the town itself. In fact, there was no uprising. It was all a diversion from the real objective: to give Heke and his men a chance to advance up the hill and cut down the flagstaff.

Now war began. Heke and his ally Kawiti retreated to establish a *pa*, an earthen and wooden palisade fort, and battled with British troops sent from Australia as well as Maori rivals backed by the Governor. Skirmishing continued for a year before Heke sued for peace. Nene gained him an official pardon, but Heke insisted on submitting formally to the governor and retired from the field.

The dynamics of Maori and Pakeha in alliance and at odds, however, had just begun. Further south, chief Te Rauparaha and his son-in-law Te Rangihaeta were already battling with settlers and the Wakefield family over land claims. In the 1850s and 1860s, assemblies of chiefs would try a "king movement" to consolidate Maori authority, and prophetic movements like the Hau Hau, led by visions of the angel Gabriel, came to embrace both religious renewal and anti-*pakeha* violence. Across the islands, some settlers and *iwi* created communities, while some slaughtered each other. But neither was going away.[10]

Heke's battles were, in some ways, just what he had tried to avoid by signing at Waitangi with the promises of British protection. He was especially suspicious of what another power might do, "the tribe of Marion," who had slaughtered so many Maori back in 1772. That incident, retaliation against an entire village, had taken place when warriors had killed and eaten the party of French explorer Marion du Fresne.

Heke was not the only one with concerns about the French. In 1835, a Baron de Thierry, like Brooke in Sarawak but without real ability, had tried to declare himself a Maori monarch. Even as the Waitangi treaty was making its rounds through the North Island for signatures, a ship of French settlers was heading for the South Island, with reports they would try to colonize and annex it. A French warship appeared in the Bay of Islands. If the British perceived threat, however, the French could point to it directly: by the Treaty of Waitangi, the British now ruled the dominant territories of Australia and New Zealand in the South Pacific. In the north, Anglo-American interests dominated Hawai'i. With few colonies or settlements, and little time to develop them, French ministers would move to acquire a Pacific Empire under the sails of admirals.

They began in 1842 in the Marquesas Islands, seeking a landfall between South America and Asia. Admiral Abel Dupetit-Thouars made his presence known with hundreds of troops and familiar European protocol: he raised a flagstaff and had the Marquesan Enata chiefs sign an official document of cession. Yet, the admiral had only a few missionaries, no settlements to protect, and no obvious population to command. In search of someone to rule, the French called at Vaitahu and declared the leader Ioete the "king." They had him sit for drawings, pressed into an ill-fitting red coat with gold braid and epaulettes and a crown of glass beads and feathers. French troops occupied his valley, and his people were made into servants and died of dysentery. Ioete took those who remained and climbed towards the mountains, leaving the conquerors behind.[11]

The French force complained, but soon moved on to the valley of Taiohae on the island of Nukahiva where they engaged Temoana as a new king. He had already traveled the British circuit from New Zealand to Australia to London, and knew the ways of Europeans. Taken as a cook on a whaling ship, he hated being a tattooed man for English curiosity, and eventually made his way back to the Marquesas. The French maintained they would restore Temoana's "royal" status and helped him build a cottage filled with furniture outside of which he flew the French tricolor. He met with officials, sold them local land at good prices, took to liquor, and became a favorite son of the Roman Catholic church. The Colonial Bureau paid him a pension, and his wife languished among nuns.

As always, there was no singular response to colonial invasion. Ioete tolerated, and then withdrew; Temoana gained what he could. It was another chief, Pakoko, who agitated to revive the Enata ways and came to symbolize violent resistance. Aggrieved by disrespect shown to their customs and practices, his men seized and killed six French sailors, sacrificing at least one to local gods. Some accounts say they had trespassed on a sacred area; other traditions claim a sailor had raped a local woman who needed to be purified in the blood of her aggressor.

French reports say Pakoko was angry about restrictions on his people made by Temoana and colonial officials. All agree that he was pursued by a massive French military response, and surrendered upon recognizing the extent of retribution and reprisals against his people's villages. After a summary trial, he requested to die by firing squad, and was executed with hundreds looking on from mountain ridges. Local lore recognizes thunder as a sign of his return.[12]

Despite its claims of empire, the French base remained as marginal as ever. Dupetit-Thouars did not wait to see what would develop in the Marquesas, if indeed he believed anything would. In command of his formidable warships, he had decided to sail where he knew of a strategic commercial port with an inviting reputation: Tahiti. The French creation of Tahiti was already legendary by the time Dupetit-Thouars arrived, shaped by generations immersed in Bougainville's images of sensual women and paradisical tropical climes. Missionaries and traders had made their claims on the political and commercial institutions of the islands, yet apart from the vociferous English missionary George Pritchard, there was no foreign colonial authority. The Pomare dynasty still ruled.

Dupetit-Thouars landed his soldiers and seized authority. French government newsletters maintained that in 1842 Queen Pomare IV and her chiefs recognized French authority and requested that the islands be put under a protectorate. It was an inviting narrative, consistent with the imagination of a tropical idyll, but far from the truth. The Queen was not the adoring and reverent Purea so lovingly detailed by Bougainville generations earlier, but the scion of a conquering dynasty, well educated by missionary teachers.

She kept her own records, and used her government ministers to send out detailed indignant letters protesting the French actions and requesting assistance, even directly addressing Queen Victoria in England as a sister monarch. She and the Tahitian chiefs denounced the documents produced by the French and the allegedly peaceful protectorate, pointedly noting that Dupetit-Thouars' threats of force meant that his authority would "begin by murdering the people!"[13]

The Queen used her best diplomacy, calling on visiting British naval officers for shipboard dinners, painting scenarios of conflict, bloodshed, and injuries to national pride both for herself and the British Crown if the French aggression were to stand. Britain declined to intervene, and the Queen, in alliance with chiefs from around the islands, prepared for conflict.

Tahiti was not an imaginary paradise. Rising resistance led to military violence in a Franco-Tahitian War of 1843–6, as Pomare's warriors took to mountains, valleys, and canoe fleets, dodging, skirmishing with, and battling French patrols with spears and muskets. The fighting soon echoed across other island chains, and in the Leewards would continue well into the 1880s and 1890s. The French navy sent frigates and steamers to support their efforts around Papeete, the only region they clearly controlled, building fortifications and sending out landing parties into the nearby archipelagos. As Tahiti was occupied by troops from the French warships, campaigns turned to other island monarchs like Queen Teri'itaria on Huahine, who massacred a French military detachment trying to claim her territories.

French battleships pounded coastal regions with cannon, and hundreds of troops made their way from beaches to interiors. Ultimately, Tahitians retreated to the valley of the Fautaua River, protected by tropical forest and rock escarpments. As with many conflicts, outcomes remained inconclusive until the French gained the cooperation of other islanders, notably Mairoto from Rapa, a rival of the Tahitians. With his knowledge of the terrain, French marines managed to gain strategic high ground on mountain ridges, forcing the Tahitians, now decimated by injury, famine, and diseases, to surrender.

Throughout, Pomare had contended with fractures in her own alliance, and in many cases the long memory of her conquering family and its collusion with European missionaries was not well regarded. Some rivals, such as Paraita, who was commissioned as a functionary in the new protectorate government, simply saw more benefit in aligning their fortunes with those of the French.[14]

What most marks Tahitian history, however, is the remarkable way in which the anticolonial wars were erased. This had begun with Dupetit-Thouars' fictional claim of a peaceful submission, and it was accelerated not by politics, but by the power of culture. With French rule came the authority of French art and literature, and the stories and images of Bougainville were revived once more, this time to embrace those of writers like Pierre Loti, Victor Segalen, and the painter Paul Gauguin.

From the late nineteenth century, the naval officer and author Loti penned a popular tale of a young Tahitian girl who falls into a liaison with a French officer and pines away after his departure. Naval doctor and scholar Segalen wrote with an almost ethnographic fervor of traditional societies losing their culture to traders and missionaries by focusing on an esteemed Tahitian storyteller who begins to forget his people's tales and genealogies.

Paul Gauguin was known as a bourgeois stock-trader with yearnings to live a savage life and be an artist. A sometime friend of the tempestuous Vincent Van Gogh, he struggled for recognition and voyaged to French colonies from the Panama Canal concession to Tahiti and the Marquesas, seeking images of other worlds. Gauguin's vibrant paintings are steeped in allegorical symbols and spiritual mysteries, presenting a French Polynesia of somberly exotic faces and lovely bodies merged with ancient statuary and luxuriant tropical backgrounds.

Through their writings, Segalen and Gauguin expressed their dismay with the colonial Pacific, and Gauguin authored blistering tracts against local administrators. Yet it was the power of the images that triumphed. Tahiti would be a story of lost love and melancholy longing for beauty, a timeless tale of inevitable corruption rather than an episode of violent imperial conquest.[15]

Tahiti developed as a strategic base, but the most expansive French Pacific response to other European powers was along the coastline of Southeast Asia. "Indochina" was the keystone of French Empire in the Pacific, a colonial domain pieced together over decades from conquered territories and collaborations with local potentates from regions that today comprise Vietnam, Laos, and Cambodia.

European knowledge of Vietnam dated back to histories of trade and exchange shared with the rest of Asia, from medieval travelers and spice contacts to pirate havens and Portuguese missionaries. Like most of Asia, the rulers of Vietnam had warred for their territories against Mongol invasions in the thirteenth century and Ming occupation in the fifteenth, finally pushing the Chinese out in 1428 under the aristocratic landholder Le Loi. Wielding a sword reportedly given him by a mystical golden turtle, Le Loi defeated the Ming armies and seated himself as first Emperor of the Le Dynasty, organizing a strongly Confucian state, codifying laws, and building monuments.

From the early seventeenth century new forces came to bear as other powerful dynastic families struggled for power, effectively dividing the country into a north ruled by the Trinh Lords drawing on a Portuguese alliance, and a south dominated by the Nguyen, supported by Dutch arms and maritime power. By the late eighteenth century French interests were on the rise, when a Catholic Bishop raised a military force to support the Nguyen, who tolerated the religion and agreed to take on European advisors. The arrangement was never secure, however, and Confucian Nguyen rulers soon repudiated the French missions, which in turn agitated for a Catholic Vietnamese emperor.

Struggles continued across the nineteenth century and in the 1850s the French Emperor Napoleon III claimed to protect the lives and interests of French Catholics by sending warships to the Nguyen territories. Troops ultimately controlled the Mekong Delta in 1867, and landed in the north in the 1870s and 1880s under succeeding French governments now engaged in a global European race for empire. The regions of Cochin China (southern), Annam (central), and Tonkin (northern) were bound together with Laos and figurehead emperors and kings into the Union of Indochina in 1887.

Over the decades, an extensive settler society developed, with land concessions, plantations, and a divided urban plan of European compounds and Vietnamese neighborhoods set among boulevards, colonial offices, and clubs. The city of Hanoi became a colonial capital with an Opera House, banks that financed merchants and overseas businesses, and a bureaucracy to move laborers around Southeast Asia and into French colonies in Oceania.[16]

Under colonialism not only social and political, but personal and intimate relations had to be negotiated. Traders and soldiers took local women as *congai* mistresses and wives, and civil records trace the ways in which the colonial administration approved or denied requests for marriage based upon presumed moral character and possibilities for financial support. Mixed couples were not unusual, so long as the man was the European master and the woman the colonial subject.

When European women began to join soldiers and administrators in the colonies, distinctions intensified. One such woman wrote of her role bringing tea-services and grand moral sentiments to the colonies – a traditional woman's role of "civilizing" men – and also the "ferocious jealousy" and disdain that so many European women held for men's Asian concubines.

Children born from mistress liaisons lived in a world of uncertain legal status. Hai-Loc, a woman from Annam, had a child with a Frenchman, a Captain Poirot. They seem to have lived well enough on his earnings, but when he died the support disappeared. Hai-Loc brought a petition to court, yet found her case dismissed. The court judged that no "act of recognition drawn up at the request of this officer" had ever been made, rendering her child Annamese, with no claims on French entitlements. Men alone could give their children rights and status; women and children without them continued to live in the status of "natives."[17]

With its long history of resistance to foreign domination, it was impossible that Vietnam would simply acquiesce. Raids, skirmishes, and battles developed across the territories called Indochina. Some, predictably, were led by former court officials and mandarins who had lost power to the French. Others were popular uprisings led by peasants and bandits. Few were organized enough to be sustained, and

28 Uneasy attachments: colonials visit an Annamese Mandarin household, French Indochina.

a generation of leaders began to look for more Asia-wide alliances. Among the most determined was a political activist who sailed to Paris in 1911 and adopted numerous aliases, finally calling himself Ho Chi Minh.

Questions of marriage, alliance, and resistance also haunted French imperial projects in Melanesia. Naval ministers wanted to build island settler colonies of farmers, miners, and traders, but developing local economies quickly needed more land and an immediate, captive labor force – of the sort that only a penal colony could provide. The French government had long been envious of Australia, where Sydney was thriving; the British seemed to be expanding while prisons in French Guiana, South America, were malaria-ridden. Emboldened by a tenuous Marist missionary presence and the overseas exile of undesirables of the European 1848 revolutions, the French government sent Admiral Febvrier Despointes to New Caledonia and the Isles of Pines, and in 1853 he carried out ceremonies to annex the archipelago.

New Caledonia, the ancient land of Lapita pottery and home to hundreds of mountain, valley, and coastal clans, was somewhat known to explorers, traders, and evangelists. A decade earlier, Ta'unga had been in the south, teaching for the London Missionary Society, about the time that French Marist missionaries landed in the far north, looking for a territory without Protestants. In Balade, they set up a shaky mission, alternately preaching, starving, or fleeing over the next years. Some chiefs, like Bwarat at Hienghene, offered land, looking to see whether the new holy men could attract traders and also protect his territories from and with French warships.

He may also have been curious about French and English dynamics; one report said that he had been to Sydney. After annexation he was labeled "hostile" to the French, who brought in Tahitian troops to battle and deport him to Papeete, where he reportedly spoke with officials in English, French, and Tahitian.

For the first decade, governors established military posts and offered concessions of land to promoters who would bring immigrants, an approach modeled on New Zealand. The consequences were similar: the local clans, collectively called *Kanaks*, resisted settlement parties. The noted governor Charles Guillain hoped for conciliation. He traded with Kanak leaders and brought socialist philosophy to the establishment of a utopian farm and workshop project. A small colony of miners, masons, carpenters, bakers, planters, and merchants were banded together to become a self-sufficient community. They built dwellings and set about their tasks to plan for a society of charitable sharing, but lack of investment, arguments, and natural disasters wrecked their crops, businesses, and dreams within a few years.

After 1864, the utopian enthusiasms gave way to the Australian model of establishing a settlement with a penal colony. Shiploads of male prisoners arrived in the bay of Noumea, an assortment of criminals, vagabonds, and political convicts. Those with long sentences were relegated for life and charged with agricultural or construction work to build up the colony. Military guards and justice maintained order, and Noumea developed into a colonial outpost with dwellings and stores set around a dusty coconut tree park and a penitentiary, where shiploads of convicts crossed the waterfront along with whalers and sandalwood traders. Over the years a town grew around the bay. Some of the convicts finished their sentences and began to cohabit with Kanak women.

Condemned French women were also part of this imperial network, routed to New Caledonia under the care of nuns and armed escort specifically to be put to labor in workhouses and married off to the men. The colonial government's hope was to create French couples who would find lives together, forget about returning to Europe, and instead dedicate themselves to becoming homestead farmers plowing fields, raising livestock, and supporting the colony with their agricultural produce.

At the heart of this was, as in Australia, a growing need of land for homesteads, farms, ranches, and grazing. But the grants and concessions given by governors took little heed of Kanak farms and reserved areas. In 1878, French colonials awoke to news of a major revolt across the New Caledonian islands, the slaughter of settlers, and the terrifying alliance of Kanak clans they had always feared. Though the scope of the violence took the colony by surprise, a report to the government by an investigating General Arthur de Trentinian blamed the settlers' own "invasion of territories indispensable to the natives for the crops necessary for their existence."

The first to die in 1878 were an emblematic group, a man, woman, and two children. What is notable is that the man, Jean Chêne, was a former convict who had served out his sentence and established a homestead, making him the very incarnation of the colonial project. More, his wife Mendon was a Kanak woman who had left her own group and the children were therefore of mixed parentage. Colonial violence was never as simple as European against Melanesian.

The leader of the revolt was the great chief Atai, who had confronted French governors and settlers for years. Illustrations show his sharp, bearded features, thin frame, and smoking pipe. Atai was known for fiery speeches to warriors, ferocity in battle, and also a marriage proposal to a lovely colonial widow whose home he protected through the Kanak attacks and the French reprisals. Anticolonial insurgency and personal sentiments remained distinct to him.

The rebellion went on for almost a year until Atai was speared and decapitated by rival clans loyal to the French. He had already made his view of empire clear, when one day he had confronted the governor with a sack of earth and one of rocks and a mordant declaration, "here is what you have taken, and here is what you have left us."[18]

"What remained" had in fact been very much a French concern as well throughout the middle nineteenth century, scrambling to annex strategic and settler colonies not claimed by other Western powers. This included almost all of the islands around Tahiti, the Marquesas, the Union of Indochina, and those territories where rival British and French settlements were developing, as in the New Hebrides, now Vanuatu.

The New Hebrides developed with two distinct European communities vying for political and commercial dominance. In 1878, as Kanak rebellion broke out in New Caledonia, France and Britain declared the Hebrides a neutral territory, a decade later establishing a joint naval commission to protect their respective interests. In 1906, they formed the awkward Condominium, a colonial state with two administrations, commercial systems, coinages, and cultural habits and holidays joined only by a common legal court presided over by a Spanish judge.

The New Hebrides government was the political comic-opera that overlay the complex histories of ancient domains, chief Roy Mata, and Quiros' New Jerusalem in Vanuatu. In the nineteenth century, the islands would also gradually become known to new actors representing religious missions and sandalwood and plantation schemes. Already, from the 1840s, the islanders of the New Hebrides, along with those of the Solomons, joined the migrations, contracts, adventuring, kidnapping, and slaving that would mark a staggering people trade across the entire Pacific.

15 MIGRATIONS, PLANTATIONS, AND THE PEOPLE TRADE

The *Sophia* was a 537-ton teak and yellow metal cargo ship built in 1819 in Calcutta, India, regularly chartered for work between Europe and the Pacific. In late 1828, she began two years of voyages unremarkable for exploring, yet which traced out the circuit of Pacific worlds increasingly drawn together. Launching from Dublin, her holds were filled with almost two hundred shackled male convicts, tossed on the months-long passage to the British prison colony in Australia. In Sydney harbor, the *Sophia* was chartered to Tonga by Captain Samuel Henry, who picked up another human load, this time laborers he recruited to sail with him to Melanesia, the island of Erromanga in the New Hebrides, to harvest sandalwood.

With its cargo, the *Sophia* sailed north to Hawai'i, where news of the valuable wood excited the attention of the Oahu governor, Boki, who launched his own ill-fated expedition to conquer Erromanga, as sandalwood had already disappeared in Polynesia. He and most of his force perished at sea or died of malaria. The *Sophia* also returned to Erromanga, but by now found the risks and returns unprofitable and sailed back to England through the New Hebrides, Singapore, and Manila. The ship's surgeon, George Bennett, returned to Plymouth with a young Erromangan girl, Elau, a chambered nautilus, and a gibbon, all of which he conflated as examples of primeval nature, contributing to Victorian debates about natural history and the possibility of educating savages.[1]

Such questions ran through many European understandings of the Pacific, where much of the framing of issues took place. By 1835, the young English naturalist Charles Darwin would be part of a crew on a survey ship the *Beagle*, where his observations would not only contribute to, but ultimately determine the course of much of European natural science. Making landfall in the Galapagos Islands off the South American coast of Chile, Darwin's writings indicate that he was disappointed by the sparse lava terrains around him. Certainly, they lacked the drama of the rain forests and jungles of the Indonesian islands studied by his contemporary Alfred Russel Wallace.

Yet the very starkness allowed Darwin to recognize that the lava on which he stood was remarkably young geologically, and that the world he was seeing might well be a "laboratory" for an entire ecology of plants and animals. Instead of finding an ancient world, he observed one still being born. Strikingly, Darwin identified up to fourteen species of giant tortoises – many of which the ship's crew ate for dinners – as well as wide variations in the islands' now famed marine iguanas, mockingbirds, and finches.

Darwin held back his conclusions that species could evolve and adapt to new environments over time; his findings ran counter to prevailing biblical views of Christian creation, and he did not publish for decades, until realizing that his colleague Wallace was coming to the same conclusion. One of the unintended legacies of Darwin's work was to see his theory of natural selection – the survival of better-adapted organisms across generations – corrupted to explain why Europeans were racially superior and duty-bound to lead, exploit, and enlighten other peoples around the world.[2]

For European colonialists dating back to Quiros, the Melanesian islands had long been such imagined places for exercising "civilizing" influences, especially if they could also be exploited for untapped labor and wealth. Such designs were not wholly European. As Boki's intervention and native agents of Christian missions had shown, aristocratic Polynesians also regarded themselves as superior to the clans and tribal groups that populated the archipelagos from the New Hebrides through the Solomons and on to New Caledonia and New Guinea. The ancient Austronesian worlds had divided millennia before, and contact was slight, the "dark islands" regarded inaccessible, the warriors hostile, and the diseases deadly.

As the *Sophia* voyage showed, however, by the middle of the nineteenth century, the worlds were nonetheless drawing together. The famous mission leader John Williams landed at Erromanga 1839 and was promptly killed. Missions blamed the earlier hostilities on previous bad experiences with sandalwood captains, whom they generally despised as unsavory and unscrupulous. Williams' death inspired the London Missionary Society to land nine Cook Islander and Samoan teachers across the Hebrides islands, including at Erromanga, Aneityum, Tanna, and Efate. They made a few inroads, but were still largely harassed and starved out or decimated by disease.

In the 1840s, both the traders and the missions began to adopt strategies which, perhaps to their horror, had striking similarities. Whereas the mission leaders had tried unsuccessfully to establish Rarotongan teachers like Vaʻa and Akatangi, they began to reach evident conclusions: they needed instead to draw on local talent that understood the customs, spoke the language, and would not die from malaria. Beginning with a small group they gave instruction to Erromangans like Nivavave and Mana, the latter of whom apparently was an effective storyteller.[3]

The sandalwood trade also adopted tactics of working directly with local islanders. While most recruiters sent ships from Sydney or Honolulu to find laborers to cut the trees, the experience of the 1830s had shown how inefficient and dangerous that could be. Rather than speculate on cargoes and Polynesian work gangs, men like James Paddon established themselves with trade goods and used land concessions to build shore station operations. For Paddon, this meant a permanent settlement in Aneityum, cattle grazing, and supplies he could sell to other traders. A small population of Europeans from New Zealand, some Chinese, and a few Maori, set up frame and palm thatch structures, landings for boats, and storage for provisions, tortoise shell, and palm oil.

Most importantly, it meant deals and interaction with local clans, who became accustomed to metal tools, woven cloth, and sometimes firearms, and took an interest in the business. In some cases, as at Inyeuc, the leaders gained trade goods by leasing an island that was spirit-haunted and so of no use to them. From shore stations set up throughout the Hebrides, Paddon and his teams built up timber stockpiles to be loaded on a single collection circuit and sailed to Sydney and Canton. By recruiting in one island group for workers to employ in another, Paddon tried to make all labor dependent on his network.

As in other parts of the Pacific, the new sandalwood circuit offered contacts, goods, and voyages. Within decades, however, it would also be recognized by islanders and colonial governors as deadly and disruptive. If Europeans and Polynesians died of malaria, greater contact meant measles, smallpox, and influenza that decimated Melanesian populations. The shore stations pulled young men away from their villages, which were left short-handed for hunting, fishing, and planting.

More, as hard-working Melanesian labor became familiar to European captains, it was the "natives" themselves, rather than wood or tropical products, that became the center of one of the most violence-ridden and brutally exploitative businesses ever seen in the islands. Part of this rose from familiar abuses, cheating, and "discipline" of laborers. But mainly it resulted from a major change in Pacific island economies. Small plots and homesteaders still dominated, but with the growth of colonial settlements and plantations, commerce was increasingly dependent on large-scale labor, and the relentless, sometimes ruthless, pursuit of a people trade.

Once established, small-time planters sometimes had islander servants, housekeepers, and workhands, and occasionally close relations with particular clans and villages. But from Australia to Fiji and Samoa, big capital companies and promoters were buying up great tracts of land for single cropping export businesses. Among the most famous was Robert Towns, who had competed with Paddon in the sandalwood trade, and was also a major land investor in the Queensland territories of Australia.[4]

His particular interest was cotton, and in April 1861 fateful events a world away resonated across the South Pacific: Confederate forces fired upon Fort Sumter in South Carolina, launching the American Civil War. The South's economy was powered by slaves and by cotton, which was sold to the industrial mills of Britain and Europe, and Union ships relentlessly moved to blockade all Southern ports. The worldwide price of cotton doubled as weavers clamored for more supply.

Robert Towns had cropping land in Queensland, and sandalwood connections in the New Hebrides and Solomons. Plantations became local sites for transnational lives tied to global markets. In 1863, the first boatload of what, over a generation, would number some sixty thousand Melanesian laborers, arrived in Australia to work the plantations. Planters in Fiji were also developing their own businesses, especially in sugar cane, which outlasted the cotton boom, and the different parties sent out captains to recruit and compete for laborers.[5]

29 Pacific plantations: pineapple field laborers in Queensland, Australia.

They did not do this by outbidding each other with good compensation and treatment. Rather, it was a cut-rate, and sometimes cut-throat, business. Ships were small, leaking, and rotten, their main attributes being their ability to operate cheaply and to have substantial cargo holds to keep, and often trap, the islanders during the voyage. Terrified laborers had to pump and bail water from the hold just to keep some ships afloat, and dysentery and other diseases were rife.

In islands with long-standing white contacts, work agreements were the standard: three years of indenture – regularly misunderstood or misrepresented as much shorter – meager wages, and repatriation. Some islands had enthusiastic and willing work gangs. In other cases, local chiefs raided and bartered off their enemies and captives to the recruiters, who offered the usual inducements of tools and guns. At times, the people trade was no more than kidnapping and slavery. Across the Pacific, it became known as "blackbirding."

Islanders would be welcomed onboard a ship to trade, and then strongarmed into the hold. Devious crews waved trade items to bring canoes close and rammed the small outriggers. A notorious technique for island traders who would not come within range was to drop pig iron weights into boats and sink them, hauling up the passengers and forcing them below deck with knives and guns. Some captains disguised themselves as missionaries to attract and seize captives. Needless to say, Church fathers themselves were outraged, and attacks on preachers by villagers were one result. As bad blood spread around the islands, some villages met any ships in their waters with hostility, and the labor trade became more tense and violent.

In 1871 came the most galvanizing incidents of the blackbirding era. An Anglican bishop was murdered in the Santa Cruz Islands, and a British warship made an inspection of a brig, the *Carl*, whose hold was unusually clean and whitewashed. In exchange for immunity and testimony, the ship's owner, James Murray, confessed that his crew had kidnapped about one hundred and fifty islanders by force, swamping their canoes and beating them in the hold so that "the bilge water was half blood."[6]

Off the island of Leli, a watchful chief attacked when his trading canoes were overrun; his warriors were blasted with musket fire and pulled on to the *Carl*'s boats and clubbed. Not waiting for their fate, the captives devised a plan to force open the hatch doors, and were met by gunfire from the crew, who shot and butchered half of them. The victims were bound with rope and thrown dead or alive into the ocean. Under pressure from the missions, political opponents, and critics of unregulated cheap labor in the colonies, the British government passed a Pacific Islanders Protection Act in 1872. This allowed for licensing, regulations, and islander testimony in courts.

The hapless "native victim" became the concern of weakly enforced patrols and inspections. Meanwhile, islanders who made the transit and had legal indenture contracts endured harsh laboring conditions, deprivation, and frequent death from disease or exhaustion in the first year or two on the plantations. Some, however, learned the plantation business and determined to build up their own trades in their home islands. Oral histories from Efate tell of Billy Mase Napau from Matoa village, who labored in Queensland. "When he returned he cleared some ground and planted coconuts. Everyone who planted coconuts produced copra, then they sold it down near Urapua to a trader who came up from Malapoa." Others started similar enterprises with their new knowledge and contacts.[7]

By far the best-known islander to learn and profit from the labor trade was Kwaisulia from Malaita. As a young man growing up on Sulufou Island in the Lau Lagoon, he was frequently around a

30 Blackbirding human cargoes: slave ship seized.

Scottish sailor named John Renton, who was shipwrecked there in 1868. Renton was protected by the local chief and remained in the islands, learning both language and practices, until a labor-recruiting boat in the area picked him up in 1875. Kwaisulia decided to accompany Renton and went aboard as a recruit for Queensland. He stayed in Australia for six years, working, learning Pidgin, and daily observing Europeans. His experiences and interactions would serve him well as recruiters began to look for knowledgeable local intermediaries to help supply bodies for the labor trade.

As a "passage master," and a mesmerizing orator, Kwaisulia proved to be very adept at negotiating for teams of laborers and gaining compensation in goods for his influence. Europeans began to call on Kwaisulia as a "coastal chief." He had tremendous local authority and an almost unique status as an islander who enjoyed the trust of both Melanesian boat crews and laborers as well as European recruiters. As a shrewd bargainer, Kwaisulia began to amass a formidable stock of goods, including metal tools and building supplies, and highly valued trade items, including tobacco and firearms. He also developed a taste for textiles and mechanical amusements, such as clocks and music boxes.

His island base, Adagege, became a protected encampment, ringed with barbed wire and organized to serve as a launching point for skirmishes with rivals and enemies around the Lau lagoon and on neighboring islands. When the British declared a protectorate over the region, Kwaisulia was praised not only as a useful partner, but as a possible colonial agent. The first Resident Commissioner, Woodford, remarked, "Qaisulia can put a large force of fighting men into the field, and if he proves to be what I expect he might be ready to arrange to keep the coast in order."

Kwaisulia was certainly willing to adopt some of the trappings of empire: "He appeared in a white drill suit, spotlessly clean, sun helmet, sash, and a broad smile." His strength, however, grew from his special role between worlds, and as direct British control and European missionary activity grew, his authority waned. In 1909 he accidentally killed himself while fishing with dynamite, but he remains an almost legendary figure.[8]

The great Queensland competitor for plantation labor was Fiji, but Chief Cakobau, who had profited from the sandalwood and tre-pang trades, had run afoul of American debt claims and never fully consolidated power against rival chiefs like Ma'afu. He managed to have himself crowned King in 1868 but remained under threat from enemies including, by now, the United States navy, which demanded payments for old losses to American property in the islands.

That year two men, Brewer and Evans, appeared in Fiji from Melbourne, Australia with an international capitalist proposal. They would pay off Cakobau's debt and confirm his status if he would grant them 200,000 acres of land, exemption from taxation, and control over banking. With Cakobau's signature, the Polynesia Company was formed, backed by Melbourne investors eager to make profits.

Blackbirding brought Melanesian islanders into Fiji plantations, while Cakobau convened a parliament of twenty-five white men, who ran up more debts trading and allocating state revenues to their own projects. Corrupt land deals and lawmakers, exploited laborers, and racial and ethnic violence characterized the "nest of robbers." European settlers, Fijian villages, and lawless guns for hire continuously battled each other. To maintain his authority as King, Cakobau looked to the British Crown to back him up, as he had decades earlier.

This time, the Empire was listening. Villages had been wasted by violence, and even the colonists, who generally preferred to keep laws and regulations distant, demanded order. The British government might have driven away unscrupulous settlers, but as one account put it, "no minister at home would send out a man-of-war and take every Briton out of Fiji." Alternatives looked to be anarchy and likely intervention by other powers. With agreements to maintain their rulership, in 1874 Cakobau and other chiefs signed over Fiji as a British colony.[9]

The British were already absorbing the expense and experience of the land wars in New Zealand, and were keen to rule through local authorities. The government appointed Sir Arthur Gordon, a career administrator by way of Trinidad and Mauritius, to develop a strategy for rule. His plan was to protect Fijian rights to land – more than 80 percent remained in native title – while simultaneously making it productive by levying taxes in produce. The system kept Fijians out of wage labor, while leaving villagers close to their communities. This was done by placing both land and populations under the authority of a Great Council of Chiefs, imposed by Gordon as a "traditional" form of rule – even though it was wholly invented by his own administration.

In this arrangement, which resembled an aristocratic and commoner system, the high-placed chiefs benefited greatly. To keep the crop shares and revenues growing, the villagers were protected from having their land expropriated by European or other settlers, yet also bound to that land with obligations of harvest labor and house building, seasonal planting of tapioca, yams, banana trees, and yaqona roots, clearing of brush and weeds, as well as service to provincial commissioners and constables.

With the native Fijian population tied to the villages, labor for an expanding plantation system was wanting, and Gordon turned to a practice he knew from his earlier governing experiences – drawing in migration from other British colonies, particularly India. The first shipload of indentured laborers arrived in 1879. Over the next forty years, 60,000 Indians made landfall in Fiji to work off a *girmit*, or agreement. This meant five years of brutal servitude, and then another five years of labor for a subsidized ticket home to India. For many, Fiji instead became home.[10]

The new population was contracted especially to the Australian Colonial Sugar Refining Company. Sugarcane grows in fibrous stalks with large quantities of sucrose concentrated in the sap. To get to that sap, plantation work was relentless and exhausting, with multiple cuttings, harvests, declining yields, and replanting. Fires burned away dead leaves and teams of workers under overseers cut the stalks with cane knives or machetes. Unlike other agricultural crops, harvesting was only the beginning, for the cane still had to be rendered, and as equipment was expensive, time lost meant falling profits and workers were pushed around the clock.

Under dangerous conditions, loads of cane were crushed by great rollers in plantation mills to release the sap and rendered in boiling houses. Brick and stone furnaces fed flaming kettles where the cane juice was successively skimmed into syrup and run through channels to cool into raw sugar. Plantations were industrial towns in the midst of island landscapes, with irrigation flumes and iron rail lines organized around a hierarchy of masters, laborers, and plantation houses scattered among palms and cane strands. Daily sights were cut, bruised, and sunburned workers, overseers on horses, and smoke from the boiling houses.

The British colonial government reinforced separation between Indian and Melanesian workers, with its land and race policies. Governing always meant keeping Fijians and Indians from politically uniting against the Empire. Though Indian Fijians settled into small businesses and built towns, they remained largely estranged from the Melanesian Fijian villages and chiefs, who were encouraged to view increasing Indian populations as political and cultural threats to their customary authority.

Laborers were given little regard; having come largely from poor, rural India to begin with, they were presumed to be little more than useful and pitiable. They lived in cramped barracks, enduring insults and whipping. Writer Vijendra Kumar relates the Indo-Fijian experience as one of sweat and tears. "Our forefathers transformed this South Pacific backwater into the most prosperous and progressive nation in the region. But their sacrifices are not appreciated today."[11] Groups struggled to maintain their cultures, and the Urdu language connected Muslims across Fiji as Hindi did similarly for the Hindu communities. Indo-Fijians developed a tradition suspended between remembrance of the almost sacred homeland of India, and the organic and emotional ties to their lives and experiences in Fiji.

Remembrances of laboring in foreign lands haunted almost all Pacific societies in the second half of the nineteenth century, even the most singular, like Easter Island. If the great Moai heads are the symbol of Easter Island's grandeur to the world, the most significant of Rapa Nui rites was the birdman festival, during which the leaders claiming primacy could swim out to the offshore rocks to claim the first swallow's egg of the season. Perhaps ironically, it was such islands that drew the mythic fate of Rapa Nui into a sordid Pacific history.

Massive seabird colonies off the coastline of Peru were the site of titanic guano deposits, some more than a hundred feet deep around the Chincha Islands. Thousands of tons of bird droppings could fertilize plantations on marginal soils, not only in Peru, but all over the world. Rich in nitrogen and phosphorus, Peruvian guano could be as profitable for extractors as the silver mountains of Spanish Potosi.

The Viceroyalty of Peru had been created in 1542 by the Spanish Crown and was highly dependent on mining using the *mita*, a forced labor system using Inca communities. Callao, on the coast, had been the launching spot into the Pacific for Spanish explorers, but new Viceroyalties in Caracas and Buenos Aires pulled the commercial power in Spain's empire to the Atlantic. By the late eighteenth century, indigenous rebellions led by the Inca leader Tupac Amaru II occupied Spanish authorities, along with revolts against the Crown by creoles and South American elites advancing liberal principles. In 1821, José de San Martin proclaimed the independence of Peru from Spain. Neighboring Bolivia and Chile also became independent, but all three countries agitated about territorial boundaries. Of particular interest were the arid coastlines of Peru and Bolivia, which preserved extraordinary deposits of guano.

Interest in guano was hemispheric. In 1856, the United States Congress passed a Guano Island Act, acting on reports that "unclaimed" islands or rock outcroppings might be sources of dense and potentially lucrative deposits. The Act took into account that the American president might use military force to defend guano sites.

Such control was serious business off the coast of South America. From 1864 to 1866, former Spanish colonies Peru and Chile fought in alliance against Spain in the Chincha Islands War for guano deposits. In 1879, Peru entered the five-year War of the Pacific with Peru and Chile over coastal territories in the Atacama region, vying for control of saltpeter and guano. Such residues and minerals had huge political stakes throughout the middle nineteenth century. With Peruvian slavery abolished in 1854, planters, mine operators, and labor contractors moved into the indenture and kidnapping business. Thousands of Chinese and Japanese came on contracts, and islanders were black-birded from the New Hebrides.

Rapa Nui villagers from Easter Island were an even easier target; there were no other nearby islands for escapes, no competing colonial powers. Peruvian and Anglo-American ships colluded with Spanish captains like Marutani, who landed at the beaches in 1862, displayed trinkets and mirrors, and signaled his men to close in on the islanders when most were "on their knees examining the trade goods." The raiding parties divided their captives into different ships, locking them in collars and numbering or tattooing their foreheads.[12]

Escaped Rapa Nui fled to caves or set fire to the brush where the slavers tried to land, but in all, more than one-third of the island's population was taken into the guano mines of Pisco. Covered with, and worked relentlessly to excavate tons of, guano, nearly ninety percent died from exhaustion, abuse, and caustic ammonia fumes poisoning, including almost all members of the chiefs and elders, who held the history and memory of the people.

Eventually pressured by the Bishop of Tahiti, the Peruvians repatriated the survivors to Rapa Nui – fifteen individuals, some infected with smallpox, which ravaged the island along with more clan warfare. In 1864, Brother Eyraud, a French priest, began a stubborn Catholic mission, and in 1888 King Atamu Tekena signed over sovereignty to Chile, whose interests were in developing a stopover for Pacific shipping companies. A Chilean businessman bought the island and transferred it to the English Williamson Balfour Company, which put up a fence around the islanders, prohibited them from fishing, and forced them to work without wages.

The contract was terminated by the Chilean government in 1953, and a decade later Alfonso Rapu Hanoa, a Chilean-educated Rapa Nui, became mayor and agitated against foreign rule, including that of the Chilean navy. In the 1980s, an Elders Committee was formed around Alberto Hotu Chavez, who continued to seek agreements for traditional language and cultural development under Indigenous Peoples Acts.[13]

Of the many schemes, plans, and enterprises that engaged Pacific laborers and marked the transition from small colonies to political and commercial empires, perhaps the most representative developed in Samoa. The Samoan islands occupied a key geographical spot in the Central Pacific and were graced with large and accommodating natural harbors at Apia and Pago Pago. For millennia, they had developed politically in trade and exchange with the great chiefdoms in the Fijian islands and the Tu'i Tonga rulers.

As the religious experience of the charismatic, millenarian preacher Siovili and of the missionary John Williams had shown in the early nineteenth century, kin networks and alliances were strong, but central authority had never been the tradition. A paramount leader could only claim rule by securing four titles held by two important rival families, Sa Malietoa and Sa Tupua, an extraordinarily difficult task. Nonetheless, in the 1830s Chief Malietoa Vai'inupo conquered his enemies and managed this feat. He protected the missions and incorporated their teachings into his ceremonial power and encouraged localized Christian instruction throughout the villages. But the four titles could not be transferred, and Malietoa's death in 1841 left not an heir, but twenty years of civil war.

In this period, the Sa Malietoa and Sa Tupua and multiple factions skirmished and warred against each other while, especially along the waterfront at Apia, a small whaling and provisioning station grew with incoming traders, beachcombers, and the general lawlessness of port towns. The Americans and British appointed resident consuls, but for influence that radiated out from Apia, little could match a more recent player in the European history of the Pacific: the Germans.

Having begun operations in 1845, the trading firm of J. C. Godeffroy and Son of Hamburg had established its headquarters in Samoa in 1857. With an ambitious and organized plan to dominate Pacific trading, the Godeffroy company started with a passenger and cargo network from Southeast Asia to Australia to the Central Pacific and Valparaiso. With low wages, low costs, and no interest in missionary or moral projects, Godeffroy soon bankrupted competitors from east to west and built a fleet of brigs and schooners that soon controlled majority trade around the Pacific.

Ruined small-time traders complained of Godeffroy's "Prussian style of discipline" and watched as the company built up shipyards and warehouses at Apia. Reports claimed that the Samoan civil wars were profitably encouraged by Godeffroy agents, who allegedly sold guns to both sides, and whose business was widely known to include an arms factory in Belgium. Sales were paid for in tens of thousands of acres of the best Samoan lands transformed into plantations on which – as all around the Pacific – contract workers labored under exacting conditions.[14]

The reputation of Godeffroy was built on copra – coconut meat – some eaten as fat, but most processed for industrial rendering into oil for soaps, candles, animal feed, confections, and some glues and lacquers. Where whalers could not fill their casks, they sometimes took on extra copra. The Godeffroy impact was to make copra into a global commercial commodity.

The meaning for a changing Pacific was striking, for nothing represented Oceania more than the coconut palm, a sacred and practical plant, literally life giving. For millennia, islanders and peoples of Southeast Asia had made food from the meat and the milk, anointed themselves with the oil, and woven mats and baskets for carrying and gift exchanges. Entire villages were built from the palm wood and thatch, and husks plaited into sennit ropes.

Samoans would know that the village of Laloata, behind Apia, was the traditional home of the folk-heroine Sina, a lovely young woman pursued by a legendary eel killed by chiefs, but whose head, planted in her garden, grew into a remarkable tree. From the tree sprang the first coconuts and the strong leaves that were woven into the mats, fans, and other creations of ceremony and everyday comfort. Tahitian and Tongan legends offer variants of the tradition, with the latter telling of the eel's warning of a great flood that would destroy Sina's village, except for her house and the spot where the coconut would grow.[15]

With coconuts systematically organized and cultivated on plantations, a tidal surge might have been a good representation of German colonial and commercial priorities of the later nineteenth century. In 1870–1, the German Chancellor Otto von Bismarck went to war with the French emperor, Napoleon III, crushing his European rival and declaring the foundation of a German Empire under Kaiser Wilhelm I, avowedly expansionist. In Samoa, the Godeffroy firm was the dominant plantation owner, and around the Pacific continued to push rival traders out. By 1874, the company controlled a staggering 70 percent of all trade and freight carrying. The company soon established itself in the western Pacific, largely unmarked by European interests. By the 1870s, Godeffroy agents had coconut and pearl shell trading interests in the islands around New Guinea and would soon annex territories in New Guinea itself.

On the mainland, the story was tenuous. Yabim-speaking people of the Huon peninsula were puzzled in 1885, when unknown strangers began to clear land and build houses on their coast rather than trade and leave, as was common. The strangers offered pieces of a black, white, and red imperial flag; they were Germans and Indonesians come to make good on a place suddenly called Kaiser Wilhelmsland, and a harbor now named Finschhafen. The German leaders offered axes and iron for land, and established stations along the coast. In some areas, peoples of Bongu, Gorendu, and Gumbu helped build a settlement. In others, canoes massed and warrior parties attacked with spears and darts.

From Berlin came orders for everything from pricing to accounting, with folios of regulations, many of which were impractical to agents on the ground. The Finschhafen station was a collection of huts, wooden stores and houses with muddy paths, a station manager, tradesmen, foresters, and Malay and Chinese laborers. Reports enthused about possibilities, but the soil was often poor, trading networks upland for foreigners not developed, and plantation labor was hard to secure. Direct contact with villages was maintained by *luluai*, headmen, who collected taxes and ensured the obedience of the people to colonial authorities. Police-soldiers, striking in their shirts, trousers, caps, and cartridge belts, were village warriors. Ordinary tribesmen and women were taken for tobacco and copra growing.

As across the Pacific, workers also came from elsewhere, thousands making crossings from the Bismarck Archipelago and the Solomons to the New Guinea mainland. The German authorities established detailed contracts, particularly for disciplinary measures including flogging, withholding of rations, and added unpaid labor. Despite the contracts, the violence that actually took place can be measured by reprisals against overseers. In 1891, one Ludwig Müller disappeared near the village of Tobenam. The same year, Malay overseers and laborers were killed at the Gorina plantation, notorious for beating workers. Skirmishes were common. As often, German authorities were drawn into local conflicts as villages defended themselves against land and trade deals that benefited rivals. More, military search parties seeking retaliation were encouraged by "informants" to attack the villages of their own enemies.[16]

Not all conflicts resulted in violence. Most discontented laborers simply did not work hard or refused to follow colonial directives. Laborers from the outer islands could not return home, but local Bongu and Gorendu villagers would work on fences or plantings that they found curious, earn some goods, and go back to their own world. They fought and raided each other over ancestral and colonial claims, but they also lived well growing sago, yams, bananas, catching fish, and raising pigs, and they ordered histories of spirits and ancestors, creating art and decoration from everything in their immediate universe. Beyond the plantation clearings, villages continued without the Germans.

The world beyond the colonial settlements is probably best known for the cultures that developed around the Sepik River, which flows more than a thousand kilometers from the central ridges of New Guinea to the Bismarck Sea. The bays near Finschhafen are famed for extraordinary bracelets and necklaces of bamboo, tortoise, and shell, and remarkable pottery carried in elaborate canoes rowed with carved paddles.

The Middle Sepik is a region of Iatmul tribal peoples, spread out among riverbank villages and waterways, sheltered by rain forests and jungles. Notable in a village is the spirit house, the Haus Tambaran, a soaring, strikingly decorated structure housing carvings and artworks accessible only to initiated warriors. As around Oceania, many carvings incorporate the substance of spirits, especially those that protect and assist local villagers and keepers of the Haus Tambaran, or are called upon for rituals and ceremonial practices. Artists master the art of carving tropical woods, often into the shapes of figures and faces, and adorn them with pig tusks, bird feathers, and plant and mineral pigments to materialize natural and ancestral presences.[17]

For Europeans, many of these became museum works, filling the collections of institutions across the world. In the 1880s, Richard Parkinson, an employee of Godeffroy and Son, took an interest in regional art and ethnography, sending collections of masks and artifacts to Europe. In addition to his company duties, he worked for, and was the brother-in-law of, a remarkable woman, Emma Forsayth, who demonstrated that some of the "German" success in the region actually came not from the mainland, but from individual planters in the surrounding islands to the north, like New Britain.

Forsayth, an American and Samoan woman educated in San Francisco, was another Pacific-wide figure of multiple heritages, part of a trading family in Apia. She and her lover and business partner, Australian Thomas Farrell, left Samoa in 1879 and built up a business in the Melanesian islands recruiting for the labor trade and establishing a trading station. Forsayth smartly bought up land and, aided by Parkinson's advice, established large-scale coconut plantations, alternated with cotton. She had many well-placed Samoan relatives join her household, and her family members married into a Pacific-wide elite. Soon dubbed "Queen Emma," Forsayth lavishly entertained traders, officials, and explorers, who were impressed by her generosity, beauty, and astute charm. In 1893, she married a German citizen, further establishing herself in the German colony.[18]

The other substantial area of German interest in the Pacific was also north of New Guinea and the Bismarck Archipelago in Micronesia, particularly around the Marshall and Caroline Islands. Godeffroy affiliates had established stations trading on the whaling and shipping circuit there, concentrating on the company's dominance in copra. Numerous firms competed by developing small plantations. Where operations folded, they were taken over by another operation, the successful Jaulit Gesellschaft, and the German government moved to annex the Marshall Islands in 1885.

As the Kaiser was making his plans in 1884, a small party of pearl divers completed their season in the waters north of Australia and came through the Ralik chain in the Marshalls. In transit, they were driven by storms to the island of Lae. Exactly what happened to them is not clear, but a British ship later came upon skeletons, clothes, and bottles with Japanese labels, and reported the findings to port officials in Yokohama. The party had apparently been murdered by local islanders. In response, the Japanese government sent two young men, bureaucrat Goto Taketaro, and former sailor and fur trader Suzuki Tsunenori, out to the Marshalls. There, they questioned and blustered with the shrewd Chief Labon Kabua, who promised to investigate and put them off. After all, in these waters, German officers on schooners made regular rounds, sometimes accompanied by New Guinea troops, reputedly chosen because they were black and terrifying to the atoll dwellers.[19]

At some point the report of Goto and Suzuki draws blank, with several weeks of activities missing. Were they spying and surveying? Some accounts say that Suzuki compelled Labon Kabua to temporarily fly a Japanese flag over his own residence. The Chief might have been humoring the young Suzuki; at this time, Japan had no oceanic colonies or influence in the region. But the history leading up to and beyond that moment of imperial ambition would shape the future of the Pacific.

16 IMPERIAL DESTINIES ON FOREIGN SHORES

In 1848, a tiny boat capsized near the coast of Hokkaido, northern Japan. Its sole occupant was rescued by fishermen of the Ainu, the aboriginal people of the region, and reported to local samurai, who incarcerated the man and sent him far south to Nagasaki, where all foreigners were detained. Ranald MacDonald may have been among the most unusual of outsiders to be cast upon Japanese shores. He had, for one, not been shipwrecked or lost at sea, but had paid a whaling captain a considerable sum to set him adrift near Hokkaido with the singular hope of visiting Japan. Nor, as his name might suggest, was he a Scotsman, but the son of a Chinook Indian woman and an official of the Hudson's Bay company, who had grown up in the Pacific Northwest, where the Chinook had thriving trade with Russian, American, British, Canadian, and Hawaiian sailors and agents. He was another typically international and intercultural Pacific actor.[1]

In 1834, three Japanese sailors, Yamamoto Otokichi, and two others by the names of Iwakichi and Kyukichi, washed up in the Pacific Northwest, having drifted in a disabled boat from Japanese waters all the way to North America. Found and enslaved by Makah Indians, they were turned over to a Hudson's Bay sea captain and reports about them impressed a young MacDonald, who followed their stories as they traveled on to England, then China, and attempted to return to Japan. This would be no easy feat. Since the early years of the Tokugawa Shoguns, when the Portuguese had been expelled and the Dutch permitted only their tiny outpost on Deshima island in Nagasaki harbor, Japanese ports had remained closed to the outsiders – including Japanese abroad.

Over the centuries, reports to the Shogun's government, the *Bakufu*, of attempted contacts would indicate a changing Pacific world, one populated by new, rising empires. In 1739, Russians had reached Kamchatka and followed the Kurile Islands to Japan's eastern coast. An official Russian expedition in 1792 was expelled after landing in Hokkaido, yet in 1805 another mission sailed into Nagasaki headed by Ambassador Rezanov. He was also turned away after months of confinement, but Russian interest only intensified. In addition to the Russians, Americans chartered Dutch ships for trade from the 1790s, and British warships entered Japanese waters in 1808 and 1824. American warships were sent in 1846 and 1849, and again were only able to collect shipwrecked sailors before being towed or forced to leave. Their captains, however, also reported on the advantages of a Japan with open harbors.

One of the most notable attempts at contact was an 1837 voyage by a group of missionaries allying with an American merchant captain in Macao to try and open preaching and trade with Japan. Their plan was to show goodwill by carrying shipwrecked Japanese sailors to Nagasaki, but Shogunal forces fired on the ship and the Japanese mariners were forced to make lives in Macao, Shanghai, and Singapore. One of them – Otokichi from the Pacific Northwest traverse – married an Englishwoman, and then a Malay, and worked as a translator and agent for a British trading company.

He was not the only Japanese between worlds from this time. In 1841, a young Japanese fisherman named Nakahama Manjiro was cast up on an island rock southeast of Japan and lived in a cave, scavenging fish until he was picked up by an American whaler. He was brought to Massachussetts, where he learned English, Western navigation, coopering, and whaling, and eventually sailed around the world.[2]

All of this inspired MacDonald, who began to identify himself with his "Indian" heritage and to think of Japan as the "land of his ancestors." Where traders, ambassadors, missions, and warships had failed, he was determined to reach across the Pacific. He signed on to a whaler and paid the captain to set him adrift off Hokkaido. Taken to Nagasaki, he saw the Dutch factory and the trading operations there that had been Japan's only sanctioned connection to the world for centuries.

Local officials rigorously followed the *sakoku* policy, but knew from their contacts that the world beyond was changing, particularly with the appearances of the British and the Americans, the latter unknown when the ports had closed in 1600. They knew especially of the Opium Wars that had humiliated the great Chinese Empire, and needed to develop the English skills of their interpreters and agents. But foreign ships were always detained and expelled, and shipwrecked sailors were generally illiterate. Along with MacDonald, Nagasaki authorities were also holding deserters from the whaler *Lagoda*; they were boisterous and ill-tempered. But MacDonald was enthusiastic and well-educated. He became a teacher for fourteen Japanese, including Moriyama Einosuke, who became his friend.

Released a year later to an American ship, MacDonald was drawn to the gold fields of Australia, then to Europe, and finally returned to North America around 1853. He and most of his Japanese fellow-travelers were largely forgotten, especially as American interest in Japan by then had a new focus. At that time, an American steam sidewheeler had left Norfolk, Virginia and was on its way to a rendezvous in Hong Kong. There, and in Shanghai, it joined forces with other warships of the East India Squadron. Commanding the fleet was Matthew Cailbraith Perry, with orders from the American government to end Japan's isolation.

Part of Perry's mission was tied to the experiences of MacDonald and the *Lagoda* crew: demands for recognition and fair treatment for shipwrecked sailors. This was an issue of major concern as the whaling industry expanded into Japanese waters and traders increasingly sailed off Tokugawa coasts between Hawai'i and China. Another part of the mission had to do with some of the very ships that Perry was sailing: they were steam-powered and needed strategic ports for taking on coal and provisions. In May 1853, he sailed to Okinawa and had his captains survey the surrounding islands for places to mine coal and develop stations. In July, his fleet made for Japan, sailing into Uraga harbor and anchoring in Tokyo, then Edo, Bay.

The black ships made a fearsome impression, and Japanese troops swarmed into the area. It was a richly recorded encounter, drawn, painted, and inked on innumerable scrolls, broadsides, prints, and canvases. Japanese prints especially emphasize the startling paddle-wheel battleships, maneuvering menacingly without the wind, and belching black smoke. Guard boats formed lines against the ships, but were easily dispersed. Fortifications and earthworks were built along the bluffs and shoreline, and antiquated cannon readied. Japanese officials offered to provision the ships with hopes for a speedy departure, but the Americans contemptuously offered instead to share their own supplies.[3]

Having learned what he could about Japanese imperial protocols, Perry refused to allow anyone to board his ships or even to see him. His officers made his demand: a letter from the President of the United States should be presented to the Emperor of Japan. The Japanese remonstrated that Perry go to Nagasaki, but the black ships did not move. After long negotiations and a threat from Perry to march on the Emperor and deliver the letter himself, Japanese officials agreed to receive the message. He presented the letter and indicated that he did not expect an immediate response, but that he would return.

Back in Hong Kong, Perry gathered together an even greater squadron, while managing to avoid being drawn into the ongoing conflicts of the Taiping Rebellion. After another trip to Okinawa, his black ships were once again in Edo Bay by February 1854. The Americans landed to gun salutes, fanfares, and a full-dress procession of hundreds of sailors and marines. While negotiations continued, displays and exhibitions occupied the parties. The Americans set up a telegraph station and a miniature locomotive, pulling sober-faced samurai around a small track that resembled an amusement park attraction. Sumo wrestlers became sources of Japanese pride by showing off their girth and strength, and the Americans staged minstrel shows of "negro" songs and dances by black sailors, as well as white sailors in black-face.

On March 31, the Treaty of Kanagawa, Japan's first with a foreign nation, was signed with much ceremony. The Shogun's officials agreed to the basic terms of an American treaty – providing for sailors and allowing provisioning as well as coaling concessions, the establishment of an American consulate, and most-favored nation status. Notably, no mention was made of trade, which the Japanese resisted and for which Perry had no orders.

Close by all this was Moriyama Einosuke, about whom a member of Perry's party remarked, "He speaks English well enough to render any other interpreter unnecessary." Moriyama impressed the Americans with his education and asked about his friend, Ranald MacDonald, from whom he had learned so much. Also drawn in on

31 Gunboat diplomacy: Commodore Perry's mission in Edo (Tokyo) Bay.

the Kanagawa negotiations was Manjiro. He had sailed back to Japan through Okinawa in 1851 and, after many long interrogations, had been released. When Perry arrived, he was summoned to Tokyo to offer intelligence on the Americans. Some reports say that the Bakufu put him in a secret room to listen in on the conversations, and he was certainly employed to quickly and accurately translate English documents.

Six months after the Kanagawa treaty, a British squadron sailed into Nagasaki to demand similar concessions. The translator was a British subject, James Matthew Ottoson; before he had taken that English name, he had been Otokichi, now settled in Shanghai after the Shogun had refused to let him return in 1837. As late as 1849 he had, actually, already made one visit to Nagasaki, pretending to be Chinese. Only by employing these identities as an Englishman and a Chinese had Otokichi, who originally inspired MacDonald, been able to return to Tokugawa Japan. Now, as the Shogun's power eroded and restive clans called for the restoration of imperial authority in Japan, Otokichi was invited to once again live in the land of his birth. He refused, and returned instead to Shanghai and the life he had made between Pacific worlds.[4]

The Japanese isolation was broken, but it was not until 1858, when the American consul Townsend Harris and the Bakufu signed an agreement for trade, that the implications were fully materialized. The closed and controlled world of Deshima was finished. Some domains and daimyo favored more interaction with the West, while others were virulently anti-foreign. With the country politically divided and pressured by the example of the Opium Wars, five Japanese ports were opened to trade, and foreigners allowed to reside directly on Japanese soil under extraterritorial rights that made them immune from Japanese law. Duties were set by foreign powers, not Japan.

The Bakufu had maintained its authority for centuries by controlling the lords and their samurai. With the Shogun's authority compromised, powerful domains like Satsuma and Choshu agitated to build a new state around "honor the emperor, expel the barbarian." Radical samurai murdered foreigners in the treaty ports and assassinated Bakufu officials, though anti-foreign sentiment did not prevent Western arms from flowing into the domains. With the imprimatur of the emperor, Satsuma and Choshu armies defeated Bakufu troops and forced the Shogun to surrender. In January 1868, the domains and the imperial court declared the beginning of the Meiji Restoration.

The period of Japan's "modernization" saw the development of a powerful imperial authority invested in ministers like Ito Hirobumi, and the acceleration of Meiji industrial development. Government missions were sent around the world and Japanese were soon studying in Europe and the United States. Fukuzawa Yukichi, the great advocate of reform, Western education, and Japanese nationalism was dispatched to San Francisco in 1860, and over the next years traveled with government envoys in England, France, Germany, Holland, Portugal, and Russia. In Japan itself, former "barbarians" were now military, administrative, and technical advisors, helping to build naval academies, schools, and factories.[5]

In the 1880s, imperial Japan became a true empire. This was not a completely new phenomenon: at the beginning of the Tokugawa era, the Satsuma domain had invaded the Kingdom of the Ryukyus for the Shogun; Hideyoshi had already attempted to conquer Korea and had designs on the Philippines, plans that were abandoned when he died. For Meiji leaders, revisiting such expansionist strategies was in step with the later nineteenth-century imperialism of the Europeans and the Americans, especially in Korea, which Japanese leaders wanted under their own influence. As the Korean Choson Dynasty traditionally paid tribute to the Chinese Ming and Qing Emperors, the Japanese supported Korean "reformers," who now looked to modernizing Japan as a model.

Deep reform currents had been waxing and waning in Korea for generations. From the sixteenth century, groups of Confucian scholars had started a *Silhak* Practical Learning movement, breaking from traditional scholarly elites and advocating political and economic reforms, including ideas of rights and social equality. By the later nineteenth century, a religious *Tonghak* movement began, extolling individual dignity and attacking government corruption and privilege. Its leader was executed in 1864.[6]

In decades of monumental change, the Korean Choson state was also shaken externally. French and American fleets attacked the Korean mainland to settle claims of insults and aggressions, and to establish colonial positions. In 1876, Japanese gunboats demanded commercial and diplomatic concessions and imposed treaties on Korea, as the Westerners had on Japan two decades earlier. Korean progressives agitated for education reform, responsible government, and national independence. Conservative Confucian officials resisted. Over two decades, the Korean government was overthrown and retaken by pro-Japanese, Choson, and Chinese factions as both the Qing and Meiji states moved troops into the Korean peninsula.

Korean activist Kim Okgyun was the adopted son of a provincial governor, and a brilliant student. Portraits show his thin face and scholar's hat. As Japanese influence spread in Korea, Kim was both impressed and alarmed by the Meiji transformations in Japan – a country long considered by Koreans and Chinese to be inferior to their own dynasties. Sent on a mission to Japan, Kim developed an uneasy and complicated politics, at once learning from, and collaborating with, Japanese officials, while strongly advocating reforms that would make Korea a "modern" state on par with both Japan and the Western powers by overthrowing the conservative Choson rulers.

In 1884, his "Independence Party" assassinated government officials, abolished Confucian noble interests, and established a constitutional monarchy. This "Gap-sin coup" heralded a progressive Korean nationalism, yet also made Kim dependent on Japanese support and interests. Already by this time, Japanese forces had begun to dominate farming and mining regions in Korea, pulling out rice, coal, and iron to fuel Meiji expansion. Famines and hardship led to riots, and more intervention. Kim's revolution was not popularly supported and lasted only three days before the conservative Min family called for Chinese Qing forces to crush the threat. Kim fled to exile in Japan.

Ten years later in 1894, with hopes of continuing his revolutionary activities, Kim boarded a ship for Shanghai but was almost immediately assassinated, reportedly by Chinese agents. The Korean patriot and Qing enemy was appropriated by the Japanese as a political martyr. When Chinese troops once again moved into Korea to help suppress other rebel movements, Japanese forces marched on Seoul and seized the royal court.[7]

The Sino-Japanese War (1894–5) began with the expectation that the great Qing Empire would crush the small, overly ambitious Japanese. But Japan's growing industrial power, tactics, and naval and army forces built upon British, French, and Prussian models were decisive. The samurai age was over; Japanese propaganda prints glorified uniformed infantry and officers. Warships, torpedo boats, and organized artillery and engineering corps strategically landed and deployed troops while the Qing, though well-armed, were poorly drilled, not well-commanded, and often unpaid. Within a year, Chinese influence in Korea was finished. By the Treaty of Shimoneseki Japan received large indemnities, forced open trading ports, and took control of Taiwan, turning it into a colony.

Taiwan had long been contested and sought as a territory by the Japanese from Hideoyshi's time. From the seventeenth century, Koxinga, pirate to some and hero to others, had established his trading and raiding base and thrown the Dutch out of Taiwan. He and his successors also harried the Qing Empire on the mainland. Over generations, the Taiwan settlement was eventually conquered by the Qing, the island becoming a Chinese prefecture. By the nineteenth century the island had a railroad line, government services, and a population heavily weighted by Chinese immigration from the mainland. When the Japanese took over, they built up the transportation system, Japanese schools, and rice and sugar cane interests, to serve imperial designs.

Japanese armies also conquered the strategic Liaodong Peninsula, but here the Russians made their southward Pacific intentions known, convincing France and Britain in a Triple Alliance to force Japan to concede the territory, which Russia would seize as its own. The Europeans had been willing to let Japan counter Russian expansion, but now allied with the Tsar to contain the surprising Japanese threat. Japan had risen as a major power, but the struggle for dominance in Asia was just beginning.[8]

Across the Pacific, David Kalakaua was an observer of Japan's transformation. Ascending to the throne in 1874, the Hawaiian King was perpetually occupied with the place of his islands in an increasingly global world. Painters and photographers captured his handsome, dignified bearing, usually in a dress uniform bedecked with medals. An elected successor to a great dynasty, he was keenly aware of his historical role, commissioning a statue of Kamehameha the Great and patronizing traditional Hawaiian culture, especially the practice of hula, martial arts, music, and surfing. Many of these had languished as Protestant missionaries had come to influence the royal court.

The sons and daughters of the early missionaries had, in some cases, benefited from political and family ties, convincing the Hawaiian monarchs to divide island lands in an event called the Great Mahele of 1848, which effectively privatized entire regions to the advantage of plantation owners and American speculators. They formed a political group called the Missionary Party that agitated for devout Christian adherence, stronger American influence in the islands, and a figurehead role for the Hawaiian monarchs.

Kalakaua, instead, promoted greater authority for Hawaiian nobles in government and embraced a traveling politics, touring his own islands to gain popular support, and meeting in Washington DC with the American President Ulysses S. Grant on a trade agreement. Like other political figures of his generation, he was deeply concerned about how to maintain and develop the independence of his kingdom in an age of imperialism. French warships had threatened to bombard Honolulu in the 1860s over questions of trade and Catholicism, and he needed to look no further than his struggles with the Missionary Party to see where concentrated opposition might lead.

With a vision of international statecraft, he determined to learn what he could abroad and became the first monarch to travel all the way around the world. In March 1881, his ship berthed in Tokyo Bay, just a little more than a dozen years into the Meiji Era. The Meiji Emperor, Mutsuhito, welcomed Kalakaua as the first visiting foreign monarch. Displays of the Hawaiian flag and renditions of the Hawaiian anthem by Japanese military bands left the visitors in tears. Over two weeks of lavish ceremony, dinners, and receptions, Kalakaua and the

Emperor exchanged official decorations and praises of friendship, and the King was particularly attentive to the evidence of Japan's new industrial and military developments.

Impressed by the value of alliances with Japan, Kalakaua made several notable proposals. One was dynastic: a future marriage between Prince Komatsu of the Japanese royal family and the Princess Ka'iulani. The imperial household declined the request, but Kalakaua also had ideas for a great league of Asian states, to confront the power of the Western empires, with Japan in the lead: "my country is a tiny cluster of islands . . . your country is exactly as I have heard – not only has your progress been truly astonishing, but the people are numerous and of a hardy disposition. That is why, if a league of the countries of Asia is to be initiated, Your Majesty must step forward and be its leader. I will serve Your Majesty as his vassal."[9]

The anticolonial vision was thoughtful, but Mutsuhito knew that the countries Kalakaua was yet to visit, Siam, Burma, India, and certainly China, would never join a Japanese-led league, and his ministers had their own ambitions for Asia. Likewise, Kalakaua's proposal for a submarine telegraph cable to link Hawai'i to Japan was not pursued. The King continued on his circumnavigation from Asia, through Egypt and Italy, Belgium, Germany, Austria–Hungary, France, Spain, Portugal, the United Kingdom, and the United States. He returned convinced he would have to form his own alliances and take leadership in the Pacific.

From the early 1880s, Kalakaua's allies in the Hawaiian legislature proposed that "This Hawaiian State is in all respects fit to take upon itself the responsibilities of an adviser, a referee, or a mediator in the affairs of the weaker but still independent divisions of the Polynesian race." High chiefs in the Gilbert Islands offered to have Hawai'i annex and protect their lands, though discussions did not continue. In the New Hebrides and the Solomon Islands, Kalakaua recommended "a Special Commissioner to several Chieftains and States, to advise them in their national affairs." Hawaiian government ministers circulated proposals in European capitals to create a Polynesian federation under Kalakaua that would be directed by a Hawaiian foreign office.

In 1886, the Hawaiian legislature appropriated considerable funds for planned consulates and commissioners from the Marshalls and Carolines to the Gilberts and Samoa. Rumors of a possible alliance between Hawai'i, Samoa, Tonga, and the Cook Islands alarmed

Western colonialists, particularly when Malietoa Laupepa in Samoa agreed to enter into a "political Confederation" with Hawai'i. The German consul in Honolulu expressed the consensus Western view that the agreements, "cannot be taken seriously by the Powers really interested in Samoa." In 1889, German, American, and British warships made the determination for themselves, formalizing the authority of three consuls in a nominally independent Samoa under Malietoa. A decade later, the islands were partitioned, dividing the German Samoan influence at Apia from the American naval and trading colony at Pago Pago.[10]

Some of this was recorded by a Scottish voyager in the Pacific, and friend of King Kalakaua, writer Robert Louis Stevenson. From the summer of 1888, Stevenson and his family had sailed on a chartered yacht around the Pacific, landing in the Gilberts, in Tahiti, Hawai'i – where he befriended the King – in New Zealand, and most notably in Samoa. In the village of Vailima in Samoa, Stevenson acquired several hundred acres of land and built an estate, taking on the name Tusitala, or "teller of tales."

Stevenson loathed the narrowness and competing colonial interests of the European and American officials, and tried without success to influence local policy. After numerous failures to be heard, he used his talent and reputation to publish A Footnote to History, a brutal overview of and protest against island politics that resulted in two colonial administrators being recalled. In declining health, Stevenson died and was buried in Samoa.[11]

Meanwhile, the Hawaiian mission had since been forced to withdraw from Samoa by German threats, and in any event Kalakaua had his own troubles at home. His diplomacy, expenses, and ambition to lead Polynesian affairs had galvanized the Missionary Party, who could see that Asian, European, and Oceanian allies would not come to his aid. Favoring an end to the kingdom and annexation to the United States, an armed militia forced him to sign a "Bayonet Constitution" in 1887 that disenfranchised most ethnic Hawaiians and all Asians, reduced Kalakaua to a largely ceremonial role, and put power in the hands of powerful white cabinet officials like Lorrin Thurston, lawyer and businessman, and the grandson of missionaries.[12]

The Missionary Party members hoped the United States would support their seizure of power in the Hawaiian kingdom, something not unreasonable to imagine for an expanding American Republic.

Across generations already, settlers had moved west across the continent, claiming territories, naming states, and displacing Native American Indian populations under the banner of Manifest Destiny. In the 1840s, US President James K. Polk was an ardent expansionist, keen to control the Pacific coast.

The Pacific claim actually began early in the nineteenth century with the Mexican War of Independence (1810–21) that ended Spanish control of territories in North America. The new country of Mexico inherited a vast claim that included California and Texas, but had limited resources to govern. Settlers from the United States moved into Texas and soon outnumbered Mexican colonists, declaring themselves an independent Republic of Texas in 1836. A decade later, the United States annexed the territory outright, an action that met with fiery protests and precipitated the Mexican–American War of 1846–8. Each side won significant campaigns, but with US forces blockading Mexican ports, conquering New Mexico, California, and marching on Mexico City itself, the Mexican government was forced to surrender.[13]

With the military victory, California, with its extended Pacific coastline, was ceded to the United States. The Treaty of Guadalupe Hidalgo, detailing the transfer of almost half of Mexico's territory over to American control, was signed in 1848. At almost exactly the same time, James Marshall was building a lumber mill for businessman John Sutter in Central California when he found glittering metal in the mill run-off. It was gold. The news spread quickly, and when President Polk made an announcement to Congress by the end of the year about the discovery, he launched a mad population rush to the west coast.

At the time of the announcement, San Francisco was a quiet seaport; within a little over a year, the population multiplied more than twenty-five times, as caravans of migrants overran the streets, and ships of hopeful miners from all over the world crowded the bay. All told, hundreds of thousands would live in or pass through San Francisco on their way to the gold fields, half of them by sea on clippers, schooners, and steamers.

Images from the time show veritable forests of ships' masts blocking the horizon, and frame houses set against scrub oak strands along dirt avenues. Some plank streets crossed the center of town, but as many muddy lanes twisted up hills and around lodgings crowded with begrimed gangs of men, smoke pouring out from cooking fires.

By summer 1849, local newspapers reported that two hundred ships were floating abandoned in the bay, their crews having deserted to seek gold. The US Navy offered rewards for missing sailors, and all across the region businesses and farms collapsed as workers, managers, and laborers went off to seek their fortunes. Boarding-houses in town stayed filled with transient visitors, and camps and settlements sprang up across landscapes crowded with tents thrown together from sail canvas, and timber and from cabins salvaged from abandoned ships.

Where local merchants found no customers, saloons and gambling taverns took over. Despite the chaos, a growing settler population overall meant greater commercial wealth in a region still known largely as the home of Indians, missions, and Mexican ranchers. Political and propertied interests in California wrote a constitution and declared the territory a part of the United States in 1850.[14]

In an era with no transcontinental railroad, hopefuls from Europe or the east coast of the Americas sailed Magellan's old track around the tip of South America, creating booming economies along the Pacific west coast in ports like Valparaiso in Chile. Gold-seeking legends were centuries old in Chile, extending back to the killing of Spanish conquistador Pedro de Valvidia by Araucanian Indians who reportedly mutilated his body and poured molten gold down his throat in 1553. Francis Drake had also assailed Valparaiso in search of riches.

In the nineteenth century, impoverished peasants in the region were tied to laboring in the fields, but landowners and overseers profited by doubling wheat planting as bread and flour demand soared in the north around San Francisco. In Valparaiso itself, ships came into a harbor crowded with American whalers and passenger barks, vessels from France and England, and transports from Ecuador, Peru, and Mexico. In the town, adobe walls and cobblestone alleyways wound around terraced hills traveled by donkeys carrying produce, squeaking ox-carts, and clusters of laborers, sailors, and shipping agents. Harbor districts were dense with new warehouses and palm-covered cheap lodgings, ringed by shops and merchants' premises, and surmounted by elegant mansions with flowering gardens, churches, theaters, and an opera house.[15]

From Callao to Acapulco and San Diego, the gold rush built speculative local economies. At each stop, and a dozen others, trade and provision houses flourished temporarily, creating rapid wealth for ambitious merchants selling tools, utensils, woolens, lamps, and pipes, as well as basic stores of sugar, salt beef, and alcohol.

In California, men like Sutter, with businesses in tanning hides and milling grain, were trampled under the onslaught of unregulated digging, tearing up and sluicing away of rivers and hillsides, and lawless claim jumping. Native American communities were pushed away from foraging lands and water sources, and began to raid mining towns, leading to severe reprisals and near extermination of entire Indian settlements.

The gold fields brought promises and conflicts to arrivals from all over the world, now officially landing in the United States. In San Francisco, neighborhoods and quarters sprang up around Irish, French, English, Mexican, and Chilean communities. Islanders from Hawaiʻi manned the ships and boats that crowded the Bay. Most notable and distinctive were the Chinese. A few hundred made passage in the early years, but by 1852 they numbered an estimated twenty thousand, who worked the gold fields but were soon pushed out by anti-foreign and anti-Asian gangs of miners and nativists.

Many worked in San Francisco, in laundries and small businesses. They built a Chinatown defined by porters with balancing baskets, and familiar streetfront vendors surrounded by paper lanterns, brass vessels, racks of cured pork, and strings of garlic and onions. They did not use schools and hospitals, but built their own; as a territorial workforce, they were favored as cheap to maintain. In the 1860s, Chinese crews labored on the Transcontinental Railroad. As California developed a white American settler population, Chinese communities were blamed for depressing wages. Violence broke out and by 1882 Exclusion Acts were passed to stop all Chinese immigration. The trans-Pacific voyage to find Gold Mountain in California ended.[16]

The search for work and opportunities, however, still continued in the mid-Pacific. The continental United States was closed, but David Kalakaua's Hawaiian diplomacy did have resonance in the ethnic make-up of his own islands. Like his European counterparts, Kalakaua had been very interested in labor migration, at one time entertaining a large-scale plan for Indian settlers to work Hawaiian plantations, a proposal that terrified American sugar interests, which feared British colonial influence in the kingdom.

The greatest influx, however, eventually came from East Asia. The year after Kalakaua's visit to Japan, two young Hawaiian brothers, James Hakuʻole and Isaac Harbottle, were studying Japanese language

and culture in Tokyo. They helped establish a worker assistance program for Japanese immigrants to the islands, who became the majority
heritage by the 1920s. They joined Chinese immigrants who had begun
arriving in the 1850s, as well as Filipinos, Koreans, Portuguese, and
Puerto Ricans, along with Norwegians and Germans, and Micronesians
and Melanesians from the end of the nineteenth century.

As elsewhere around the Pacific, yet with even greater diversity,
the cane fields were the true site of international and intercultural
experiences. Some of these were manifested in totems of cross-cultural
exchange, such as songs and tales, a polyglot language of Asian and
European terms, and the famed mixed-plate lunches that came to
incorporate rice, Chinese chow fun, Hawaiian *kalua* pork, or Japanese
shoyu fish.

Just as often, the experiences were divisive. Caucasian overseers, the *lunas*, wielded the whip, and Portuguese, Japanese, Korean,
Chinese, Hawaiian, and Filipino men labored for different rates of
already meager wages. Women field hands earned less than even that.
Depending on the politics or prejudices of the plantation, particular
groups were assigned the most backbreaking or hazardous work.
Japanese women stripped leaves, hoed plantings, and loaded cane;
others washed laundry or were assigned cooking, scrubbing, and
ironing. In the dust, heat, and spiny leaves of the cane gulches, one
women's song cycled, "My husband cuts the cane stalks / And I trim
their leaves / With sweat and tears we both work / for our means."[17]

Everyday life was company-controlled and also culturally
organic. Shacks and board bungalows provided minimal housing, with
common laborers piled on top of each other in barracks in rainy or
searing weather. Debts were contracted with inflated prices for food
and goods at company stores. Company policemen knocked, shouted,
and threw laborers out of bed at 5 a.m. and insulted or slapped "slow"
workers. All were closely supervised and fined or beaten for talking,
smoking, or taking breaks without permission. *Lunas* addressed
workers only by numbers on tags, which all workers were obliged to
wear around their necks. Communities were organized around nation-
alities and languages, but were often tense, fatigued, and always overcrowded and susceptible to epidemics.

Still, through a pidgin of English, Hawaiian, Portuguese, and
Asian tongues, members of different camps communicated. Camp
members told stories, shared packages from their home countries

32 Immigrant struggles: Hawaiian cane field workers.

of tea or herbal remedies, and planted vegetable gardens. They ate Portuguese bread and danced Japanese Obon. Chinese immigrant Len Wai supported his wife Len Mau Nin in China, and also started another family with a Hawaiian woman. On seven-year cycles, he voyaged back to China and tried to hold together his trans-Pacific families, joined by a father but separated by an ocean. Immigrant communities built temples, formed church congregations, and sometimes had plantation schools to learn basic literacy and preserve languages and customs.

Out in the fields, laborers bided their own senses of justice and limit. Supervision was brutal, but more than one overseer was assaulted in return by gangs of laborers with hoes and cane knives, and some were murdered. Everyday strategies took advantage of plantation systems themselves. Chinese workers counterfeited the coupons they were given to make purchases from the company store. Laborers injured by accidents or felled by sicknesses were joined by those who learned to imitate symptoms. Some work gangs regularly smoked opium, and almost all distilled their own rough liquors like "swipe wine" from molasses, water, and yeast. Chinese and Japanese gambled at cards; Filipino men staged cockfights after work.

Toward actually improving conditions, the greatest weapon of the laborers was the strike, but organization was difficult and overseers pushed back hard. Whip-bearing police crushed some protests by beating the workers and destroying their camps, as in Kapaʻau in 1891. Managers were also quick to exploit grievances by encouraging race pride and hatred, especially between Japanese, Koreans, and Chinese.

In 1898 on Maui, Japanese with sticks and clubs drove Chinese workers out of camps. Riots ended with killings and maimings. Japanese plantation laborers were the dominant strikers in 1900 and 1909 for better conditions and wages, and planters brought in Filipinos and Koreans to replace them. The Korean associations made it clear that, "we are opposed to the Japanese in everything." The Filipino leadership eventually allied with the Japanese on labor demands, forming a powerful union in Hawaiʻi.[18]

At the end of the nineteenth century, the Filipino and Hawaiian worlds were already drawn together by more than labor questions; they were both becoming territories of an imperial United States. In 1887, as King Kalakaua signed the Bayonet Constitution at gunpoint, his sister Liliʻuokalani was in London; she had been sent there with a royal party to attend the Golden Jubilee of Queen Victoria. While courtesies and glittering honors were exchanged between the Hawaiian and English monarchs, the Missionary Party was taking power in the islands by force.

When Kalakaua died in 1891, Liliʻuokalani, daughter of a line of chiefs, became Queen. Portraits and statues invariably concentrate on her regal bearing, and she remains a powerful symbol for Hawaiian sovereignty movements. As with the King, the Americans had looked forward to a figurehead monarch, but like her brother, Liliʻuokalani was determined to rule for the Hawaiian people. Building on petitions and grievances from supporters, she drafted legislation to overturn the Bayonet Constitution, return executive power to the monarch, and restore voting rights to Hawaiians and Asians.

Needless to say, the reaction from the white plantation, business, and missionary interests was immediate. They constituted themselves a Committee for Public Safety and spread rumors of violent threats to American lives and property. Critically, they convinced US Government Minister John L. Stevens to order sailors and marines from the USS Boston to leave their ship and take up military positions in Honolulu. The stated cause was to maintain order, but the intended and actual effect was to force the Queen to declare war on American troops if she wished to carry out her reforms. She declined, and was deposed in January 1893.

In yielding, however, Lili'uokalani ignored the new "Provisional Government" and instead surrendered to "the superior force of the United States of America." Grover Cleveland, the American president, declared the overthrow illegal and ordered his government to restore the Queen. The Provisional Government had expected to become part of the United States; in defiance, the conspirators rejected the American directive and instead declared themselves an independent republic, with plantation and pineapple magnate Sanford B. Dole as president.[19]

Following all this was Robert William Kalanihiapo Wilcox, a dashing and cosmopolitan Hawaiian artillery officer and engineer. Trained in Italy, he married an Italian Baronesa and then a princess of the Kamehameha family, and lived in Turin, San Francisco, and Honolulu, all the while agitating in favor of Hawaiian rights. After the Bayonet Constitution, he and other activists rebelled against the new government, and Wilcox also staunchly supported Lili'uokalani's attempts to challenge the American oligarchy.

In 1895, he and supporters mounted an armed counter-revolution against the Republic, but were quickly defeated and tried for treason. Wilcox was pardoned and turned to politics, serving as a delegate to Washington DC for the US Territory of Hawai'i from 1901 to 1902. As he moved from officer of the Hawaiian state, to rebel against the Republican government, to political defender of indigenous rights and claims, he embodied the shifting status of Hawaiians at the close of the nineteenth century.[20]

The American status of Hawai'i that defined Wilcox's last role was partly shaped by the machinations of Dole's regime, as the US annexed Hawai'i in 1898 and made it a US Territory in 1900. The larger picture was a reframing of the global imperial order, as American rule replaced the Spanish from the Caribbean to the Pacific. Since the centuries of the "Spanish Lake," the power of Spain had been fragmenting, under challenge from the Dutch and British, and significantly shattered by the independence of the Latin American states in the early nineteenth century.

In 1898, American political attention was focused on Cuba, where anti-Spanish rebel movements had led to serious military repression and an inflamed American "yellow press" reporting on Spanish atrocities. With tensions in the Caribbean and the notorious sinking of the USS Maine in Havana Harbor, the 1898 Spanish–American War erupted, driving the collapse of Spanish rule in Cuba and Puerto Rico, and American colonial expansion toward the Pacific. Hawai'i, more than ever a strategic prize for an oceanic empire with interests in Asia, was annexed by the United States.

But Hawai'i was only one part of a series of conquests. Though focused on events in Cuba, the first shots of the Spanish–American War came in the Philippines, where Commodore George Dewey gathered a battle squadron and steamed toward Manila Bay to confront Spanish naval forces. Dewey's ships were coming in by cover of night when soot in the funnel of the support vessel *McCulloch* briefly caught fire while passing Spanish fortifications. Chief Engineer Francis Randall worked the overheated engine room trying to contain the blaze, suffered a stroke, and died. He was the famous one American life lost during Dewey's campaign.

The Spanish were not so fortunate, losing all of their vessels and hundreds of lives to Dewey's superior cruisers in a naval battle that lasted seven hours. The antiquated Spanish ships were all sunk, abandoned, or used in futile attempts to run the American blockade toward the open sea. Admiral Patricio Montojo y Pasaron reportedly placed his ships in strategically poor shallow waters, partly to be covered by shore batteries, but also so that his sailors would be able to swim for their lives when outgunned by the American squadron.[21]

The real battles would be in the streets and jungles of the islands. In spite of American declarations to liberate the Philippines of Spanish tyranny, the United States was joining a rebellion already a generation old, and an armed revolution that had begun two years earlier. The Spanish had staked their claim with Magellan in 1521, and come to stay with Legazpi in 1565. Over three centuries, the *barangays* had been reshaped by Catholic missions and the relentless labor of the *encomiendas*. Muslim wars and Chinese trading communities formed the boundaries of a historical identity tied to a Spanish colonial society framed by Iberian doctrines and the trans-Pacific trade of the Manila galleons.[22]

By the nineteenth century, middle-class Spanish and Chinese–mestizo families were attentive to liberal ideas from Europe, as well as the reform and revolution changes in Latin America and much of the former Spanish Empire. The most distinguished of the younger generation were well-traveled, educated, and presented themselves as enlightened – they were the *Illustrados*.

The national hero of the Philippines was one of them, not a general, conqueror, nor even strictly speaking a statesman. He was an ophthalmologist, artist, thinker, writer, and poet of great eloquence and conviction: José Rizal. Not a Spanish grandee, Rizal was a son of prosperous farmers, a man whose personal heritage drew from many cultures and histories, making him a syncretic, Pacific-wide figure. The patrilineal descendant of a Chinese merchant, Rizal also had ancestors who included Japanese settlers, Malay farmers, the Rajah of Tondo, and mixed-blood Spanish and Chinese mestizos. Educated, beginning in Manila, Rizal learned surveying and was a superior student in philosophy and letters. In 1882 he traveled to Madrid, Paris, and Heidelberg, earning degrees in medicine and studying anthropology and linguistics.

His is one of the most famous and mythologized deaths in Pacific history: he was executed by a Spanish firing squad in 1896. Imprisoned and sentenced for his scathing novels and essays against the Spanish Empire and Catholic friars, he penned a final poem, *Mi Ultimo Adios*, "I go where there are no slaves, no hangmen or oppressors, where faith does not kill." He alluded to secret writings he had hidden to be revealed after his death. He may or may not have married the woman he loved, or retracted his anti-Catholicism at the last moment. His executioners were reportedly struck by his calm sense of destiny at the moment of death. His body was spirited away and buried in secret to avoid exactly the sorts of legends and reverential commemorations that grew up immediately around his martyrdom.[23]

All of this had sprung from Rizal's formidable presence, in which he drew on the many cultures and languages of his own lineages and his education from Asia to Europe to articulate a distinctly Filipino identity. He was inspired by the contradictions that had built up in Spanish colonial society. The Catholic Church was built on conversion and trained an increasingly well-educated population of native disciples and teachers. Yet, socially and politically, aspiring local priests were kept in subordinate positions, excluded from joining religious orders and becoming pastors. In 1872, three native priests were executed for raising grievances that the government condemned as anti-Spanish.

Rizal agitated for reforms, using his talent as a writer to make his nationalistic points and draw attention. His 1887 classic *Noli Me Tangere* was a satirical and inflammatory chronicle of a progressive family suffering abuse and injustice at the hands of a corrupt Spanish Church, and his sequel *El Filibursterismo* brought back the central character as a tragic, vengeful figure bent on violent revolution. Copies circulated in Spain and were smuggled into the Philippines, where Rizal was condemned by authorities and lauded as an activist and eloquent critic of "bad government." For many, his legacy would be not his politics but his role as a champion of a unique Filipino culture, challenging Iberian scholars whose research claimed that no history or literature of value existed in the Philippines before the Spanish.

With his reformist mission, Rizal provoked harassment for himself, his relatives, and friends, from Spanish officials. He agitated for representation in courts and government, for freedoms of assembly and speech, and for Filipino priests to replace Spanish friars in parishes. He wrote petitions against friar-landlords for tenants. His actions got his family evicted, and his civic reform *Liga Filipina* banned by the governor. He was exiled to Dapitan, where he ran a hospital, and taught languages, agriculture, surveying, sculpturing, and painting, as well as martial arts, and natural history. He connected Mindanao with erudites around the world, and called upon his students to help him create cartographic and engineering plans for the region.

A fierce agitator for reform, Rizal never personally embraced revolutionary violence, but his contemporaries did. In 1896, Spanish authorities were alerted to a well-developed secret anticolonial organization, the *Katipunan*, led by Andres Bonifacio. With a program of secession and the support of local government leaders across the islands, the *Katipunan* declared an armed revolution and attack on Manila in August 1896. The main military force was defeated by Spanish defenders, but allied rebels commanding the surrounding provinces had some notable successes, particularly those from Cavite, under General Emilio Aguinaldo. In a power struggle, Aguinaldo arrested Bonifacio and had him executed, setting up his own revolutionary government before being himself forced into exile in Hong Kong.

Skirmishes between Filipino and Spanish forces continued. Rizal, who disagreed with the armed rebellion, was distancing himself by sailing for Cuba when he was arrested. The *Katipunan* had long sought his endorsement and Bonifacio had forged his name on declarations. Rizal was tried and executed, and his name became an inspiration for Filipino nationalists, reformers, and revolutionaries, and later advocates of non-violent global anticolonialism like Mohandas K. Gandhi in India.[24]

33 Rebel with a cause: monument to a martyred José Rizal, the Philippines.

In the Philippines, final Spanish overthrow came with the Americans, and a story not of liberation, but of substitution, as a European imperial power was replaced by an American presence claiming progressive rule over a decadent colony. In May 1898, a military vessel was sent on a traverse to Singapore and Hong Kong. Its mission was to transport Emilio Aguinaldo back to Manila. Conferring with US consuls and with Dewey himself, Aguinaldo came to understand that the Americans wanted him to complete the Philippine Revolution, ousting the remaining Spanish and loyalist forces. Reportedly assured by Dewey that "America is exceedingly well off as regards territory, revenue, and resources and therefore needs no colonies," Aguinaldo routed Spanish forces in the northern Philippines and established himself as president.

But Spain was humiliated to be beaten by a popular revolution and made a deal to surrender to the United States instead, after an agreement to stage a mock battle for the capital of Manila. Already an uneasy partner with the Americans, Aguinaldo was furious, but bided his time. In February 1899, as arguments continued and tensions rose, an American patrol fired on, and killed, three Filipino soldiers.

The Philippine Revolution and Spanish–American War became the Philippine–American War.[25]

As American forces advanced across the island of Luzon, Aguinaldo retreated from fighting with a standing army and organized guerrilla commands; his forces could not match the US military, and instead opted for a conflict of attrition, hoping the Americans would leave. Aguinaldo's troops were strongest in Central Luzon and allied with other forces in the Tagalog regions and Visayan islands against the Americans. Fought in skirmishes, ambushes, and reprisals, the war became infamous for its brutality. Witnesses reported shootings of surrendering combatants, torching of villages, and bayoneting of villagers. Both sides found corpses of soldiers hacked apart, and journalists reported that some American commanders tortured prisoners to death. Most of the US generals were veterans of Indian Wars that had decimated native populations across the American continent.

American propaganda dedicated to "lifting the yoke of Spanish oppression" from noble and courageous Filipinos became racist. The southern islands pledged neutrality, but as the battles spread south, American troops began fighting in Mindanao with the Sultan of Sulu, and anti-Islamic reports decrying the savagery of "bloodthirsty Moros" became headlines. As many as 200,000 civilians died, some from combat, most from famine and disease.

In March 1901, Aguinaldo was captured by Philippine forces allied with the American military. As terms of surrender, he pledged his allegiance to the United States and officially called for an armistice. Not all forces heeded him, and fighting continued in some regions into the next years, but a new history was already being created. In the twentieth century, the legacy of Rizal was adopted by both Filipino nationalists and American colonial governors, beginning with William Taft, to shape a patriotic history of resistance, sacrifice, and martyrdom to the former Spanish empire.[26]

By immediately buying out the landed estates of the hated Catholic friars, Taft positioned the American colonial government on the side of progress, even though most of the lands were sold back to elites and great landlords. A Filipino legislature in 1916, and a 1934 plan for granting independence established the foundations for "democratic rule." Trade monopolies and old commercial restrictions were dissolved, and free markets that benefited US exporters opened. American products and cultural influence became paramount; the legacies of a new imperial age were just being born.

17 TRADITIONS OF ENGAGEMENT AND ETHNOGRAPHY

In 1907, William Jones made his way up the Cagayan River in northern Luzon Province of the Philippines. In a letter posted back to the United States he wrote, "I am sojourning with a Negrito-Malay people called Ilongots, who dwell in lofty booths on poles and in the forks of trees." He was excited to be among a headhunting jungle society, yet also repelled by the "savagery" that he witnessed. Two years later he was speared and cut down with bolo knives at a bend in the river by Ilongot warriors.

The attack came in response to unfortunate events that might have been reminiscent of the fate of James Cook: Jones had argued about boats, been impatient and unwise in dealing with local clans and, at the last moment, seemed to be taking a local elder, Takadan, hostage until he could have his demands satisfied. In Jones' case those demands centered on balsa rafts that the Ilongot were supposed to build and guide for him downriver. The need for so many rafts was unusual, but Jones had a large cargo: extensive collections of baskets, weapons, fish traps, and models of local dwellings bound for the Field Museum in Chicago.

Jones was not a trader or colonial official in the Philippines. He was, rather, a Harvard and Columbia-trained anthropologist, a PhD student of the renowned Franz Boas, and one that knew something of American colonialism, for he had been born on the Sauk and Fox Reservation in Indian Territory, Oklahoma, in a family line that included an English–Welsh grandfather married to the daughter of the Fox chief, Wa-shi-ho-wa. An enthusiastic linguistic scholar and collector of materials from the Indian Territories, he was a personally ambivalent, outwardly assimilated product of scholarly professionalism and American patriotism. He brought his transcultural background to the Pacific and American Empire.

Though Jones' Philippines mission was scientific and did, in fact, provide rich ethnographic data when his notes and collections were recovered, he could not avoid the ties that developed between anthropology and the colonial government. Since annexation in 1898, American interests had been heavily invested in organizing and reshaping life in the Philippines. The first civil governor, William Howard Taft, established public services, English-language and manual training schools, and political districts and elections for "tutelage" in democracy. "The national policy is to govern the Philippine Islands for the benefit and welfare and uplifting of the people of the Islands."

In 1901, the US Philippine Commission also established a Bureau of non-Christian tribes with an object to "conduct systematic work in the anthropology of the Philippines, and the recommendation of legislation on behalf of these uncivilized peoples." Jones entertained informal conversations about taking on "governorship of a sub-province of wild people," with the idea that a trained scientist with "sympathy" for local culture could bring about "the right attitude toward the government and its purposes."

That plan never developed, and like most field researchers, Jones devoted his time to noting the customs, tools, and practices of the "wild, naked folk." Such study of culture was always fraught. Even as anthropologists moved in, colonial "pacification" continued. Jones and his colleagues may have been aggrieved to know that the immediate consequence of his death was a vicious military reprisal by the Philippine Constabulary, with the wholesale burning of villages and rice stores, and an aggravation of headhunting raids and violence between displaced and rival Ilongot tribal groups.[1]

The collusions and tensions between anthropology and colonial projects accelerated in the early twentieth century around the Pacific, as decades of settlements, trading posts, and military conquest formalized into administrations and established colonial societies. In some cases, colonial and scholarly imperatives directly overlapped. The official Papuan Collection of the National Museum of Australia – some hundreds of cane cuirasses, waistbands, arm-bracelets, grass skirts, stone clubs, shields, masks, and fire-starting devices – was

34 Collecting cultures: art, artifacts, and implements from New Guinea.

assembled over a quarter century by officials and employees of
Sir Hubert Murray, the Papuan territorial governor, who went on field
expeditions with visiting researchers. Historians have suggested that
the ordered nature of such collections was intended to display the
colonial administrator's own presumably ordered rule over both the
local terrain and the local people.[2]

In 1907, Murray wrote to the Australian Minister for Home
and Territories with a project in mind. He had amassed a considerable personal collection and wanted to have it recognized as an
ethnological museum and specially displayed in Port Moresby, the
colonial capital. Murray believed that it was his scientific and
imperial duty to preserve the elements of the local cultures that
were, he thought, destined to disappear in confrontation with Western
civilization. For this, he sought assistance from researchers and
the support of Alfred Court Haddon, a like-minded Cambridge
anthropologist.

Murray's patrol officers worked like field researchers, sent out
to "obtain information as to the customs and habits of the natives and

to collect curios." They traveled the rivers, setting up possible exchanges: "we anchored off some native houses and went ashore. Inside were many stuffed heads, sago bags, fish nets and other odds and ends ... I did not touch anything in the shelters but left one or two old tomahawks in the hope of making friends with the people upon my return." At other times, the patrols were less scrupulous, simply taking what they wanted and leaving their own trade goods.[3]

While collecting, the main function of the patrols was still to establish communications and alliances with the clans, and to map out the territories, most completely unknown to Europeans. In 1914, a young Polish anthropologist arrived in Port Moresby. Bronislaw Malinowski and Murray did not get along well: the governor looked down on most academic men of science, and Malinowski found Murray a caricature of a British colonial officer. Yet they had common interests, and Malinowski had a dilemma. He was by birth an Austrian national, and when the First World War broke out in Europe he was suddenly an enemy, faced with the prospect of spending years in a prison camp. Murray, for his part, was always interested in field researchers who could provide him with more knowledge of linguistics, customs, and village ties. He found Malinowski useful, and recommended his fieldwork in New Guinea and in the nearby Trobriand Islands.

Malinowski is noted for his attention to meanings, the richness of his frameworks, and especially for creating the very image of the anthropologist as "participant-observer," in exotic and unknown cultures. His major first work famously proposed, "Imagine yourself suddenly set down surrounded by all your gear, alone on a tropical beach close to a native village, while the launch or dinghy which has brought you sails away out of sight." This was the image that would remain of the early years of field anthropology: the moment of isolation and new contact.

Yet that was not exactly correct, as Malinowski himself noted, "Since you take up your abode in the compound of some neighboring white man, trader or missionary, you have nothing to do, but to start at once on your ethnographic work." Anthropology came late to Pacific histories, developing in tandem with political and colonial change. As he landed in the lagoon of Kiriwina island, the Trobriands, Malinowski set foot not on the sandy beach, but on a coral jetty built by labor from the local prison.

He was obliged to introduce himself to the magistrate, and was attended to in an enormous compound of barracks, a hospital and dispensary, food warehouses, and orchards of fruit and flower trees. The magistrate, Raynor Bellamy, was hard at work developing trepang and pearl fishing industries, requisitioning villagers to level roads, and imprisoning those who practiced sorcery or did not help him develop his hundreds of miles of coconut tree plantations.

Malinowski set off for Omarakana, a village of dwelling huts and yam storehouses. He erased Murray and the European settlement from his writings, even as his supplies were brought in by prison porters, and his famous tent – symbol of the lone adventuring scientist – was borrowed from Bellamy's colonial store. From this base began the work that, instead, plunged readers into a world of trade, kinship, religion, and magic that made Malinowski world-renowned.[4]

Twice each year, Trobriand islanders set out, often across hundreds of miles of sea, to exchange and barter. Arm bands and necklaces of white and red shells were passed from canoe to village in opposite directions around a great island ring of exchange called Kula. Acquiring a particular Kula item carried significant prestige, but it also had to be passed along, taking on new values through its travels in time and space, the status of its holders, and the power of their magic. Malinowski dismissed suggestions that Kula items were somehow like money. He saw that Kula voyages were quests for status and magical power that created networks of political stability through exchange.

The Kula work dazzled the world. Here was an island world not driven by commodities and competition, an alternative to Western modernity. Malinowski defended the revelatory interweaving of ancient practice and belief. "Destroy tradition, and you will deprive the collective organism of its protective shell, and give it over to the slow but inevitable process of dying out."[5]

The question of tradition and disappearance haunted all anthropological work of his era. In 1922, the Oxford-trained Francis Edgar Williams joined Hubert Murray's staff as a full-time government anthropologist, focused on everyday objects like fishing floats and coconut containers, while chronicling the faces and lives of villagers in richly detailed photographs. Like Murray and Malinowski,

35 The myth and magic of anthropology: Malinowski's campsite in the Trobriand Islands.

Williams felt a duty to protect the peoples he worked with from exploitation by European planters and traders, and he marveled at the richness of their languages, art, and culture. More in common with Murray, though, he worked to eliminate practices he thought objectionable such as sorcery and "unsanitary" burial practices, head-hunting, and seclusion of widows.

Williams' scholarly work shows a fine attention to meanings and practices in the Papuan world, yet his news bulletin, *The Papuan Villager*, reinforced colonial hierarchies by offering advice to his neighbors about learning English, "so that you can talk to the white man and get a good job," and cultural difference: "You can never be quite the same as a white man; and you will only look silly if you try to be." As some historians have remarked, Williams' genuine regard for Papuan cultures did not admit that those cultures could respond to historical change. "He admired them for what they were, not for what they might become."[6]

When innovative responses arose, they ran into defenders of tradition – often the colonials themselves. Protection and paternalism were remarkably enlightened in societies where landless laboring, religious indoctrination, and legal codes enforcing white superiority against indigenous peoples were the norm. But the idea that islanders could change and develop their own economies and politics was too much to imagine. More, it was threatening to colonial establishments.

As might be expected, notable cases early on took place in Pacific colonies that had long and complicated histories of interaction between local communities, Westerners, and Asians. The Fijian islands were a good example, as governor Gordon had created a colonial Fijian society based on the "traditional" Council of Chiefs, which he had in fact invented himself to allow indirect British rule. Once established, the chiefs and their allies were pleased to command their subjects and gain the harvest benefits of villages, according to "custom."

The white colonial society took up the charge of studying this now-ordered "traditional" world, examining oral histories as literary tales and studying ceremonial and common trade items not as parts of lives, but as art objects. Gordon's cousin, the intrepid solo traveler, writer, and watercolorist Constance Gordon-Cumming, reported to friends and family, "All our rooms are like museums, adorned with savage implements, and draped with native cloth of beautifully rich patterns, all hand-painted."

In 1904, colonial official Sir William Allardyce donated his own collection to the Suva Town Board with the idea of displaying and preserving "traditional Fijian culture." In 1908, a research group, the Fijian Society, was formed and regularly published papers on sacred stones, firewalkers, fishing and net making, place names, spirits and origin tales, and a running series of encounters with Dakuwaqa, the famed shark god. Some British officials wore the *sulu* skirt and popularized ceremonial toastings of *kava*.[7]

Yet many Fijians were not content with, and did not live in, an ethnographic world of tales and artifacts. Neither a glorious, mythologized past, nor a "traditional" present of chiefly rule and colonial domination suited their desires. It was a Melanesian commoner, Apolosi Nawai, who defied both the British and the collaborating chiefs. He knew that the only path to advancement in Fijian colonial society was through the government's Native Administration, where regional commissioners and headmen were appointed from chiefly families. Apolosi, from the village of Narewa, was a commoner and would be hard pressed to rise in such a system, but he was a gifted preacher and reportedly had a vision telling him to lead the Fijians to a "new era." Charismatic prophets were not uncommon in the islands, but Apolosi was unusual in that he offered not only spiritual direction, but a sophisticated, anticolonial business plan.

As anthropologists pursued research of Pacific Island peoples, Apolosi had in turn been studying the Westerners, and formed a group targeting the international banana and produce market. Calculating how much profit European traders made by buying from farmers and then shipping bananas overseas, Apolosi created a company in 1914, the Viti Kabani, to compete with them. More correctly, he forced them to compete with each other by cutting them out as middleman distributors, declaring "Fiji for the Fijians." The Viti Kabani instead organized farmers to pool their capital, and reinvest in their own profits. With teams of supporters, Apolosi did what the white traders could not: he circulated through the islands, from village to village, convincing chiefs and farmers to buy shares in the company.

His subscriptions were immediately popular, raising more than a thousand pounds sterling and attracting the business interests not only of Fijians, but of Europeans, who could see a good profit and had themselves appointed as a board of directors. The colonial government watched suspiciously, and the Great Council of Chiefs opposed the clever commoner who challenged their authority and compromised their crop revenues and work exactions.

Apolosi continued to organize ever more successful meetings of subscribers. Reporting on one, a colonial newspaper noted "a larger and more enthusiastic meeting of natives than any governor could hope to do – so much for the Native Office influence." Indeed, the meetings were community consultations, and as spirits rose, so did proposals beyond simple business, with demands that "there should be no dealing with Europeans," and that "customary" labor and church levies be abolished. Company leaders exhorted subscribers not to work for the chiefs, and talk turned to the Company serving as an alternative government for Fijians, with its own police and judges.

As the Viti Kabani grew stronger and more profitable, fractures appeared in colonial society. Some headmen and commissioners of the chiefs resigned their positions to take up roles in the Company. European business interests, under pressure for harvests, agitated fiercely against the policies that prevented them from buying up native land titles. White prestige suffered as poorer settlers and planters were outclassed by Apolosi's influence. An Australian journalist and supporter, Stella Spencer, was jailed for slapping a business rival, though her trial was clearly about whether a white woman should associate so closely with Fijian men.[8]

Also called to trial was Apolosi himself, on general insinuations of business fraud brought by his enemies. Papers reported that he was "clad in European clothes with tennis shirt and artistic fancy tie, with his hair cropped close." Colonial authorities not only preferred, but encouraged Fijians to wear "traditional" clothes and the big hair of the old "cannibal kings." Apolosi challenged that ethnographic image, and his attackers were strident. Charges and counter charges flew, suggesting that the Company was a massive swindle, and an illegal affront to the colonial government. Supporters were intimidated with more exacting labor laws, and Apolosi was repeatedly detained. Ultimately, he was convicted of sedition and deported to exile in Rotuma.

Apolosi's challenge to the chiefs and the colonial government had not only given him a popular base of support, it had been a direct assault on the policies that maintained the fictions of a romanticized Fijian tradition, which tied families and clans to their local villages. More, he had created a model community that looked beyond the colonial government, and beyond the Fijian islands, to an international trading circuit for its market and profits. The popular fashion for a past Fiji of artifacts and noble warriors betrayed an insular colonial world threatened by Pacific peoples with broader connections.

Some of these concerns had actual bases. In parallel with the Viti Kabani, Fiji's Indian communities were also showing that they were not isolated in grim plantation hardship and furtive memories of the subcontinent. The indentured laborer Totaram Sanadhya had arrived in 1893 like many others, impoverished and tied to a contract signed with false promises. For five years, he labored at the Colonial Sugar Refining Company, always short of food, regularly abused by overseers, and forced to beg to survive.

After the term of the contract, he was in debt but, determined to improve his position, borrowed money, and set himself up as a small cane farmer. He learned trade skills in wood and metal, and made deals for books to begin studies as an Indian priest. As he attracted a following, he worked closely for the welfare of Indians, forming an assistance group, and petitioning the Governor for Indian education and political rights. When he left the islands he had a wide reputation and addressed the Indian National Congress in Madras.[9]

One of Sanadhya's legacies was to take his grievances beyond Fiji to a wider political network, asking for help from abroad. His success was ably demonstrated by the arrival in 1912 of Manilal Maganlal Doctor. He was a barrister – an advocacy lawyer – born in India, educated in London, and a practitioner in the British colony of Mauritius, and was greeted by hundreds of Fijians and honored with songs, dances, and orations. His commitment was legal assistance for Indian communities, and he represented a circuit of activists and political figures that linked Europe to British interests in India, South Africa, and the Pacific islands. All of this was enough to attract the attention of Fijian authorities, but there was something else: he had been sent specifically to Fiji by Mohandas K. Gandhi.

Active in the Home Rule Society and freedom politics in India, Manilal spent three years on the island of Mauritius, taking cases and petitions on behalf of Indian contract laborers and challenging uneven sentencing guidelines. Over the next years, he published an activist newspaper in the Hindi language and sailed to Bombay and South Africa. In Fiji, Manilal drafted documents, letters, and petitions for poor Indians and defended them in court. He also worked against abuses of the indenture system by side-stepping colonial bureaucracy and sending cases to allies at the Anti-Slavery Society of London. As president of the Indian Imperial Association – a successor to Sanadhya's earlier assistance group – Manilal filed regular reports on indenture conditions in Fiji, attracting the attention of the British Labour Party, and leading to investigations by the Indian government. Fiji became a local site of transnational interest.

By 1920, the Fiji indenture system was abolished, largely by pressure from Indian nationalists with a coalition of officials and British progressives. One of the dreams of Sanadhya and Manilal was realized. But only one. In January of that year, Indian laborers for Public Works in Fiji saw their work hours abruptly increased and went on strike. Manilal guided meetings seeking a negotiated settlement, but after initial successes, police and strikers clashed. The government used the incident to prevent Manilal from having contact with Fijian Indian settlements.

After weighing internal exile, Manilal left the islands. Refused the right to practice as a barrister in Australia, New Zealand, Ceylon, and Malaysia, he continued on in lower courts in India and supported Socialist and Communist organizers before moving on to Aden in the

Middle East. His global circuit connecting the Pacific to activism across the Indian Ocean continued.[10]

The tensions between a Pacific of isolated anthropological cultures and strident worldwide politics continued into the late 1920s in the Samoan islands with the arrival of a woman who would become the most famous anthropologist in the world. Margaret Mead, like William Jones, was also an American student of Franz Boas, and in search of field study that would help her examine the supposedly "natural" turmoils of adolescence in girls and young women. In 1925, she settled for nine months in a community on Tu'a Island in American Samoa, where she observed and participated in everyday life, interviewed female subjects, and formulated daring conclusions about youth and open sexuality.

Her 1928 *Coming of Age in Samoa* made her instantly famous, a visibility she would embrace for more than a half century as a public figure, becoming an advisor to academics and institutes, and commenting widely as an international celebrity on issues of child-rearing, sex, health and ecological challenges, feminism, and global justice. The questions of whether sexuality and adolescence were culturally flexible made her a cult figure and also attracted a legion of critics, who claimed that her research was naïve, superficial, or fabricated.

Whether Mead was correct about life cycles on Tu'a island, she created an ethnographic image of "Samoa" with lasting impact, based on her desire "to conduct a human experiment," under controlled and comparative conditions. She shared and promoted the idea that "for such studies the anthropologist chooses quite simple peoples, primitive peoples, whose society has never attained the complexity of our own."

"Samoa" was never more than Tu'a villages for many readers, yet even as Mead was writing and publishing, different confrontations over sexuality and social values were taking place around the Samoan islands. One outcome of the First World War and the military defeat of Germany was the loss of all the Kaiser's colonies to other powers. German Samoa had been mandated to the government of New Zealand, and was the sort of complicated Pacific place that Mead specifically avoided.[11]

In this other Samoa, New Zealand ruled a colony of Samoans, mostly German planters and settlers, and Chinese indentured laborers. The military administrator Robert Logan had his own ideas of maintaining traditional cultures. Thinking to keep the Samoan race "pure," he was hostile to Chinese men cohabiting with Samoan women and issued orders outlawing Chinese from entering Samoan houses. His government became increasingly unpopular as he forced the Chinese out of the islands, broke up the German firms that produced his islands' main revenues, and incompetently allowed influenza-ridden passengers from the steamship *Talune* to disembark, leading to a gruesome epidemic that killed more than seven thousand islanders.

Subsequent administrators also faced discontent and questions of sex, race, and culture. General George Richardson was not keen on Samoan and white "half-caste children," arguing that "the European father finds himself drawn back into the native or semi-native circle and ultimately gives up the struggle to maintain the prestige of his race." He also fostered great resentment by reorganizing village common lands and by prohibiting customary exchanges of fine woven mats. More, he dared banish and take away the titles of chiefs; this was an affront that had led to rebellions decades earlier under German rule. Now, restive Samoan leaders stirred again.

One determined Samoan was Olaf Frederick Nelson. His father had been a Swedish merchant, but he was proudly transcultural, carrying himself as Samoan "by birth, blood, and sentiment." He was a rich man, well traveled and educated, but excluded from any real governance role because of his mixed background. General Richardson thought of him as a "half-caste" who was not quite European, but also not a real "native." In 1926, Nelson and supporters organized public meetings and founded a Samoan League to highlight grievances and challenge the authority of colonial New Zealand rule. The opposition movement was called the O le Mau a Samoa – the firm opinion of Samoa.

The Mau movement began resistance to the administration by ignoring its edicts. There had been an earlier Mau movement under German colonial rule, and there was also an anti-naval Mau in American Samoa. In such cases, district councils, women's groups, and other committees simply stopped meeting. Colonial officials found themselves without information or collaborators. During the anti-New Zealand protest, laborers did not show up for work, and panicked plantation owners watched as crops of bananas and coconuts fell and rotted in the heat. Village officials no longer filed local business and civil documents, and many Samoans conveniently forgot to meet requisitions or pay taxes. Instead, villages appointed "talking men" and organized around chiefs to handle their own commercial and political affairs.

Estimates suggest that more than 80 percent of the Samoan population stopped cooperating with the colonial government in the late 1920s. General Richardson arrested hundreds, but hundreds more voluntarily surrendered and overwhelmed the jails and guards, forcing him to release everyone.[12]

By 1928, Margaret Mead finished her manuscript and *Coming of Age in Samoa* was published, sparking ethnographic debates about lives and customs in Tu'a. Meanwhile, the Mau movement in American Samoa stretched across the entire decade of the 1920s and continued. Across the water in Apia, Olaf Nelson was deported to New Zealand, where he published *The Truth About Samoa*, setting forth the grievances and platform of the Mau. The same year, he gained the support of the New Zealand Labor Party and sailed to Europe to present a petition for action to the League of Nations in Geneva. Like his predecessors in Fiji, his island identity was rooted in custom and heritage, but connected to a global political circuit.

Mead, the anthropologist, was not the only one with ideas on Samoan youth development. In Apia, General Richardson was replaced by Colonel Stephen Allen, who argued, "the main thing to remember is that the Samoan never grows up, but always retains the mind and intellect of a child." He imprisoned and exiled opponents, and on December 28, 1929, had his military police fire on a demonstration, killing Mau leader Tupua Tamasese Lealofi III. Men fled the towns until a truce a year later, and the Mau continued under Tamasese's widow Alaisala and other prominent women. Mead's work became a classic reference for a simple, primitive "Samoa" in much of the world, even as complex local struggles continued to evolve over the future of the islands.[13]

As the Mau was organized in 1926, it adopted a singular slogan: "Samoa for the Samoans." The popular suggestion of a common identity and purpose was one of the hallmarks of a phenomenon that developed in tandem with political and cultural change in the early twentieth century: nationalism. There was no single model around Asia and the Pacific, but everywhere it was based on championing a shared heritage and was opposed in varying degrees to colonial authority.

The 1868 Meiji Restoration in Japan provided a strong "modernizing" example, while José Rizal and the Philippine Revolution embraced both political reform and armed resistance to Spanish rule

36 For the Samoans: leaders of the Mau movement, Tupua Tamasese Lealofi III seated, center.

respectively. Apolosi Nawai's charismatic initiatives in Fiji directly competed with European interests, and Indian Fijians saw their cause taken up by Gandhi and other opponents of empire.

In China, wracked across the nineteenth century by the Opium Wars and Taiping Rebellion, anti-foreign militancy grew. In 1900, popular bands of fighters, with leaders trained in spiritual disciplines and the martial arts, took up a call to expel foreigners from China. Their athletic, disciplined attacks on foreign legations earned them the name of "Boxers." Aggrieved by insults, foreign domination of Chinese territory, and the intrusion of Christian missions, the Boxers massacred foreign civilians, officials, and religious congregations with the assent of the Empress Dowager Cixi. Only some twenty thousand troops sent in by Western nations allowed the Boxer Rebellion to be quelled with severe repressions.

In the aftermath, greater sanctions were placed on the Qing government, including a crushing indemnity. The weakening of the Qing state permitted movements for alternative governments to arise.

By 1911, the Qing were overthrown by the Chinese Revolution of Dr Sun Yat Sen, who declared a new Republic. Sun was born in China and spent many years in Hawai'i with a brother who had been an earlier laborer immigrant. Sun studied arts and sciences and the English language during the reign of King David Kalakaua, and at the turn of the nineteenth and twentieth centuries, pursued revolutionary activities in China, while facing exile in Europe, North America, and Japan. His global itineraries were not uncommon as nationalist sentiments sparked all across Asia and the Pacific.[14]

In colonial Southeast Asia, familiar Western policies of attempting to isolate villagers in stable, "traditional" societies began to fragment in the face of parallel changes. Everywhere a minority in the territories they ruled, colonial officials were tied to urban centers for trade and communications, and dependent on local elites as well as trained and educated native clerks, notaries, and teachers. Export crop economies meant that villages were linked along jungle and highland roads to commercial centers and ports by chains of purchasers, transporters, and merchants speaking Malay, English, and Chinese.

These connections could mean restive populations. Villages were not completely separable from urban settlements, just as towns were not isolated from news and ideas from abroad. Where grievances combined with aspirations, sentiments of common purpose developed. When they occurred, rebellions were not yet particularly "nationalistic," usually locally focused on poverty, and disputes over unmet community obligations between different social ranks, yet men and women, often separately, wrote to each other and in towns and cities created mutual interest groups. These increasingly took the form of voluntary associations around trade, religion, and culture, imagining new "national" identities and futures.[15]

Glimpses of change could be seen in the publication of letters by a young Muslim woman, Raden Adjeng Kartini, advocating female education and advancement in Java. In 1911, the same year that Sun Yat Sen declared his Chinese Republic, Kartini made a challenge to imperial priorities. The Dutch continued to rule through local elites, which – as in Fiji – they regarded as "traditional," but whose authority created concentrations of power that had not existed previously. Debates in the Netherlands over tax revenues, however, and a more liberal government led to a reorientation away from the commercial exploitation of the Cultivation System toward something called "Ethical Policy." The approach claimed to protect indigenous populations by offering them European education while still respecting, indeed advocating, traditional cultural practices.

The "traditional" part followed the strained collusion of science and politics in colonial territories everywhere. In 1914, the Dutch director of the Anthropology section of the Colonial Institute in Amsterdam announced that his mandate would be to "acknowledge and accommodate" indigenous societies. While presented as progressive, Ethical Policy advocates knew that better understanding also allowed more sophisticated manipulation of *adat*, the complex of customary law, conventions, and practices in hundreds of regions all across the Indonesian islands. Colonial administrators reinvented *adat* "traditions" of rulership, by claiming that their system of rule was culturally authentic and justified by ethnographic science.

The Ethical Policy mission as such sought to demonstrate that progressive values could be woven into the very fabric of traditional culture. In this, a focus on women was central, for women were presumed to be the very core of a customary society, "naturally" living out tradition in daily rituals and practices of family and religion.

R. A. Kartini became the woman who stood at the crossroads of Ethical Policy, women's rights, and nationalism. Well-born into the Javanese aristocracy, she was notable for her intelligence, voluminous letter writing, and for what she could not do. Despite her status and education, her family refused to let her attend medical school in Batavia, or to travel and study abroad. From the age of twelve, she was secluded at home, a common practice, to prepare her for marriage. Her father eventually gave permission for her to become a teacher, plans that were abandoned when she was married off as the fourth wife to a regency chief in central Java. She died in 1904, after giving birth to a son, at the age of 25.

Kartini was an elegant prose stylist in Dutch, and devoted her energies to letter writing, setting forth frank criticisms of a world in which "We, Javanese girls, are not allowed to have ideals." She also attacked her own traditions, which meant "everything for the man, and nothing for the woman." Her refinement and strong views made her a favorite of Ethical Policy supporters, and inspired nationalists, who emphasized the messages of greater autonomy and legal equality, with all of their implications.[16]

37 National heroine: Raden Adjeng Kartini memorialized, Jakarta.

Some nationalists found her unremarkable: she was not an anticolonial rebel. Yet she represented another nationalism, that which was building communities through literacy and print. She read and commented on newspapers, journals, novels, and feminist and pacifist literature as a Javanese woman with "modern" aspirations. Letters traveled back and forth, developing circuits of connection. After she died, her letters were published and became a common reference for movements of political and social reform in the Indies as well as the Netherlands, making her a transcultural figure. Friends followed her example and established a foundation in Kartini's name to build and support schools for women. Kartini would later be declared a national heroine of Indonesia and her birthday made into a holiday.

Ethical Policy and schools were only one way to imagine change. What inspired ambitious reformers was the challenge of revering great traditions while giving them "modern form and modern insistence." Founded in 1908, the Budi Utomo was an organization that also wanted to "raise up" ordinary people, with a plan to revive monarchy and celebrate Java's Hindu–Buddhist past.

Islamic associations were widely reputed in the archipelago for their charity, teaching, and community work, and they were also a consistent connection with a wider oceanic world, as students traveled to Mecca and to Egypt for worship, education, and business, bringing back new teachings. In fact, global maritime networks were integral to colonial challenges within the Indies. A Muslim population meant an annual circuit of voyagers between the Indonesian islands and the Arabian peninsula for the *hajj* – the pilgrimage of faith for every able-bodied Muslim. Dutch transport lines vied for this lucrative transport trade, yet also kept surveillance over contacts between Arab sheiks, teachers, and Indonesian pilgrims, fearing "contamination" of political and Pan-Islamic ideas. In the 1930s, the Islamic reformist organization Muhammadiyah made plans to run ships under its own charter and religious principles, generating resistance from the monopolistic Dutch-backed companies.[17]

Commercial interests also initially directed trader Hadji Samanhoedi in 1911 to found an Islamic Trading Association to aid Muslim merchants in *batik* textile competition with Chinese merchants. The mission was quickly outgrown and the group became the Sarekat Islam, a mass organization championing an Islamic identity for the Indies.

In 1913, the Sarekat Islam ruled to accept only indigenous Muslims in its membership. It was a nationalism of a particular sort: not one that embraced all groups, faiths, and ethnicities in a country, but rather one that identified the Indies with Islam itself. This created suspicion within the Dutch colonial government, for recognition of *adat* was supposed to apply to "pure indigenous culture," not Islamic law, which was regarded as part of an Arabic tradition.

The Sarekat Islam grew as a social and economic welfare network, and the government approved its local community chapters, but steadfastly refused to recognize it as a national organization. The superb orator Haji Umar Said Cokroaminoto addressed crowds of thousands as head of the group, organized religious programs at mosques, helped communities pay bills, boycotted Chinese businesses, contested taxes, and gained a reputation for planning to exile all Christian influence and "foreigners" from an Islamic state. The nature of political nationalism was complicated, however, and Cokroaminoto also entertained cooperation with the Social Democrats and alliance with the Communist Party while struggling to maintain membership.

One of Cokroaminoto's legacies was to have as his student a young Sukarno, who in 1927 would be one of the founders of the Indonesian Nationalist Association and, after 1945, the first president of an independent Indonesia.[18]

The marking of 1945 is important, for in the 1920s and 1930s, "ethnographic" and "custom" peoples asserted claims on education, global political ties, and forms of national consciousness, but concerted political opposition to colonial regimes was still weak. It would take more than a common faith, set of political principles, or petition of grievances to shift the balance of authority. As large groups rallied, clandestine resistance movements also began to grow, and European agents reported anxiously on communist and nationalist operatives traveling a maritime circuit around the colonial world, reportedly meeting in Asian capitals like Shanghai.

The change that came was, in fact, accelerated from Asia, and came with a military blow, as Japanese forces attacked Pearl Harbor, the Solomons, New Guinea, Burma, Singapore, Malaya, Indochina, Indonesia, the Philippines, Manchuria, and China in their own bid for imperial dominion.

18 WAR STORIES FROM THE PACIFIC THEATER

In the twelfth century, the Javanese king Joyoboyo penned commentaries and dictates on lontar leaves. He left a record of tales, including a famed story of struggle between two clans performed as a *wayang*, the shadow play in which finely crafted puppets gesture in light behind screens, suggesting imponderabilities of meaning. Joyoboyo was also a prophet, and inscribed for the future predictions of the return of a righteous king and ships sailing the skies.

In 1941, the nationalist Mohammed Tharmin addressed the Volksraad in Indonesia, a consultative body to the Dutch colonial government. He invoked for the crowd the prophecy of Joyoboyo that a yellow conqueror would come from the north and drive away the white skinned buffalo, remaining for the crop cycle of maize, after which an era of prosperity would reign. Dutch officials imprisoned Tharmin, fearing the popular fervor that the prophecy could stir. One year later, Japanese forces landed in Indonesia, overwhelming the disorganized Dutch, sending them off on work gangs and imprisoning them in concentration camps. Indonesians waved small Japanese flags and lined routes under the new military command, excitedly calling out "Joyoboyo" to the imperial troops. Scholars debated interpretations of the prophecy that foretold the coming of a yellow peacock, while the nationalist leader Sukarno claimed a new era of righteousness. In prison camps, Dutch internees remembered prophecies of yellow, bow-legged monkeys. All agreed, though, that the white buffalo would be driven out.[1]

As Japanese forces invaded the Indonesian islands, General Imamura Hitoshi and the Sixteenth Army supported the vision of change, claiming common ancestry of all Asians. The Japanese empire had, after all, been expanding under a singular slogan of being the "leader, protector, and light of Asia." An ideology of *Hakko Ichiu* placed Japan as a father figure under the emperor, gathering Asian charges into a Greater East Asian Co-Prosperity Sphere of ambiguous sovereignty for peoples and political and economic leadership – or domination – from Tokyo.

There was reason to believe Japanese claims. Having warred with China over Korea in 1895 and also annexed Taiwan, Japanese naval and military forces had come to dominate East Asia. Following the violence and repression of the Boxer Rebellion in 1900–1, however, new challenges arose. Russian troops had occupied Manchuria and threatened Japanese interests in that region and in Korea, building up a fortified presence on the Liaodong Peninsula at a strategic natural harbor called Port Arthur.

Tensions heightened when the Japanese demanded a Russian withdrawal, or at best an agreement defining Japan's paramount authority in Korea. The Russian Tsar refused. In a surprise offensive, the Japanese imperial navy attacked the Russians at Port Arthur. When the Tsar sent his Baltic fleet all the way to Asia, the Japanese navy astonished the world by defeating the great Tsar in an epic battle and sending the fleet to the bottom of Tsusushima Straits in 1905. An Asian power, within memory too weak to defend itself against Commodore Perry, was now destroying a "Western" navy. Europeans in treaty ports in China watched with amazement and more than a little concern as a weakening China conceded its final tributary authority over Korea, and Japanese armies seized the peninsula for its colonial empire.

Concluding peace with a defeated Russia under the eye of US President Theodore Roosevelt, Japanese militarists established Korea as a protectorate in 1905, abolishing its military and Ministry of Foreign Affairs. Japanese colonists took over Korean lands, and Korean resistance movements launched thousands of attacks, but were overwhelmed. In 1909, Korean nationalist An Jung-geun assassinated the Japanese Resident-General, Ito Hirobumi. In less than a year, the Korean Emperor Sunjong was forced to sign a treaty of annexation, and in August 1910, the Choson Dynasty disappeared. Japanese colonial rule fell across Korea.[2]

Yu Gwan Sun was a 17-year-old girl at Ewha Women's School in Seoul when it was closed by Japanese authorities. Returning to her home town, she joined with her parents and rallied thousands of neighbors to a marketplace protest against Japanese rule, aligning herself with a nationwide independence movement on March 1, 1919. Traveling among local villages, she drew in greater numbers from around the region and indicated that she would light a beacon on a hill to give a sign for the protests to begin.

Yu is today a Korean national heroine, and chronicles glorify her actions. At the appointed time, she set out her beacon and took her place in the market to lead crowds in cries in favor of independence. Japanese police broke up the rally, killing Yu's parents and condemning her to prison. Some of the best-known pictures show her in traditional Hanbok dress, very much the student; grim prison photographs capture her determined stare against a brick wall. She continued to agitate against Japanese rule, was beaten, tortured, and finally died. Her body was not released until her school threatened exposure of her treatment to the world. Today, museums, monuments, and commemorations claim her as a patriot. Colonial rule over the country tightened, and thousands were arrested and imprisoned.[3]

Nominal cooperation between Japan and Western states collapsed in the late 1920s and Japan, breaking with the League of Nations, began to develop former German territories mandated it after the First World War, building plantation, settler, and military bases in Micronesia in the 1930s. In 1931, the Japanese Kwantung Army overran Manchuria after claiming a Chinese attack and established the puppet state of Manchukuo, with Henry Pu Yi, the last of the Qing emperors, as its head. Six years later in 1937, Japanese armies staged the Marco Polo bridge incident, seizing northern Chinese territories from the embattled Nationalist government of China and opening up full-scale war.

In Korea, all freedoms of speech, press, and organization were abolished by the Japanese colonial government, and Korean students were taught to be obedient, imperial subjects in Japanese-language schools. Family names were taken away, and workers drafted into agricultural work and labor in coal mines.

In China, offensives against Shanghai and Nanjing followed and overwhelmed armies withdrew. The Japanese seizure of Nanjing became historic for its brutality. Chinese survivors and horrified witnesses in a foreigner's zone recorded tens of thousands of women raped and killed, indiscriminate slaughter of civilians, pillage, and destruction. Military tribunals gathered records and photographs of violated women, mass graves, decapitated heads, and bound captives used for bayonet practice. Some Japanese nationalists and government leaders have tried to maintain that the reports and pictures are fabrications; sharp disputes about war crimes and apologies continue.[4]

Asian nationalists were at once horrified and awestruck by Japanese power. European states were aghast, and they had problems at home. In 1939, Nazi armies invaded Poland and Belgium and routed resistance in weeks. The Netherlands government also surrendered and headed for exile in London. The German blitzkrieg overran France in 1940, occupying Paris and setting up a collaborationist government run from the southern French city of Vichy. Japanese forces meanwhile took over French Indochina, setting up another cooperating colonial state as Communist leader Ho Chi Minh, with support from China, began to organize Vietnamese resistance to both Japan and France.

Japan's imperial armies were spreading at a staggering speed, powered by aircraft and battleships. Keeping all of this moving was oil and aviation fuel; much of Japan's came from the rich fields and refineries of Indonesia. The Dutch colonial government cut off exports in agreement with American authorities seeking to maintain their own hegemony, and Japanese military strategists accelerated their plans to move their wars out of mainland Asia and into the Pacific islands.

George Maelalo lived in a village in the Solomon Islands. He knew something of the conflicts, but in 1941, "The only war that was covered on the radio was the one in Europe. I was still in Yandina when the government started sending back all the people on all the plantations ... it was at that time that I heard that there was war in the Pacific. It was between Japan and the U.S. because Japan had bombed a place in Hawai'i called Pearl Harbor."[5]

In a tactical strike, Admiral Yamamoto Isoroku tried to destroy the American Pacific fleet at anchor, gain time for Japanese advances, and likely force the US to agree to a negotiated peace, recognizing Japanese annexations and a sphere of influence. Dive-bombing Japanese planes destroyed or crippled twenty-one fleet ships, blasted hundreds of military aircraft, and killed almost 2,500 sailors and civilians. American forces suffered a devastating blow, but major aircraft carriers were out at sea during the attack, and fuel and supply facilities remained undamaged. Hawai'i was put under martial law, Japanese immigrants and territorial citizens interrogated and put under surveillance. Some were deported to mainland internment camps as enemy aliens, and shore and air defenses in the islands were prepared against an imminent invasion.

But Hawai'i was not a Japanese priority. The focus was Southeast Asia, with its enormous labor and natural resources. As bombs fell on Pearl Harbor and the United States declared war, Japanese forces invaded and overran the Philippines, forcing the retreat of the commander, General Douglas MacArthur. Remaining forces capitulated in the largest military surrender in American history. More than 75,000 Filipino and American troops were sent on a forced "Death March" from Bataan to prison camps, with tens of thousands dying or being executed along the way. Politician and judge José P. Laurel ran a Japanese-sponsored Philippine Republic, while Communist leader Luis Taruc organized a guerrilla resistance, the Hukbalahap, against both Japanese and American colonialism.

British Malaya soon fell to Japanese forces, and after punishing air bombardments, thousands of British troops surrendered at the heavily fortified military and naval base at Singapore. Thailand and Burma were both occupied. With France and the Netherlands under the military rule of Nazi troops, the greatest threats for resupply and resistance came from Britain and the United States. Japanese forces moved to isolate the great Anglo outposts of the South Pacific, New Zealand, and Australia, bombing Australian cities, and concentrating enormous military forces within striking distance in New Guinea and the Solomon Islands. Commanders of the imperial forces drew up plans to strike towards Fiji and Samoa.[6]

The First World War in Europe a generation earlier had left little impact on the Pacific: colonial societies were challenged for resources, a German gunboat shelled Tahiti, and Japan took over Germany's Micronesian possessions, but the colonial order was not seriously shaken. The conflicts beginning in 1941, on the other hand, would change everything. Where colonial planters and governors had ruled over chiefs, villages, and towns, unprecedented numbers of foreign troops landed on beaches to set up military bases, build harbor facilities, landing strips, and supply stations. Europeans fled or were evacuated from plantations and towns. Battles ripped across entire island chains. Former colonial skirmishes and battles for outposts and control of trading ports paled in comparison to the staggering fleets of

38 Cargo and strangers: massive military build-up in the Pacific islands.

transports that landed troops, and the battleships, cruisers, submarines, and warplanes that attacked, destroyed, and sank each other off the coasts of Java and Luzon, near New Guinea in the Coral Sea, or the Central Pacific around Midway.

The conflicts are recorded and remembered in thousands of documents and memoirs of admirals and generals, marine companies, and common sailors, soldiers, and pilots, conveying distinctive experiences. Watching an amphibious assault on the Marianas island of Tinian, American Admiral Harry Hill reported, "Three regiments of troops plus a battalion with their equipment had been landed successfully at cost of only 15 dead and 240 wounded ... with so many troops ashore in a short time, we knew that our plan was assured of success."

On patrol in Guadalcanal, Japanese platoon leader Inui Genjirō wrote in his diary, "10:40, a counterattack on our front, but drove back. We didn't sleep a wink and looked in the direction of enemy's camp from dusk till dawn, but we could find neither a sign of our victory or even a small fire. An anxious night." Louis Ortega of the US navy medical corps remembers crouching in foxholes with soldiers: "With two people in there you learn one thing. Look at that sonofabitch, he's scared as hell. And he's looking at you and saying the same thing ... You knew when an air raid was coming. Every fly, bird, every insect seemed to head for a foxhole. And sure enough, soon the bombs started falling. I don't know how the insects knew it."[7]

Also reconstructed from accounts and oral histories are the experiences of the displaced, exiles and refugees, prisoners and forced laborers. These included populations fleeing the violence, gang crews building roads and bridges in jungles, and women sent to military brothels as sex slaves. It also prominently included those who did not always distinguish "between the U.S. and Japan," but found themselves in between, changing alliances as servants and agents, guides and caregivers, collaborators and nationalists with programs of their own liberation, to push out colonial rule.

The meaning of authority, and survival, were at times chaotically uncertain. One of the most striking and immediate consequences of the Pacific War was for comfortable colonial families to suddenly be living in fear and starvation, subordinate to Japanese commanders. As a young girl during the war in Indonesia, Elizabeth Van Kampen remembered the years of occupation in waves of emotion, particularly registers of terror and despair. Hiding behind roadside coffee bushes as a convoy passed, she was shocked to hear screaming and saw trucks with large bamboo baskets, "not used for pigs but for men as they were laying crammed ... all piled up three to four piles of baskets high."

As she herself was sent to prison camp she remembered the changes that had come abruptly upon her world. "Along the road sides were many young Indonesians calling us, the Dutch women and children of our transport, all sort of names, they shouted at us that they were happy that the Dutch were captured by the Japanese. Slowly tears were coming into my eyes and I bowed my head ... This was happening in Malang, the town where I had been to school, where I proudly had received my two swimming certificates, where I had walked with my friends ... where I had bought all sorts of sweets and peanuts from the Indonesian street vendors."[8]

In the camp, the women and children were crowded into dirty rooms, given small bowls of soup and starch, and watched the elderly and ill die. Some women were given kitchen work and Elizabeth was assigned to grass cutting, while a guard stood by with a whip. Boys emptied sewers and camp latrines, and night meant quarrels,

39 A world upside down: Dutch family prisoners of the Japanese.

hopelessness, dirty mattresses with thousands of bed bugs, and diarrhea and malarial fevers from mosquitoes. On good days, some of the women scratched out wild plants during their work duties and boiled what snails they could find. The upside-down world tormented Van Kampen's recollections of warm relations with servants and neighbors, and she was stunned to learn that her father's former barber was also a Japanese colonel and interrogation officer.

Everywhere, worlds were being overturned. Men were rousted from towns, villages, and camps on work duties from which many never returned. Prisoner and civilian conscripts became known as the *romusha*, over a million forced laborers, who were at times herded to ships and sent to other Japanese colonies for jungle clearance and road building, dying from starvation, disease, and exhaustion. *Romusha* from Malaya, Burma, and Thailand, and Allied prisoners of war built the infamous Burma–Thailand Railway, and tens of thousands were sent from Java all over Southeast Asia to work and die. In the camps, it was the Dutch who were now punished for their own starvation, forced to watch their fellow prisoners beaten for hiding or stealing food.[9]

The most notorious of war experiences for women were the abuses under sexual slavery. From Indonesia to New Guinea, and most famously across China and Korea, Japanese military commanders established brothels of "comfort women," to be taken for the pleasure of soldiers. Administration and politics built the comfort stations, fueled by concerns about venereal disease and spies in public brothels, and in occupied areas, resistance from local populations if soldiers assaulted women outside of military control. Commanders also feared revolt from their own soldiers, many brutalized by Japanese military training.

"Comfort stations" were built in Shanghai in 1932, board barracks with small spaces separated by hanging sheets. Men waited in lines to receive tickets and condoms. The first followers of the armies were Japanese prostitutes, but deception, coercion, and force under the military police rapidly developed to procure more women. Police could make arrests for unsubstantiated crimes and have a woman sent to a station. Some were kidnapped. Felicidad de los Reyes was a 14-year-old in the Philippines when Japanese soldiers visited her school and told her to come to their garrison. She was held in the compound, beaten, and sexually assaulted by both military and civilian men.

Where large military units occupied territories, commanders made direct requests for women to fill brothels. A majority of the tens or hundreds of thousands of comfort women were from Korea, where they were colonial subjects under Japanese rule. Others were recruited or taken from China and across Southeast Asia, including Indonesia and the Philippines. As with other labor practices, what was forced prostitution began as a business, initially handled by recruiters who placed print advertisements and set up agents to entice young women, largely teenagers.

Japanese colonial rule in Korea was stringent, with heavy taxes, labor exactions, and cultural repression. There was little work or opportunity. Kidnapping by direct force was not always necessary for starving, desperate, or dutiful girls who wanted to help themselves or their families and were promised jobs as servants, nurses, or as factory workers overseas. Some signed contracts in exchange for small payments of yen and were loaded into trucks and on boats with fear and expectation.

Pak Kumjoo was about 17 when she heard about women being recruited for factory work from Korean officials acting on Japanese orders. To her shock, she and other women were taken instead to a military brothel in China. Pak's story is a mixed tale of fear and rage, despair and defiance. "Whether it was morning or night, once one soldier left, the next soldier came. Twenty men would come in one day ... We would try to talk each other out of committing suicide, but even with that, women still did. There were women who stole opium and took it. If they took a lot of it, they would vomit blood and die ... There were also people who hanged themselves with their clothing when inside the toilet."

Six months into her ordeal, Pak confronted an army colonel, "'Do you think we are your maids and your prostitutes? How can you be a human being after making us do such things? We came because we were told we were going to a factory, and we didn't come knowing we would be prostituted.' I spat in his face. From there, that soldier said, 'It is the command of the army. The country's order is the Emperor's order. If you have something to say, you can say it to the Emperor.' Then he beat me. I was in a coma for three days."[10]

Pain, anger, and Japanese denials of responsibility after the war kept the experiences and debates alive. Korean victims began to speak out in the 1990s, and a Korean Council for Women Drafted for Military Sexual Slavery filed legal claims. Japanese government representatives protested that the brothels were the work of contractors operating without official sanction, and Japanese courts rejected lawsuits. But archives said otherwise. In 1991, researchers working at Japan's Defense Agency turned up documents that forced the government to concede that, "The Japanese military was directly or indirectly involved in the establishment and management of the comfort stations and the transfer of the women."

In 1995, Japan established an "Asia Women's Fund" for redress of claims in the form of reparations provided by private donations. However, the fund was unofficial, leading many comfort women to refuse compensation; they continued their campaigns for recognition and settlements. Survivor and activist Kang il-chul was deeply suspicious of Japanese journalists, even those who seemed sympathetic. "They want to show us weak and dying ... Especially the camera crews. They follow the oldest, sickest women around." She told one journalist, "You must show us strong."[11]

The Korean women in Asia are the best-known voices of the forced prostitution system, which spread across the Pacific from Asia to

Melanesia with Japanese military conquest. In Rabaul, the island capital of New Guinea, one former "boss boy" for a plantation, Chouka of Manus, recounts of the women in the brothels, "Some were Japanese girls, but the majority were Koreans. I was used as general labourer and cut wood, etc . . . during the day time the soldiers visited the brothels all day long."[12]

Rabaul was a tumultuous world for many New Guineans, not only because of the brothels and crowded neighborhoods, but because, like much of Melanesia, it was an uncertain terrain, shifting back and forth between American, Australian, British, and Japanese forces. Around key strategic regions in Papua New Guinea, Chief Moll of the Ablemam people remembers renting canoes and guides to Japanese platoons, and bartering for requisitions of yams and pigs, while wondering over the disappearance of the colonial masters.

Moll, one of the "big men" chiefs of the Sepik District, can recall a life extending to the colonial era, as one of the first in his area to become a laborer in the plantation system. He traveled the foothill jungle roads as a cargo carrier for European gold miners, and held a post as a domestic servant for Australian government officers before the Pacific War. During the war, as the Japanese armies overran the Sepik, he became a cook for imperial troops, switching to engagement as a guide for Allied troops as control of islands shifted back and forth. Throughout the colonial period, he served as an intermediary with occupying authorities, and became a court chairman upon the independence of Papua New Guinea. His life story is both personally extraordinary and, historically, unremarkable: his changing alliances kept him alive, and broadly incarnated the experiences of many islanders during the Pacific War.

In 1942, as Japanese troops first began to land on the northern coast of the island, the Australian administration evacuated. The Allies were on the run as a combined American, British, Dutch, and Australian fleet was devastated by Japanese warships in the battle of the Java Sea. In the area around Moll's village, about 15,000 troops held positions through 1945. Armed resistance to the foreigners was out of the question, and like many peoples caught up in the Pacific War, Moll and his fellow villagers tried working with Japanese troops and, where untenable, fled.

In personal recounting, Moll began with a sense of his daily reality, "The Japanese would catch all these really small fish, dry them well, put them in bags, and send them over to us. We would take them out of the bags and make a kind of soup out of them." When Moll's friend Ndunjamba was nearly beaten to death for "stealing" some of the fish, however, Moll decided he could no longer accept Japanese treatment and stole off into the bush with his companions. At their village, some families remained and pretended to maintain cordial relations so that the Japanese would not suspect any mass flight or abandonment of the territory.

But the Japanese position was not secure either. Within months of establishing bases in New Guinea and the Solomons, imperial troops were faced with tremendous military offensives by Allied forces. The naval Battle of the Coral Sea in May 1942 was strategically inconclusive, but the following month, north of Hawai'i, the epochal Battle of Midway with the US navy saw the loss of four Japanese aircraft carriers, hundreds of planes and pilots, and an increasingly defensive Japanese military. Allied marines launched their major South Pacific campaign in the Solomons in August 1942, landing thousands of troops on the beaches of islands like Guadalcanal. In New Guinea, Japanese forces from the northeast battled for months in the jungle with mostly Australian troops coming across the mountains along the Kokoda Trail from the colonial capital of Port Moresby.

Chief Moll remembered that as the Japanese were cut off from their supply lines, they became more desperate. "They were trapped. So they began to raid our gardens, and steal our food, and, eventually, they began to kill and eat local people. They killed a number of men from Kalabu and ate them." Reports of cannibalism were verified after the war. Moll also recalled, however, one Japanese soldier who prevented an entire village from being massacred, "He tried to talk the other soldiers out of killing us by reminding them that we had not done them any wrong ... Finally he said, 'I will stand up with these people, and you shoot me first.'" The villagers were released.[13]

For islanders like Moll, the war meant negotiation and constant attention to changing fortunes, with the ability to deal with deprivation, commandeered gardens and catches, starvation, and ever-present danger from artillery shelling, bombing raids, starvation, traps, and mines. Japanese and Allied fighting meant tens of thousands of villagers perished from gunfire, starvation, and execution. Military offensives were times of terror, as Alfred Duna of Konje at Buna describes, "there was no time to go to your village to gather your family or collect your valuable belongings. Wife ran naked without her husband and children. Husband ran naked without his wife and children. A child ran without his parents ... All ran in different directions into the bush. All ran like rats and bandicoots in the Kunai grass."[14]

In the Langa Langa lagoon in the Solomon Islands, the artificial island of Laulasi was built up by ancient peoples who separated from the mainland, carved canoes, wove from sago palm, and polished a widely traded shell money. Priests in spirit houses called the incarnations of ancestors, who appeared as sharks rising to the surface of the lagoon. Worlds collided in 1942, as the Allied invasion of the Solomons began. American warplanes dropped bombs and incendiary clusters on the villages, killing dozens of children in a mistaken mission on a Japanese encampment. Islanders have not forgotten and are still asking for redress.

The terror of battles was facing distant, alien powers: atrocities under harsh Japanese supervision and brutal American assaults. As one villager reported, "At the finish there was not a single coconut standing ... all of us were in the holes ... the U.S. warriors were not straight in their work. They came to the shelter of ours, guns ready, and looked toward us inside. So great was our fear that we were all in a corner ... they yelled and threw in a hand grenade."[15]

Not all islanders fled the conflict; some made the fighting part of their lives. In Papua New Guinea, some 3,500 islanders filled the ranks of infantry battalions to become the Pacific Islands Regiment. In closely contested territories, where Japanese and Allied forces overlapped patrols, fighters from some regions found themselves skirmishing with neighboring villages under rival enemy commanders. Some island troops, like Fijians, were feared for their warrior reputations, and two thousand were moved to join operations in the Solomons. Pohnpeians fought alongside Japanese. Nor were all of the alliances or conflicts localized in the Pacific. A famed Maori Battalion from New Zealand was called up to fight in North Africa and Italy, and a French-led Bataillon du Pacifique also sent Kanak New Caledonians and Tahitians to the Mediterranean war theater.

In addition to the soldiers who took up arms, Allied armies were especially supported by Melanesian scouts, guides, porters, sentries, nurses, and sometimes spies. Australian military history records the importance of the "Fuzzy Wuzzy Angels" to campaigns in New Guinea along the Kokoda Track. Named for their hair and for their attentive help to the wounded, men from the villages portered supplies, moved artillery pieces, and in particular earned the personal gratitude of Australian soldiers and flyers in the field by carrying them over treacherous terrain for medical aid. As one witness respectfully reported, "They carried stretchers over seemingly impassable barriers ... if night finds the stretcher still on the track, they will find a level spot and build a shelter over the patient. They will make him as comfortable as possible, fetch him water and feed him if food is available, regardless of their own needs."[16]

In the Solomon Islands, rescues, battles, and strategies often turned on the "Coastwatchers," islanders recruited to gather intelligence and report enemy movements, often in areas where only locals could move in safety. The most noted is Jacob Vouza. Born in Guadalcanal and educated in a mission school, Vouza had already worked for the British Protectorate government when the Japanese invaded. As a scout for the US Marines, he was captured by a Japanese detachment. At times, islanders could make good use of their "native" status. As contemporaries said of Mostyn Kiokilo, a big-man of Buala, "When he first went to see the Japanese, he wore only a loincloth. He wore a coconut frond visor and a loincloth. And even though he could speak English, he acted as if he didn't know how to speak and just used sign language ... so they trusted him."[17]

This unfortunately did not work for Vouza, who was found to be carrying a small American flag in his own loincloth. Viciously bayoneted and left to die, Vouza staggered back to the American lines. The Allied victory at the Battle of Tenaru is largely credited to Vouza's warning information and the Coastwatchers became part of military history. American President John Kennedy, then a patrol torpedo boat commander in the Solomons, was also rescued by islander scouts Biuku Gasa and Eroni Kumana – and the help of a secret message carved on a coconut – after his craft and crew were rammed and sunk by a Japanese destroyer.

Of the cooperation between islanders and military, perhaps the most resounding consequences came not only from experiences of heroic feats, but also from striking transformations of everyday life, as thousands of troops and cargo ships landed on island beaches.

For some islanders in the Solomons the military – in the form of bases and camps – meant benefit owing to the enormous material

40 Island wars in black and white: Fijian commandos and Allied soldiers.

wealth of the American forces. Logistical and military support units not only rested in, but transformed the landscape, engaging contract labor to help move provisions into jungle airbases and camps. Islanders were paid and given trade items for unloading ships and carrying supplies, stretcher bearing and medical assistance, cultivating crops, logging, and helping construct roads, airfields, and buildings. They also were employed in mosquito abatement, laundry, janitorial, and garbage details. The work was hard and discriminatory, but it was also not colonial plantation slavery or indenture.

At times, islanders became involved with supporting the military community building up around their islands. In Palau, villagers donated funds to the Japanese war effort, and Tongans helped pay for a British fighter plane. Fijian Indian communities took it as a point of pride to raise money for a bomber that would have the name *Fiji Indina*. Around American bases, GIs were happy to part with surplus cigarettes, rice, generators, engine parts, and mosquito netting in exchange for bananas, pineapple, sugarcane, yams, and chickens.

Islanders also soon found that in spite of their apparent material wealth, soldiers at military bases, particularly Americans, would trade for very local items, such as carved spears and sticks, baskets, sea shells, and pig tusks. Sir Frederick Osifelo of Malaita remembered being 14 years old and "actively involved in making walking-sticks, combs, and grass-skirts. At night we went out to the reef with torches or lit coconut leaves in search of sea-shells. Sometimes we sent our stuff to Lunga with relatives working in the Labour Corps so that they could sell them for us; at other times we sold them ourselves when the warships visited Auki." Many buyers were fascinated by "traditional" arts, though few knew or cared if they had been created specifically to be sold to military personnel.[18]

One of the most profound consequences of interactions through military encampments came not from objects, but from new faces. Companies of African American soldiers from the US armed forces were trained in segregated units and suffered discrimination in rank and assignments, but Melanesians noticed this much less than the uniforms and weapons of the black men. As the future anticolonial leader Jonathan Fifi'i of Malaita recounts, "We saw the black soldiers there, and they all wore shirts, and they wore trousers. And their job was to work just like the white soldiers. Even we worked with the white soldiers ... Any kind of thing that the whites did, they could do it too."

With ideas and contacts to a world beyond colonial Melanesia, Fifi'i made friends with some of the black soldiers. In his memoirs, he recalls one who told him about education and jobs for blacks in the United States – though not in terms of American wealth and generosity. "He started using a word that was new to us: 'struggle.' You have to struggle against the Government. If you confront them strongly, the Government will have to pay attention ... then you can start moving ahead, the way we black people did in America."[19]

Fifi'i kept these lessons and continued to work around the military base. Allied forces pushed on, engaging in bloody battles in the "green hell" jungles of Guadalcanal, and "island hopping" to murderous combat for strategic positions in Iwo Jima and Okinawa. Civilians were slaughtered in the crossfire. Victoria Delos Reyes Akiyama, a Japanese and Chamorro woman from Saipan, remembers her house disintegrating in a bombardment. "My sister Teruko just disappeared. I never found any trace of her after that. I looked over to where my stepmother and baby brother were. His head was cracked open ... I am sure he was dead, but his lips were still moving as if sucking on his mother's breast."[20]

Staving off coming defeat, Japanese naval forces launched kamikaze fighters against American ships. Seaman First Class Fred Mitchell remembers trying to stay alive: "Just as I hit the deck, the plane crashed into our gun. There was a tremendous explosion, and debris was falling all around me ... I felt my arms and legs to make sure they were still there. I wiped my face and felt blood. A mate rushed by, and I asked him if my face was gone. He said it was cut but nothing serious. Then he hurried away."

The Japanese kamikaze pilots sent final letters to their families. One closed, "Living for an eternal noble cause. Protecting always our country from the despicable enemy." Many more are like that of Lieutenant Uemura Sanehisa, who wrote to his daughter, "In my airplane, I keep a charm doll you had as a toy when you were born. So it means Motoko was together with Father."[21]

Defense forces prepared the Japanese islands for an imminent invasion. American bombers incinerated Tokyo with firebombs, killing a hundred thousand people in a single evening. The scale of the growing carnage reached a final point in August 1945, as atomic bombs dropped on Hiroshima and Nagasaki. A terrifying new threshold had been reached. The Japanese military and Emperor Hirohito capitulated to an "unbearable" defeat, and a treaty of surrender was signed on the deck of the USS Missouri anchored in Tokyo Bay. For the event, the navy sent out and displayed an old, nineteenth-century American flag: it had flown on Commodore Perry's flagship in 1853.

Military chronicles, commemorations, and monuments mark the memory of the war. In the islands, it is remembered also in other ways, in songs, personal stories, and small village ceremonies. Here and there, some material traces remain: fortifications, artillery pieces, hulks of ships rusting in jungles or on the bottom of lagoons. There are also smaller fragments: helmets, old mess kits, souvenirs given and exchanged representing stories of relationships between islanders and outsiders.

Some of these are collected. About twelve miles along the coast from Honiara, the capital of the Solomons, a dirt road leads to a grassy compound built up with walls of Marsden matting, the material of wartime airbases cleared out of the jungle. The Vilu War museum is the work of Fred Kona, and is filled with guns, helmets, mortars, cannons, and assemblages of crashed planes, each attached to a personal narration. In other places, the past is formalized. On Skyline Ridge a US World War II fiftieth anniversary committee conceived a marble monument overlooking major battlefields. It draws the eye away from a nearby Japanese "Peace Memorial." Across the Central Pacific, monuments still mark histories of European, American, and Japanese wars and occupations.[22]

For the historical Pacific War that ended in 1945, somewhere away from the monuments and headlines, are the individual and shared experiences of unremarkable, yet resonant, stories. In the Solomons, George Maelalo's Pacific War began when the resident commissioner called on him, "Do not ask any questions. I cannot answer them for you. There is one thing I have to tell you and it is this, go to the armory now and get your uniforms and equipment." This was the beginning of Maelalo's war: "I heard the word soldier but I did not know what it meant ... I knew what a policeman was. But a soldier, what is he? What kind of person is this?"[23]

Four years later, in Indonesia, Elizabeth Van Kampen remembers the end of the war from the gates of a prison camp. Her world had disappeared with the Japanese conquest, rising Indonesian nationalism, and great uncertainty for the colonists. As the Dutch families straggled out, "Several Indonesian women came into our prison, looking for work. My mother, who had hidden a little bit of money, was very happy to find an Indonesian woman willing to help her, because she was too weak to do anything at all." The struggling and surviving women found each other, though not exactly as before. "Our neighbors advised my mother not to take this Indonesian woman to help her, because she had a Merdeka badge, which meant that she was against the Dutch. Merdeka stands for political freedom." Van Kampen's mother formed a trust with the woman. Van Kampen says the woman reminded her of a former servant; she also says that the woman "felt so sorry for us."[24]

19 PROPHETS AND REBELS OF DECOLONIZATION

In 1942, in northwest Papua, healer and prophetess Angganita Menufleur spoke of a new order and renewal of history. The islands and territories of Papua had for centuries been nominally ruled by the Sultan of Tidore for the Dutch Empire in the Indies, and the coastal clans subjugated to feudal exactions and plantation labor. Angganita preached against the foreign overlordship and foretold a time when the world would be upside down: trees would grow their fruit underground, black and white people would exchange skins, ancestors would return, and ships bearing cargo would bring the Papuans prosperity as never before.

Her followers danced and sang, spoke in tongues, and waited for Mansren, an old man who had long ago captured the Morning Star and been given magical powers. He had sloughed off diseased skin, become new, and, in the company of a young wife and miracle child, created the lands of Papua. His return would herald the new age.

From the 1860s, stories about Mansren and his cargo were known to European missionaries. The development of colonial trading routes through the area boosted the movement's popularity, but followers noticed that the wealth never reached them. Preachers explained that the Dutch were taking the cargo sent by ancestors, just as they had removed the sections of the Bible showing that Christ was a Papuan. By the early twentieth century, villagers were encouraged not to pay taxes or to show up for labor assignments, and confrontations were put down by force.

Angganita continued the contests. She was arrested by Dutch officials in 1942, but both she and her successor Stephen Simopyaref had reasons to be optimistic: Japanese forces landed, announcing a new Asian empire. As they pushed out the Dutch, it appeared Mansren had returned. The excitement did not last long. Angganita was taken away by the Japanese, and colonial exactions continued, worse than ever. Simopyaref organized warriors to liberate the prophetess, and to drive away all foreigners. His army united as *Koreri*, the new order, under the sign of the Morning Star.

In October 1943, they anointed themselves with magic oil, and attacked Japanese forces with hatchets, spears, and clubs. Hundreds, or perhaps thousands, were slaughtered by machine-gun fire. The remainders of the army fell back, but in June 1944, in an island a little further south, other strangers landed in the lagoon and began to build facilities and an enormous warehouse. American ships carrying tons of cargo began to arrive, and military actions pushed the Japanese back. Perhaps this was Mansren?[1]

To the east, American forces were also launching across the Solomons toward the New Hebrides. On islands like Tanna, they found villagers who had followed the charismatic leader Manehivi, and a movement called John Frum, that spoke of a new age in which whites would leave and Melanesians would acquire all food, houses, and possessions. The enigmatic "John from ..." had appeared in a previous time and would return. In 1941, missionaries found churches and schools empty as John Frum followers abandoned villages and plantations to feast, dance, and plan for the coming change.

As American forces established bases and covered beaches with ships, transports, and landing craft, the cargo landings astounded islanders – entire field compounds, food stocks, provisions and supplies, motor pools, refrigeration, and military equipment were all taken ashore. Particularly intriguing were the regular airdrops and runs of supply planes, and Tannese began to clear spaces to attract their own planes, building replicas from wood and coconut fiber and cutting semblances of runways through the jungle.

Such movements long fascinated Westerners, who found them irrational and puzzling. Popular accounts drew on thinking as old as the death of James Cook: "natives" thinking white men are gods. Collectively, the movements were called "cargo cults," and they were less about deities than popular responses across generations and Pacific territories to colonial conditions and changing political circumstances.

41 Waiting for the return: followers of John Frum drill on Tanna Island, Vanuatu.

From the 1880s, the prophet-priest Navosavakadua had led a movement predicting cataclysmic change in Fiji, and the 1919 "Vailala Madness" of the Papuan Gulf featured ecstatic followers and prophesized a ghost steamer piloted by ancestors returning with cargo. Mansren and John Frum came out of known traditions. All of the movements had elements that were millenarian and at times apocalyptic, focusing on a returning figure or ancestor, with promises of a new era of unbounded prosperity in which the existing world is upended and believing communities restored to their rightful places. None were merely spiritual or concerned with salvation, cosmology, and doctrine. All offered explanations of colonial society, industrial goods, and islander poverty, and had plans to acquire wealth.

They wove together intricate local beliefs with elements from Christian missions, and rites and practices that mimicked and appropriated the behavior of powerful strangers, constantly adapting to the times. During the Pacific War, this meant an emphasis on military drill, sitting in chairs around tables, signing documents, and building boat landings and air strips. Most notable, in a mix of expectation, religious faith, and lookout duty, were endless days staring at the horizon for signs of something.[2]

The movements continued to develop through the postwar period, and some, like the John Frum community, are world renowned, thanks to soldiers and anthropologists. Questioned about the odd waiting for John Frum, Tannese simply ask Christians when Jesus is supposed to return. The impact of the movements was never limited to yearning. Angganita and her followers rebelled against taxation and plantation labor, and John Frum followers abandoned their churches and fields. Simopyaref organized a disciplined, if overmatched, military force under the sign of the Morning Star. Islanders created unique institutions to challenge European rule and communities of believers overlapped with developing trade unions and customary native councils.

As the war ended on the island of Malaita in the Solomons, Jonathan Fifi'i was one who wanted change. He knew the preachings of Noto'i, a prophet with visions of a great cataclysm. The war certainly brought that, but Fifi'i had more than spiritual questions. He had thought himself a well-regarded member of the Labor Corps serving American military bases until the black *nigiru* soldiers made him see how poorly paid and treated he was. They wore uniforms, where his clothes were torn off by British colonial officials, who told him that "natives" wear only loincloths. The trade goods he received as gifts from soldiers were worth more than his tiny pay, and officials confiscated them all.

Fifi'i and his companions Nori and Aliki Nono'oohimae complained to Major Sandars, the British commander. Nori talked about pay, education, and the right to sit with Europeans: "other black people aren't treated like dirt, the way we are." Sandars tried to be diplomatic, "If you want to learn how to organize a union so you can bargain for higher wages, I can show you how to go about it. I'll help you." But Fifi'i noted, "He acted as if all we wanted was higher wages."

The question was no longer about being a plantation worker or laborer after the war. Fifi'i wanted power for the chiefs, and representatives "to speak for our land." He told Sandars, "You come and hold courts and judge cases. But ... you don't know the laws of our customs. So you go against our custom."

The three men formed Maasina Rule – from a word for brotherhood – an organization dissatisfied with colonial government, and staged acts of disobedience to work demands, taxes, and new codes and rules. Europeans called it "Marching Rule," because of its threatening, disciplined character, and planters rumored it was "Marxian Rule," a communist plot led by Australian radicals. Though not connected to international communism, Maasina Rule did send out "patrols" to raise funds with a plan to buy lands for Malaitan people and improve their housing, education, and medical care.

Islands were divided into districts headed by chiefs and, most critically, charged with compiling local genealogies, customs, folklore, titles, and histories, so that a society could be rebuilt on the laws and traditions of the ancestors. Some villages and towns were surrounded by fences and gates and guards posted, leading to confrontations with colonial police.[3]

Mass public meetings attracting thousands were forums for unrolling initiatives to take over native courts and cases, and to push for higher standards of living and more political freedoms, even if independence itself was still too risky a demand. The British colonial government responded with attempts to persuade, threaten, and intimidate, and then in 1947 arrested the Maasina Rule leaders. Most were sentenced to years of hard labor, but the disobedience campaigns and tax boycotts continued. Thousands of arrests did not break the movement, and in 1951, the British government began to negotiate with the leaders in prison. Later the same year the Maasina Rule leaders were released, with a deal for a Malaitan Congress and self-government, with the incorporation of custom rule.

Conflicts over differing traditions and agitation for self-rule also manifested themselves in Southeast Asia, in one incident, through the singular figure of a young girl. Maria Hertogh was born in Bandung, Java, the daughter of a Dutch Catholic military man and a Eurasian mother, giving her elements of a European and Malay heritage. During the Pacific War, her parents were interned by the Japanese, and Maria lived with a family friend, Aminah binte Mohammed, a Muslim Malay woman from Java, who raised her from 1943. At the war's end, Maria's mother, Adeline Hertogh, could not locate Maria, finally tracing her to Singapore in 1950. Raised by Aminah as a Malay child in the Muslim faith, Maria expressed no desire to be reunited with her birth mother.

Court battles ensued with conflicting testimonies as to whether Maria had been given up for adoption or was being forcibly held. Political, cultural, and religious struggles erupted around a conflict between mothers. Maria married a young Muslim man, but this only intensified the controversy. Islamic organizations admired Maria's evident Muslim piety, but the marriage was annulled and they were outraged when she was separated from Aminah and sequestered in a Catholic convent pending legal decisions. Custody was awarded to Maria's Dutch parents and when an appeal was dismissed, riots broke out in Singapore.

Malay police hesitated to act, and the British government called in troops. Buildings and vehicles were burned and eighteen lives were lost in the violence. Rioters were arrested and condemned to death. Colonial reports emphasized the rights of the birth parents and Maria's "better" future raised as a European, while Muslim community leaders underscored Maria's attachment to Aminah and what they called insults to Islam. The incident gained worldwide attention and soon involved members of the United Malays National Organization, including Tunku Abdul Rahman, who would become the head of an independent Malaya (later Malaysia) in 1957. He pressured the government to offer clemency to the rioters.[4]

Maria Hertogh, the young Dutch girl raised a Malay Muslim, briefly catalyzed many of the tensions taking place under weakening colonial rule. She represented the possibilities of joint cultures, and also their extreme separations, as imperial subjects made demands for self-determination and claims for cultural recognition. Maria was ultimately taken to the Netherlands, where she was schooled as a European, married, and raised a large family as a Dutch Catholic. She was later acquitted of a plot to kill her Dutch husband.

The Singapore events unfolded in the context of shifting fortunes involving the British colonial government, Malay nationalists, and Chinese communists struggling for authority as European empire was losing legitimacy in an age of *Merdeka* – independence. Moves toward decolonization, self-determination, and eventual independence developed differently across decades in the Pacific, some in collaboration with colonial governments and some in civil strife and contests for power. Changes were sweeping across Asia, and the geopolitical conflicts called the Cold War had already begun, drawing all anti-colonial and nationalist struggles into disputes about whether they were communist- or imperialist-inspired.

The range of upheavals was striking and profound. The Philippines had gained independence in 1946, but as landlords returned to their village estates, poor tenant farmers with guerrilla experience rejected the old system of rents and crop taxes. The Japanese resistance Huk units became a People's Liberation Army and allied with a growing National Peasant Union, a popular movement the Philippine government branded as communist.

On the Asian mainland, there was no question of communist power. Since before 1945, Nationalist and Communist parties had waged civil war for control of China. The Marxist Mao Zedong's peasant insurgent forces grew into a formidable People's Liberation Army in the 1940s, gaining popularity and strategic advantage, and pushing Chiang Kai-Shek's rival Kuomintang forces off the mainland to Taiwan, surrendered by the Japanese in 1945. Under Mao, the People's Republic of China was established as a communist state in Beijing in 1949. Chiang established a rival Republic of China in Taiwan under a martial law government and the "two Chinas" vied for authority and international recognition during the Cold War.

Tensions were also strong along the border of a divided Korea, which had been occupied from the north by the Soviet Union and from the south by the United States in 1945. After three years, American military occupation ended with the inauguration of Dr Rhee Syng-man as president of the Republic of Korea, with a government at Seoul. At the same time, Korean communists in the north declared a Democratic People's Republic under Premier Kim Il-sung. In 1950, North Korea launched an attack on its neighbor that would drag on through three years of inconclusive conflict, draw the Americans back in, and leave the country as divided as before.

Further south, French colonial forces in Vietnam struggled to maintain their "Indochina" empire, engaging in guerrilla warfare with Viet Minh revolutionaries. Miscalculating their opponent's strength and tactics, the French army would lose the major battle of Dien Bien Phu in 1954, ending their rule in Vietnam. As the French withdrew, Americans replaced them, wary of what they saw as communist expansion. This led to the partition of the country into a South under US-backed Emperor Bao Dai, and a North under a victorious Ho Chi Minh.[5]

As the tumultuous geopolitics of the postwar period indicate, not all of the contests for independence pitted local populations against former European colonial masters, and of those many evolved into internal or civil conflicts. But imperial legacies everywhere shaped the ways that recent and ancient pasts – tradition, custom, and history – would be used for political change.

In December 1961, a New Guinea Council raised the Morning Star flag as its symbol of coming independence from the Dutch. The consequence was a military strike from an Asian state: the government of Indonesia. The Jakarta government claimed the territory for its own newly independent nation, leading to vicious guerrilla warfare and a new subjugation of the Papuan people by force.

The immediate conditions for all of this lay in a dynamic that ultimately would fail: the attempts of colonial powers to return to rule in their old territories. In 1945, British armies had landed in Indonesia, focused on disarming and repatriating defeated Japanese forces, while the Netherlands struggled with the end of Nazi occupation in Europe. But the British had concerns about their own colonies, especially India, and little interest in holding on to Indonesia for the Dutch. Throughout the war nationalist leaders Sukarno and Mohammed Hatta had collaborated with the Japanese, and in the last years secured a pledge for the independence of Indonesia from a faltering Japanese administration, which they announced in 1945, just after Japan's surrender.

Strongly pushed by the radical *pemuda* youth groups, the new leaders rallied their forces to quickly control political districts and military units, and form an Indonesian government. The Dutch clearly intended to return and revive their colonial rule and denounced Sukarno and Hatta as Japanese puppets. Some rajahs and officials who had benefited from the old patronage system supported the Dutch, but their forces were overrun as Sukarno and the *pemuda* declared a National Revolution. In late October, major violence in Surabaya, Eastern Java, took thousands of lives including hundreds of British troops. Dutch military forces were increasing, but they were forced to accept that the Revolution had popular support.

In 1946, the Dutch proposed the Linggajati Agreement, by which they would recognize republican rule on Java and Sumatra, with other islands and territories held in loose federation through a Netherlands–Indonesian Union under the Dutch Crown. The agreement was signed reluctantly in 1947, but within months had broken down and a bloody Dutch "police action" pushed most republican forces to Central Java by 1948. At the same time, the Islamic mystic Kartosuwirjo declared a breakaway Muslim theocracy in Western Java, while in Eastern Java communist leaders Musso and Tan Malaka attacked the republicans for collaborating with imperialists. Fighting on all fronts, the National Revolution leaders were captured and exiled by the Dutch.[6]

But there would be going no back to the old system. If the struggles for power within the archipelago were familiar, those in the world had changed. The United Nations condemned the Dutch actions and resolved that the Netherlands return the republican government and withdraw by 1950. Protests were registered by newly independent India, and by regional power Australia.

Nor was there support in the Security Council. The US government, in particular, paid close attention to the republican war against the Indonesian communists, and calculated a useful ally. For a Cold War American administration watching developments in Asia and Indonesia, the National Revolution of Sukarno was sufficiently anti-communist, and seemed a better opportunity for influence than a discredited European colonial regime.

In December 1949, the Dutch withdrew from Indonesia but did not leave the Pacific. Dutch colonial authorities could still imagine a role in the region by maintaining a colony in the western half of Papua New Guinea. They established themselves in that remaining vestige of their empire with a plan to build up a Dutch-advised, self-governing Papuan administration as the country moved toward independence.

In Jakarta, the nationalists of Greater Indonesia were never reconciled to these plans. In 1961, as the Morning Star flag was raised, Sukarno sent a "liberation" military force to attack both Papuan and Dutch forces.

Since the beginning of the National Revolution, Sukarno's supporters had envisioned an Indonesia centered in Java that included Sumatra, Bali, and all of the eastern territories of the former Netherlands Indies, as well as Portuguese Timor, North Borneo, and the Malay peninsula. Breakaway movements against Java's domination of politics in Sumatra, Sulawesi, and the Moluccan Islands were put down by force. The justification for integrating Papua was more contested. Melanesian culture and history back to ancient Papuan and Austronesian migrations connected east and west New Guinea together, but there was less to suggest why the forest and island peoples should be part of the Malay and Islamic world of Java.

Sukarno's campaign did not rely simply on claiming the boundaries of the former Dutch Indies. Six hundred years earlier, in 1365, the poet Prapanca had written an epic eulogy to the Javanese empire of the

Majapahit. He praised a royal court of sophisticated ritual, great temple compounds, and a king reincarnated from Buddhist and Hindu deities. The Majapahit ports harbored traders, spices, and produce from all across Southeast Asia and chroniclers from the time recorded vast populations and dazzling entertainments. Courtiers and holy men ate off of plates of gold, patronized fine terra cotta art, and presided over important rituals to bless rice harvests. Most important, Prapanca's cantos described a maritime empire of tributary states extending from the Malay peninsula, north to the islands that became the Philippines, and east to Wanin, the Bird's Head Peninsula of New Guinea.

Indonesian nationalists avidly promoted this vision and other historical contacts with western New Guinea. From the sixteenth century, village headmen were vassals to the Sultan of Tidore, and Muslim coastal communities developed with Malay homes, dress, and customs. Majapahit chronicles, and generations of maritime interaction and cultural exchange between the Malay and Melanesian worlds were now taken up by nationalists to "return" Papua to Indonesia.[7]

As Indonesian troops landed in West Papua, they were met by Dutch and Papuan forces. The United Nations enforced an interim settlement, sending an Executive Authority administration to oversee a transfer of authority from the departing Dutch to Indonesia and an eventual "free choice" vote among Papuans. As the Dutch withdrew in 1962, Indonesian officials moved quickly to replace Papuans in the government, and Sukarno threatened charges of treason and reprisals against supporters of an independent state. Troops harassed and intimidated Papuans, and the Jakarta government gave work and land concessions to Indonesian immigrants, many of them former military personnel.

When the United Nations removed its own administration in 1963, armed struggle began again, this time between the Indonesians and the Papuans. Everywhere the Morning Star of Mansren's voyages was raised, fighting broke out and Indonesian troops, exhorted by the Majapahit maritime empire tales, moved in. Militant rebels of a Free Papua Movement (OPM) took their battles to the jungle. Brutal killings and reprisals followed between Indonesian military and Papuan guerrillas, with scores of civilians kidnapped, tortured, and killed. By the time the vote came in 1969, "free choice" was a fiction, and the coerced vote allowed the Indonesian government to take full control over Papua, renaming it Irian Jaya, and claiming restoration of the Majapahit vision.

The Dutch withdrawal from Papua also altered the boundaries of the Pacific islands. That was recorded by the South Pacific Commission, a regional organization founded at Canberra, Australia in 1947 to provide coordination for technical and economic development assistance to the Pacific region. In 1962, the artificial nature of Pacific borders was made starkly clear as the Netherlands left New Guinea and resigned from the SPC. For the Commission, the Papuan peoples immediately became part of Southeast Asia, "moving a population of 728,000 outside the Pacific Island region." Historic identity changed more slowly: even after forty years as part of Indonesia, a West Papuan Presidium member, Franzalbert Joku, could still remark on "our natural habitat, the South Pacific."[8]

1962 also saw another indicative change for members of the South Pacific Commission: Western Samoa became the first Pacific Island state to declare independence. After German colonialism, the Mau movement, and New Zealand mismanagement through the early twentieth century, the postwar Auckland government had worked competently with Samoan political leadership for a transfer of power.

Decolonization was the temper of the time. The larger political forces driving change had been made clear in 1955, when representatives of restive Asian and African states gathered in Bandung, Indonesia, for an unprecedented conference to jointly oppose colonialism. At the invitation of Sukarno and with the sponsorship of India, Burma, Pakistan, and Ceylon (Sri Lanka), delegates from Afghanistan, China, Egypt, Ethiopia, Iraq, Thailand, North and South Vietnam, and more than twenty other nations denounced imperialism and declared for "world peace and cooperation," forming the basis of a non-aligned movement in the Cold War.[9]

Pacific Island states also met with each other under the auspices of their SPC colonial sponsors France, the Netherlands, Australia, New Zealand, the United Kingdom, and the United States. At the 1950 meeting in Suva, Fiji, Marcus Kaisiepo and Nicholas Jouwe of West Papua were seated beside Prince Tu'ipelehake of Tonga, Ratu Sir Edward Cakobau of Fiji, and Albert Henry representing the Cook Islands. SPC meetings were by charter "non-political," but by 1971–2 island leaders created their own South Pacific Forum for exchange on economic, resource, political, and cultural issues critical to the coming decades. As island nationalists agitated for self-determination, colonial governments promoted commonwealth plans: political independence within treaty frameworks of representative government and special trade and development agreements. Nauru, Fiji, and Tonga gained sovereignty by 1970, and Australia administered Papua New Guinea in 1975. Most of these were peaceful, administrative transfers of power, marked by flag ceremonies and ecstatic celebration in the islands.[10]

The Tongan case suggests the importance of historical memories in the Pacific, for the ending of a British protectorate in 1970 was never regarded as decolonization. Celebrated in songs, orations, and school programs, Tongan history is officially taught through the ancient maritime empire of the Tuʻi Tonga rulers, and the warrior and statesman Taufaʻahau, who united the islands in 1845, took the baptized title King George, and established a constitutional monarchy. His edicts prohibited slavery and asserted "there shall be but one law in Tonga, one for the Chiefs, and commoners, and Europeans and Tongese." Though a 1900 Treaty of Friendship put the islands under a protectorate, the monarchy continued through generations, and the long-reigning (1918–65) Queen Salote Tupou III embodied a court that patronized culture and history, supported archeological work and kept the royal genealogies intact.

The ending of the protectorate in 1970 was not an anti-imperialist moment. As one government minister has put it, "We are proud of our heritage. We are the only Polynesian country in the South Pacific that was never colonized, and that is very important." The narrative of an unbroken past remains the core of Tongan identity. This contrasts sharply with other experiences around the Pacific. As one Tongan commentator argued, "Once you remove the safeguards of a Monarchy, you no longer will have the power to stop foreigners and Big Business taking over... like the Hawaiians."[11]

In fact, Hawaiians, like the Maori of New Zealand and the Aborigines of Australia, are often cited as particularly dispossessed minorities within their own homelands. Under military rule during the Pacific War and a territory governed by Washington DC afterwards, the islands were incorporated into the United States in 1959. US President Dwight Eisenhower displayed an American flag with fifty stars, while newspapers reported wild celebrations by crowds in Honolulu and sailors stationed at Pearl Harbor. Many Hawaiians refused to vote on the statehood question and instead honored the legacy of Liliʻuokalani, the last queen of the islands, overthrown in 1893. *Famous Are the Flowers*, a song written at the time of the overthrow, seemed particularly resonant. "We back Lili'u-lani / Who has won the rights of the land / She will be crowned again / Tell the story / Of the people who love their land."[12]

The decades following statehood were characterized by the build-up of massive Cold War military facilities and the dramatic acceleration of a state-guided tourist industry. Beachfronts, especially at Waikiki on Oahu, became characterized by hotels and highrises, packaged Polynesian dance and music entertainments, and a native population pushed even further away from historic lands by American and Asian businesses.

But in 1976, efforts to restore a Hawaiian past to the islands also became strikingly visible. Far from the commercial metropolis of Honolulu, a small group in a boat crossed from the island of Maui to the smallest of the Hawaiian Islands, Kaho'olawe. This "occupation" was an illegal act, for Kaho'olawe was a training and bombing range site for the US Navy. Thousands of troops had practiced maneuvers there before heading out for Iwo Jima, the Korean War, and the Vietnam War, and the landscape was littered with unexploded ordnance. An *'ohana* – family – movement developed to protect the island, not simply demanding restoration of territory and an end to US militarism, but recognition of the desecration done to an ancestral terrain discovered to have thousands of shrines and other sacred places.

Native Hawaiian activists organized. Luana Busby explained, "The island has a lot of mana. As soon as you step on it you feel it . . . it is like a birthing spot, like a womb. The whole of Polynesia is connected to it." Appeals to culture and spiritual protection also ran through the work of philosopher and musician George Helm and had an impact with indigenous rights and ecological supporters around the world. Litigation and protests led to agreements with the military and state government for preservation and reforestation.[13]

Kaho'olawe was also known to have been the location of teaching for one of the most revered practices in all Polynesia: celestial navigation. This was tremendously important, for the revival of voyaging as sacred and historic journey as well as maritime feat of transit was about to be realized with the launching of the *Hokule'a*. A replica of a double-hulled ancient sailing canoe, the *Hokule'a* was the project of the Polynesian Voyaging Society founded in 1973 by Dr Ben Finney, an anthropologist and surfer from California, Herb Kawainui

Kane, a historian and artist of Hawaiian life and tradition, and seafarer Tommy Holmes. The canoe was built to contest the then popular ideas that Polynesians could only have settled widely distant island groups by accidental sailing, or that they had drifted with currents from South America.

At the time of the maiden voyage to Tahiti in 1976, no long distance voyaging canoe had been built or sailed from Hawai'i in more than six hundred years, and at question were the connected heritages of the Oceanian world, the traditions of ancestors who had brought human settlement, agriculture, and gods to landfalls from New Zealand to Hawai'i, from Tahiti to Easter Island. The only man known who could guide such a voyage was the Micronesian wayfinder Mau Piailug. For more than a month at sea without instruments, he navigated by the stars, the motion of the sea and winds, signs from birds, and a cosmology of moving islands.

When the *Hokule'a* appeared off the coast of Tahiti, half the population of the island, cheering and in reverence, came out to witness their own history restored. On subsequent voyages under navigator Nainoa Thompson, the *Hokule'a* also sailed to New Zealand, the Marquesas, the Cook Islands, Tonga, Samoa, Easter Island, and to Micronesia and Japan. Another canoe, *Hawai'iloa*, revived connections to the Pacific Northwest of the Americas, being carved entirely from giant spruce trees felled with sacred observance and donated by the Tlingit people of Alaska. A Pacific of "isolated" islands seemed a relic of colonial thinking and boundaries.[14]

As political regimes changed and historical pasts were reimagined, new voices began to narrate this re-connected cultural experience of the Pacific. Whereas previous generations had only known the works of great European and American authors like Herman Melville, Robert Louis Stevenson, or Pierre Loti, local authors and poets began to write back. The question of smallness was interrupted by new thinking about the Pacific, notably articulated by Tongan writer and anthropologist Epeli Hau'ofa's reconsideration of the vast, interconnected Oceanian world. Commenting on tradition, economic development, and institutional religion, Hau'ofa described populations circulating between Asia, Europe, and the Americas – manifesting the hybrid cultures of the region, speaking with eloquent and challenging voices.

Writers and artists with reputations as part of a global Oceanian literature, from Alan Duff to Sia Figiel to Albert Wendt, Patricia

Grace, and Subramani, wrote in idioms not of European representations of Pacific lives, but of their own experiences, often between worlds. Hauʻofa's ribald and ironic tales of islanders embracing and exploiting Western religion, development aid, and manners in *Tales of the Tikongs* cast comic and sobering light upon questions of who is teaching whom about the future of Pacific relations.

Patricia Grace, in works from *Potiki* to *Cousins*, has explored personal ancestry, communities facing commercial developers, family experiences from the Pacific War, and women's challenges in multi-racial lives and loves. Alan Duff earned a global reputation for his *Once Were Warriors*, the searing tale of a Maori family struggling with its own heritage, torn between past and present. Equally, Albert Wendt, in classics like *Sons of the Return Home* (1973) and *Leaves of the Banyan Tree* (1979), explored family challenges, spiritual and metaphysical collisions, and characters trying to deal with traditions and cultural identities in European-influenced societies. His figures travel between islands and continents, crossing political and cultural boundaries around not only Oceania but the world.[15]

Many Pacific island writers became known not only for their novels and stories, but also for poetry, theater, chanting, and dance. The past and present were united and embodied in their performances. As the voyages of the *Hokuleʻa* kept alive ancient practices by enacting them once again, so writers and artists employed gestures, songs, and movements as evidence to transmit heritage and identity. They sought alternative forms to "write" and make histories.

Making histories in a decolonizing Pacific could take resonant turns. One of the most expressive examples of Oceanian identity came not from a writer or artist, but from a political figure, Ratu Kamisese Mara, one of the great chiefs from eastern Fiji, and a founder of the South Pacific Forum. As the acknowledged "father" of Fijian independence, he not only led his country for decades, but articulated what he called a "Pacific Way" of acting politically with strong attention to custom, consensus, and respect for multiple cultures.

This "Pacific Way" was never a systematic program, but an approach to leadership that grew from indigenous experiences and traditions of community consultation. Formulated by a figure of the chiefly elite, it was especially effective in rallying islanders across many new states to oppose interference in their affairs from former colonial powers.[16]

As new expressions flourished, isolation and separation were things of the past in the decolonizing Pacific, but the legacies of colonial policy were not gone. Nowhere was this more starkly illustrated than in Ratu Kamisese Mara's homeland, Fiji, where the "traditional" rule of the Council of Chiefs invented by Arthur Gordon conflicted with changes in the Indian and Melanesian Fijian populations.

In 1987, ten masked soldiers in combat gear broke into a meeting of the Fijian parliament and announced a military takeover. Their leader, Colonel Sitiveni Rabuka, was already waiting in the public gallery of the hall in a suit jacket and *sulu* skirt. He got up, took an automatic weapon, and led the ministers outside to two military trucks. He was supported by a militant movement known as the Taukei that barricaded streets, called rallies, and accused the sitting government of "dispossessing Fijians in their own country." The Taukei leaders called themselves nationalists and promoted a racial politics based on fear of Indians.

The background for the coup dated back generations. Though Indian indentured labor had been in the islands since the late nineteenth century, the Indian community developed largely separated from the Melanesian Fijians who held title to all lands under the chief system of indirect rule maintained by the British colonial government. After 1931, when indenture was abolished, a new generation of Indians, born and raised in Fiji, established itself economically and politically, but without real representation. Whereas Fijians under the chiefs rallied to the British cause during the Second World War, "Indo-Fijians" led campaigns for greater equality first, and strikes and protests earned them a reputation as "disloyal" to the crumbling Empire.

In 1970, Fiji became independent under the political leadership of Ratu Kamisese Mara. He envisioned a state with cooperation between the ethnic Fijians and the Indo-Fijians, but the system was set up by electoral communes to guarantee that Melanesian Fijians would have the advantage in representation. Tensions developed. In the middle 1980s, a physician and trade unionist, Dr Timoci Bavarda, won election with a politics of social justice for all groups. Though an ethnic Fijian himself, he drew strong support from many Indo-Fijians, and a wide-ranging coalition of workers, laborers, and business people. Key cabinet posts went to Indo-Fijians and ethnic Fijians who were not traditional chiefs.

Within a month, Bavarda's opponents denounced him in parliament, declaring "Our chiefs are really the guardians of the peace in Fiji," and "Fiji for the Fijians." Rabuka and his gunmen made their move. In the name of tradition, "Fijian" meant the rule and patronage of eastern chiefs. Indians, though born in the islands, were foreigners. Trade unions and workers' groups were labeled "Communist inspired" and enemies of custom.[17]

The coup stunned the South Pacific Forum and world media began to report on "trouble in paradise." News outlets blamed race hatred between Fijians and Indo-Fijians, while ignoring the crossover coalitions between groups. Complaints about chiefly patronage and favoritism from both Fijians and Indo-Fijians were labeled as examples of "ethnic" strife. Rabuka declared himself head of state of a new Republic of Fiji. Under his rule, a new constitution was approved by the Council of Chiefs, requiring that government leaders and most voting districts be ethnic Fijian.

Power sharing was not reinstituted until 1997. Two years later, Mahendra Chaudhry, the first Indo-Fijian prime minister, was elected. The Taukei movement again became active, warning of Indian domination. One year later, an unsuccessful Fijian businessman, George Speight, led a force of criminals and soldiers to Parliament and overthrew Chaudhry. Speight had lost millions on planned timber contracts when the government changed, but claimed that he was acting to protect Fijians.

The Fijian military high commander, Commodore Voreqe Bainimarama, did not support the coup, but his troops were unable to break the hostage situation or the rioting against Indian businesses by Speight's supporters for months. Bainimarama then declared martial law, arrested Speight, and fled an assassination attempt from some of his own troops before taking control himself. A caretaker government, and an unending series of court challenges and shifting cabinets continued to characterize Fijian politics. In Fiji, nationalism protected oligarchies, and tradition was used to enforce discrimination. The suspicion between ethnic Fijians, Indo-Fijians, and the chiefs and commoners ensured that terms like "custom" and "indigenous" continue to defy easy definition.

As the first decades of the independent Fijian state unrolled, other Melanesian islands struggled with their own appropriations of custom that pitted different politics of the past against each other. Since

1906, the New Hebrides had been ruled by the farcical joint French and British administration of the Condominium, which pointlessly duplicated almost all government offices and services for the benefit of small settler colonies. A Spanish judge who understood neither the European nor the local languages was supposed to adjudicate disputes, and rituals like flag raising and lowering had to be done simultaneously.

The New Hebrides had been hard hit by the blackbirding and slaving trades of the nineteenth century, and plantation owners who gambled with their workers' contracts were part of local history. During the Pacific War the islands were occupied by Allied troops, and the John Frum movement concentrated desires for change.

As the New Hebrides moved to become the nation of Vanuatu in 1980 under the Anglican priest and politician Walter Lini, some Vanuatuan leaders rejected independence and instead agitated for a conservative, *kastom-* (custom-)based village society. Primary among these was Jimmy Moses Tubo Pantuntun Moli Stevens, a mesmerizing orator who established his own compound on the island of Santo and urged his followers, and other islands, to withdraw from Vanuatu. He already had notoriety from opposition to the expansion of European coconut plantations and created his own flag and plans for a separate form of authority called Nagriamel, named after local plant leaves, that symbolized the people and the law. He championed village life and pig exchanges and denounced Lini and other nationalists as elite collaborators of the West, who would destroy the Vanuatuan people with money and non-island values.

Hampering Stevens' cause was his choice of allies: French colonial officials who would be happy to see independence collapse, and curiously, an American right-wing interest group, the Phoenix Foundation, that hoped to establish a free-enterprise state in the islands behind a millionaire property developer and a libertarian professor of philosophy. Skirmishing, raids, and riots followed. While French authorities hoped for the worst, Vanuatu declared its independence. Lini looked to his own neighbors for help and, to the dismay of the Europeans, Stevens was quickly routed by troops from Papua New Guinea.

The Vanuatu episode reminded Pacific Island leaders of the hazards that lay in navigating issues of sovereignty and tradition in their quests for new nations. While moving ahead with a politics that supported liberation movements in Africa and the Middle East, the

Vanuatu government adopted symbols of local tradition for its identity. The national logo was designed to show a proud warrior with a boar's tusk around his neck and a spear in hand.

The assertion of independence was evident, but to Vanuatu women's councils, so was their own absence. The poet and politician Grace Mera Molisa put a critical eye to independence: "Free: Men are Free, Women are chattels; Self-Determined: Men determine, Women go along." She wrote extensively about proud, nationalist men and abused, unequal women. She called this "The Nature of the Nation's Melanesian Values." Vanuatu showed that the very definition of independence itself was at stake in the decolonizing Pacific.[18]

Even getting to that step was difficult where strong settler populations also made historic claims to land and history. French officials had actively supported the Nagriamel secession in Vanuatu out of fear that cultural assertion and nationalist activism would inspire similar movements for change in the French colony of New Caledonia.

Not that the Kanak needed inspiration. Since the Great Rebellion under chief Atai in 1878, successive colonial governors had authorized the military seizure of lands, forcing the Kanak to reservations and marginal territories. A strict Native Code imposed legal segregation, prohibiting Kanak from entering many European areas, outlawing feasts and dances unless approved, and making crimes of "lack of respect for authorities" and failure to engage in mandatory labor on road building. Individuals were subject to arbitrary arrest, required to pay colonial taxes, and subject to a 9 p.m. curfew.

By the turn of the century, as Kanak populations declined, the New Caledonian economy was expanding, thanks to one of the largest concentrations of nickel in the world. Mining operations brought in laborers from Java and from Japan, and new settlements of Europeans, who expanded the ranks of locally born colonists who claimed New Caledonia as their familial homeland.

But the expanding colonial settlements led to more clashes with the already marginalized Kanak populations and another rebellion that claimed lives on both sides in 1917. During the Pacific War, New Caledonia was occupied by American troops. As in the Solomons, this led to new political ideas for greater rights, claims that were buttressed by Kanak veterans who returned from fighting for the Free French armies of General Charles De Gaulle.

In the 1950s, a liberal politician, Maurice Lenormand, helped rally a number of contentious political movements into a Caledonian Union that promised governance in the name of "two colors, one people," but settler enemies forced him out. A younger generation of Kanak activists educated in Europe witnessed the student rebellions of 1968 and took their inspiration from Paris radicals. Nidoish Naisseline, the son of a chief, organized demonstrations and published pamphlets denouncing "French imperialism and white prejudices," honoring the historic spirit of Atai. Other groups called specifically for unconditional return of lands and Kanak independence.

Within the movements, questions of tradition and the true meaning of a state called Kanaky were disputed. Susanna Ounei agitated with Naisseline and was imprisoned for her politics, but she also remembers Kanak meetings with men: "Every time women tried to talk, they would say it was against the custom or that it was a waste of time ... We have to fight hard to make men understand that a free Kanaky is for everyone. Not only independence for men but independence for everyone." As in Vanuatu, the complexities of a future built upon a revolutionary past were not yet fully examined.[19]

At the same time, conservative settler groups favored independence for no one, rallying around their own colonial history. They developed militant strategies to oppose any French retreat by advancing appeals to business, tourist, and farming interests. New Kanak leaders, led by former priest, sociologist, and poet Jean Marie Tjibaou, continued to push for independence. In November 1984, Kanak leaders boycotted elections and smashed ballot boxes, arguing that local patronage politics discriminated against Kanak voters. Two months later, ten Kanak men were murdered in an ambush as they drove from a political meeting. After settler suspects were arrested, the investigating magistrate reasoned that they had acted in "self-defense" and released them.

With tensions high, Tjibaou insisted on a peaceful road to independence, and took his case internationally. He discussed land issues with other Pacific Islanders, and also Native American Indian councils. He traveled abroad and made unlikely allies with farmers in the heartland of France threatened by plans for a military base, and Japanese rice planters who were being evicted by an airport development plan. But progress was slow, and in 1988, Kanak militants captured and held French gendarmes hostage. Troops stormed the

42 Nationalist challenges: Kanak villagers and French soldiers in New Caledonia.

militants' cave; three soldiers and nineteen Kanaks died. Paris finally agreed to negotiate the Matignon Accords, leading to land reforms and a future referendum on independence. Tjibaou signed the compromise, and outraged Kanak extremists assassinated him.

Tjibaou had never fully embraced armed politics. In the 1970s, he had appreciated the power of language, culture, and tradition to shape history and had organized an unprecedented festival to showcase largely unknown Melanesian dance, song, and ritual. Men and women staged their customary and spiritual lives in costumes of brightly colored printed cloth and raffia, and stark historical tableaux of giant puppet colonists. Tjibaou's forward-looking *Melanesia 2000* vision would become his politics as he sought to move ahead by embracing the traditions and history of a living culture. As around the Pacific, agitation for rights, nationalism, and decolonization intersected with assertions of cultural pride, and competing political claims on the past.[20]

After Tjibaou's death, the French government commissioned a stunning cultural center in his honor. Equally important, a follow-up to Matignon, the Noumea Accord, created local Kanak autonomy in some provinces. More, it acknowledged that long before European settlement, Kanak "men and women" had already developed "their own civilization, with its traditions and languages, in which custom, which governed social and political life, prevailed." It noted that Kanak spiritual and cultural life were realized in creative expression, and specifically asked for decolonization as a way for "Kanak people to establish new relations with France ... reflecting the realities of our time."[21]

20 CRITICAL MASS FOR THE EARTH AND OCEAN

Three hours north of Auckland, New Zealand, in the waters around Moutapere Island lies one of the most famous wrecked ships in the world. The *Rainbow Warrior* is today an artificial reef, encrusted with polyps and festooned with kelp and sea grass, the ocean home of schooling fish, fluorescent jewel anemones, and speckled moray eels. This seems appropriate for a ship once registered to Greenpeace, the globally activist environmental organization. How the ship came to be lying under more than eighty feet of ocean is a story that goes back at least to the final days of the Pacific War and engages the history of colonialism and decolonization, especially in the French and American territories.

On August 6, 1945, the American B-29 bomber *Enola Gay* passed over the Japanese city of Hiroshima and dropped a single weapon, the "Little Boy." As the atomic bomb exploded, some 70,000 Japanese were instantly killed and a square mile of the city incinerated. Much more of the city went up in flames and as many as 140,000 people staggered out with trauma and injuries, dying in the next few months. The blast collapsed buildings, melted steel, and left shadows on stone buildings where passers-by had been instantly vaporized. Survivors were left with disfiguring burns. The atomic bomb also brought something never seen before in warfare, with the power to terrify across generations: radiation sickness, and a growing documented record of leukemia, cancer tumors, birth defects, and deformities, some immediate, some developing over the course of years.[1]

The power of atomic weapons was immediately recognized and feared around the world, and the consequences of their use was evident to occupying forces in Hiroshima and in Nagasaki, where a second bomb was dropped on August 9th. But as the Pacific War officially ended, American military and atomic scientists argued that there had never been a "controlled" test of the weapons, and no knowledge of their effects on naval forces in the open ocean.

A little less than a year after the bombing of Hiroshima, in the summer of 1946, the US Navy moved Operation Crossroads, an enormous fleet of warships, target vessels, and transports with scientists, dignitaries, media, sailors, and technical equipment into the Marshall Islands. The Marshalls were becoming a US Trust Territory, and with the authority of a colonial power, the navy designated the Bikini Atoll as an optimum protected anchorage, largely "uninhabited," for its testing. The military governor of the atoll visited the islanders after church and asked them to "temporarily" leave, "for the good of mankind and to end all world wars." King Juda agreed on behalf of his people.

The 167 Bikini residents were moved to Rongerik Atoll, which seemed ideal to the navy, as it actually was uninhabited. For good reason: the terrain was too small to collect enough fresh water, the fishing was poor, the coconuts small. The atoll was traditionally haunted by demon sisters who had power over spirits and nature. Malnourished and uncomfortable, the Bikinians petitioned for a return to their home islands within months.

By 1947 the Bikinians were near starvation, and finally convinced the navy to move them to the Ujelang Atoll, to build a new community. But the US needed more testing sites and relocated other islanders there instead. The Bikinians were sent to Kwajalein Atoll and lived in tents next to a military airstrip. They moved on to Kili, which also had no lagoon or fishing and starved again, living on transported goods and even at times surviving on airdropped food rations. Return to Bikini did not occur until 1974, when families were allowed to resettle. Soil was cleared, trees planted, and houses built, to give the community a new start. After four years, alarming levels of radiation in their bodies from contaminated fish, crabs, and coconuts, forced their evacuation again, to live scattered around the Marshall Islands and across the Pacific.

In 1983, a Nuclear Claims Tribunal was established to adjudicate for damages, medical care, personal injury, and education related

43 Global fallout: American nuclear testing in the Marshall Islands.

to the testing. Legal grievances continue, though for most of the world that history means little. Bikini is best known for inspiring the name of fashion designer Louis Réard's new bathing suit, introduced at the time of Operation Crossroads in 1946.[2]

The Crossroads blast was just the beginning of testing in Bikini. By 1954, the United States was ready to detonate a newer, more destructive technology: the hydrogen bomb, code-named Bravo. On March 1st in the early morning, inhabitants of the Rongelap Atoll, east of Bikini, were astonished to see two suns on the horizon. At the Bravo blast site, a cloud rose more than twenty miles into the atmosphere and the concussion generated fiery winds that battered the surrounding islands at hundreds of miles per hour. Millions of tons of radioactive sand and coral drifted over the Marshalls in clouds of ash and dust. On Rongelap, the dust covered the island two inches deep, while children played in the strange atmosphere and water turned yellow. Naval observers watched as winds pushed the radioactive cloud further into populated areas. In two days, the Rongelapese were evacuated to medical facilities, as their hair fell out and they collapsed from vomiting and diarrhea.

The radioactive debris also fell where it would create an immediate international outcry. Just outside the restricted zone, a Japanese fishing boat, the *Fukuryu Maru* (Lucky Dragon), was pulling in a tuna catch. The fishermen were soon covered at sea with the radioactive ash.

Their skin itched, and they were beset by nausea and vomiting. Returning to port in Japan, the fishermen were diagnosed with acute radiation sickness and their contaminated catch destroyed. One died and the rest remained hospitalized.

Despite the news photos of nuclear blasts in the world media, little was known about the actual Pacific tests outside of military circles, and the Bravo fallout caused a global storm of outrage. Men, women, and children a hundred miles from an explosion were sick and dying, raising tensions about the American military and occupation in Japan, Pacific Island colonialism, and the poisoning of the world's oceans. What had been a question for soldiers and debates in the United Nations was now a threat to families, the environment, and the food supply of the entire world. The "small" islands had become local places of very global concern. Government scientists issued statements on "harmless levels" of radiation, while critics publicized research on long-term illnesses, disabilities, and genetic mutations.[3]

Political resistance developed, but the testing did not stop. The western Pacific powers made effective use of their colonial authority in Micronesia and the South Pacific islands. Until 1958, the United States detonated sixty-seven atmospheric nuclear devices in the Marshalls, including twenty-three at Bikini and forty-four in the Enewetak Atoll region. In the following four years, Great Britain exploded a dozen more nuclear bombs on Johnston Atoll in the Central Pacific and a dozen in Australia. The United States ended Pacific testing by treaty in 1963.

France began its testing in Algeria, and after losing that site to Algerian independence, moved to Tahiti. From 1966, the French government exploded 46 atmospheric bombs in the Pacific, and 146 more underground at Moruroa and Fangataufa reefs. The nuclear issue galvanized island peoples across the Pacific, but direct opposition was at first difficult; except for Samoa, Nauru, and the Cook Islands, there were few independent states before 1970. That year, Fiji and Tonga raised their flags, and a South Pacific Forum of island heads began appeals directly to France to end atmospheric testing.

Governments in Australia and New Zealand were also concerned about both radioactive and political fallout from the French initiatives, and had to weigh their future relations with newly independent island neighbors, as well as their own citizens. Street protests developed in Melbourne, Sydney, and Auckland, and labor unions began to refuse the unloading of French ships. In 1972, a Canadian living in New Zealand sailed his yacht into the test site and was rammed by a French minesweeper. He was working with two antiwar Americans living in Canada, Jim Bohlen and Irving Stowe, who had formed an activist organization called Greenpeace.

New Zealand protested French policy, and in 1972 Canberra and Auckland led an appeal to the International Court of Justice to ban French testing in the Pacific, and New Zealand even sent naval frigates into the Moruroa test areas to protest and observe first-hand. The French relocated their tests underground and continued.[4]

In 1975, New Zealand opened discussion with the South Pacific Forum for a proposed South Pacific Nuclear Free Zone. Flotillas of small boats were already blocking American warships and submarines from entering Auckland harbor. The antinuclear movement in the Pacific is particularly notable because it moved politically upwards, from local activism, and then in parallel to state actions. The Nuclear Free Zone idea had developed from a People's Charter drafted at Suva, Fiji, organized by citizens' committees from the University of the South Pacific, Pacific Theological College, and the Fiji YWCA. While the national governments debated policy, the Charter and its meetings moved around the Pacific, drawing in an international network of activists. Conferences at Pohnpei in 1978, and Kailua, Hawai'i in 1981, framed greater anticolonial sentiments and established resource centers, including fund raising for medical aid to the Marshall Islands, which the United States refused to provide.

A fourth meeting at Port Vila, Vanuatu in 1983 produced a Charter that declared, "Our environment continues to be despoiled by foreign powers developing nuclear weapons for a strategy of warfare that has no winners ... we call for an immediate end to the oppression, exploitation, and subordination of the indigenous people of the Pacific." The People's Charter for a Nuclear Free and Independent Pacific indicated that French testing was inseparable for many Pacific peoples from the Kanak and West Papuan struggles, American militarism in Hawai'i and the Philippines, and environmental damage from weapons testing, mining, foresting, and toxic dumping by all nations across innumerable islands and ocean zones.[5]

As Papua New Guinea and Vanuatu declared independence, they also endorsed the principle of a "Niuklia Fri Pasifik" by 1981. The

Marshalls and Micronesian states staged symbolic occupations of restricted islands and voted for nuclear-restrictive constitutions despite intense American pressure. The anti-testing initiatives also created alliances with even broader-based nuclear disarmament groups around the Pacific. Popular movements supported each other below the governmental level. Demonstrators in the Philippines came out in the streets against American naval bases, especially at Subic Bay. Buddhist peace organizations, citizen councils, and youth groups in Japan staged rallies and easily gathered tens of millions of signatures on antinuclear petitions. There, and in Australia, townships used their local authority to declare municipalities nuclear free, putting pressure on elected officials.

In New Zealand, church congregations, women's groups, Maori councils, and labor organizations stood behind antinuclear proposals. In 1982, unions stopped work and shut down ports when warships tried to enter, and the following year, 25,000 women marched up Queen Street in the largest political gathering of women in New Zealand history. Even those who did not avow feminist or anti-militarist views were attracted to the cause by moral, religious, or personal welfare concerns. Bridget Roberts of a British women's antinuclear network reported, "Pacific women are the backbone of the movement . . . We have been moved to act – not only in support of them, but for ourselves and our own communities."

Women became the most striking voices of the movement. News from Rongelap or Bikini, regularly drawn from the clipped reports of admirals and technicians, was matched by the testimonies of Lijon Eknilang, who suffered seven miscarriages, thyroid and kidney damage, and the loss of her homeland. She described the sufferings of her community and warned, "I have come to share my experience with you because I want you to see your future – what is going to be – through me." Darlene Keju-Johnson of the Marshall Islands also spoke out: "Now we have this problem, what we call 'jelly-fish babies.' These babies are born like jellyfish. They have no eyes. They have no heads. They have no arms. They have no legs. They do not shape like human beings at all." The testimonies generated outrage and the support of women's groups around the world.[6]

In New Zealand, the government responded, declaring itself completely nuclear free under Prime Minister David Lange in 1984, a move that would cause the United States to denounce Lange as no longer an ally. The more cautious Australian Prime Minister Bob Hawke proposed a South Pacific Nuclear-Free Zone Treaty to the South Pacific Forum in 1983. The aim was to focus discontent on French Pacific bomb testing and leave flexible issues of Australian uranium mining and port visits by nuclear warships.

The treaty was signed in Rarotonga in August 1985, on the 40th anniversary of the bombing of Hiroshima. It was an impressive assemblage of Pacific states: Australia, Cook Islands, Kiribati, New Zealand, Fiji, Niue, Tuvalu, and Western Samoa all joined. But it was hardly a People's Charter. Nauru, Papua New Guinea, Tonga, the Solomon Islands, and Vanuatu refused to follow. Micronesia was not included at all. Neither France, Great Britain, nor the United States agreed to abide by any of its provisions, and the resolutions allowed individual states to invite warships to transit their territorial waters. Critics called it an "empty gesture." Supporters praised the possibilities of a new cooperative politics in the region.[7]

The incident that really galvanized the antinuclear movement and anti-French sentiment that summer was not the treaty signing, but the sinking of a ship. Greenpeace founders Bohlen and Stowe had read a Cree Indian woman's prophecy of a time when the peoples of the world would unite as rainbow warriors to save the earth. Their Greenpeace flagship had pursued that vision around the world, sailing into the firing line of whaling vessels, and escaping from arrest by the Spanish navy and Russian destroyers. In spring 1985, the *Rainbow Warrior* agreed to help relocate the population of Rongelap to Kwajalein for "decontamination." After this effort, the ship sailed to Auckland harbor in preparation for action in conjunction with an upcoming French nuclear test at Moruroa Atoll. Already, protests had begun in Tahiti and around the Pacific.

On July 10, 1985 in Auckland harbor, two blasts ripped open the *Rainbow Warrior* below the waterline. A photographer was killed and the ship sank in minutes. Accusations flew. The French government immediately denied any connection, and French journalists published stories suggesting that the ship's crew were Soviet sympathizers or mercenary supporters of Kanak liberation bent on embarrassing Paris. But French agents with forged passports were soon tracked down in Auckland and arrested. The true story came out: French military divers had planted magnetic mines on the ship and escaped by submarine. A Greenpeace office worker had been a French spy.

World condemnation was swift, unanimous, and incredulous. The French had attacked a civilian ship in the home waters of a peaceful nation. President François Mitterand forced his Defense and Secret Service ministers to resign, and Prime Minister Laurent Fabius made a meaningless promise of full accountability. Paris offered an apology and reparations, but also threatened to cut off New Zealand exports to the European Union. The agents were released to French custody and after a short imprisonment at a military base were flown back to France as patriotic heroes.

The sinking of the *Rainbow Warrior* did not end French testing, but it galvanized hundreds of movements and made the realities of colonial power and the stakes of a nuclear-free Pacific starkly visible to the entire world. When the government of President Jacques Chirac sought to revive French testing in 1995, the mayor of Fa'a, Tahiti, Oscar Temaru, organized huge demonstrations in the islands, "to show that we are the people of this country, not France."[8]

Temaru's movement drew on the inspiration of anti-foreign resistance under Queen Pomare in the 1840s, and the legacies of Tahitian nationalist Pouvana'a O'opa, a distinguished World War II veteran who had fought for Free French armies and expected colonial reforms to follow Liberation in France. When the French government instead sent Paris officials to take jobs that could have gone to Polynesians, O'opa organized strikes and became a popular politician, giving Tahitians a voice. It was taken away by a colonial government that tied him up with accusations of fabricated crimes, banned his party, and finally imprisoned and exiled him. A generation later, working against pro-Paris Tahitian governments, Temaru rallied his supporters to end nuclear testing and demand independence for Tahiti.

The independence issue was not engaged by other major powers, but the public outrage over the testing forced them to question and pressure France for a solution. The most widespread impact came in a reversal of the economic threats against New Zealand ten years before. Consumers worldwide poured French wine into streets, and companies in sensitive areas refused to do business with French firms. The proposed tests were cut short and in 1996, France, the United States, and Britain agreed to sign in favor of the South Pacific Nuclear Free Zone. The same year, the United Nations adopted a Comprehensive Nuclear Test Ban Treaty.

It was a moment of remembrance for some, as at Moutaperi Island where, in 1987, the *Rainbow Warrior* had been towed to become an artificial reef. After blessings and traditional Maori burial rites, the ship was flooded and slowly sank to the bottom. For the Test Ban Treaty, no particular leader could claim credit. After decades of forums, rallies, marches, charters, and tragedies across the Pacific and around the world, the US Ambassador to the United Nations, Madeline Albright, best captured the moment: "This was a treaty sought by ordinary people everywhere."[9]

Perhaps the lasting legacy of the Nuclear Free Pacific movement was that it engaged so many different political constituencies that somehow found common cause. The People's Charter supported antinuclear groups, but also independence struggles. For every antitesting group there was also a coalition concerned with general nuclear disarmament, military base expansions, and local sovereignty questions.

For some communities, as in the Mariana Islands, the key issue was military occupation that should have ended with the close of the Pacific War and decolonization. As it became a multi-hemispheric power, the United States maintained a dominant position in the Pacific by linking together air and seapower bases in California, in Hawai'i, at Subic Bay in the Philippines, and in the Japanese islands of Okinawa. As political pressures closed the bases at Subic Bay in 1992 and reduced the American presence in Okinawa, large numbers of troops were relocated to Guam, to buttress the already formidable naval and air force facilities at Pearl Harbor.

Around the Marianas, Chamorro residents allied with labor groups and international activists from Micronesia and the Philippines to protest the use of their islands. They saw a decision taken in Washington and Tokyo to move an unpopular military presence out of Japan by putting it in Guam. Old American and Asian adversaries, now allies, faced resistance to their continuing dominance in the Pacific islands. In Guam, much opposition was led by *maga'hagas*, eldest daughters of a clan, a term referring to a traditional strong woman leader. The contests stretched across generations. In 2007, a group of *maga'hagas* met with US Congressional representatives to protest against the expansion of naval and air force bases, and the relocation of more American bombers and nuclear submarines to the islands, along with thousands of military personnel.

The following year, Chamorro activists spoke to the United Nations. One reflected on the brown tree snakes that had stowed away during the Pacific War on US cargo ships, multiplying in the islands to devastate local wildlife. The continuing influx of American troops, chemical and nuclear hazards, political discrimination, and economic imbalance in the islands made for a pointed analogy, "more foreign snakes, fewer native birds."[10]

In the face of challenges, the legacies of Pacific activism meant global contacts for regional groups, many of them concerned with issues that overlapped political and natural hazards. Delegates for anti-militarist campaigns or medical relief in the Marshalls traveled on circuits followed by women's rights activists and environmentalists. These new coalitions took up issues ranging from land ownership and economic equality to anti-whaling campaigns and customary sea tenure.

Some groups, like the Pan-Pacific and the South East Asian Women's Association, drew on these legacies, forming across regional boundaries to advance agendas of human development and women's rights. As the recovery of Kahoʻolawe island and the anti-testing movement had demonstrated, this would be a politics of respect for the natural environment, often with reverence to local custom. In the 1990s, Suliana Siwatibu spoke of Fijian communities "that are capable of calling up from the depths of the sea pink sea prawn and turtles. The animals concerned respond to simple chanting of ancient verses." Some called this an application of tradition and folklore to cultural identity. She called it nature conservation.[11]

The politics of conservation grew to embrace new appreciations of localized sea-harvesting practices. Many were studied and celebrated. Around the Kiribati islands, coastal clans followed complex obligations on sharing fish traps and minding material and cosmological boundaries along lagoon contours and channels. Particular fish like the ray were not eaten by healers, sailors, or navigators, as they were understood to carry the spirit of Nei Tituabine, goddess of the sea and health.[12]

In the Solomons, men in canoes knew coral reefs around lagoons and mangrove inlets, and around Marovo Lagoon, generations were known for their guardianship and social interactions with sea creatures. Baraulu women from Roviana Island harvested most of the shellfish and taught collecting skills to children. For coastal fishing, entire village settlements in the Philippines gathered on shore to drag nets up on the beach or into coves. Malayan and Indonesian littorals still featured *kelongs*, the timber and bamboo fishing platforms that sat miles out in the ocean, catching fish in suspended nets and harvesting mussels.

The "traditional" world, however, was changing. Across the Pacific, many of the transformations were coded "development," as governments embraced, or were promised, revenues for building projects, urbanization, and market economies. The result was cultures in tension. This was especially true for the most famed of the sea people, the Orang Laut. Yang Asseng, of Kampung Bakar Batu Danga, spoke of an altered world for his people. "I was born in a small dugout or pau kajang. I have lived off the sea all my life but I never dreamed that the sea around me would die in my lifetime." He could remember back a half century, when "one could hardly look at any stretch of the Tebrau Straits without spotting tens or even hundreds of our tribesmen's boats floating in the water." But a causeway divided the waters, and the fish, mud crabs, and mangroves disappeared, along with most members of his clan, who gave up fishing to try and find new lives on the land.

The Orang Laut had long been called sea nomads, or sea gypsies, and some had historic reputations as pirates or "indentured defenders" of maritime routes for the sultans. In the twentieth century, they became nominal citizens of nation states, but always as marginal "ethnic minorities," mooring houseboats crowded with children and animals along beaches and lagoons, floating communities outside the interest of central governments. Children were born on the water in vessels of plank and board, covered with palm. Spaces were small and cluttered but the boat itself was only part of a world that was open to the horizon of sky, water, and light, and that moved with the monsoons and revered the deep. Hantu spirits were everywhere under water, in rocks and in the rain, all needing proper attention and ritual. Islam and other faiths drifted through communities but did not stay with the roving fleets of families and kin.[13]

Governments praised, ignored, or tried to erode these practices, calling them traditional, artisanal, or backwards, but in all cases looked to larger scale operations. The rugged underwater terrain and extreme depths around Fiji prevented it from becoming a site for shrimp trawling, but a good-sized business did develop for boats in the seas around Papua New Guinea. All of these enterprises, though, were minuscule compared to the leviathan of Pacific marine challenges: industrial tuna fishing.

Tsukiji, in downtown Tokyo, is the largest wholesale fish and seafood market in the world. Under acres of lights in the early morning, more than two thousand metric tons of sardines, mackerel, halibut, squid, eels, clams, crabs, seaweed, caviar, and other marine plants and animals in hundreds of varieties are stacked on ice and moved out every day. At the heart of the business are the famous tuna auctions, the meeting point of giant fleets depositing their catches and the buyers and chefs of Japan's supermarkets and restaurants. Fresh tuna is at the core of modern Japanese identity, the foundation for a thousand sushi bars and sashimi restaurants in Tokyo, across the country, and around the world.

As everywhere in the Pacific, Japanese fishing was small scale until the early twentieth century. In the 1920s and 1930s, the Japanese used their League of Nations mandate in Micronesia to develop commercial pole-and-line operations in Palau, the Marianas, and the Marshalls. After the Pacific War, much like earlier whaling stations, Japanese tuna fleets set up bases from Vanuatu and New Caledonia to Fiji and Tahiti. Most of the catch at that time went to American processors for canned tuna. Korean, Taiwanese, and Chinese albacore boats followed into the business in the 1970s. At the same time, Japan's "economic miracle" brought new prosperity to an upwardly mobile population and a consumer boom. Japanese fleets outfitted boats with freezers and began fishing deeper for bigeye sushi and sashimi tuna, depleting their stocks.

Changes over tuna exemplify the growth of a Pacific-wide industrial fishing business. The financial stakes have increasingly risen for the fleets. The largest fishing ships are floating factories, launched at a cost of millions of dollars. Crews make use of sonar equipment and spotter planes to sight fish schools and breeding grounds in the open ocean. The fuel alone to maintain the ships at sea can run to thousands of dollars every day, and maximum catches are needed to pay off costs.[14]

Most controversial has been the use of driftnet fishing, an ancient technique still preferred by many small boats and coastal fishermen around the Pacific. A buoyed and weighted net is floated behind a boat so that fish entangle themselves; the method is simple and can produce large catches. As employed by industrial ships towing nylon mesh up to thirty miles long, however, driftnet fishing attracted

44 Industrial fishing: tuna for auction at Tsukiji Fish Market, Tokyo.

worldwide condemnation and resolutions at the United Nations. Targeted on tuna and squid, the nets ensnared millions of other fish that were discarded as of no commercial value. The nearly invisible nets also killed seabirds, turtles, and drowned a host of marine mammals, particularly dolphins. Already under pressure for continued industrial whaling, the Japanese government announced a moratorium on drift-net fishing in 1992.[15]

The connections between tuna and politics continue, however, as Pacific Island states use economic partnerships with Asian governments to further "development." This has been critical in poorer states, for some of the richest fishing areas in the Pacific fall within the territorial waters and economic zones of the Federated States of Micronesia, the Marshall Islands, Papua New Guinea, and the Solomon Islands. To have access to those seas, Japanese and Chinese officials have made fishing agreements with local governments. Where colonial and nuclear politics are in disfavor, commercial payments and deal-making continue. But the exploitation rights and development aid usually do not go to build up local economies; rather, they generate export businesses and low-quality jobs.

In Fiji, these again are women's questions. Not the calling of the pink shrimp, but the port town of Levuka, where trucks bring in hundreds of village women every morning to leave their children at the factory gates of the state-owned tuna cannery. The rest of the day the women labor over conveyer belts, picking apart cooked and rotten fish for processing. Pay is small – "women's wages" – and many are in poor health. They are not supposed to talk, are limited in toilet visits and are fired for taking time to care for a sick child. The women are expected to meet cleaning quotas. Esiteri, a senior line worker, says, "if you haven't got the 300 kilos a day, you are laid off." The women have gone on strike, but they also do not have other ways to earn a living.[16]

As they labor for the tuna company, traditional Fijian practices and industrial harvesting come full circle in telling ways. Tuna boats supplying the factory are manned with lines and hooks needing bait, and the small fish of the ancestors are depleted in local waters for the big fish of the world's commercial markets.

In Aotearoa New Zealand, issues about fishing were also about questions of sovereignty. By the Treaty of Waitangi, Maori had historic guarantees over their own land and fisheries, but as elsewhere, commercial fisheries had gradually encroached upon these rights. In 1975, an advisory body known as the Waitangi Tribunal was established specifically to hear grievances and claims related to violations of the Treaty. Following claims and petitions, the government in 1989 transferred partial fishing quotas, shareholding in fishing companies, and cash to a Waitangi Fisheries Commission, pending distribution to the different Maori *iwi*. Three years later, a second agreement gave Maori representatives 50 percent of Sealord Fisheries and additional shares and cash. The first major settlement between government and Maori interests took place over marine resources.

The struggles in Aotearoa, New Zealand, over environment and politics were not only in the sea, but across the land. Among the most famous of Maori figures for a half century was Whina Cooper, born in the late nineteenth century in the far north of New Zealand, yet achieving some of her most lasting impact in 1975, at the age of 80, when she led a coalition of Maori groups on a march to Wellington, to protest land alienation. She was active in community politics already in the 1930s and 1940s, and in 1951 was elected head of the new Maori Women's Welfare League, focused on health and family issues in conjunction with all New Zealand women. Much of her work was dedicated to culture and history education, and she was instrumental in promoting and establishing Maori language education schools.

Already a revered figure, she became the nationally known "Mother of the Nation" for leading thousands on the 1975 Maori Land March to the steps of Parliament, presenting a petition, and calling for an end to the loss of traditional lands. Some of the Maori heads had resisted a woman leading the march, but her presence had an impact on the entire country. She remains an iconic image, a wizened, determined figure with a cane, and the Waitangi Tribunal was established that year, to hear Maori claims. Not all were satisfied. Still more radical women like Titewhai Harawira decided to also camp in front of the Parliament, arguing, "our old people are unaware of Pakeha politics and do not have the courage to meet the Pakeha and his tricks head on."[17]

The sentiment for direct action would be engaged two years later when lands of the Ngati Whatua people were put up for sale in Auckland for a development to build upper-income housing. Since the nineteenth century the lands had been sold off or claimed by the government, and Whina Cooper's associate Joe Hawke led an occupation of the area, called Bastion Point, or Orakei. For 506 days, protestors camped in sheds and trailers, growing gardens, and building a *wharenui* meeting hall to claim the spiritual and ancestral right to the land. Men took on political leadership, while women organized, spoke, and pushed against "traditional" support and cooking roles.

In 1978, the government sent 700 police and military troops to evict 222 male and female Maori and Pakeha occupiers while the country watched. Elders holding fast to the posts of the *wharenui* were dragged away, and an earth-moving machine knocked it to the ground. But the message on reverence and rights had been delivered. By 1984 the Waitangi Tribunal reached a settlement, the government apologized, and the land was restored for a public park.

In the late 1980s, the confluence of political sovereignty struggles, land tenure disputes, activist women, and protection of the environment reached a flashpoint in island Melanesia. In Bougainville, north of the Solomon Islands, the Panguna region is the homeland of matrilineal Nasioi and Nagovisi Melanesian clans, who pass land across generations through mothers and daughters, a practice recognized in local custom as "woman to woman." German imperialists came in 1885 and the Australian military in 1914. Japanese troops briefly occupied the region during the Pacific War, but were forced out by Allied forces. After the war, the island was typically neglected until prospectors uncovered a unique deposit of copper ore. The British and Australian mining conglomerate Rio Tinto began extensive surveys in the 1960s.

In the Nasioi clan system, both men and women have authority to plant and settle land, but all rights to its use must be approved by female members of the clan. In 1965, a Rio Tinto expedition team was expelled for setting up camp in Nasioi territory without seeking permission. The Australian colonial government responded with force and jailed two hundred villagers.

Four years later, along the coast at Rorovana, the local women refused to allow a Rio Tinto subsidiary, Bougainville Copper Limited, to build port facilities on their land. The colonial government set a price for acreage and palm trees, and moved to seize the land when the offer was refused. Community practices and indigenous knowledge were once again dismissed in the name of development. Riot police were flown in to protect surveyors, and arrested women who broke the cordon to pull out the company's boundary markers. Crowds clashed with police, who fired tear gas canisters and charged with truncheons. Village women massed at gates, and threw themselves in front of heavy equipment to block roads. As communities were evicted, villagers organized a Panguna Land Owners Association to protest and negotiate.[18]

Australia was the colonial authority in Bougainville, but as Papua New Guinea became independent in 1975, it transferred the island to the new nation. The people of Bougainville, who considered themselves part of the Solomons, were not consulted. Papua New Guinea built its economy on the enormous returns of the mine, which it shared with Bougainville Copper Limited; the people in Bougainville themselves got almost nothing. Bougainville islanders agitated to come out from under what they regarded as a new colonialism, and in 1975 tried declaring an independent Republic of North Solomons, but were not recognized.

By the 1980s, grievances were strong against Papua New Guinea and Australia, and anger became centered on the Panguna mine. An open pit extraction operation, the mine was a seven-mile-around wasteland of dust and mud, crowded with smoke, heavy machinery, and a company town of industrial labor from across Melanesia. Regional communities like the Nasioi lived in villages and supported their clans through gardening, small farming, and fishing.

45 In the name of the land: Rorovana women protest the Bougainville mine.

The impact was tremendous. Crimes and intimidation of women increased with the inflow of male laborers and gangs of men with no clan ties in the area. Alcohol abuse and domestic violence descended on families evicted from their ancestral homes. Children began to suffer from sharp rates of asthma and tuberculosis.

Most critically, the land itself began to die. The stripping of the watershed created landslides, flooding, and sinking. Women filed suit, but the company invoked mining ordinances that gave them ownership of all mineral rights; the women held customary titles, but the company claimed everything in the earth underneath them. The mining contract allowed the company to dump its waste in the local rivers, where, according to officials, it would be washed down to the sea and carried away by the currents. Instead, chemicals contaminated the entire Jaba River basin.

Copper and gold processing at the mine released cyanide discharge and sulphuric acid run-off as tailings and waste debris blocked channels, spilling toxic floods into the surrounding watershed. Rain forests rotted in oozing swamps, and farmlands were polluted. At the Rorovana delta, dead fish floated in contaminated water, and mussels, clams, and birds disappeared. Villagers were no longer able to feed themselves from land or sea.

In 1988, Perpetua Serero and her cousin Francis Ona formed a new, more militant Panguna Landowners Association. They protested to the company, the government, and, when available, to international journalists, asking for greater shares in mining revenues and an end to environmental destruction. Serero described the alienation of an entire society: "We don't grow healthy crops anymore, our traditional customs and values have been disrupted, and we have become mere spectators as our earth is being dug up, taken away and sold for millions." The company rejected the claims and Francis Ona rallied supporters to a Bougainville Revolutionary Army. When Serero died, Ona decided to take matters into his own hands.[19]

Ona had been a mine employee and knew the operations, including the storage of dynamite. In 1989, he launched an armed insurrection, destroying the power sources to the mine and engaging in guerrilla attacks against facilities. He was aided by a former soldier, Sam Kauona, as the rebellion splintered into dozens of armed groups. The campaign brought the deployment of police and then army troops from Papua New Guinea who fought for towns and villages and terrorized the population.

After one year, reports of human rights abuses were so damaging that the army was recalled and a military blockade of the island began. Fighting for resources and power, the Bougainville factions erupted into civil war, while Papua New Guinea closed off all aid and continued to occupy sections of the island. Women were left with starving families and sick and dying children. For the next decade they organized internationally to lift the blockade and try to restore peace.

Drawing on clan and church organizations, the Bougainville Catholic Women's Federation became active, supporting travel of women's delegations to Papua New Guinea for negotiations on peace initiatives. A 1994 Bougainville Transitional Government included a female representative, and the following year delegations from both militant and government-controlled areas of the island attended the fourth annual Global Conference on Women in Beijing, China.

Felecia Dobunaba made her Beijing appeal as the protector of a family and condemned both sides of a conflict waged largely by men. "The destruction of health and educational facilities by the militants and the imposition of sanctions by the Papua New Guinea Government created further hardship for women and children. Women were not able to go to collect food from gardens nor cultivate food out of fear for their lives. Many women and children died due to lack of medicines and facilities." She saw that women would have to take on "additional roles as peace-makers and negotiators in order to restore peace on the island."[20]

Peace conferences were held in Australia in 1995, but ambushes, assassinations, massacres, and broken promises continued. The following year, the Australian government recognized that a military victory was not possible and withdrew support for the Papua New Guinea campaign. In 1997, the PNG Prime Minister, Julius Chan, hired mercenaries from a British firm, Sandline, who had previously contracted themselves out to fight in civil wars in Africa. Protests from across the Pacific, and from some of his own generals forced him out of office. A new government, with the support of Australia and New Zealand, signed a peace treaty in 1998. An Autonomous Government was elected in 2005, with a future vote on independence.

Through that date, the fate of the Panguna mine remained undetermined. Francis Ona's troops stayed on guard around the site and resisted reopening the place that had meant so much bloodshed and destruction. After his death, his successors held their positions, though the Autonomous Government itself looked to restart operations.

In 2008, the president signed an agreement to open the mining operations to a Canadian company. The deal was not reviewed by the Parliament and the majority of revenue would go overseas. Helen Hakena, head of the women's development agency Leitana Nehan, offered a history lesson: "Women own the land in Bougainville. They own the land on which the Panguna mine is situated. For too long, men have negotiated and made arrangements about our land without our input or permission." The Women's Minister in the government, Magdalene Toroansi, was the only cabinet minister to oppose the decision. She was fired. A new generation of women and men debated the conditions for re-opening the mine. Leaders from the mine region, Joan and Linet Ona, announced, "We are not opposing the menfolk or threatening the negotiation ... all we want is to have a woman's say in every decision made." The struggle continued.[21]

21 SPECTERS OF MEMORY, AGENTS OF DEVELOPMENT

The smallest island nation in the world is Nauru, twenty-one square miles completely encircled, lying northeast from Papua New Guinea, paired with Banaba. It is an archetypical Micronesian reef island, palm fringed, yet one bearing the marks of its own history since being first settled by twelve tribes of legendary seafarers in canoes. Over the centuries, traders and beachcombers landed, and by the nineteenth century, the islanders fell into warfare after the European introduction of firearms and alcohol. A German protectorate from 1888 and British, Australian, and New Zealand mandates from 1914 built up a rich, singular mining economy in phosphates, as in Peru. A Japanese air base during the Pacific War and the center of intensive American bombardment, the island became one of the earliest independent Pacific states in 1968, but with the phosphate fields dwindling, heavily dependent on external aid and support.

In 2001, the Australian government received a distress call from international Pacific waters and requested any nearby vessels to search and rescue. A Norwegian cargo ship, the *Tampa*, came upon the floundering *Palapa*, an Indonesian fishing boat packed with more than four hundred sick and desperate passengers, including pregnant women and almost fifty children. They were, it turned out, refugees and asylum seekers, largely from wars, conflicts, and persecution in Afghanistan and Iraq.

As the ship waited in international waters, the Australian government denied entry. The captain decided to move forward anyway and was boarded by special forces of the Australian navy. The passengers were removed, and Conservative leader John Howard raised fears of "border protection" and unwanted refugees reaching Australian shores. To keep the refugees away from the continent and legal process, millions in aid went to another country – Nauru. The "Pacific Solution" was an uneasy partnership: the scheduling of foreign assistance to small island states in exchange for their becoming detention facilities – part refugee camp, part prison, for stateless peoples.

The *Tampa* group was joined by other boatloads of refugee Iranians, Chinese, and Vietnamese, as governments reviewed human rights and United Nations political asylum conventions. The dilemma of the refugees linked Asia, Oceania, and the rest of the world into debates on international "burden sharing," as states like Malaysia, Indonesia, Thailand, and the Philippines agreed to grant asylum if other countries provided their own resettlement quotas. Discussions continued as the refugees languished in guarded camps.[1]

Every crisis generates not only its own misery, but its own historical memory. Many of those memories come from conflicts, some forgotten or erased, but also relentlessly remembered by survivors. The question of Pacific refugees revived stories from a generation before, when Southeast Asian political history had become globally visible as human tragedy. After the collapse of French forces at the battle of Dien Bien Phu in 1954 and the end of colonial Indochina, American military advisors took over in South Vietnam. In an escalating conflict, the communist forces of Ho Chi Minh in the north battled the South Vietnamese for control of the entire country. In 1964, American President Lyndon Johnson claimed an attack on US ships in the Gulf of Tonkin and received congressional authorization to wage an undeclared war.

As the American presence increased, the economies of Japan, South Korea, Hong Kong, the Philippines, and Singapore profited from hosting and supplying for the military. The Australian government sent troops and New Zealand contributed a token force. Despite years of strategic maneuvers and a "Rolling Thunder" campaign of massive bombing, a 1968 Tet Offensive attack by North Vietnamese forces demonstrated that American military power was not winning the war. The conflict was widely condemned as guerrilla movements and American bombers expanded operations into neighboring Laos and Cambodia. Dwindling support for the war driven by a strong

46 Oceanic exile: Vietnamese boat people at sea.

worldwide protest movement led to American withdrawal by 1973. War quickly renewed without the Americans, and in 1975, the South Vietnamese capital of Saigon fell to the victorious northern armies of the Viet Minh.[2]

In the new Vietnam, the Communist government harassed and exiled supporters of the South to "re-education" camps, where tens of thousands were tortured and abused and many died. The American war had also destroyed much of the countryside, leaving millions to succumb to poverty, disease, and starvation. Desperate, terrorized, or fearful families in the South and in Cambodia bribed officials and smugglers for places on fishing junks and small cargo boats. In some cases, trawlers set out with hundreds of refugees, in others, small, rotten craft launched barely above the waterline. Some had objectives of reaching refugee stations in Thailand or Malaysia. Others aimed to follow straits and coastlines as far as Hong Kong, the Philippines, or Australia. All were dangerously overcrowded and minimally equipped for bare survival. They hoped to drift eventually into international shipping lanes and be picked up by freighters on their way to maritime Asian ports.

Survivors told grim tales of hunger, thirst, and sickness. All remembered storms, deadly heat, and being crammed against other terrified strangers in tiny holds and on decks. Some reported cannibalism and drowned bodies at sea from other capsized boats. Even hope of relief brought terror as told by one woman: "We saw a boat! Everybody was so grateful, we used all kinds of cloth, towel, t-shirt to wave and scream ... but when we saw it clearly we started to be afraid because there was a fishing boat with more than a dozen mean looking men, carrying weapons and speaking Thai language." The men, dreaded pirates or simply brutal seafarers recognizing the helplessness of the refugees, stole everything and abused the women. This might happen many times to one craft.[3]

Some women were taken from weeping families at sea and never seen again. Many boats drifted full of the sick and dying until wrecked on the Malaysian coast. Bidong became one of the best-known islands to become a government refugee camp with the assistance of the United Nations and the Malaysian Red Crescent Society. The refugees, especially fleeing Vietnam and Cambodia, became known worldwide as "the Boat People," and starkly demonstrated the impact of regional conflicts well beyond the borders of any nation. Government heads met to debate a humanitarian crisis that could only be addressed with international action.

In the 1970s, more than a quarter of a million Vietnamese and Cambodians ended up on Bidong Island, a singular, local place of overlapping transits and lives. Stories of flight from murderous regimes and terrifying sea passages filled news stories. The survivors and victims meanwhile began to rebuild their lives. At Bidong, refugees built longhouses, workshops, and consecrated temples and churches. Teachers took on groups of students, and families set up small markets for noodles and rice with aid agencies. Merchants traded with local fishermen and contraband smugglers in the stalls and plank sheds of "Little Saigon."

Over the years, individuals and families lived as reluctant colonists, building up transitory island communities, before being moved into resettlement lives. Bidong refugees took residence and work offers from Malaysia to the Philippines, while some were accepted in the United States. The *Tampa* survivors were also gradually resettled, most integrated into the Australian population. The camps they left behind bear witness to the desperation and resilience of the stateless and largely unwanted. The sea and their battered boats gave them visibility, following maritime routes in search of new lives.

Some of the Vietnamese and Cambodian boat people were relocated to the Philippines; this was a place of new safety for them, but one just as entangled in memories and conflicts over a north and a south as the world they had fled. In 1968, students in Manila held a protest and vigil in front of the Presidential Palace over an open and empty coffin labeled "Jabidah." The students were Moro, Muslims from the southern Philippines and part of a culture that encompassed Mindanao in the Philippines, as well as parts of Malaysia and Indonesia down through the Celebes Sea. Their ancestors harked back to the Arab and Malay seafarers who had settled the archipelagos of inter-island Southeast Asia and the sultans whose Islamic territories shaped regional trade and politics.

The students had long-standing grievances against the Philippines since Magellan and Legazpi and Spanish Catholic forces had designated the Muslims "Moros" and tried to convert, exterminate, or push them out of the islands. Famed figures like Sultan Kudarat gained the enmity and respect of the Spanish for their warrior resistance to the missions and settlements in the seventeenth century. In 1898, southern Muslim rulers fought to not be transferred to American rule, but were occupied nonetheless.

The Pacific War was marked by Japanese occupation and tremendous bloodshed between Filipino, American, and Japanese forces. An independent Philippines raised its flag in 1946, but recognition for the Muslim populations of the south was not part of the new sovereignty. Rather, population growth, land pressures, and conflicts with farmers led the Manila government to encourage Christian migration settlements and leases in the south, with favorable terms often pushing out long-standing Muslim communities.

Philippine leaders also had expansionist ambitions overseas. In 1963, President Diosdado Macapagal challenged Malaysia over control of Sabah, the northern territory of Borneo, rich in timber, oil, and cacao. Macapagal claimed that it was Philippine land dating back to the Sultan of Sulu, and established a special military unit to try and destabilize Malaysian rule in Sabah. In 1965, the lawyer, senator, and war veteran Ferdinand Marcos was elected president. He also favored an elite force invasion of Sabah, and had his commanders recruit about two hundred Tausug and Sama Muslim men for a commando unit called "Jabidah."

The recruits were enthusiastic for the recognition and chance to participate in a special military operation, but it was not until they were sent for special training on the island of Corregidor that they fully understood the mission: to battle and kill other Muslims in Sabah, and even other Tausug and Sama kin. The men rebelled, and demanded to be paid and released. The military called it mutiny, but the rebels were not arrested and court-martialed. Instead, in March 1968, they were taken out at night to a desolate airstrip and systematically machine-gunned by the Armed Forces of the Philippines. One man, Jibin Arula, escaped.[4]

Attempts to cover up the massacre fell apart and protests exploded. Official records contend that about thirty men were murdered, and some ineffectual charges were brought. Some estimates proposed upwards of two hundred victims. That latter claim was made by radical Moro intellectuals like Nur Misuari. The Jabidah massacre had at least one undeniable effect: it so outraged and catalyzed the Philippine Muslim communities that support rallied behind Misuari and a new, armed organization: the Moro National Liberation Front (MNLF).

The MNLF drew on long-standing Moro resistance traditions and anticolonial, peasant insurgencies updated with communist guerrilla tactics from all across Southeast Asia to form military units and battle government troops for land and political control in the south. A revolutionary image was championed: circulated photographs showed the MNLF fighters in their battle fatigues, displaying mortars and brandishing automatic weapons.

In the midst of the conflicts in 1972, President Marcos declared martial law in the Philippines and established an authoritarian dictatorship. He required that his portrait be displayed in schools and public buildings. His edicts required all weapons to be surrendered to the government, a position that only hardened the stance of the MNLF. In the early 1970s, Misuari could claim upwards of 30,000 armed fighters, and as the conflict escalated, tens or hundreds of thousands of civilians died in battles, from starvation, or disease.

In 1976, the Philippine government called for peace talks, while the international Organization of the Islamic Conference brokered a deal for Moro autonomy, including local control over courts, schools, and administration, with some independence in economic and security matters. The agreement was contested among different Moro leaders, and eventually caused the MNLF to break into separatist organizations. A secure autonomy agreement would be twenty years in the future, though even that would not end the claims and grievances drawn from a long, entangled history.[5]

As Marcos and the Moro nationalists clashed, yet another memory from yet another war was returning to haunt the present in the Philippines. There, on Lubang Island in 1974, an unexpected figure emerged from the jungle. He was Onoda Hiroo, an officer of the Japanese Imperial Army, and he had never surrendered.

Onoda's reappearance stunned the world, and global media descended on the story of, alternately, a loyal or fanatical soldier of the Emperor who had continued to obey orders for a Pacific War guerrilla mission given him thirty years before. He had fought after the atomic bombings, surrender, and American Occupation of Japan. He had hidden in the Lubang jungles, dismissing news of the end of the war as "a trick," and lived by foraging and raiding long past the 1964 Tokyo Olympic Games, Prime Minister Ikeda Hayato's "income doubling" policies, and the global rise of the Sony and Toyota corporations.

Originally part of a small squad tasked with surveillance and harassing the enemy, Onoda's companions either gave up or were killed over the years by police or search parties. Onoda remained on the run, reading airdrops of letters, surrender documents, and news clippings as hoaxes. Notably, what changed his mind were not official proclamations, but a Japanese college dropout, Suzuki Norio. A youth of the postwar, he had traveled to Lubang for fun, hoping to find Onoda or "the Abominable Snowman." Onoda found Suzuki so odd and harmless that he agreed to have his photograph taken. When Suzuki reached Tokyo with the pictures, the Japanese government sent Onoda's former commanding officer to relieve him of duty.

Onoda was an instant celebrity in Japan, but with an uneasy legacy. As he saluted his commander, he still wore his officer's uniform; his rifle was oiled and in working order; he declined to stand down until the old imperial ceremony was completed. Japanese newspapers and television programs praised him as a hero – but not all. For many, Onoda raised the dark legacy of Japanese militarism and glorification of war. Conservative veterans and politicians portrayed him as a loyal samurai retainer and liberal critics questioned his unthinking devotion, while a younger generation was puzzled by the old-fashioned values of a man from a history they barely knew. Filipinos on Lubang were outraged when Philippine President Marcos pardoned Onoda for the locals he and his men had killed during the war – and after it had ended.

A few months after Onoda's return, another soldier was caught in the jungles of Indonesia. But Nakamura Teruo was not an officer. He was in fact a Taiwanese who had been forcibly conscripted into the Japanese Imperial Army and had been living in a hand-made shack fenced in by bamboo. He had not spoken to another human being in twenty years. His appearance raised again the unresolved legacies of Japanese colonialism, especially when Nakamura declined to live in Japan, preferring to return to Taiwan.[6]

At the heart of "straggler soldier" debates was a confrontation about the ways Asian and Pacific countries should deal with their histories. The Japanese government's refusal to address its imperialist past continued to embitter war survivors and veterans in Korea, the Philippines, the Pacific islands, and especially China, countries that the Japanese had invaded and tyrannized under military rule. The controversies had become conflicts over historical memory. For decades already, the Japanese historian Ienaga Saburo had been pursuing lawsuits against the Ministry of Education for revising textbooks that played down Japanese responsibility for invasions and war crimes. China and Korea also had regular diplomatic feuds with Japan over official textbooks, and visits by Japanese officials to Yasukuni, a shrine they said glorified Japanese militarism. The past was far from past.[7]

Onoda himself was critical of the Japan to which he had returned, though not specifically concerning the war. He was uncomfortable for other reasons in the Japan of the 1970s and left for Brazil, where other members of his family had settled, telling the press, "people don't respect the ways of the past anymore."[8]

Onoda's departure marked a particular moment in the mid-1970s as the Pacific, Korean, and Vietnam wars stubbornly became history. As debates continued to rage about memory and regard for the past, new generations asked about the future, questioning the relationship between "tradition" and "modernity." Some Asian leaders claimed to straddle both. The Prime Minister of Singapore, Lee Kuan Yew, became a major postwar figure for leading the transformation of the island state from a British colony to part of the Malaysian Federation, and then into one of the premier independent financial and commercial centers of Southeast Asia.

A controversial and admired leader, he would become widely known for espousing what he called "Asian values" as the keys to his success, criticizing Western and undeveloped countries that did not adhere to supposedly "Confucian" precepts of thrift, hard work, filial piety, family loyalty, and respect for learning.[9] In this, he claimed to shape a dynamic capitalist future precisely by reimagining classical Asian precepts.

Other Asian states nominally adopted parts of this philosophy – particularly regarding hard work and loyalty – to control workers and drive economies. Through the 1970s and 1980s, the industrial and commercial expansion of East and parts of Southeast Asia would gradually be formulated by policy makers, government officials, and large capitalist business interests into an idea that would frame the last decades of the twentieth century: the Pacific Rim. In this "new" conceptualization, the Rim would become a state and capitalist engine of the region, effectively separating itself from both continental Asia and the developing or impoverished Oceanian islands, heralding a "Pacific Century."

Pacific islands themselves, such as the postwar US Trust Territories in Micronesia, were themselves placed under the 1960s to 1970s "development" vision of the new imagined Pacific. Governed by statistics, islands from Yap and Pohnpei to the Marshalls would be under the tutelage of a great power like the United States, seeing the build-up of infrastructure, agriculture, marine products, and tourism into a "rational" economy.

Development became the creed of a generation, though cash and market systems did not always correspond to local cultural practices in the islands. In Asia, where large labor forces and industry did take hold, the new societies came not only with economic "development," but with social changes. The Republic of Korea, emerging from war, and Taiwan, were experiencing lower birth rates, increased capital investment, and a more mobile workforce. In the immediate postwar period, Taiwan had been what the Japanese Empire had established: an agricultural colony producing sugar, rice, tea, and tropical fruits. The 1949 Nationalist government had, however, resettled there with significant reserves from the mainland, as well as large numbers of business and intellectual leaders fleeing from the Communist advances. With a cheap labor force, they encouraged exports, foreign investment, and Western patronage, and by 1962, industrial production became dominant, along with an urban society.

As the regional economies developed, companies across Asia subcontracted work for the undisputed postwar economic giant, Japan, whose Ministry of International Trade and Industry advanced the historic co-prosperity vision by leading the Pacific Rim. The Japanese postwar period saw the withdrawal of the divine Emperor and the rise of a state-guided export economy characterized by giant corporations, lifetime company employment, and the rapid expansion of material goods: a consumer society.[10]

By 1962, ten million Japanese households gathered around televisions for their entertainment and news, and the *Mai ka* – my car – was the symbol of a new middle class. In the early 1970s, regulations were necessary to regulate air and water pollution, and Japanese cities were infamous for their smog and congestion. When global oil shocks hit after 1973, jobs and businesses collapsed as the Japanese government was investigated for misused funds, corruption, and bribery. Public debates grew heated over materialism, greed, and "selfishness." The critic Kitazawa Masakuni would describe the "spiritual emptiness" of these years, and the agitation for new, or renewed, values in a changed society.[11]

Onoda captured the temper of those who looked back to an ideal of loyalty and self-sacrifice. From the early 1970s, other groups sought to limit the damage done by industry and consumerism by supporting environmental organizations. Some rallied for the Nuclear Free Pacific. In the commercial economies of Asia and the West, urban middle classes began to join coastal communities and trade unions in ecology and conservation campaigns.

Australian coalitions led actions to protect the Great Barrier Reef from industrial pollution, and organized "Green Ban" work shutdowns against building projects. Leaders of island communities championed local traditions and the virtues of village societies, present and past. Scholars and conservationists took interest in ancient resource organization, praising practices such as the Hawaiian *ahupua'a* integration of upland watershed with coconut strands and brackish and seawater fish ponds. In the midst of re-examinations of culture, development, tradition, and anxieties over a lost or disappearing world, an astonishing encounter – like Onoda's also in the Philippines – suddenly captured the imagination of the globe.[12]

In July 1971, at the very southern tip of the island of Mindanao, Manuel Elizade Jr. put down in a helicopter in a forest clearing. Elizade worked for the Ferdinand Marcos government in an office charged with overseeing the interests of the Philippines' many tribal peoples and their lands. As the Moro National Liberation Front organized and Marcos planned for martial law, he came at the request of a trapper and frontiersman named Dafal, who had met a most unusual people out in the jungle.

The group were called the Tasaday, and a few had accompanied Dafal to the encounter. They were amazed and terrified by the helicopter, as they had never seen machines. Elizade offered them rice, corn, and other field crops, but they had no familiarity with agriculture. They admired his colored beads and steel knives, and showed their own stone tools and wooden sticks. They did not speak any of the known tribal languages, and translators exploring dialects and later compiling vocabularies said the Tasaday had no ideas of enemies, or words for war.

Researchers were called in and the "discovery" of the Tasaday shook the world of anthropology. Studies suggested a people that had been out of contact with the rest of the world for generations, perhaps millennia. World media tried to present the Tasaday as a living prehistoric clan, surviving from an ancient stone age. Even judicious journalists and film crews focused on groups living in caves, crafting stone tools, and making fire with sticks. Tasaday were pictured foraging for roots and plants, and catching crabs and frogs from a stream. Major organizations like the National Geographic Society sent crews out to photograph and record the world of the Tasaday, introducing millions to the smiling Lobo and Siyus eating and playing with flowers, Belayem the spirited mimic, and naked, dusty Tasaday families clustering on rock outcroppings or leaping among vines in the mouth of a cave.

47 A world of yesterday? Tasaday people as cave dwellers in Mindanao.

The primeval Eden made the Tasaday instantly famous and world-beloved, and Marcos' government set aside forty-five thousand acres of rainforest to create a reserve to protect them. Here, isolated from civilization, was a peaceful, uncorrupted culture. But there were questions. Elizade was not only a government official, but a member of one of the Philippines' richest families. He openly courted publicity, investments, and wealthy donors for his work. By creating a reserve, the Marcos government gave itself direct control over lands known to be of interest to logging and mineral companies, while gaining significant global goodwill at a time of political turmoil for his government.

Field anthropologists found that the Tasaday did not have mythic or poetic traditions, and no middens, the refuse dumps found in most sedentary tribal cultures. As questions and requests for more investigation intensified, Elizade canceled all visits from outsiders, citing the welfare of the Tasaday, and Marcos made it illegal to try and contact them.

It was not until 1986 that outsiders once again found the Tasaday. Journalists trekked into Mindanao and returned with stories that were almost as stunning as the first encounter: the Tasaday were not real. Television crews followed, interviewing young men who said they were from the tribal Tboli and Manobo groups and had been asked by Elizade to pretend they were Tasaday. Charges and counterclaims flew as defenders and critics of the Tasaday attacked each other's evidence in books, at conferences, through lawsuits, and in the media. Supporters defended the original group of twenty-six men, women, and children. Skeptics and opponents of the Marcos regime denounced a cruel hoax in which impoverished local villagers had been hired to live in caves and act as primal peoples for the benefit of cameras.[13]

The debates have never been settled on the question of conspiracy, but consensus developed that the Tasaday were never the inhabitants of the stone-age Eden so widely publicized. Global attention faded. This allowed the Tasaday to be real, rather than simply manipulated actors in a government scheme or timeless children of idyllic nature. They were a forest group fairly separate from others, but also one that had migrated, settled, and married over generations like – and with – other clans. They were interested in material goods. Lobo made statements that the Tasaday were invented, and that they were real. Questioners seemed to want different things and he tried to earn favors from his translators.

Later visitors were disappointed or eager to point out Tasaday with cotton clothes, shoes, and wooden houses. But as Udelen's family got a motorbike and Belayem a gun, it largely demonstrated the Tasaday's own concerns; debates about plots and paradise were only one part of their own interests in a changing world.

Desires for an encounter with an authentic, unspoiled culture permeated the initial and immediate popularity of the Tasaday. It was a story as old as "first contact" tales from jungles, forests, and beaches around the Pacific dating back centuries. By the 1970s in some places it was not only institutionalized, it was big business.

No one understood this better than the Mormon community of Laie, Hawai'i. There, an 1865 missionary settlement and temple were developed along with Brigham Young University, an institution with majorities of students from the Pacific islands. Throughout the 1940s visitors were invited to communal fishing activities and treated to a celebratory *luau*. Seeking ways to put students to work and support mission activities, the elders proposed what would become a widely imitated plan: to create a Polynesian Cultural Center (PCC), a great showcase of lagoons and "villages" in which students would learn traditional arts, rituals, dances and oral tales, and perform them for visitors.

The PCC opened its gates in 1963 and was put on the Oahu Tourist Bureau circuit in 1967. An unprecedented commercial success, by the 1970s it was the largest and most profitable enterprise of its kind in the Pacific, and has been studied for projects in Fiji, Thailand, Korea, Indonesia, the Philippines, Pohnpei, China, and Alaska. The center championed its mission to "preserve and portray the cultures, arts, and crafts of Polynesia." Scholars called it "ethnographic tourism." Critics said the PCC was a "theme park." No one denied it was popular.[14]

The history of many regions of the world can be told without serious mention of tourism, but not the Pacific, in particular the islands. The Asian world shares representations linking it to many other parts of the globe: the Asia of the mysterious Orient, temples from Angkor to Borobudur, paralleling monuments of the Pharaohs, or god-kings of the Aztec and Inca. Asia is also night markets, crowded harbors, and vertiginous urban districts of glass and neon. The "Pacific islands" have a more singular and generic identity, made up of palm trees, sandy beaches, and native cultures: Paradise.

As might be expected, organized tourism in Oceania took root early in the twentieth century, as the Pacific empire developed. Actual tourist boards in 1920s Fiji grew out of initiatives of the White Settlement League, which hoped to attract investors to the European colony. Steamship lines in the following decades accommodated well-to-do voyagers making tours of colonial capitals, from Sydney and Suva to Honolulu. The Pacific War had a tremendous impact, both north and south of the equator, bringing populations of military men and women to bases on islands and atolls for months at a time, building roads, airfields, housing, and facilities. As former workers for the Labor Corps in the Solomons recounted, the presence of so many soldiers created local markets in something entirely new: souvenirs. Rare masks and artifacts favored by colonial officials gave way to the popularity of grass skirts and carved coconuts.

The extensive bombing and fighter runs of the Pacific War also left another legacy: demobilized aviation firms, and the postwar development of long-distance commercial aircraft. The 1960s and 1970s became the "Golden Age" of Pacific air travel, organized for

48 Island smiles: performing at the Polynesian Cultural Center, Hawai'i.

middle-class families and, quite often, veterans returning to islands where they had known military service.

What visitors would find at venues like the Polynesian Cultural Center would be a colorful assemblage of structures and performances, dedicated to "culture." The forty-acre grounds of the PCC were landscaped into distinct areas, each representative of a major Polynesian island group: Hawai'i, Samoa, Aotearoa, Fiji, Tahiti, Tonga, and the Marquesas.

As crowds circulated through the villages or were poled along the central, engineered lagoon, students and real islander chiefs performed songs and dances, and demonstrated local skills pounding bark cloth, fishing, husking coconuts, and making fire. Where needs in programming arose, shifting student populations took on roles as different kinds of islanders. Cultural styles, however, were fixed for each island. The reconstructions of dwellings and practices, researched from archeological and ethnographic records, were exacting, and were also intended to create a particular effect: "the Islands as you always imagined they would be."[15]

The PCC was proud of its role in "preserving vanishing traditions," yet it also froze them, carefully ignoring new tools, weapons, and habits brought by trade, and certainly any indications of colonial practices, except one: a sample missionary house and exhibit. More, the picture of preserved culture selected out other noted traditions such as cannibalism and strong taboo restrictions. This vision of culture, like the one that enveloped the Tasaday, was organized around a world of chants, native costumes, and nature-based arts. It was rich in folkloric imagery and historically void.

Centers like the PCC did play a mediating role. The founders, with some justification, saw their island enactments as an antidote to the far more generic Polynesian floor shows of many tourist hotel bars, where hula meant dancing girls and music a crooner with a ukulele. But these were not only issues of representation. Debates over tourism were always struggles over culture and tradition in the Pacific islands, and in most cases also over elemental questions of land and water.

Hawaiian activists like Haunani Kay Trask have called tourism "cultural prostitution," and attacked the "use of replicas of Hawaiian artifacts like fishing and food implements, capes, helmets, and other symbols of ancient power to decorate hotels," while criticizing the "unfettered 'primitive' sexuality" that represents Hawaiian men and women in tourist promotions. Trask offers an "understanding of life as a relationship between the spirit of the land and the people of the land, between material survival and cultural expression." The community need of a land base for the transmission of culture and religion is obstructed by Hawaiian post-statehood development, when "burgeoning tourism led to an overnight boom in hotels, high-cost condominium and subdivision developments, and luxury resort complexes."

As decolonization unrolled after the 1960s, new economies had to be built in the Pacific, but smaller islands could not compete with the industrial exports of Asian and Western states, or pay for their consumer "modernity." Even fishing was often controlled by extra-territorial powers. One of the most significant economic resources of some new states lay not in the former colonial commodities of copra, sugar, or pearl shell, but in the selling of local culture. Development agencies like the World Bank encouraged this trend, often in ways that seemed to replicate colonial policy: large loans would be granted, but mostly for hotels, airports, and roads between the two. Little went into business aid at neighborhood levels or education. Large construction contracts were ripe for bribery and abuse, and the new jobs created – always a goal – were often for low-wage service workers and housecleaners in hotels and resorts.

Not all tourism followed the luxury hotel model, and small-scale Samoan *fale* accommodations in coastal communities had some success, along with the development of eco-tourism, particularly in Borneo and New Zealand. The package tour business expanded the ethnographic vision of the Polynesian Cultural Center for tourists who were interested in their own on-site experiences. Not only did such tours move from a controlled setting into island terrains, they also catered to precisely the elements erased by the PCC: fascinations with cannibalism, headhunting, and the "savage" rather than "idyllic" representation of the Pacific.

Predictably, tourism of this sort turned away from the bronzed bodies and sandy beaches of Polynesia and concentrated in the Solomons, Vanuatu, New Guinea, and other "dark islands" of Melanesia. One operator in Vanuatu called Hawaiian Polynesian dance shows "totally commercial," whereas a "custom village" on Tanna Island was "their daily culture. That's just how they live."[16]

Such "cannibal tours" promised direct encounters with real villagers rather than performers, though the distinction was ambiguous. Already from the 1880s, villages like Tambunum on known trading circuits along the Sepik Valley in Papua New Guinea had produced artifacts and displays for the benefit of visitors. Tourists after the 1970s arrived to experience life in the bush and found that artists sold carvings to pay for things they found useful to themselves: radios, school fees, and outboard motorboat oil.

In some cases, islanders were perfectly willing to play with expectations and assumptions. Ethnographers have recorded Chambri artifact sellers sitting inside a Walindimi men's house, waiting for tourists. As one rolls a cigarette and takes out a disposable gas lighter, a conversation ensues: "'Where did you get that expensive white man's lighter?' 'A tourist gave it to me.' 'Yes, I know he did – I told him to. I told him he should feel sorry for you since you were a poor bush native who had to walk around with a big burning stick to light your cigarettes.'" At the same time, local Sepik Valley artists could also see a larger global picture: "We carve because we do not have real development here."[17]

Development was a key issue, for although tourists asked for amenities like furnished rooms and air-conditioning, it was the opportunity to see other people living without such things in forest and jungle villages that was the draw of explorer tourism. The most "unspoiled" visiting sites were thus often without means, and lost popularity with operators when they acquired utilities and services, and began to look poor rather than authentic. In some cases communities were entirely absent, having been removed or barred from occupying designated lands in order to promote another significant tourist market: nature.

The commercial potential of land- and seascape tourism encompasses rainforest treks, volcano climbs, and ocean and river sojourns in passenger boats. Dive sites are also very popular around Asia and the Pacific. Stunning emerald islands like Sipadan in the Celebes Sea off Borneo rise from coral crowns and underwater limestone caves, hosting hawksbill turtles, eagle rays, and glittering *trevally* in azure seas. The effect can be otherworldly, though tourists seeking experiences of nature can sometimes find themselves instead trapped inside politics.

Tour operators are not the only ones to know the value of foreign visitors. In April 2000, high-powered speedboats landed at Sipadan; they carried not tourist parties, but heavily armed guerrillas of the Abu Sayyaf Group, an Islamist separatist organization operating out of the southern Philippines. Eleven resort workers were kidnapped, along with ten international tourists – Germans, Japanese, Finns, South Africans, and Lebanese. The Abu Sayyaf had formed in 1991 from elements of the larger Moro National Liberation Front, pursuing Muslim autonomy from the Philippines in Mindanao.

The hostages were forced into the boats and eventually taken to Jolo Island of Mindanao. Over the course of months, they were ransomed for millions in "development aid." Some analysts found ties with the Indonesian Jemaah Islamiyah militant group, which supported armed struggle for an independent Muslim state across Southeast Asia, principally in parts of the Philippines, Malaysia, and Brunei. Others pronounced the Abu Sayyaf a straightforward kidnapping and ransom criminal organization. There was no doubt that they had international ties and that their tactics earned them enormous payouts for boats, weapons, and the planning of sophisticated operations. Another raid involved American hostages, triggering US military assistance to the Philippine government and joint military exercises involving thousands of troops.[18]

Though focused on the careful packaging of timeless cultures, natives, and natural wonders, the Pacific tourism industry was no more immune to the grievances and conflicts of the region than had been boat people, survivors of war, or agitators for ecological justice. Old claims and controversies overlapped with ancient cultures and modern politics, and tourism became both the expression of the tensions and their target.

This was true even in a place like Bali, the "Island of the Gods." Bali was settled by Austronesian seafarers and colonized by ancient Hindu Majapahit rulers, who moved from Java with the expansion there of Islam. Dutch colonizers began to stake claims in the nineteenth century and in a legendary 1906 show of defiance, the nobility of Denpassar burned their own palaces and marched into Dutch guns in their jewelry and ceremonial vestments. Japanese invasion and liberation marked the Pacific War, but Bali had always been less known for its history than its arts: the intricate, decorative work of headdresses and temple facades, the vibrant allegories of Barong dance, the dense tones and rhythms of Gamelan music, the mystical allusions of the Wayang Kulit shadow puppets, all rooted in Balinese Hindu cosmology.

The presentation of arts still permeates the Bali atmosphere, including in seaside towns like Kuta, whose other attractions are budget lodgings, surfing, beautiful sand beaches, and a famed nightlife scene. All of this made Kuta an international locale when, in 2002, a backpack bomb went off inside a club. As panicked crowds ran outside, a one-ton car bomb exploded in the street, collapsing buildings, igniting fires, and killing more than two hundred tourists and vacationers, the great majority Australian. Emergency services were overwhelmed and airlift evacuations began to Jakarta, Australian cities, and medical facilities across Southeast Asia.

Bali police tracked down members of the Jemaah Islamiyah group, piecing together phone and chemical evidence, arresting and trying a large number of suspects before convicting and executing three members. The reputed spiritual leader of the organization, Abu Bakar Bashir, denied involvement, but was convicted on a compendium of "treason"-related charges and imprisoned for a few years.[19]

The bombings came a year after the September 11, 2001 airplane attacks on the World Trade Center in New York. The small tourist enclave of Kuta became a memory site for the global "war on terror" of American President George W. Bush, supported by the Australian Prime Minister John Howard. Memorials were erected in multiple Australian cities, including the federal capital, Canberra. Kuta itself established an elaborate monument on the site of the bombings. After a disappearance of foreigner business, Kuta and its natural and cultural spectacles began to once again attract families and vacationers, now with other reasons to make sojourns in the Land of the Gods.

22 REPAIRING LEGACIES, CLAIMING HISTORIES

In 1995, Flor Contemplacion was hanged by the government of Singapore. Accused and convicted of a double murder, Contemplacion's execution set off a storm of protest in her home country, the Philippines, and resulted in a diplomatic crisis, attempted intervention by the Philippine president, and the breaking of international contracts and agreements. Contemplacion was not a known figure, nor was her crime political. She was a low-paid, overseas domestic worker with a job in Singapore away from her own family. The victims had been a fellow overseas worker and a little boy in her care. What the death of an "ordinary" woman meant to the Pacific world was a story of very old and unresolved histories.

Those histories centered on the question of labor. The transit of peoples across the Pacific is a narrative that includes legendary feats of navigation, dark records of slavery and blackbirding, and desperate flight. The nineteenth century was profoundly marked by the oceanic circuits that brought Chinese laborers to California and Australia, Japanese, Koreans, and Filipinos to Hawai'i, and Indians to Fiji to work in mines, or on railroads and plantations. The twentieth century saw Javanese slave labor populations working in gangs across Southeast Asia, and the postwar economic migration of workers into factories, sweatshops, and domestic labor jobs.

The movement of workers has long characterized a Pacific world whose economies and cultures are not contained within territorial borders but often extend far overseas. Chinese communities, often marked by the sights and sounds of a local "Chinatown," are familiar in almost every part of the globe. Some are little more than ethnic enclaves, restaurants, and small shops. Others have earned reputations – often exaggerated – as neighborhoods for wealthy merchants. In Malaysia, Indonesia, and Singapore, they are a dominant presence, and at times targets of nativist, anti-foreign violence.[1]

There are also hierarchies within communities themselves. In Malaysia and Hong Kong, middle-class Chinese families can often have domestic help, young women from poorer regions in Eastern Indonesia. Some are driven by a desire to help their families, as Susana, who told a researcher about an earthquake in her home province: "Our house was destroyed. I wanted to go and earn money ... I met a cousin who had been a domestic worker... that was how it started and then I made up my mind to travel overseas." One young woman, Rika, liked traveling because "who knows we may meet someone new" and was drawn by the chance to see the world beyond her village.

Many others found work abroad trying. Netti reported, "one day my parents said that many had commented on my going away, saying that I had sold myself into prostitution." It was not an unwarranted fear; stories circulated widely through villages and towns of young women being held captive by syndicates in cities like Kuala Lumpur and trafficked as sex slaves. Usually, they were picked up by recruiters who offered jobs as nannies or housecleaners, had their documents stolen, were sometimes drugged, and locked into guarded, urban brothels.

Even where the work was legitimate it could be like indentured labor. Women found their jobs overloaded, some were beaten, and many faced the abuse of families. News reports followed the stories of women who were held for years or gravely injured trying to escape by jumping from apartment buildings.

News and criminal investigations followed workplaces all around the Pacific. In American Samoa, the owner of a clothing factory was charged with "physical beatings, inhumane conditions, and forced labor" of his virtually prisoner Vietnamese and Chinese employees. The workers were not paid or were charged "fees" from their paychecks, locked in and starved for days at a time. Those that resisted were beaten by security guards. The clothing was made by a Korean contractor and sent to buyers in Los Angeles.[2]

But where poverty was widespread, danger and risk did not keep poorer Pacific countries from developing working populations abroad. In states like the Philippines overseas workers became part of national identity for contributing directly back to the home country through a remittance economy. In this, Filipino workers on extended contracts, notably in the United States, the Middle East, Malaysia, and Canada, sent money back to family in the islands. The savings generated by their work abroad became part of the Philippine economy. Immigration checkpoints in Manila airport have special lines for overseas workers, and media accounts relate the pride and the pressures of these workers who have some of the populist status of folk heroes.[3]

As president then dictator of the Philippines, Ferdinand Marcos encouraged a romantic and loyal definition of Filipino character, speaking of Filipinos living abroad as *balikbayan*, from Tagalog words for sentimental attachment to home and extended family. They represented both the imagined vision of traditional Filipino kinship and culture while also living in a world with access to Western consumer goods, salaries, and education that Filipinos presumably wanted but did not have. Developing that vision at home became part of national policy.

But Marcos also built a personality cult around his rule, gave favors and contracts to close associates, and forced opponents out of the country. Political and economic discontent simmered as his strong-arm tactics became dictatorial rule in 1972, outlawing all dissent. In 1983, one of Marcos' key political opponents, Benigno Aquino, returned from exile to challenge the dictator. As he stepped out of his airplane at Manila airport to the cheers of a crowd, he was shot dead.

It was the beginning of the end for the Marcos regime. Benigno Aquino's widow, Corazon, was not a political leader, had no experience in government, and was an unlikely challenger to the powerful Marcos. She seemed to have no claim to leadership other than to be the widow of a murdered man. Educated in Catholic school, studious, and self-described as "plain," with tousled looks and big glasses, Corazon Aquino nonetheless showed she was quick with words, a strong speaker, and had a manner that attracted genuine affection from Filipinos disgruntled with the imperious Marcos. They called her "Auntie."

Marcos derided her for being just a woman, but he gravely miscalculated the surge of national pride focused on her image as a strong, pious, and reverential widow, recapturing the sacred qualities of José Rizal's legacy of principled resistance to tyranny. As a prayerful

49 People power: Corazon Aquino's supporters rally in the Philippines.

Catholic, Aquino displayed her spirituality, and incarnated a non-violent image of resistance. She became adept at challenging Marcos rhetorically, pointing out that she had no experience of lying, stealing, or murdering.

She was also not exactly the neophyte of her image. She had married into a well-connected political family, and was the one figure capable of uniting the fractious opposition, leading protests, rallies, and then a movement that became "People Power." Her presence galvanized massive street demonstrations with the ability to shut down urban centers. Marcos pushed for a vote to confirm his power in an election marked by obvious fraud, and escalating confrontations with police and authorities. In 1986, he was forced from office by collapsing support at home and pressure from abroad. Corazon Aquino became the eleventh President of the Philippines in 1986.[4]

The new government was a watershed in Philippine popular politics, though little was altered in the entrenched institutions of power. One particular thing that did not change was the larger challenge of global work and labor. Around the Pacific islands, policy makers spoke of Polynesian and Micronesian MIRAB states – migration, remittances, aid, and bureaucracy. These were dependent upon emigrant workers sending checks home and foreign governments providing aid. Some

MIRAB experiences were built around Oceanian families, who calculated which family members to send abroad as workers. These practices created international networks of kin and remittances crossing economic, political, and cultural boundaries.

In the Philippines, Aquino, like Marcos, recognized the importance of overseas foreign workers to the economy of the Philippines. These were not the *balikbayan* living abroad, agitating for rights or citizenship in their new homes, but migrants on contracts who brought their money and businesses back to families in the Philippines.

In this there was opportunity, and also great hardship. Through the preceding decades, industrial countries had been enjoying a postwar boom of "economic miracles" built with the revival of civilian industry and the labor of low-paid guest workers from all over the world, especially former colonies. Aquino tried to navigate the realities of poverty in a globalized economy. As a woman, she took special interest in meeting with domestic helpers in Hong Kong in 1988 and declaring "You are the new heroes."[5]

It was an indicative moment for trying to generate respect for Filipino workers abroad. Though many were teachers, nurses, doctors, and engineers, governments regularly regarded Filipinos as dispensable, low-skill servant labor. March 1995 brought all of those tensions and bitterness into international focus when Flor Contemplacion was hanged. Contemplacion was a domestic worker for a Singaporean family, an acquaintance of another Filipina worker, Delia Maga, who had been found strangled. The little boy Maga cared for was also found drowned in a bathtub. Police arrested Contemplacion on charges of double murder and she confessed to both crimes.

But some witnesses said she had been bullied and framed by her employer. A storm of protest challenged the Singapore courts and rocked the Philippine administration of then President Fidel Ramos. Contemplacion became a rallying figure for thousands of overseas workers and their families suffering from disrespect, neglect, and abuse. Through her Singapore work, she had been supporting four children back in the Philippines. Ramos took the extraordinary step of personally asking the Singapore government to stay the execution, but was declined. Ramos' opponents attacked him for caring more about business with Singapore than the lives of Filipina workers, and the Manila government broke off a series of contracts and ventures. Contemplacion was executed, and her body returned to the Philippines.

At the airport, the president's wife, Amelita, met the cortege, and thousands followed the body to the town of San Pablo, where Bishop Teodoro Bacani conducted an overflow mass, intoning, "She is a symbol of millions of Filipinos driven by poverty to take their chances abroad." Journalist Conrado De Quiros wrote for the *Philippine Daily Inquirer* that Contemplacion's execution "encompasses all the abuse that the nation has had to endlessly endure." For an aggrieved country demanding justice he did not offer a lament, but a caution for a long history and continuing challenge: "We are mad."[6]

Flor Contemplacion's case drew attention to well-known but often unstated global inequities in the late twentieth century. Labor was key among them, but there were also many other claims, as requests, petitions, and then demands surfaced across the Pacific on issues of sovereignty, territorial rights, and cultural and historical recognition. The 1990s were a worldwide decade of change. The Berlin Wall had fallen in 1989; in 1990 Nelson Mandela was released from prison in South Africa and the legal apartheid system began to come down. Political decolonization dating from the postwar was matched with clamor for rights.

Activists raising claims of historical injustice began to overturn precedents, gain apologies, and sometimes settlements between Pacific peoples and governments, often their own. In June 1992, the road linking the villages of Meriam people in the Murray islands was crowded with locals calling out and whistling to each other. They were celebrating a landmark legal decision, in a case fought for ten years, conferring upon them something that they already knew: they were possessors of their own land. The case had been brought by a local, Eddie Koiki Mabo, and the victory was bittersweet: after years of struggle, Mabo had died of cancer just a few months before the decision.

The case, simply called "Mabo," confirmed title in a uniquely Pacific place. The Murray islands lie in the Torres Strait, the waterway between mainland Australia and New Guinea and so are historically the product of both, culturally and ethnically Melanesian, Aboriginal, and influenced by neighboring Indonesia. The Meriam people are islanders of many traditions: sedentary cultivators also known for their seafaring and fish traps. Eddie Mabo grew up in the islands and pursued local work before taking a position as a gardener in Townsville, Queensland at James Cook University.[7]

At this institution named for the "discoverer" of British Australia, Mabo fell into discussions with faculty and students about his homeland and was stunned to learn that it fell under the legal doctrine of *terra nullius*: his lands belonged to the Crown, having been "unoccupied" before the British presence. The Australian judicial system had never pretended there were no prior inhabitants, just that they had no social organization and therefore could not make legal claims. The law had allowed the almost absolute dispossession of the Aboriginal cultures.

In 1982, Mabo and other islanders filed a case to challenge the law. A decade of legal proceedings brought to public attention the operation of land allotments bounded by real and imaginary lines, natural markers and landscape features, held together by religious and mythical commandments of customary practice. Missionary and anthropological records were brought by plaintiffs to reference continuities in the custodianship of land, culture, and knowledge across generations in ways distinct from, yet just as enforceable as those of European property rights. Islanders testified and their knowledge was heard in court and debated in the press.

Over ten years, courts considered and ruled on multiple arguments and challenges, including one from the state of Queensland that annexation of the islands in 1879 had voided all previous legal practice. Courts rejected this colonial argument and in 1992 ruled that "native title" existed, and that pre-European peoples had customary forms of law, rights, and entitlements. Significantly, the Australian High Court also overturned the doctrine of *terra nullius*, erasing the fiction that Europeans had settled an "empty" continent.

Mabo did not live to see the legal victory, but he was buried and awarded posthumous honors in Townsville. When his grave was vandalized he was reburied in the Murray islands in a ceremony, unpracticed for generations, befitting royalty. The vandals had marked Mabo's grave with slurs against Aborigines. Opponents of the decision warned of "the ambitions of communists for a separate Aboriginal State" that would plunge law, property, and the country into chaos.[8]

While celebrating the victory, even some Aboriginal activists had reservations. The case had established principles for land claims in the Torres Strait, but done nothing for dispossession and discrimination involving nearly a quarter of a million Aboriginal people living across the continent. Others read the decision as a call to action. Kimberly communities in Western Australia announced territorial claims within months of the ruling, as did the Yolngu people far north in East Arnhem Land, against mining interests. Advocates for cultural and economic independence sat down with municipalities, state land councils, and members of the national government. The case had introduced a generation to the heritage of another Australia. The Mabo decision had, in fact, resolved little specifically; but negotiations were now beginning.

By the 1990s, island states from Samoa and Fiji to the Solomons and Vanuatu were independent. But many peoples also lived on lands as part of societies that they did not accept as their own; nor were they themselves always accepted. The year 1993 had particular resonance in Hawai'i, for exactly a century earlier, in 1893, American commercial and missionary interests, with the collusion of the forces from a US warship, had overthrown Queen Lili'uokalani, the last monarch of the islands. For a hundred years Hawaiian patriots, beginning with the Queen herself, had sought recognition for stolen lands and culture. Such claims were taken up strongly again in the 1970s and 1980s by a new generation of Hawaiian activists. In 1993, they took to the streets in protests, vigils, and commemorations. Especially at stake was what Lili'uokalani and the kingdom had lost: sovereignty.

There had never been a single "Hawaiian" position on the question, or even definition of sovereignty. The 1978 Office of Hawaiian Affairs began as a funded department of the state government to assist and administrate on behalf of Kanaka Maoli – Native Hawaiians – on issues of education, home ownership, public lands, and betterment of conditions. Another group, Ka Lahui, was formed in 1987 by lawyer Miliani Trask and her sister professor Haunani-Kay Trask, as a grassroots activist campaign seeking to have Hawai'i decolonized along with other Pacific states according to United Nations guidelines. Dr. Kekuni Blaisdell created Ka Pakaukau to advocate for complete independence for Hawai'i by American withdrawal. Dozens of other groups supported versions of local rule, state-within-a-state self-determination, independence, and Hawaiian leadership dependent upon indigenous ancestry.[9]

In 1993, backed by a resolution in the US Congress, American President Bill Clinton formally apologized on behalf of the government for the overthrow of the Hawaiian monarchy. The apology did not mandate any actual political or territorial changes in Hawai'i, and critics scoffed, but it did call for continued negotiations to address historical wrongs. Native Hawaiians seemed to have a champion when Daniel Akaka, himself Hawaiian, was elected to the United States Senate.

Beginning in 2000, Akaka made multiple legislative proposals to have Kanaka Maoli recognized as an indigenous or First Nation people, as had self-governing American Indian tribes on territorial reservations and Alaska Natives who negotiated land and compensation claims through indigenous corporations. While such groups were protected under special legal status, the US government maintained that Hawaiians were an ethnic minority, not a nation. Akaka's decade of attempts met opposition from legal and political groups that argued the legislation would sanction the creation of a race-based state in which economic and political power would belong to those of specific heritage or blood. More critically, however, his bills pulled the otherwise divergent Hawaiian sovereignty campaigns into unified opposition.

Why Hawaiian rights activists should oppose one of the first legislative attempts at self-determination puzzled the sponsors. Different provisions of the bills, on grievance claims, revenues, and voting rights satisfied or alienated the constituencies of different groups, but the central, common argument against Akaka became clear. The bill would give Hawaiians federal recognition like Native American Indians, yet Kanaka Maoli did not see themselves as indigenous Americans. As Hawaiians, the groups commonly agreed that they had never ceded their sovereignty or identity, and that the history of the 1893 overthrow up through statehood and the present was nothing more than part of a prolonged colonial occupation of Polynesia.

The legislation had benefits: it would require the federal government to allocate support and resources for Hawaiians. But the Kanaka Maoli in turn would concede their claims of being an independent nation, and instead work with the Department of Interior, subject to federal, state, and county laws. This appealed to some, but activist Henry Noa posed a familiar question: "Aren't we already subjugated to that?"[10]

One of the more visible responses to the sovereignty question came not at the legislative level, but on the ground in Waimanalo, Hawai'i. There, a working-class town of about 10,000 was built up by Hawaiian and part-Hawaiian neighbors, speaking the language, going to jobs, and being disinterested in and unfriendly towards the tourist world. In the hills above the town, Bumpy Kanehele came in 1994 to build a community. Kanehele seemed like a statistical snapshot of too many native Hawaiians growing up: few opportunities, angry youth, school dropout. In 1987, he began agitating on behalf of Kanaka Maoli causes, was imprisoned, and became more militant.

For the commemorations of 1993 he occupied Makapu'u beach near Waimanalo with supporters. After a year, the local government negotiated, agreeing to give his group land in the hills if he withdrew. Above Waimanalo town, Kanehele staked out Pu'uhonua o Waimanalo, a community that suggested what an independent Hawaii might actually look like. On forty-five acres, his crews cleared their own dirt roads, set small houses and sheds along the hills, dug and irrigated muddy *taro* and *ti* patches, and created a world crossed by children, animals, and birds. Run by a four woman "council of aunties," the community was immediately and effectively self-governing; state officials kept a distance, families and individuals were assigned duties, cleaning, provisioning, and planting. Children were required to learn the Hawaiian language from others, as well as traditional arts and practices of hunting and fishing.[11]

But the world was not merely folkloric. Cars and old trucks carried residents and supplies, children in shorts played basketball, disputes and evictions needed meetings, and work had to be found for residents, many supporting themselves with outside trades. Still, it was all locally run. Kanehele's ambition was to establish more Kanaka Maoli communities. His view of the mountains and sea from his own land, he said, was his own definition of sovereignty.

Questions of land and sovereignty also remained central to Maori and *Pakeha* disputes in Aotearoa, New Zealand. On February 5, 1995, a magnitude 7.0 earthquake struck offshore North Island, New Zealand, and was followed by twenty-one additional events. Over the next weeks a series of "prolific aftershocks" continued, progressing from north to south. The seismic events were named the "Waitangi Day Sequence," for the annual commemoration, and would be a telling indicator for what unfolded that year.

Waitangi Day ceremonies had begun in the 1940s to commemorate the 1840 document that created New Zealand as a British territory with presumed protection of all Maori and *Pakeha* citizens under the Queen of England. Early commemorations featured a naval party and government officials, and Maori ceremony and participation became part of the proceedings in the 1950s. In 1974, the day was legislated a national holiday.

Speeches and presentations every February by officials generally tried to offer New Zealand's self-image to the world: a multiracial society governed by law and cooperation. After the Maori–Pakeha wars of the nineteenth century, New Zealand had little of the vicious ethnic and religious sectarian violence common in so many parts of the world, from the Balkans to South Asia. But Maori activists also regularly found the commemoration a moment to raise questions of continuing injustices. Through the 1980s activists tried to bring more attention to the Treaty, and by the 1990s began to question its validity altogether, turning Waitangi Day into an occasion for visible protests.

The official harmonious view had already been fraying for decades as Maori activists and liberal Pakeha began to publicly question race and inequality questions in New Zealand society, and the issue of whether the country would be a small Britain of the southern hemisphere, or an independent oceanic, Pacific Island society. These matters had already been given airing in 1981, when hundreds of thousands of New Zealanders engaged in debates, protests, and street battles for and against a singular event: a tour of the South African rugby team, the Springboks.

Sport was a source of national pride in New Zealand, whose famed All Blacks teams played in fierce rivalries with the world's champion squads like the Springboks. Tours between the two countries had raised passions since the 1920s, but by the 1970s and 1980s, in the midst of decolonization and social change, one point about the matches stood out above all: South Africa was run by an *apartheid* government of legal discrimination, race separation, and white supremacy, and sporting teams were also selected along those lines.

When the Springbok team planned to tour New Zealand in summer and fall of 1981, the country divided between ardent supporters, government officials who argued that sport and politics could be separated, and opponents who condemned South African policies. Conservatives following the traditional line argued that the South Africans would learn by the good example of New Zealand's multiracial society. Critics asked for greater examination of racial realities in New Zealand.

The tour proceeded, though not without incident. Fans watched matches as large crowds demonstrated outside of stadiums. Riot police were issued special gear, and on at least two occasions protestors tore down fences to invade the pitch. Matches were postponed or canceled, and broadcast facilities sabotaged. During one match a small private plane flew in low over the stadium and dropped flour bombs.[12]

The Springbok controversy died down, but the questions that split New Zealand and, for some, the taint of ignoring race and inequality, did not. The Waitangi annual commemorations absorbed these issues, though most ceremonies featured crafted remarks, with protestors kept away behind police cordons. In 1990, the Anglican Archbishop Whakahuihui Vercoe was invited to offer words before the Prime Minister as well as Queens Te Arikinuki and the visiting Elizabeth II. Maori protesters jeered his introduction, but fell silent as he told the dignitaries "Since the signing of the treaty ... our partners have marginalized us. You have not honored the treaty ... The language of this land is yours, the custom is yours, the media by which we tell the world who we are, are yours." He was never invited back.

The sharpness of disputes became acute in 1995 as the government prepared to legislate a "fiscal envelope" to settle Maori claims. The plan outraged Pakeha conservatives, who saw the potential $1 billion fund as an example of special treatment, race favoritism, and weakness in the face of militants and grievance politics. Maori communities protested it was another government plan made without their consultation, or discussion of local authority and sovereignty. At the *Te Ti'i marae* where Waitangi Day events were held, Maori leader Kingi Tairua roundly criticized the assembled officials, Tame Iti spoke and spat at the feet of the Prime Minister, and Joe Murphy trampled on a New Zealand flag.[13]

The following weeks saw national debates about the actions, and the questions lingered on through the next decade even as alliances came and went, and claims were made to the Waitangi Tribunal. Who was being insulted? Some said it was the government or all of New Zealand; others said it was the Maori who, like Archbishop Vercoe, remembered the unmet promises of the treaty.

Still, treaties and agreements continued to be signed and written, for negotiations with former and present colonial powers around the Pacific were not only over land and sovereignty, but over control of cultural and natural inheritance, and the issue of who would benefit. The question was who would be drafting the language. Strong statements of principle were made in 1993, when the Nine Tribes of Mataatua of Aotearoa New Zealand convened the First International Conference on The Cultural and Intellectual Property Rights of Indigenous Peoples.

Delegates from fourteen countries attended, representing the range of indigenous peoples around the Pacific region including the Philippines, Ainu from northern Japan, Australian Aborigines, and many Polynesian islands. At issue were general commitments to indigenous knowledge and custom, particularly practices of environmental management, as well as the protection and development of arts, music, and cultural forms. In addition, discussions also centered on the promises and challenges of biodiversity and biotechnology.

Well-known cases had long convulsed the domain of culture, where indigenous peoples petitioned to protect sacred dances, chants, and ritual practices from commercial exploitation, and fought with museums and anthropologists over repatriating artifacts, objects, and especially human remains. The question of whether these were specimens or ancestors filled court briefs and public demonstrations. The conference affirmed indigenous rights to specific heritage and property, while also indicating that, "the knowledge of the Indigenous Peoples of the world is of benefit to all humanity." This principle also defined a position on what in some cases was called "biopiracy," and called for an end to the "exploitation of indigenous peoples, indigenous knowledge, and indigenous cultural and intellectual property rights."[14]

A case arose in Hawai'i in 2002 as the University of Hawai'i signed an agreement with a San Diego biotechnology company, Diversa Corporation, for "unique molecules from the unusual environments within our biodiversity access network," according to the firm's president. The company proposed to use its genetic technology to examine samples from unstudied island environments with interests in developing pharmaceutical and antibody applications.

The heritage controversy came because of Diversa's agreement, which stipulated that the company "shall own all right, title and interest to any and all Diversa inventions," in effect claiming ownership and eventual patent over "novel products" developed from prospecting and sampling in the islands. In a commentary delivered for a legal brief, lawyer Liliani Trask cited Diversa claims that it had "exclusive rights to Hawaii's unique marine resources ... directing all research interests and venture capital investors to their offices in San Diego."[15]

The ownership and profit questions already had a history. In 1995, the Canadian Rural Advancement Foundation International broke news that the United States had issued a patent on a line of genetic material collected from a member of the Hagahai people of Papua New Guinea, a group with little regular encounter with the outside world until 1984. At that time, many died of diseases brought through contact. Medical researchers saved lives with innoculations while noting that the Hagahai seemed to have little history of leukemia or neurological disorders. Their genetic material was studied in the United States and used to create potentially useful antiretroviral therapies.

The research benefits seemed incontestable. Chemicals useful for supporting immune cells from the AIDS virus were also extracted from plants in Samoa with the knowledge of a woman healer. Yet the legal ownership of individual DNA was troubling. Critics denounced the action as "the U.S. government patenting an indigenous person from Papua New Guinea." Some called it a new form of colonial exploitation, the state or private ownership of human biology. Patent claims were also made for the human T-cell line of a woman from Marovo Lagoon and a man from Guadalcanal in the Solomons.

As with the indigenous property conference in Aotearoa New Zealand, one of the responses was a call for Pacific-wide cooperation and action. Lopeti Senituli, at the Pacific Concerns Resource Center in Suva, Fiji, helped draft a treaty. The initiative was to approach Pacific governments for support in regulating and setting policy on questionable practices. The document drew on the tenets set forth by the indigenous property conference, but also took its inspiration from a slightly older legacy of grassroots action, as Senituli explained: "It contained about 50 percent of our Nuclear Free and Independent Pacific Treaty."[16]

Pacific Islanders were not the only people reclaiming heritages with an eye on the future in the 1990s. Parallel actions were taking place in maritime Asia. In 1997, another treaty – this one British colonial – was reviewed, and in this case, canceled. In July, one of the last major European outposts in Asia disappeared as the administration of Hong Kong was transferred to the Chinese government.

Since being seized during the Opium Wars, and "leased," the British crown colony had been a free trading port and developed an international European and Asian population, though privileged British residents established themselves around the Victoria Peak, away from regular contact with the majority Chinese. Built around a series of islands, the colony was famed for its crowded markets, tram cars, restaurants, hawker stalls, and constant movement of junks and cargo ships across the linking waterways.

Many of the commercial and legal institutions were built by the Four Big Families, Li, Ho, Hui, and Luo, and hospitals, schools, and financial centers established by immigrant communities. Japanese forces invaded during the Pacific War and overran British positions with bombardments and an occupation that led to mass starvation, disease, and tremendous loss of civilian lives. At the end of the war, the territory was taken under British rule once again, with immigrants, refugees, and businesses hoping to escape from conflicts on the mainland between the Chinese Nationalists and the Communists. When the Communists under Mao triumphed, even more mainlanders fled to Hong Kong fearing persecution.

A colony and product of European Pacific empire, Hong Kong remained notable in the postwar period by expanding as not only a regional, but as a global entrepôt of consumer goods and financial transactions. From the 1970s, with a strong educational system and cheap labor, it was discussed as one of the four "Asian Tigers," along with Singapore, South Korea, and Taiwan, and with Japan reshaped the late twentieth-century history of the "Pacific Rim" and "Pacific Century." Planners in states like the Marianas, Fiji, and Samoa also entertained projects to keep up with the "Pacific Century" by importing raw materials and using cheap labor and authoritarian rule to create export economies.

Both islands and Asia had some common interests. Japan and Taiwan in particular solicited contracts with Oceania. The Taiwanese government actively courted the developing Pacific island states, offering aid and gaining contracts and diplomatic recognition from the Solomon Islands, the Marshall Islands, Nauru, Kiribati, Tuvalu, and Palau. Hong Kong banking firms and trading emporiums flourished, leveraging capital for projects in Asia and the islands. In a glittering port filled with skyscrapers, Hong Kong Chinese raised families and kept households with Filipina servants and maids.

On June 30, 1997, following a decade of negotiations, tensions, and the uncertainty of millions – some of whom fled overseas – the British surrendered their expiring leasehold. Jiang Zemin and Li Peng, the President and Premier of the People's Republic of China, sat on a red stage and dais with Charles, the Prince of Wales, representing Queen Elizabeth II. Also in attendance was Tony Blair, the prime minister of the United Kingdom. With ceremony and solemnity, Prince Charles read a declaration of British departure, and the British and Hong Kong colonial flags were lowered to the strains of *God Save the Queen*. A new flag for Hong Kong was raised, along with that of the People's Republic of China. As the clock registered midnight and became July 1, Chinese President Jiang Zemin gave a speech on "one country, two systems," to indicate Hong Kong's new status as a special administrative region under Chinese rule. Fireworks were launched as the British sailed away.

For many political and media observers, the transfer was rich with historical meaning. The British had come in the nineteenth century with their gunboats and unequal treaties to create an empire that would rule over the China trade, stretch from the Indian Ocean across the Pacific islands, and encircle the globe. Now almost all of that empire was gone. In the late twentieth century, China had created a ferociously competitive and rapidly expanding industrial base and export economy fueled by cheap labor, which Japan watched with trepidation.[17]

For another thirteen years after the Hong Kong transfer, Japan would remain the unchallenged giant of Asian economies, dominating the world with global brand names in automobiles and electronics, and enrapturing generations with graphic novel *manga* and pop-culture animated films and programs. A change, however, had already begun.

In the 1970s and 1980s, prime ministers Deng Xiaoping and Zhao Ziyang had shifted communist China's agrarian and industrial priorities to special economic zones on the Pacific, instituting a Coastal Development Strategy focused on global maritime export trade. As glittering showcases like the futuristic Pudong district of Shanghai began to develop postmodern skylines along with spectacular poverty, social stress, and environmental degradation, the rest of the planet – and the twentieth-century hegemons in Russia, the United States, and Western Europe – watched with disquiet and fascination.

Though regularly acknowledged as a rising power, China's eminence was less a new history than a recapturing of an almost traditional position. The long history of the Ming treasure fleets, the silk trade, the early modern tea monopoly, and the domination of global exchange with Spanish silver through Canton were formidable evidence of that past. Interrupted by the Opium Wars, the galleons,

50 Pacific Century? Shanghai, showcase of twenty-first-century China.

clippers, and junks had disappeared; now they returned as mammoth container ships and tankers, once again drawn to the busiest ports in the world.

In Oceania, Beijing negotiated fishing and resource contracts while financing new projects across the islands. The Cook Islands, Fiji, Samoa, Papua New Guinea, and Vanuatu all received support for new sports stadiums, and subventions to construct government facilities. Heads of state were invited to, and lavishly entertained in, China. Asia was once again a center of island politics and interests. As the British departed, China was a dominant partner, commanding as it had for so many centuries the trade and attention of the world.[18]

The Pacific Century that China was expected to dominate in the coming decades immediately showed what the future might hold in the new millennium. Within twenty-four hours of Hong Kong being transferred to the People's Republic of China, economies began to collapse all over Asia. The timing of the 1997 Asian Financial Crisis was notoriously symbolic: the relentless export-driven optimism of the Pacific Rim and the Asian Tigers would have to account for an even newer Pacific of frighteningly interdependent financial markets that could not only ruin economies, but destabilize entire societies and topple political regimes.

News of the Tigers and reports on Asian "economic miracles" had for decades excited foreign investors attracted by returns on high interest rates offered by local and national governments. The returns, however, were often not supported by actual economic growth, but only by financial speculation that drove property and stock market prices to unrealistic levels. This was the case in Thailand, where the economy had for some years been driven by increasing real estate values. In 1997, as credit stalled and buyers began waiting for prices to fall rather than chase them as they rose, the value of the Thai economy, along with its currency, the baht, began to tumble. Finance companies collapsed, construction stopped, and thousands of foreign workers had their visas and permits canceled. Thai laborers in urban areas went back to villages.

Panic selling and uncollectable debts and loans dropped property, stock market, and business values, and the currencies of Thailand, the Philippines, South Korea, and Malaysia all fell by 30 to 40 percent in a year. In Indonesia, currency values fell by 80 percent as businesses began to abandon the unstable rupiah in favor of dollars. For common people, it meant having to buy goods with money that was worth less and less.

As the Asian Financial Crisis spread, credit disappeared, businesses and shops closed, unemployment increased, and runs on stores pushed up prices. Riots broke out across the country, and in Jakarta, mobs looking for scapegoats attacked Chinese districts, murdering residents and burning businesses. Thousands died. Witnesses said that the mobs had been organized and backed up by military personnel. Rocked by looting and violence, and unable to contain the deteriorating situation, President Suharto came under fire. While the country plummeted into near chaos, he and his family were widely believed to hold billions from illegal business contracts.[19]

As the violence escalated, districts like Aceh, Riau, and Irian agitated against Jakarta's central power. The military feared civil war and some generals lost confidence in Suharto. Without their backing, Suharto was forced to resign, and was replaced by his Vice-President, B. J. Habibie. The Asian Financial Crisis starkly demonstrated the workings of the Asian Pacific at the turn of the millennium. Global markets produced great wealth and also threw entire nations into turmoil with brutal rapidity. Recovery would take years and place many countries into even greater and dependent relations with the bankers and directors of the International Monetary Fund.

Indonesian President Habibie spent a fair amount of time just surviving challenges to his authority and restructuring his country's finances. He also did something unexpected, announcing in 1998 that the people of East Timor could decide whether to remain a part of Indonesia. The news was so startling that it was greeted with some praise and a great deal of suspicion.

Timor is the largest of the Lesser Sunda Islands, to the far eastern extremity of the Indonesian archipelago. Like many other places in the zone between Asia and Oceania, it had been settled by ancient Austronesian and Malay peoples and had been a trading entrepôt for sandalwood, beeswax, and slaves. The population was composed of multiple ethnolinguistic groups across the valleys and plains, notably the Tetum in the east. From the sixteenth century, the island had been settled by Portuguese traders who established maize, coffee, and taxes, and politically held on to administering the eastern half of the island as the imperium of the Dutch East India Company settled over the west.[20]

As Indonesia became independent, all of the former Dutch territories became part of the new state, but East Timor remained under Portugal. The global impact of decolonization would finally be felt in 1974, as Lisbon gave up its remaining colonies. Focused on the withdrawal from their African territories in Zimbabwe and Angola, the Portuguese gave little attention to exiting East Timor. When they did, the East Timorese split, some favoring ties to Portugal, others to Indonesia. But, as had been the case in West Papua, Indonesia immediately claimed the territory as a part of the historic Majapahit empire.

Ruthless, independent military commanders sent large forces to crush any independence claims, terrorize the population, and exterminate opposition. They battled East Timorese Tetum nationalists and leftist militias while the United States and Australia stayed on the sidelines, seeing the action as a defense against communism. The Suharto regime let the military have an open hand in running East Timor, allowing officers to create an occupied state with themselves in critical administrative positions. After 1975, the Portuguese language and local animistic religions were outlawed.

To offer East Timor a chance to decide for special autonomy or independence, Habibie was going against the interests of his own military. Some thought him unusually brave, but as a former associate of Suharto, many more questioned him for not acting sooner, and for not reining in the military units and their militia supporters. He seemed to personally believe in self-determination, and as a non-elected president with little political future, had a chance to stabilize one part of Indonesia and settle a volatile issue that had brought so much international condemnation.

In 1991, a massacre of civilians in the East Timor capital of Dili had raised global outrage, and in 1996, Timorese activist José Ramos Horta and Bishop Carlos Filipe Ximenes Belo received the Nobel Peace Prize for their non-violent push toward independence, gaining more worldwide attention. Indonesia found itself the target of human rights investigations, and faced challenges in securing aid and loans for its economy.

In 1999, the East Timorese voted almost 80 percent in favor of independence. But the military and pro-Jakarta Timorese militias were not finished. They rampaged and raided across the island, killing thousands, in an attempt to seize full control and drive the population into refugee camps. Crowds were massacred as they clustered in church compounds; Francisco de Jesus da Costa testified, "When I was outside I saw dead bodies scattered on the ground, children, women, young and old people. I was walking among those corpses." This time, backed by the vote, and with an understanding that intervention would not lead to war with Indonesia, the United Nations led by Australia agreed to send troops as a peacekeeping force.[21]

After the destruction and killing, almost nothing was left. Years of rebuilding, negotiations on power sharing, and constitutional drafts followed under a United Nations administration. The preceding decades had seen many battles for sovereignty across Asia and the Pacific. In 2002, East Timor was recognized as an independent state and became the world's first new nation of the twenty-first century.

AFTERWORD: WORLD HERITAGE

At midnight on January 1, 2000, the world's attention turned toward an unlikely place: a small, uninhabited island, part of the Kiribati group in the Pacific. There, as the day changed across the International Date Line, President Teburoro Tito lit a torch and welcomed the world to the new millennium. Within hours, the Date Line would pass toward the western Pacific, triggering celebrations in New Zealand, the Melanesian Islands, and on toward Australia. In Aotearoa, Maori communities greeted the night with chants and songs. In longitudinal sections just hours apart, celebrations began in Sydney harbor with tall ships and fireworks, in Tokyo with the ringing of ancient bells, and in Hong Kong with cheering flotillas. It was a moment for the world.

As peoples of the Pacific celebrated the new millennium in great Asian metropolises and small island towns and villages, Kiribati pondered its future. The archipelago, encompassing the Gilbert, Ellice, Phoenix, and Line Islands, is officially the Republic of Kiribati. The islands are for the most part low lying atolls, but their encompassing waters are enormous, about the size of the continental United States. In the west, the capital, Tarawa, lies adjacent to the Marshall Island of Micronesia and north of the Solomons and Vanuatu of Melanesia. The republic stretches north of Fiji, Tonga, Samoa, and the Cook Islands. The Line Islands at the eastern end lie between Hawai'i and French Polynesia. The islands fall both north and south of the equator and in the eastern and western hemispheres, giving them a unique claim to focus the Pacific and the world.

In an age of the "Pacific Century" and the "Pacific Way," Kiribati officials posed a very particular question, especially to Australia and New Zealand: would those countries accept Kiribati citizens as refugees? Climate change had come, and with it the phenomenon popularly known as global warming. Worldwide debate raged as to whether environmental changes were real, imagined, natural, or man-made. But one thing was incontestable: low-lying islands were disappearing under the ocean.

As sea levels rose and regional drought intensified, saltpans formed across islets and lush palm strands died from contamination. In 2008, Kiritabi President Anote Tong hosted a United Nations environmental forum in New Zealand and made his point starkly. "To plan for the day when you no longer have a country is indeed painful but I think we have to do that." The first Pacific place of the new millennium might, perhaps, also be one of the first to disappear.[1]

Remedies could not come from just the islands themselves. The United Nations-sponsored Kyoto Protocols entered into force in 2005. The agreements set targets for carbon emissions and allowed nations to "cap and trade" output credits with other countries, but disagreements about the responsibilities of major powers like the United States and growing Pacific economies in Asia left the issue uncertain. In 2010, China surpassed Japan to become the world's second largest economy. The leader, the United States, had long been a disproportionate consumer of global energy and creator of atmospheric pollutants, but conservative governments there argued that regulations would hamper industrial and economic growth, and refused to sign.

Increasing attention was also paid to India and China, where staggering rates of development were accompanied by widespread environmental devastation. In China, this meant the poisoning of rivers, the depletion of coastal waters, and billions of tons of carbon dioxide emissions from burning cheap coal to power industry. These combined with sulfur contaminants released into the atmosphere, to create acid rain, hazardous health conditions in China, and accelerated changes in ocean temperature.

Coral bleaching and poisoned seas led to the collapse of marine life habitats and the washing away of natural breakwaters. Coastal regions eroded. Kiribati and other low-lying island countries signed and ratified environmental treaties, including Kyoto and its successors, with complaints about the lack of mechanisms to enforce compliance in a globally dependent world.[2]

A tiny state with fewer than 100,000 citizens spread across all of its archipelagos, Kiribati looks small, yet has an islander history that is nonetheless very much a trans-local place of the Pacific and the world. Located at the intersection of the major cultural and trading zones, the islands were long the crossroads of wayfinding paths. The I-Kiribati Micronesians settled in the great migrations out of Asia millennia ago. Like most Oceanian peoples, they were seafarers and navigators, inhabiting a connected world.

On Tarawa, stories tell of voyagers from Samoa, or even Sumatra and Indonesia, and records track invasions from Fijian and Tongan warriors. European merchants and slave traders came followed by whalers, giving the populations a unique but not unusual blend of Micronesian, Polynesian, Melanesian, and European backgrounds. Spaniards brought the majority Roman Catholic faith, and Protestant evangelicals followed.

The major island groups have a colonial history, having been taken as British protectorates beginning in the nineteenth century, and some fell under Japanese imperial rule during the Pacific War. The Tarawa atoll was noted for its bloody battles, and the Line Islands were used during the Cold War for nuclear weapons testing. In the decolonizing Pacific, independence in the 1970s brought self-government but also separation and claims for autonomy between different island groups. The Gilberts became primary in the Republic of Kiribati, while the Ellice Islands declared themselves an independent Tuvalu. Banaba Island has sought to secede and become part of Fiji.

Most of the islanders continued to work in subsistence farming and fishing, some migrated into tourism, small business, and copra production. The main population centers became overcrowded. Problems of urban life, displacement, employment, and education challenged peoples of palm strands, lagoons, and sandy beaches.

Marine products remained principal exports, with fish and seaweed going to Japan, Taiwan, Australia, the United States, and Western Europe, and manufactured goods being imported from the same and from China, Korea, and New Zealand. Because of Kiribati's equatorial location, Japan and China established satellite tracking telemetry facilities there, and the Chinese compound was rumored to be eavesdropping on American missile and military operations in the nearby Marshall Islands. Diplomatic relations with China were broken off when Kiribati recognized Taiwan as a country, and Kiribati has raised the question of resettlement there as the oceans rise. Revenues come in from development aid, agreements with Asian factory fleets, and remittances sent back to the islands by overseas workers. The seas around Kiribati are marked by overlapping historical transits. The islands were and are global Pacific places.[3]

Though small in population and land surface, Kiribati could nonetheless try to influence the heritage of the world by understanding that Pacific histories are finally about the ocean, its challenges and possibilities. In 2008, the government created one of the world's largest protected marine reserves, more than 150,000 square miles of coral reefs, fish and bird breeding regions, turtle sanctuaries, and rich pelagic zones. It was a bold statement of conservation over development. The decision meant millions in lost state revenues from commercial fishing licenses, and enforcement depended upon foreign aid contributors seeing the value. Governments pledged to help, and Kiribati made its case for a possible future.[4]

Across the islands are visible the legacies of many familiar Pacific histories of epic voyaging, trade, invasion, colonialism, war, migration, Asian economics, and imagination. Oceania, Europe, the Americas, and Asia all have crossed, and continue to act, struggle, and create in these islands. The palm-fringed shores are marked by overlapping histories and reminders: rusting artillery fortifications, tinned fish, Japanese electronics and motorbikes, *pandanus* baskets, Sunday mass, dubbed television, dances to honor the frigate bird, ancient outriggers. The Pacific brings and takes them all. Children greet strangers with their own favorite question: "Where are you going?"

NOTES

Introduction

1 Alisi's story in Pamela Stewart and Andrew Strathern (eds.), *Identity Work: Constructing Pacific Lives* (Pittsburgh, 2000); Vicki Luker and Brij V. Lal, *Telling Pacific Lives: Prisms of Process* (Canberra, 2008); Cathy A. Small, *Voyages: From Tongan Villages to American Suburbs* (Ithaca, NY, 1997); also K. R. Howe, *Vaka Moana, Voyages of the Ancestors: The Discovery and Settlement of the Pacific* (Honolulu, 2007); George Kuwayama, *Chinese Ceramics in Colonial Mexico* (Los Angeles, 1997).

2 Matt K. Matsuda, "AHR Forum: The Pacific," *American Historical Review*, 111, 3 (June 2006).

3 Oskar Spate, "European invention," in *The Pacific Since Magellan* (Canberra), vol. I, *The Spanish Lake* (1979), ix ; vol. II, *Monopolists and Freebooters* (1983); vol. III, *Paradise Lost and Found* (1989); also Mark Borthwick, *Pacific Century: The Emergence of Modern Pacific Asia* (Boulder, 2007); Rob Wilson and Arif Dirlik (eds.), "Introduction," *Asia-Pacific as Space of Cultural Production*, (Durham, 1995); for definitions, see Brij V. Lal and Kate Fortune (eds.), *The Pacific Islands: An Encyclopedia* (Honolulu, 2000); Donald Denoon, Malama Meleisea, Stewart Firth, Jocelyn Linnekin, and Karen Nero, *The Cambridge History of the Pacific Islanders* (Cambridge, 1997); for historiography, see Matsuda, "AHR Forum: The Pacific," and John Mack, *The Sea: A Cultural History* (London, 2011).

4 Epeli Hau'ofa, "Our Sea of Islands," in *We Are the Ocean* (Honolulu, 2008), 27–40; also Heather Sutherland, "Geography as Destiny? The Role of Water in Southeast Asian History," in Peter Boomgaard (ed.), *A World of Water: Rain, Rivers and Seas in Southeast Asian Histories* (Leiden, 2007), 27–70; Robert Borofsky (ed.), *Remembrance of Pacific Pasts* (Honolulu, 2000); Jerry Bentley (ed.),

Seascapes: Maritime Histories, Littoral Cultures, and Transoceanic Exchanges (Honolulu, 2007); Richard Feinberg (ed.), *Seafaring in the Contemporary Pacific: Studies in Continuity and Change* (DeKalb, 2005). For "Southeast Asia," see Barbara Andaya, *The Flaming Womb: Repositioning Women in Southeast Asia* (Honolulu, 2006).

5 Barbara Andaya, "Oceans Unbounded: Transversing Asia Across 'Area Studies,'" *The Journal of Asian Studies*, 65, 4 (November 2006), 669–90; Dennis O. Flynn and Arturo Giraldez (eds.), *The Pacific World: Lands, Peoples and History of the Pacific, 1500–1900*, 17-volume set (London and Burlington, 2009).

6 "Ocean 'Supergyre' Link to Climate Regulator," www.csiro.au/news/ OceanSupergyre.html; see also Sabrina Speich, Bruno Blanke, Pedro de Vries, Sybren Drijfhout, Kristofer Döös, Alexandre Ganachaud, and Robert Marsh, "Tasman Leakage: A New Route in the Global Ocean Conveyor Belt," *Geophysical Research Letters*, 29, 10 (2002), 55/1–4.

1 Civilization without a center

1 Albert Wendt, *Inside Us the Dead: Poems, 1961–1974* (Auckland, 1976); Patrick Vinton Kirch, *On the Road of the Winds* (Berkeley and Los Angeles, 2000).

2 Margaret Jolly, "Routes," and "Imagining Oceania: Indigenous and Foreign Representations of a Sea of Islands," *The Contemporary Pacific*, 19, 2 (2007), 508–45; also Elizabeth Bott, *Tongan Society at the Time of Captain Cook's Visit* (Honolulu, 1982), 89; Paul D'Arcy, *The People of the Sea: Environment, Identity, and History in Oceania* (Honolulu, 2006).

3 See the research of Patrick Nunn, *Vanished Islands and Hidden Continents of the Pacific* (Honolulu, 2008); Kirch, *Road of the Winds*; also Donald Freeman, *The Pacific* (London and New York, 2010), 8–34.

4 See Reed Wicander and James Monroe, *Historical Geology* (Belmont, 2003).

5 Peter Bellwood, "The Spread of Agriculture in Southeast Asia and Oceania," in *First Farmers: The Origins of Agricultural Societies* (Oxford, 2005).

6 Peter Bellwood, James Fox, and Darrell Tryon, *The Austronesians: Historical and Comparative Perspectives* (Canberra, 1995); James Fox and Clifford Sather (eds.), *Origins, Ancestors, and Alliance: Explorations in Austronesian Ethnography* (Canberra, 1996); for the Malay world, see Jean Taylor, *Indonesia: Peoples and Histories* (New Haven, 2003), 14.

7 Kirch, *Road of the Winds*, 92; Andaya, "Oceans Unbounded," 677; also A. D. Couper, *Sailors and Traders: A Maritime History of the Pacific Peoples* (Honolulu, 2008).

8 Joel Bonnemaison, *The Tree and the Canoe* (Honolulu, 1994).

9 Jerry Wayne Leach and Edmund Ronald Leach, *The Kula: New Perspectives On Massim Exchange* (Cambridge, 1983); Per Hage and Frank Harary, *Exchange in Oceania: A Graph Theoretic Analysis* (Oxford, 1991).

10 For Lapita, see Kirch, *Road of the Winds*, 85–116.

11 John Tunui, in Margo King Lenson (ed.), *Pacific Voices Talk Story*, vol. 1 (Vacaville, 2001).

12 J. Koji Lum, James K. McIntyre, Douglas L. Greger, Kirk W. Huffman, and Miguel G. Vilar, "Recent Southeast Asian domestication and Lapita dispersal of sacred male pseudohermaphroditic 'tuskers' and hairless pigs of Vanuatu," *Proceedings of the National Academy of Science*, 101, 24 (2004), 9167–72; Jonathan S. Friedman, *Genes Language, and Culture History in the Southwest Pacific* (New York, 2007).

13 Patrick V. Kirch and Roger Green, *Hawaiki: Ancestral Polynesia* (Cambridge, 2001); Douglas Oliver, *Polynesia in Early Historic Times* (Honolulu, 2002); Juniper Ellis, *Tattooing the World: Pacific Designs in Print and Skin* (New York, 2008).

14 K. R. Howe, *Where the Waves Fall* (Honolulu, 1984), 44–67; Patrick V. Kirch, *The Evolution of the Polynesian Chiefdoms* (Cambridge, 1984).

15 D'Arcy, *People of the Sea*, 27.

16 D'Arcy, *People of the Sea*, 75, 82, 120; also K. R. Howe, *The Quest for Origins: Who First Discovered and Settled the Pacific Islands?* (Honolulu, 2003).

17 For the *Hokule'a* story, see Ben Finney, *From Sea to Space* (Palmerston North and Honolulu, 1992); David Lewis, *We the Navigators: The Ancient Art of Landfaring in the Pacific* (Honolulu, 1994); Polynesian Voyaging Society website, http://pvs.kcc.hawaii.edu/

2 Trading rings and tidal empires

1 Kirch, *The Road of the Winds*, 172; also Glenn Petersen, *Traditional Micronesian Societies: Adaptation, Integration, and Political Organization* (Honolulu, 2009).

2 For foraging circuits see D'Arcy, *People of the Sea*, 53; Petersen, *Traditional Micronesian Societies*, 13; for Yap stone terraces, see Kirch, *Road of the Winds*, 193.

3 For Saudeleur history, see David Hanlon, *Upon a Stone Altar* (Honolulu, 1988).

4 John Fischer, Saul Riesenberg, and Marjorie Whiting (eds. and trans.), *The Book of Luelen* (Honolulu, 1977); Petersen, *Traditional Micronesian Societies*, 206–7.

5 General history in Edwin Ferdon, *Early Tonga as the Explorers Saw It, 1616–1810* (Tuscon, 1987); also Shankar Aswani and Michael W. Graves, "The Tongan Maritime Expansion: A Case in the Evolutionary Ecology of Social Complexity," *Asian Perspectives: The Journal of Archaeology for Asia and the Pacific*, 37 (1998).

6 Story of sacrifice in Bott, *Tongan Society*, 93.

7 Penelope Schoeffel, "Rank, Gender and Politics in Ancient Samoa: The Genealogy of Salamasina o le Tafaʻifa," *Journal of Pacific History* 22 (1987), 3–4.

8 Leonard Andaya, *The World of Maluku* (Honolulu, 1993), 6; Herman C. Kemp, *Oral Traditions of Southeast Asia and Oceania: A Bibliography* (Jakarta, 2004); also Lenore Manderson (ed.), *Shared Wealth and Symbol: Food, Culture, and Society in Oceania and Southeast Asia* (New York, 1986); Ian Glover and Peter Bellwood (eds.), *Southeast Asia: From Prehistory to History* (Abingdon, 2004).

9 See Jeffrey McNeely and Paul Sochaczewski, *Soul of the Tiger: Searching for Nature's Answers in Southeast Asia* (Oxford, 1988); George Coedes, *The Indianized States of Southeast Asia* (Honolulu, 1968); Peter Bellwood, *Prehistory of the Indo-Malaysian Archipelago* (Honolulu, 1997).

10 Latika Lahiri, *Chinese Monks Who Went to India* (Delhi, 1986); Lynda Norene Shaffer, *Maritime Southeast Asia to 1500* (Armonk, 1996), ch. 3.

11 O. W. Wolters, *The Fall of Srivijaya in Malay History* (Ithaca, 1970), 97; O. W. Wolters, *Early Indonesian Commerce* (Ithaca, 1967); Nicholas Tarling (ed.), *The Cambridge History of Southeast Asia*, 2 vols. (Cambridge, 1992).

12 Kenneth Hall, *Maritime Trade and State Development in Early Southeast Asia* (Honolulu, 1985), chs. 4–5; Lynda Norene Shaffer, *Maritime Southeast Asia to 1500* (Armonk, 1996); Wolters, *Fall of Srivijaya*, 10–12.

13 R. Soekmono and Jacques Dumarcay, *Borobudur: A Prayer in Stone* (London, 1990).

14 M. C. Ricklefs, *A History of Modern Indonesia since 1200* (Stanford, 2001); Nicholas Tarling (ed.), *The Cambridge History of Southeast Asia*, vol. 1, part 1 (Cambridge, 1992).

3 Straits, sultans, and treasure fleets

1 Wolters, *Fall of Srivijaya*, 108–27; Donald B. Freeman, *The Straits of Malacca: Gateway or Gauntlet?* (Quebec, 2003).

2 Leonard Andaya, *Leaves of the Same Tree: Trade and Ethnicity in the Straits of Melaka* (Honolulu, 2008); also Charles Corn, *The Scents of Eden: A History of the Spice Trade* (New York, 1999).

3 For Arab voyaging, see Jean Gelman Taylor, *Indonesia: Peoples and Histories* (New Haven, 2004), 72–3; George F. Hourani, *Arab Seafaring in the Indian Ocean in Ancient and Medieval Times* (Princeton, 1951); also Markus P. M. Vink, "Indian Ocean Studies and the 'New Thalassology,'" *Journal of Global History*, 2, 1 (March 2007), 41–62.

4 Wen-Chin Ouyang, "Whose Story Is It? Sindbad the Sailor in Literature and Film," *Middle Eastern Literatures*, 7, 2 (July 2004), 133–47.

5 Hussin Mutalib, *Islam in Southeast Asia* (Singapore, 2008); Eric Tagliacozzo (ed.), *Southeast Asia and the Middle East: Islam, Movement, and the Longue Durée* (Singapore, 2009), chs. 2–4.

6 For Ibn Battuta's chronicles, see *Travels in Asia and Africa, 1325–1354* (Abingdon, 2005), 272–3; Samuel Lee (ed.), *The Travels of Ibn Battuta* (New York, 2009), 211–15.

7 Anthony Reid, "Islamization and Christianization in Southeast Asia: The Critical Phase, 1550–1650," in Anthony Reid (ed.), *Southeast Asia in the Early Modern Era: Trade, Power, Belief* (Ithaca, 1993).

8 See Yaneo Ishii (ed.), *The Junk Trade for Southeast Asia, 1674–1723* (Canberra, 1998); Louise Levathes, *When China Ruled the Seas* (New York, 1994); also Samuel Wilson, *The Emperor's Giraffe* (Boulder, 1999); Tan Ta Sen and Dasheng Chen, *Cheng Ho [Zheng He] and Islam* (Singapore 2009).

9 For contemporary representations of Malay identities, see Rick Hosking, Susan Hosking, Washima Che Dan, and Noritah Omar (eds.), *Reading the Malay World* (Kent Town, Australia, 2010).

4 Conquered colonies and Iberian ambitions

1 For Ibn Majid and the Portuguese connection, see Hourani, *Arab Seafaring in the Indian Ocean*; Tabish Khair, Martin Leer, Justin D. Edwards, and Hanna Ziadeh (eds.), *Other Routes: 1500 Years of African and Asian Travel Writing* (Oxford, 2006); see also K. N. Chaudhuri, *Asia Before Europe: Economy and Civilization of the Indian Ocean from the Rise of Islam to 1750* (Cambridge, 1990); Sugata Bose, *A Hundred Horizons: The Indian Ocean in the Age of Global Empire* (Cambridge, MA, 2006).

2 A. J. R. Russell-Wood, *The Portuguese Empire: A World on the Move, 1415–1808* (Baltimore, 1998); Sanjay Subrahmanyam, *The Portuguese Empire in Asia, 1500–1700* (Longman, 1993); also Corn, *The Scents of Eden*, 15; Taylor, *Indonesia*, 115–24; Baily W. Diffie, Boyd C. Shafer, and George D. Winius, *Foundations of the Portuguese Empire, 1415–1580* (Minneapolis, 1977), ch. 16.

3 Laurence Bergreen, *Over the Edge of the World: Magellan's Terrifying Circumnavigation of the Globe* (New York, 2003), 53; R. A. Skelton (ed.), Antonio Pigafetta, *Magellan's Voyage: A Narrative Account of the First Circumnavigation* (New Haven, 1969).

4 Charles E. Nowell, *Magellan's Voyage Around the World; Three Contemporary Accounts [by] Antonio Pigafetta, Maximilian of Transylvania [and] Gaspar Corrêa* (Evanston, 1962).

5 Linda Newson, *Conquest and Pestilence in the Early Spanish Philippines* (Honolulu, 2009), ch. 7.

6 William Henry Scott, *Barangay: Sixteenth Century Philippine Culture and Society* (Quezon City, 1994); also O. D. Corpuz, *The Roots of the Filipino Nation* (Quezon City, 2005), 15–20, 94.

7 Alfonso Felix Jr., *The Chinese in the Philippines, 1570–1770* (Manila, 1968); Andrew Wilson, *Ambition and Identity: Chinese Merchant Elites in Colonial Manila, 1880–1916* (Honolulu, 2004); Richard Chu, *Chinese and Chinese Mestizos of Manila: Family, Identity, and Culture, 1860s–1930s* (Brill, 2010).

8 Kudarat: Corpuz, *Roots*, 177–81; Michael O. Mastura, *Muslim Filipino Experience: Essays* (Ministry of Muslim Affairs, 1984).

5 Island encounters and the Spanish lake

1 Elizabeth Reitz, C. Margaret Scarry, and Sylvia J. Scudder, *Case Studies in Environmental Archaeology* (New York, 2008); Lewis Spence, *Myths of Mexico and Peru* (Charleston, SC, [1913], 2008).

2 Oskar Spate, *The Spanish Lake* (Canberra, [1979], 2004), 87–110; for the Spanish Empire as a global maritime phenomenon, see Carla Rahn Phillips, *The Treasure of the San José: Death at Sea in the War of the Spanish Succession* (Baltimore, 2007); Pablo E. Pérez-Mallaína (Carla Rahn Phillips, ed. and trans.), *Spain's Men of the Sea: The Daily Life of Crews on the Indies Fleets in the Sixteenth Century* (Baltimore, 1998); Carla Rahn Phillips, *Six Galleons for the King of Spain: Imperial Defense in the Early Seventeenth Century* (Baltimore, 1986); also Antonio Barrera, *The Spanish American Empire and the Scientific Revolution* (Austin, 2006); Hugh Thomas, *Rivers of Gold: The Rise of the Spanish Empire from Columbus to Magellan* (New York, 2003).

3 Thor Heyerdahl, *Kon Tiki: Across the Pacific by Raft* (New York, [1950], 1990).

4 For Mendaña and Quiros, see Thomas Suárez, *Early Mapping of the Pacific* (Singapore, 2004), 74–6; Byron Heath, *Discovering the Great South Land* (New South Wales, 2005), 56–62; Mercedes Maroto Camino, *Producing the Pacific: Maps and Narratives of Spanish Exploration, 1567–1606* (New York, 2005), 34–6.

5 Marquesas described by Greg Dening, *Islands and Beaches: Discourse on a Silent Land, Marquesas, 1774–1880* (Honolulu, 1980).

6 Dening, *Islands and Beaches*, 52–63; Spate, *Spanish Lake*, 44; Kirch, *Road of the Winds*, 236–65; Barry Rollett, "Voyaging and Interaction in Ancient East Polynesia," *Asian Perspectives*, 41, 2 (2002), 182–94.

7 Spate, *Spanish Lake*, 61, 136.

8 José Garanger, "Oral Traditions and Archaeology," in R. Blench and Matthew Spriggs (eds.), *Archaeology and Language: Theoretical and Methodological Orientations* (London, 1997); Kirch, *Road of the Winds*, 139.

6 Sea changes and Spice Islands

1 Story of Afo, *The Jakarta Post* (Jakarta, July 4, 1999).

2 Taylor, *Indonesia*, 131–3; Jack Turner, *Spice: The History of a Temptation* (New York, 2004).

3 Williard Anderson Hanna and Des Alwi, *Turbulent Times Past in Ternate and Tidore* (Ann Arbor [reprint], 2008), 90–5.

4 Ernst van Ween and Leonard Blussé (eds.), *Rivalry and Conflict: European Traders and Asian Trading Networks in the 16th and 17th Centuries* (Leiden, 2005); Thomas Suárez, *Early Mapping of Southeast Asia* (Singapore, 1999), 177–82; Taylor, *Indonesia*, 139–40; Robert Parthesius, *Dutch Ships in Tropical Waters: The Development of the Dutch East India Company (VOC) Shipping Networks in Asia, 1595–1660* (Amsterdam, 2010).

5 J. Redhead, *Utilization of Tropical Foods: Trees* (United Nations, 1989), 1–5; Richard Finn, *Nature's Chemicals: The Natural Products that Shaped Our World* (Oxford, 2010), 27–9.

6 Leonard Blussé, *Bitter Bonds: A Colonial Divorce Drama of the Seventeenth Century* (Princeton, 2002); Leonard Blussé, *Strange Company: Chinese Settlers, Mestizo Women, and the Dutch in VOC Batavia* (Dordrecht, 1988); Jean Gelman Taylor, *The Social World of Batavia: Europeans and Eurasians in Colonial Indonesia* (Madison, 2009); Ulbe Bosma and Remco Raben, *Being "Dutch" in the Indies: A History of Creolisation and Empire, 1500–1920* (Singapore, 2008), 33–65.

7 Gerrit J. Knaap, *Shallow Waters, Rising Tide* (Leiden, 1996), 1–2, 16; Gerrit J. Knapp and Heather Sutherland, *Monsoon Traders: Ships, Skippers, and Commodities in Eighteenth-Century Makassar* (Leiden, 2004); Els M. Jacobs, *Merchant in Asia: The Trade of the Dutch East India Company during the Eighteenth Century* (Leiden, 2006); Kerry Ward, *Networks of Empire: Forced Migration in the Dutch East India Company* (Cambridge, 2009).

8 J. C. Beaglehole, *The Exploration of the Pacific* (Stanford, 1968), 127–37; also Sir Peter H. Buck (Te Rangi Hiroa), *Explorers of the Pacific: European and American Discoveries in Polynesia* (Honolulu, 1953).

9 Vincent Lebot, Mark Merlin, and Lamont Lindstrom, *Kava – The Pacific Elixir: The Definitive Guide to its Ethnobotany, History, and Chemistry* (New Haven, 1997); on insignificance, Ronald Love, *Maritime Exploration in the Age of Discovery 1415–1800* (Westport, CT, 2006), 98.

10 James Belich, *Making People: A History of the New Zealanders from Polynesian Settlement to the End of the Nineteenth Century* (London, 1996), for moa, see 51–2.

11 Ngati Tumata history in tdc.govt.nz/Tangata/Whenua/History; Anne Salmond, *Two Worlds: First Meetings Between Maori and Europeans, 1642–1772* (Honolulu, 1991); Anne Salmond, *Between Worlds: Early Meetings Between Maori and Europeans 1773–1815* (Honolulu, 1997).

7 Samurai, priests, and potentates

1 John Nelson, *A Year in the Life of a Shinto Shrine* (Seattle, 1996); Donald F. Lach, *Asia in the Making of Europe: The Century of Discovery* (Chicago, 1965).

2 K. W. Taylor and John K. Whitmore (eds.), *Essays Into Vietnamese Pasts* (Ithaca, 1995).

3 Jonathan Porter, *Macau, the Imaginary City: Culture and Society, 1557 to the Present* (Boulder, CO, 1996).

4 Olof Lidin, *Tanegashima: The Arrival of Europe in Japan* (Honolulu, 2002).

5 For Francis Xavier's work, see Ikuo Higashibaba, *Christianity in Early Modern Japan: Kirishitan Belief and Practice* (Leiden, 2001), ch. 1.

6 Joseph Francis Moran, *The Japanese and the Jesuits: Alessandro Valignano in Sixteenth-Century Japan* (London, 1993); Po-chia Hsia, *The World of Catholic Renewal, 1540–1770* (Cambridge, 1998).

7 Po-chia Hsia, *The World of Catholic Renewal*, 181–206; J. S. A. Elisonas, "Nagasaki: The Early Years of an Early Modern Japanese City," in Liam Matthew Brockley (ed.), *Portuguese Colonial Cities in the Early Modern World* (Farnham and Burlington, 2008); Leonard Blussé, *Visible Cities: Canton, Nagasaki, and Batavia and the Coming of the Americans* (Cambridge, MA, 2008).

8 Stephen Vlastos, *Peasant Protests and Uprisings in Tokugawa Japan* (Berkeley and Los Angeles, 1990); John Whitney Hall (ed.), *The Cambridge History of Japan*, vol. IV, *Early Modern Japan* (Cambridge, 1991), 326–34.

9 James Bryant Lewis, *Frontier Contact between Choson Korea and Tokugawa Japan* (Abingdon, 2003); Jae-un Kang, *The Land of Scholars: Two Thousand Years of Korean Confucianism* (Paramus, 2003).

10 Samuel Hawley, *The Imjin War: Japan's Sixteenth-Century Invasion of Korea and the Attempt to Conquer China* (Berkeley, 2005); Robert Finlay, *The Pilgrim Art: Cultures of Porcelain in World History* (Berkeley and Los Angeles, 2010), 182–6.

11 Yoshi S. Kuno, *Japanese Expansion on the Asiatic Continent* (Berkeley, 1938), 308–12; Lyle W. Schurz, *The Manila Galleon, 1565–1815* (New York, 1959), 104–5.

12 For ancient Ryukyus and Ah Xiang, see George Kerr, *Okinawa: The History of an Island People* (2000); Gregory Smits, *Visions of Ryukyu: Identity and Ideology in Early Modern Thought* (Honolulu, 1999).

13 Willem R. van Gulik (ed.), *In the Wake of the Liefde: Cultural Relations Between the Netherlands and Japan since 1600* (Amsterdam, 1986); C. R. Boxer, *The Christian Century in Japan, 1549–1650* (Berkeley, 1951), chs. 7–8; Stephen R. Turnbull, *The Kakure Kirishitan: A Study of their Development, Beliefs, and Rituals to the Present Day* (Surrey, 1998).

14 Matthew Keith, "The Logistics of Power: Tokugawa Response to the Shimabara Rebellion and Power Projection in Seventeenth-Century Japan," unpublished PhD dissertation, Ohio State University (2006); George Elison (Jurgis Elisonas), *Deus Destroyed: The Image of Christianity in Early Modern Japan* (Cambridge, MA, 1973); Ivan Morris, *The Nobility of Failure: Tragic Heroes in the History of Japan* (New York, 1975).

15 Leonard Blussé and Willem Remmelink (eds.), *Deshima Diaries: Marginalia 1740–1800* (Tokyo, 2004), these citations, 19–21, 236, 245.

8 Pirates and raiders of the Eastern seas

1 Pirate descriptions: Stephen Turnbull, *Pirates of the Far East 811–1639* (Botley, 2007); Gertrude L. Jacob, *The Rajah of Sarawak, An Account of Sir James Brooke* (London, 1876), 146.

2 See Dian Murray, *Pirates of the South China Coast, 1790–1810* (Stanford, 1987), 9, 23, 24.

3 For the Lim Ah Hong legend, see Cesar V. Callanta, *The Limahong Invasion* (Dagupan City, 1979); Chang-Hsing-lang, "The Real Limahong in Philippine History," *Yenching Journal of Chinese Studies*, 8 (1930), 1473–91.

4 Tonio Andrade, *How Taiwan Became Chinese: Dutch, Spanish, and Han Colonization in the Seventeenth Century* (New York, 2008), 8.

5 Zheng Zhilong in Andrade, *How Taiwan Became Chinese*, 12, 46.

6 Zheng Zhilong in Andrade, *How Taiwan Became Chinese*, 21–6.

7 Joan Druett, *She Captains: Heroines and Hellions of the Sea* (New York, 2000), 55–63; Robert Antony, *Like Froth Floating on the Sea: The World of Pirates and Seafarers in Late Imperial South China* (China Research Monograph, 2003).

8 Atsushi Ota, *Changes of Regime and Social Dynamics in West Java* (Leiden, 2006), 125–7; also James Francis Warren, *Iranun and Balangingi: Globalization, Maritime Raiding, and the Birth of Ethnicity* (Singapore, 2000).

9 Warren, *Iranun and Balangingi*, 64; see J. F. Warren, *The Sulu Zone, 1768–1898* (Honolulu, 2007); also Eric Tagliacozzo, *Secret Trades, Porous Borders: Smuggling and States along the Southeast Asian Frontier, 1865–1915* (New Haven, 2005).

10 Raffles, introduction to *Malay Annals Translated from the Malay Language by the Late Dr. John Leyeden* (London, 1821), ix. See also David Sopher, *The Sea Nomads: A Study of the Maritime Boat People of Southeast Asia* (Singapore, 1965); for comparative work, Adam Young, *Contemporary Maritime Piracy in Southeast Asia: History, Causes, and Remedies* (Singapore, 2007); Stefan Eklöf, *Pirates in Paradise: A Modern History of Southeast Asia's Maritime Marauders* (Copenhagen, 2006).

9 Asia, America, and the age of the galleons

1 Harry Kelsey, *Sir Francis Drake: The Queen's Pirate* (New Haven, 2000);
William Lytle Schurz, *The Manila Galleon* (New York, 1939), 307–8;
Peter Gerhard, *Pirates of the Pacific, 1575–1742* (Lincoln, NE, 1980); Kris
E. Lane, *Pillaging the Empire: Piracy in the Americas, 1500–1750*
(Armonk, 1998).

2 Dennis O. Flynn and Arturo Giráldez, "Born with a 'Silver Spoon': The Origin
of World Trade in 1571," *Journal of World History*, 6 (Fall 1995), 201–21;
"Cycles of Silver: Global Economic Unity through the Mid-Eighteenth
Century," *Journal of World History*, 13 (Fall 2002), 391–427; *China
and the Birth of Globalization in the 16th Century* (Burlington and
London, 2010).

3 Floro L. Mercene, *Manila Men in the New World: Filipino Migration to
Mexico and the Americas from the Sixteenth Century* (Honolulu, 2006);
Schurz, *The Manila Galleon*, 357–60; also O. D. Corpuz, *The Roots of the
Filipino Nation* (Quezon City, 2005), 185–215; Robert Reed, *Colonial Manila:
The Context of Hispanic Urbanism and Process of Morphogenesis*
(Berkeley, 1978).

4 Robert Rogers, *Destiny's Landfall* (Honolulu, 1995), and Anne Perez Hattori,
Colonial Dis-Ease (Honolulu, 2004).

5 Rogers, *Destiny's Landfall*, 70–1.

6 Rosina C. Iping, "The Astronomical Significance of Ancient Chamorro Cave
Paintings," *Bulletin of the American Astronomical Society*, 31 (1999), 671;
Deryck Scarr, *A History of the Pacific Islands: Passages through Tropical Time*
(Richmond, Surrey, 2001), 58.

7 Crouchett, *Filipino Sailors in the New World*; Mercene, *Manila Men*.

8 Robert Jackson and Edward Castillo, *Indians, Franciscans, and Spanish
Colonization: The Impact of the Mission System on California Indians*
(Albuquerque, 1995).

9 Mercene, *Manila Men*, 6; Yen Le Espiritu, *Filipino American Lives*
(Philadelphia, 1995).

10 Leslie Bauzon, *Deficit Government: Mexico and the Philippine Situado, 1606–
1804* (Tokyo, 1981); Spate, *Spanish Lake*, 106.

11 Schurz, *Manila Galleon*, 362–3, and 373–5.

12 Catarina de San Juan, in Tatiana Seijas, "The Portuguese Slave Trade to
Spanish Manila," *Itinerario*, 32, 1 (2008), 19–37; also Nora Jaffary (ed.),
Gender, Race, and Religion in the Colonization of the Americas (Burlington,
2007); Nora Jaffary, *False Mystics: Deviant Orthodoxy in Colonial Mexico*
(Nebraska, 2004).

13 Nicholas Tracy, *Manila Ransomed: The British Assault on Manila in the Seven
Years War* (Exeter, 1995); Alan Frost, *The Global Reach of Empire: Britain's*

Maritime Expansion in the Indian and Pacific Oceans, 1764–1815 (Carlton, Victoria, 2003); Lauren Benton, *A Search for Sovereignty: Law and Geography in European Empires, 1400–1900* (London, 2010).

14 James Cloghessy, *The Royal Philippines Company* (Chicago, 1956); Norman Owen, *Prosperity Without Progress: Manila Hemp and Material Life in the Colonial Philippines* (Berkeley and Los Angeles, 1984).

15 Lewis Bealer, "Bouchard in the Islands of the Pacific," *Pacific Historical Review*, 4, 4 (1935), 328–42; John Charles Chasteen, *Americanos: Latin America's Struggle for Independence* (New York, 2008).

10 Navigators of Polynesia and paradise

1 Missed Hawaiian contacts in Deryck Scarr, *A History of the Pacific Islands: Passages through Tropical Time* (Richmond, Surrey, 2001); also Deryck Scarr, *The History of the Pacific Islands: Kingdoms of the Reefs* (South Melbourne, 1990), 58; Thomas Suárez, *Early Mapping of the Pacific* (Singapore, 2004).

2 John Waiko, *A Short History of Papua New Guinea* (Oxford, 1993).

3 For Hawaiian society, see Patrick V. Kirch, *The Evolution of the Polynesian Chiefdoms* (Cambridge, 1984); for New Guinea, see Scarr, *Passages through Tropical Time*, 62.

4 William Dampier, *A New Voyage Around the World*, http://gutenberg.net.au/ ebooks05/0500461h.html#ch5; also Chapell, *Double Ghosts*, 27; Geraldine Barnes, "Curiosity, Wonder, and William Dampier's Painted Prince," *Journal for Early Modern Cultural Studies*, 6, 1 (2006), 31–50; Derek Howe (ed.), *Background to Discovery: Pacific Exploration from Dampier to Cook* (Berkeley and Los Angeles, 1990).

5 Stephen Fischer, *Island at the End of the World: The Turbulent History of Easter Island* (London, 2005); Jared Diamond, *Guns, Germs, and Steel: the Fates of Human Societies* (New York, 1997); P. V. Kirch, *The Growth and Collapse of Pacific Island Societies* (Honolulu, 2007); Terry Hunt and C. Lipo, "Ecological Catastrophe, Collapse, and the Myth of 'Ecocide' on Rapa Nui (Easter Island)," in P. A. McAnany and N. Yoffee (eds.), *Questioning Collapse: Human Resilience, Ecological Vulnerability, and the Aftermath of Empire* (Cambridge, 2009), 21–44.

6 Patrick V. Kirch and Roger Green, *Hawaiki: Ancestral Polynesia* (Cambridge, 2001); Robert W. Williamson, *Religion and Social Organization in Central Polynesia* (New York, [1937], 1977).

7 Dennis Kawaharada, "1992 Voyage: Sail to Ra'iatea," http://pvs.kcc.hawaii. edu/1992/raiatea.html

8 Rod Edmond, *Representing the South Pacific* (Cambridge, 1997); Vanessa Smith, *Literary Culture and the Pacific: Nineteenth Century Textual Encounters* (Cambridge, 1998), 87.

9 Michael Sturma, *South Sea Maidens: Western Fantasy and Sexual Politics in the South Pacific* (Westport, 2002); Harry Libersohn, *The Traveler's World: Europe to the Pacific* (Cambridge, MA, 2008), 28.

10 On Tahitian encounter, see Peter Brooks, "Gauguin's Tahitian Body," in Norma Broude and Mary Garrard (eds.), *The Expanding Discourse* (New York, 1992).

11 Anthony Pagden, *European Encounters with the New World: From Renaissance to Romanticism* (New Haven, 1993), 127–30; Dodge, *Islands and Beaches*, 42–3.

12 Glyndwr Williams (ed.), *Captain Cook: Explorations and Reassessments* (Suffolk, 2004); Nicholas Thomas, *Cook: The Extraordinary Voyages of Captain Cook* (New York, 2004).

13 Joan Druett, *Tupaia: Captain Cook's Polynesian Navigator* (Westport, 2010); Margarette Lincoln (ed.), *Science and Exploration in the Pacific: European Voyages to the Southern Oceans in the Eighteenth Century* (Suffolk, 1998).

14 Michelle Hetherington, *Cook and Omai: The Cult of the South Seas* (Canberra, 2001).

15 Atlasov and Dembei in David Schimmelpenninck van der Oye, *Russian Orientalism: Asia in the Russian Mind from Peter the Great to the Emigration* (New Haven, 2010), 37; Walter McDougall, *Let the Sea Make A Noise* (New York, 1993).

16 This remains a major controversy; see Gananath Obeyesekere, *The Apotheosis of Captain Cook: European Mythmaking in the Pacific* (Princeton, 1992); Marshall Sahlins, *Historical Metaphors and Mythical Realities* (Ann Arbor, 1981); Marshall Sahlins, *How "Natives" Think: About Captain Cook, for Example* (Chicago, 1995).

17 Sidney Mintz, *Sweetness and Power: The Place of Sugar in Modern History* (New York, 1985); Greg Dening, *Mr Bligh's Bad Language: Passion, Power and Theatre on the Bounty* (Cambridge, 1992).

11 Gods and sky piercers

1 For Maretu, see Marjorie Crocombe, *Cannibals and Converts: Radical Change in the Cook Islands* (Suva, 1983), 5, 13; David Hanlon, "Converting Pasts and Presents," *Reflections on Histories of Missionary Enterprises in the Pacific*, www.hawaii.edu/cpis/files/Hanlon-Converting_Pasts.pdf

2 For native agents, see Crocombe, *Cannibals and Converts*, 18–19; also Doug Munro and Andrew Thornley (eds.), *The Covenant Makers: Islander Missionaries in the Pacific* (Suva, 1996); also Raeburn Lange, *Island Ministers: Indigenous Leadership in Nineteenth Century Pacific Islands* (Canberra, 2005).

3 For Spanish and English LMS, see Dodge, *Islands and Empires*, 85–9.

4 Ian Campbell, *Gone Native in Polynesia: Captivity Narratives and Experiences from the South Pacific* (Westport, 1998), 47–51.

5 Pomare and Nott in Howe, *Where the Waves Fall*, 90, 141.

6 Native agent status in Norman Etherington, *Missions and Empire* (New York, 2005), 139.

7 In Crocombe, *Cannibals and Converts*, 12.

8 Siovili in Vanessa Smith, *Literary Culture and the Pacific: Nineteenth Century Textual Encounters* (Cambridge, 1998); also Howe, *Where the Waves Fall*, 236; Garry W. Trompf (ed.), *The Gospel is Not Western: Black Theologies from the Southwest Pacific* (New York, 1987).

9 In Crocombe, *Cannibals and Converts*, chs. 4–5, ms. sections 123–4.

10 For Ta'unga and disease, see Ron and Marjorie Crocombe, *Works of Ta'unga* (Honolulu, 1968); Smith, *Literary Culture and the Pacific*, 87.

11 For Ta'unga, see Crocombe, *Works of Ta'unga*, 83; also Marjorie Tuainekore Crocombe, *Polynesian Missions in Melanesia: From Samoa, Cook Islands and Tonga to Papua New Guinea and New Caledonia* (Suva, 1982).

12 Crocombe, *Works of Ta'unga*, 21–2; John Garrett, *To Live Among the Stars: Christian Origins in Oceania* (Suva, 1985).

13 Elekana in Norman Etherington (ed.), *Missions and Empire* (Oxford, 2005), 139; Michael Goldsmith and Doug Munro, *The Accidental Missionary: Tales of Elekana* (Christchurch, NZ, 2002).

14 Poate Ratu in Crocombe, *Polynesian Missions in Melanesia*, chs. 5, 7, 8; Etherington, *Missions and Empire*, 141; David Wetherell, "Pioneers and Patriarchs: Samoans in a Nonconformist Mission District in Papua, 1890–1917," *The Journal of Pacific History*, 15, 3 (July 1980).

15 Harvey Whitehouse, *Arguments and Icons: Divergent Modes of Religiosity* (Oxford, 2000); also Clive Moore, *New Guinea: Boundary Crossings and History* (Honolulu, 2003), 15–56.

16 A point made by Ernest Dodge, *Islands and Empires* (Minneapolis, 1976), 97.

17 See Howe, *Where the Waves Fall*, 156–8; Patrick V. Kirch and Marshall Sahlins, *Anahulu: The Anthropology of History in the Kingdom of Hawaii* (Chicago, 1992), chs. 2–4.

18 Noenoe K. Silva, *Aloha Betrayed: Native Hawaiian Resistance to American Colonialism* (Durham, 2004), 28–30; Juri Mykkänen, *Inventing Politics: A New Political Anthropology of the Hawaiian Kingdom* (Honolulu, 2003); Jocelyn Linnekin, *Sacred Queens and Women of Consequence: Rank, Gender, and Colonialism in the Hawaiian Islands* (Ann Arbor, 1990).

19 Sally Engle Merry, "Kapiolani at the Brink: Dilemmas of Historical Ethnography in Nineteenth-Century Hawai'i," *American Ethnologist*, 30, 1 (2003), 44–60; Linnekin, *Sacred Queens and Women of Consequence*, 32.

20 Dodge, *Islands and Empires*, ch. 5, "Whalers Ashore."

21 Harrison Wright, *New Zealand, 1769–1840: Early Years of Western Contact* (Cambridge, MA, 1967).

22 Anne Salmond, *Between Worlds: Early Meetings Between Maori and Europeans 1773–1815* (Honolulu, 1997), 405; Angela Middleton, *Te Puna: A New Zealand Mission Station, Historical Archaeology in New Zealand* (Dunedin, 2008); James Belich, *Making People: A History of the New Zealanders from Polynesian Settlement to the End of the Nineteenth Century* (London, 1996), 140–4.

23 John B. Williams, *The New Zealand Journal, 1842–1844* (Salem, Peabody Museum, 1956).

12 Extremities of the Great Southern Continent

1 Greg Dening, "Deep Times, Deep Spaces," in Bernhard Klein and Gesa Mackenthun, *Sea Changes: Historicizing the Ocean* (New York, 2004).

2 Verna Philpot report in *Cook's Log*, Captain Cook Society, 18, 2 (1995), 1140; Glyndwr Williams (ed.), *Captain Cook: Explorations and Reassessments* (Suffolk, 2004), 239.

3 Mark McKenna, *Looking for Blackfella's Point: An Australian History of Place* (Sydney, 2002), 158; Annie Coombes (ed.), *Rethinking Settler Colonialism* (Manchester, 2006).

4 For literature on the Dreaming, see Patrick Wolfe, "On Being Woken Up: The Dreamtime in Anthropology and in Australian Settler Culture," *Comparative Studies in Society and History*, 33, 2 (1991), 197–224.

5 For prehistoric Australia, see Ian McNiven, "Saltwater People: Spiritscapes, Maritime Rituals, and the Archaeology of Australian Indigenous Seascapes," *World Archaeology*, 35, 3 (2003), 329–49.

6 Geoffrey Blainey, *The Tyranny of Distance* (Melbourne, 1966), 2; also Stuart MacIntyre, Anna Clark, and Anthony Mason, *The History Wars* (Melbourne, 2004), 83–90.

7 Stephen Nicholas (ed.), *Convict Workers: Reinterpreting Australia's Past* (Cambridge, 1988); Deborah Oxley, *Convict Maids: The Forced Migration of Women to Australia* (Cambridge, 1996).

8 Mike Walker, *A Long Way Home, The Life and Adventures of the Convict Mary Bryant* (Hoboken, NY, 2005); Nance Irvine, *Molly Incognita: A Biography of Mary Reibey* (Sydney, 1983); Kay Daniels, *Convict Women: Rough Culture and Reformation* (Crows Nest, 1998).

9 As noted in Dodge, *Islands and Empire*, 131.

10 Cases of Henry Kable, John Randall, and Edward Pugh archived at http://members.iinet.net.au/~perthdps/convicts/con137.htm

11 Judy Campbell, *Invisible Invaders: Smallpox and Other Diseases in Aboriginal Australia, 1780–1880* (Melbourne, 2002); Grace Karskens, *The Colony: A History of Early Sydney* (Crows Nest, 2009), 32–61.

12 Jane Carey and Claire McLisky, *Creating White Australia* (Sydney, 2006); Laksiri Jaysuriya, David Walker, and Jan Gothard (eds.), *Legacies of White Australia: Race, Culture, and Nation* (Perth, 2003); Hsu-Mind Teo and Richard White (eds.), *Cultural History in Australia* (Sydney, 2003); Manning Clark, *A History of Australia* (Melbourne, [reprint] 1997); Frank Sherry, *Pacific Passions: The European Struggle for Power in the Great Ocean in the Age of Exploration* (London, 1994); Dampier, *A New Voyage*, 410.

13 See Suvendrini Perera, *Australia and the Insular Imagination* (New York, 2009); David Walker, *Anxious Nation: Australia and the Rise of Asia, 1850–1939* (St Lucia, 1999); archeological finds: Julian Holland, "The Search for a Continent," in *Pacific Voyages* (New York, 1971), 336.

14 Miriam Estensen, *The Life of Matthew Flinders* (London and Crows Nest, 2002), 264–6.

15 Regina Ganter, Julia Martinez, and Gary Lee, *Mixed Relations: Asian–Aboriginal Contact in North Australia* (Crawley, 2006), 14–16; Alison Mercieca, "From Makassar to Marege to the Museum: Trepang Processing Industry in Arnhem Land," www.nma.gov.au/audio/transcripts/ NMA_Mercieca_20080709.html

16 C. C. Macknight, *The Voyage to Marege: Macassan Trepangers in Northern Australia* (Melbourne, 1976); circuit records, 98, 116.

17 Macknight, *Voyage to Marege*, 204.

18 Ganter et al., *Mixed Relations*; www.Aiaa.org.au/news/news15/seacucumber.html

19 See Stuart MacIntyre, Anna Clark, and Anthony Mason, *The History Wars*, (Melbourne, 2004), 103.

20 Ganter et al., *Mixed Relations*, 33.

13 The world that Canton made

1 Joseph Waterhouse, *The King and People of Fiji* (London, 1866), 24.

2 Marion Diamond, "For all the Tea in China," in *America, Australia, and the China Tea Trade*, special edition of *Mains'l Haul: A Journal of Pacific Maritime History*, 39, 2 (Spring 2003), 47–55; also Max Quanchi and Ron W. Adams, *Culture Contact in the Pacific* (Cambridge, 1993).

3 Fa-ti Fan, *British Naturalists in Qing China: Science, Empire, and Cultural Encounter* (Cambridge, MA and London, 2004), 17.

4 On the Canton harbor system and the Hoppos, see Paul Van Dyke, *The Canton Trade* (Hong Kong, 2005), 16–25; K. N. Chaudhuri, *The Trading World of Asia and the English East India Company, 1600–1760* (Cambridge, 1978).

5 For Canton merchants, see ocw.mit.edu/ans7870/21f/21f.027/rise_fall_canton_01/ cw_essay03.html. See Weng Eong Chong, *The Hong Merchants of Canton: Chinese Merchants in Sino-Western Trade* (Richmond, 1997).

6 Mary Dusenbery and Carol Bier, *Flowers, Dragons, and Pine Trees: Asian Textiles in the Spencer Museum of Art* (Manchester, VT, 2004), 118; villas and gardens, Fa-Ti Fan, *British Naturalists in Qing China*; Yong Chen, *Chinese in San Francisco, 1850–1943* (Stanford, 2000), 37.

7 Yen P'ing Hao, *The Comprador in Nineteenth Century China: Bridge Between East and West* (Cambridge, 1970), for work and culture, see 48–9, 75–6, 87, for Robert Ho Tung, see 182.

8 Daniel Peacock, *Lee Boo of Belau: A Prince in London* (Honolulu, 2007); for Kaiana, see David Chappell, *Double Ghosts: Oceanian Voyagers on European Ships* (New York, 1997), passim chs. 6–9.

9 Chappell, *Double Ghosts*, chs. 3–5.

10 Susan Lebo, "Native Hawaiian Whalers in Nantucket, 1820–60," *Historic Nantucket*, 56, 1 (Winter 2007), 14–16.

11 Rev. Henry Cheever, *The Whale and His Captors* (New York, 1853).

12 For Melville and global literature, see David Chappell, "Ahab's Boat," in Bernhard Klein and Gesa Mackenthun, *Sea Changes: Historicizing the Ocean* (New York, 2004), 75–90.

13 For Nootka encounters and Maquinna, see Dale Walker, *Pacific Destiny: The Three Century Journey to the Oregon Country* (New York, 2000); also David Igler, "Diseased Goods: Global Exchanges in the Eastern Pacific Basin, 1770–1850," *American Historical Review* 109 (June 2004), 693–719.

14 For Barkley, Frances, and Winnee, see Chappell, *Double Ghosts*, 19–20; also Jean Barman and Bruce McIntyre Watson, *Leaving Paradise: Indigenous Hawaiians in the Pacific Northwest* (Honolulu, 2006).

15 For Kamehameha's trade policy, see Dodge, *Islands and Empires*, 62, 160–1.

16 Gavan Daws, "The High Chief Boki," *Journal of the Polynesian Society*, 75, 1 (1966).

17 R. Gerard Ward, "The Pacific Bêche-de-Mer Trade with Special Reference to Fiji," in Ward (ed.), *Man in the Pacific Islands* (Oxford, 1972), 91–123.

18 Trepang trade in "The Disappearing Dri," *The Fiji Times* (July 28, 1988); also Richard Tucker, *Insatiable Appetite: The United States and Ecological Degradation of the Tropical World* (Berkeley, 2000).

19 Robert Gardella, *Harvesting Mountains: Fujian and the China Tea Trade* (Berkeley and Los Angeles, 1994); Yong Liu, *The Dutch East India Company's Tea Trade with China, 1757–1781* (Leiden, 2007); tea history is always a popular subject: see Roy Moxham, *Tea: Addiction, Exploitation, and Empire* (New York, 2004); Laura Martin, *Tea: The Drink that Changed the World* (North Clarendon, 2007); Beatrice Hohnegger, *Liquid Jade: The Story of Tea from East to West* (New York, 2006); Alan Macfarlane and Iris Macfarlane, *The Empire of Tea: The Remarkable History of the Plant that Took Over the World* (New York, 2004); Victor Mair and Erling Hoh, *The True History of Tea* (London, 2009).

20 For the Qing and the English barbarians, see Harry Gregor Gelber, *Opium, Soldiers, and Evangelicals* (New York, 2004), 29–30; Alain Le Pichon, *China Trade and Empire: Jardine, Matheson & Co. and the Origins of British Hong Kong, 1827–1843* (Oxford, 2006).

21 Yangwen Zheng, *The Social Life of Opium in China* (Cambridge, 2005); David Anthony Bello, *Opium and the Limits of Empire: Drug Prohibition in the Chinese Interior, 1729–1850* (Cambridge, MA, 2005); Gelber, *Opium*, 35–40.

22 Lydia He Liu, *The Clash of Empires: The Invention of China in Modern World Making* (Cambridge, MA, 2004), 235; Hsin-pao Chang, *Commissioner Lin and the Opium War* (New York, 1970); Arthur Waley, *The Opium War through Chinese Eyes* (Stanford, 1968); W. Travis Hanes and Frank Sanello, *The Opium Wars: The Addiction of One Empire and the Corruption of Another* (Naperville, IL, 2002).

23 Jonathan Spence, *God's Chinese Son: The Taiping Heavenly Kingdom of Hong Xiquan* (Norton, 1997); Anthony Reid (ed.), *The Chinese Diaspora in the Pacific* (London, 2008).

14 Flags, treaties, and gunboats

1 Carl A. Trocki, *Prince of Pirates: The Temenggongs and the Development of Johor and Singapore* (Singapore, 1979); Hong Lysa and Huang Jianli, *The Scripting of a National Story: Singapore and its Pasts* (Singapore, 2008); C. E. Wurtzburg, *Raffles of the Eastern Isles* (London, 1954).

2 Peter Carey, *The Power of Prophecy: Prince Dipanagara and the End of an Old Order in Java, 1785–1855* (Leiden, 2008); Nancy Florida, *Writing the Past, Inscribing the Future: History as Prophesy in Colonial Java* (Durham, 1995); Michael Adas, *Prophets of Rebellion: Millennarian Protest Movements against the European Colonial Order* (Chapel Hill, 1979).

3 For the Cultivation System policy, see R. E. Elson, *Village Java under the Cultivation System, 1830–1870* (Sydney, 1994); C. Fasseur, *The Politics of Colonial Expansion: Java, the Dutch, and the Cultivation System* (Ithaca, 1992).

4 John H. Walker, *Power and Prowess: the Origins of Brooke Kingship in Sarawak* (Honolulu, 2002), 14, 113; Benedict Sandin, *The Sea Dayaks of Borneo before White Rajah Rule* (East Lansing, 1967).

5 Gertrude L. Jacob, *The Rajah of Sarawak, An Account of Sir James Brooke* (London, 1876); Steven Runciman, *The White Rajahs: A History of Sarawak from 1841 to 1946* (Cambridge, 1960).

6 Jacob, *The Rajah of Sarawak*, 174.

7 Claudia Orange, *The Treaty of Waitangi* (Crows Nest, 1987); Donald F. MacKenzie, *Oral Culture, Literacy, and Print in Early New Zealand:*

The Treaty of Waitangi (Wellington, 1985); Paul Moon, *Te ara kī te Tiriti (The Path to the Treaty of Waitangi)* (Auckland, 2002); Ranginui Walker, *Ka whawhai tonu matou (Struggle without End)* (Auckland, 2004).

8 James Belich, *The New Zealand Wars and the Victorian Interpretation of Racial Conflict* (Auckland, 1986); Angela Ballara, *Taua: Musket Wars, Land Wars, or Tikanga: Warfare in Maori Society in the Early Nineteenth Century* (Auckland, 2003); Ron Crosby, *The Musket Wars: A History of Inter-Iwi Conflict, 1806–1845* (Auckland, 1999); Dorothy Ulrich Cloher, *Hongi Hika, Warrior Chief* (Viking, 2003).

9 Marshall Sahlins, *Islands of History* (Chicago, 1985), 54–72; Paul Moon, *Hone Heke: Nga Puhi Warrior* (Auckland, 2001).

10 Angela Ballara, *Te Kīngitanga: The People of the Maori King Movement* (Auckland, 1996); Belich, *The New Zealand Wars*; James Liu, Tim McCreanor, Tracey McIntosh, and Teresia Teaiwa (eds.), *New Zealand Identities: Departures and Destinations* (Wellington, 2005).

11 Greg Dening, "Writing, Rewriting the Beach," in Alan Munslow and Robert Rosentstone (eds.), *Experiments in Rethinking History* (New York, 2004), 44–5; also John Dunmore, *Visions and Realities: France in the Pacific 1695–1995* (Waikanae, 1997).

12 For Pakoko, see Dening, "Writing, Rewriting," 50–1.

13 Pomare and the chiefs' protests: Colin Newbury, "Aspects of French Policy in the Pacific 1853–1906," *Pacific Historical Review*, 27, 1 (February 1958); also Colin Newbury, "Resistance and Collaboration in French Polynesia: The Tahitian War: 1844–7," Appendix 1, 21–5, cited here, 23.

14 Colin Newbury, *Tahiti Nui: Change and Survival in French Polynesia, 1767–1945* (Honolulu, 1980); Matt Matsuda, *Empire of Love: Histories of France and the Pacific* (New York, 2003).

15 Robert Nicole, *The Pen, the Pistol and the Other: Literature and Power in Tahiti* (New York, 2001), 167–202; Lee Wallace, *Sexual Encounters, Pacific Texts, Modern Sexualities* (Ithaca, NY, 2003).

16 Nicola Cooper, *France in Indochina: Colonial Encounters* (Oxford, 2001); Panivong Norindr, *Phantasmatic Indochina: French Colonial Ideology in Architecture, Film, and Literature* (Durham, 1996); Kathryn Robson and Jennifer Yee (eds.), *France and "Indochina": Cultural Representations* (Lanham, 2005).

17 See Matsuda, *Empire of Love*; also Julia Clancy-Smith and Frances Gouda (eds.), *Domesticating the Empire: Race, Gender, and Family Life in French and Dutch Colonialism* (Charlottesville and London, 1998); Ann Laura Stoler, *Carnal Knowledge and Imperial Power: Race and the Intimate in Colonial Rule* (Berkeley, 2002).

18 Roselène Dossuet-Leenhardt, *Terre natale, terre d'exil* (Paris, 1976).

15 Migrations, plantations, and the people trade

1 Lamont Lindstrom, "Sophia Elau, Ungka the Gibbon, and the Pearly Nautilus," *The Journal of Pacific History*, 33, 1 (1998), 5–27.

2 Charles Darwin, *Voyage of the Beagle* (London, [1839], 1989).

3 For native agent missionaries in Erromanga, see report by George Bennett in *The Asiatic Journal and Monthly Register* (January–April, 1832), 120–5.

4 See Dorothy Shineberg, *They Came for Sandalwood* (Melbourne, 1967) and *The People Trade: Pacific Island Laborers and New Caledonia* (Honolulu, 1999); also Tracey Banavanua-Mar, *Violence and Colonial Dialogue: The Australian-Pacific Indentured Labor Trade* (Honolulu, 1997).

5 Gerald Horne, *The White Pacific: U.S. Imperialism and Black Slavery in the South Seas After the Civil War* (Honolulu, 2007).

6 For the *Carl* incident, see report in John M. Bennett, *Sir William Stawell, Second Chief Justice of Victoria* (Sydney, 2004), 147.

7 For Billy Mase Napau, entrepreneur, see http://arts.anu.edu.au/arcworld/vks/BLAKSTOR.HTM

8 Kwaisulia reported by Peter Corris, "Kwaisulia of Ada Gege: A Strongman in the Solomon Islands," in J. W. Davidson and D. Scarr (eds.), *Pacific Islands Portraits* (Canberra, 1970), 253–65; Roger Keesing, "Kwaisulia as Culture Hero," in James Carrier (ed.), *History and Tradition in Melanesian Anthropology* (Berkeley, 1992), citations 175–82. Nigel Randell, *The White Headhunter* (New York, 2003).

9 Joseph Waterhouse, *The King and People of Fiji* (Honolulu, [reprint] 1997); Anthony Trollope, *The Tireless Traveler: Twenty Letters to the Liverpool Mercury, 1875* (Berkeley, 1989), 187–9.

10 For Arthur Gordon, the Great Council of Chiefs, and the Indian *girmit*, see Brij Lal, Doug Munro, and Edward Beechert (eds.), *Plantation Workers: Resistance and Accommodation* (Honolulu, 1993).

11 See Subramani, *The Indo-Fijian Experience* (Suva, 1979); Vijendra Kumar in Brij V. Lal, *Bittersweet: The Indo-Fijian Experience* (Canberra, 2004).

12 For *guano* histories, see Harry Evans Maude, *Slavers in Paradise: the Peruvian Slave Trade in Polynesia, 1862–1864* (Stanford, 1981), 15–17; also *Pacific Voices Talk Story*, 243–7.

13 Stephen Fischer, *Island at the End of the World: The Turbulent History of Easter Island* (London, 2005).

14 J. C. Godeffroy and Son of Hamburg; C. Brundson Fletcher, *Stevenson's Germany: The Case Against Germany in the Pacific* (New York, 1920); and Brij Lal and Kate Fortune (eds.), *The Pacific Islands: An Encyclopedia* (Honolulu, 2000), 216.

15 For the Sina legend, see Vilsoni Hereniko and Jasper Schreurs, *Sina and Tinilau* (Suva, 1997); J. M. Mageo (ed.), *Cultural Memory; Reconfiguring History and Identity in the Postcolonial Pacific* (Honolulu, 2001), ch. 3.

16 Stewart G. Firth, *New Guinea Under the Germans* (Carlton, 1983), 20–33, 73–9, 136–41; Rainer Buschmann, *Anthropology's Global Histories: The Ethnographic Frontier in German New Guinea, 1870–1935* (Honolulu, 2008).

17 Anita Herle, Nick Stanley, Karen Stevenson, and Robert Welch (eds.), *Pacific Art: Persistence, Change, and Meaning* (Honolulu, 2002); Anthony Forge, "Style and Meaning in Sepik Art," in Victor Buchli, *Material Culture: Critical Concepts in the Social Sciences* (London, [1973], 2004).

18 Emma Forsayth in R. W. Robson, *Queen Emma: The Samoan-American Girl Who Founded an Empire in Nineteenth-Century New Guinea* (Sydney, 1965).

19 For the Goto and Suzuki mission, see Mark Peattie, *Nan'yo: The Rise and Fall of the Japanese in Micronesia* (Honolulu, 1988); also August Ibrun K. Kituai, *My Gun, My Brother: The World of the Papua New Guinea Colonial Police* (Honolulu, 1998).

16 Imperial destinies on foreign shores

1 Ranald MacDonald in Frederik Schodt, *Native American in the Land of the Shogun: Ranald MacDonald and the Opening of Japan* (Berkeley, 2003); Peter Mills, *Hawaii's Russian Adventure: A New Look at Old History* (Honolulu, 2002).

2 Kawada Shoryo (Junya Nagakuni and Junji Kitadai, trans.), *Drifting Toward the Southeast: The Story of Five Japanese Castaways* (New Bedford, MA, 2003); John Van Sant, *Pacific Pioneers: Japanese Journeys to America and Hawaii, 1850–1880* (Chicago, 2000).

3 William G. Beasley (ed.), *Perry's Mission to Japan, 1853–1854*, 8 vols. (Richmond, [1952], 2002).

4 For the treaty of Kanagawa, Moriyama, and Otokichi, see Ruth Roland, *Interpreters As Diplomats* (Ottowa, 2001), 83–121.

5 See Kenneth Pomeranz (ed.), *The Pacific in the Age of Early Industrialization* (London and Burlington, 2009).

6 Andre Schmid, *Korea between Empires, 1895–1919* (New York, 2002); Peter Duus, *The Abacus and the Sword: The Japanese Penetration of Korea, 1895–1910* (Berkeley and Los Angeles, 1995).

7 K. Hwang, *The Korean Reform Movement of the 1880s: A Study of Transition in Intra-Asian Relations* (Cambridge, MA, 1978); Ki-jung Pang, Michael Shinn, and Yong-sop Kim, *Landlords, Peasants, and Intellectuals in Modern Korea* (Ithaca, 2005).

8 Sino-Japanese War and Taiwan colonization: Yuko Kikuchi, *Refracted Modernity: Visual Culture and Identity in Colonial Taiwan* (Honolulu, 2007).

9 For Hawaiian politics, see Lilikala Kame'eleihiwa, *Native Lands and Foreign Desires: How Shall We Live in Harmony?* (Honolulu, 1992); for Japan, see

Donald Keene, *Emperor of Japan: Meiji and His World* (Columbia, 2002), citations from 346–51; for Kalakaua's travels, see Keene, *Emperor of Japan*, 348; also Ralph Kuykendall, *The Hawaiian Kingdom 1874–1893* (Honolulu, 1967), 312–17.

10 Kuykendall, *The Hawaiian Kingdom*, 316–17; Gerald Horne, *The White Pacific: U.S. Imperialism and Black Slavery in the South Seas after the Civil War* (Honolulu, 2007), 115–16.

11 For Stevenson's life in the Pacific, see Vanessa Smith, *Literary Culture and the Pacific: Nineteenth Century Textual Encounters* (Cambridge, 1998).

12 For the Bayonet Constitution, see: Noenoe Silva, *Aloha Betrayed: Native Hawaiian Resistance to American Colonialism* (Durham, 2004); Jonathan K. Osorio, *Dismembering Lahui: A History of the Hawaiian Nation to 1887* (Honolulu, 2002).

13 For American expansion, see Bruce Cumings, *Dominion from Sea to Sea* (New Haven and London, 2009); also Arthur Power Dudden, *The American Pacific* (New York, 1992); Jeffrey Geiger, *Facing the Pacific: Polynesia and the U.S. Imperial Imagination* (Honolulu, 2007).

14 James Delgado, *Gold Rush Port: The Maritime Archaeology of San Francisco's Waterfront* (Berkeley and Los Angeles, 2009); David Igler, *Industrial Cowboys: Miller and Lux and the Transformation of the Far West, 1850–1920* (Berkeley and Los Angeles, 2005); David Igler, "Global Exchanges in the Eastern Pacific Basin: 1770–1850," *American Historical Review*, 109, 3 (June 2004).

15 Jay Monaghan, *Chile, Peru, and the California Gold Rush of 1849* (Berkeley and Los Angeles, 1973), chs. 1–2, 14–16.

16 Madeline Yuan-yin Hsu, *Dreaming of Gold, Dreaming of Home: Transnationalism and Migration Between the United States and China* (Stanford, 2000); Susan Lee Johnson, *Roaring Camp: The Social World of the California Gold Rush* (New York, 2000); Yong Chen, *Chinese San Francisco, 1850–1943: A Trans-Pacific Community* (Stanford, 2000).

17 Ron Takaki, *Pau Hana: Plantation Life and Labor in Hawaii* (Honolulu, 1983); also Yong-ho Ch'oe, ed., *From the Land of Hibiscus: Koreans in Hawai'i, 1903–1950* (Honolulu, 2006); Ron Takaki, *Strangers From a Different Shore: A History of Asian Americans* (Boston, 1989); Gary Okihiro, *Margins and Mainstreams: Asians in American History and Culture* (Seattle, 1994); Evelyn Hu-Dehart, *Across the Pacific: Asian Americans and Globalization* (Philadelphia, 2000); Sucheng Chan, *Remapping Asian American History* (Lanham, 2003).

18 Takaki, *Strangers from a Different Shore*, 154.

19 Silva, *Aloha Betrayed;* Osorio, *Dismembering Lahui.*

20 Lauren L. Basson, *White Enough to be American? Race Mixing, Indigenous People, and the Boundaries of State and Nation* (Chapel Hill, 2008), ch. 3 on Wilcox.

21 David F. Trask, *The War with Spain in 1898* (New York, 1981), 96–8.

22 Samuel K. Tan, *A History of the Philippines* (Quezon City, 1997).

23 Maria Stella Sibal Valdez, *Dr. José Rizal and the Writing of His Story* (Manila, 2008); for critiques of *Ultimo Adios*, see Eva-Lotta E. Hedman and John T. Sidel, *Philippine Politics and Society in the Twentieth Century: Colonial Legacies, Post-Colonial Trajectories* (London, 2000).

24 Leon Maria Guerrero and Carlos Quirino, *The First Filipino: A Biography of José Rizal* (Manila, 1974); Reynaldo Clemeña Ileto, *Pasyon and Revolution: Popular Movements in the Philippines, 1840–1910* (Quezon City, 1979); Michael Cullinane, *Illustrado Politics: Filipino Elite Responses to American Rule, 1898–1908* (Quezon City, 2003).

25 Dewey's quote, *The Quarterly Journal of the Library of Congress*, 27 (Washington DC, 1970); David Silbey, *A War of Frontier and Empire: The Philippine–American War, 1899–1902* (New York, 2007).

26 Allan Punzalan Isaac, *American Tropics: Articulating Filipino America* (Minneapolis, 2006); Stuart C. Miller, *Benevolent Assimilation: The American Conquest of the Philippines* (New Haven, 1984); also Julian Go, *American Empire and the Politics of Meaning: Elite Political Cultures in the Philippines and Puerto Rico during U.S. Colonialism* (Durham, 2008).

17 Traditions of engagement and ethnography

1 For Taft quote, see Thomas McHale, "American Colonial Policy Towards the Philippines," *Journal of Southeast Asian History*, 3 (1962), 24–43; for William Jones and ethnography, see Renato Rosaldo, *Ilongot Headhunting 1883–1974* (Stanford, 1980), citations 1–9; also David Barrows, *The Bureau of Non-Christian Tribes for the Philippine Islands* (Manila, 1901).

2 Collecting described by Nicholas Thomas, *Entangled Objects: Exchange, Material Culture, and Colonialism in the Pacific* (Cambridge, MA, 1991); also Jan van Bremen and Akitoshi Shimizu (eds.), *Anthropology and Colonialism in Asia and Oceania* (Richmond, 1999); for ideas of custom and "decentralized despotism," see Mahmood Mamdani, *Citizen and Subject: Contemporary Africa and the Legacy of Late Colonialism* (Princeton, 1996), chs. 3–4.

3 Sylvia Schaffarczyk, "Australia's Official Papuan Collection: Sir Hubert Murray and the How and Why of a Colonial Collection," *reCollections: Journal of the National Museum of Australia*, 1, 1 (2006); Amira Henare, *Museums, Anthropology, and Imperial Exchange* (Cambridge, 2005).

4 Bronislaw Malinowski, *Argonauts of the Western Pacific* (London, 1922); also *The Sexual Life of Savages in North-Western Melanesia*, 3rd edition (London, 1932).

5 Cited by Talal Asad in George Stocking (ed.), *Colonial Situations: Essays of the Contextualization of Ethnographic Knowledge* (London, 1991), 51.

6 Michael Young and Julia Clark, *An Anthropologist in Papua: The Photography of F. E. Williams, 1922–1939*, 23, 25; Nicholas Thomas, *Out of Time: History and Evolution in Anthropological Discourse* (Ann Arbor, 1996).

7 See Constance Gordon Cumming, *At Home in Fiji* (Edinburgh, 1881), 147, 345; see also Margaret Jolly and Nicholas Thomas, "The Politics of Tradition in the Pacific": Introduction, *Oceania*, 62 (1992), 241–8; Lamont Lindstrom and Geoffrey M. White (eds.), *Chiefs Today: Traditional Pacific Leadership and the Postcolonial State* (Stanford, 1997); Lamont Lindstrom and Geoffrey M. White (eds.), *Culture, Kastom, Tradition: Developing Cultural Policy in Melanesia* (Suva, 1994).

8 For Apolosi Nawai, see Brij V. Lal, *Broken Waves: A History of the Fiji Islands in the Twentieth Century* (Honolulu, 1992), 48–54; J. Heartfield, "You Are Not a White Woman," *Journal of Pacific History*, 38, 1 (June 2003), 69–83; John Garrett, *Footsteps In the Sea: Christianity in Oceania to World War II* (Suva, 1992), 176–7; Robert Nicole, *Disturbing History: Resistance in Early Colonial Fiji, 1874–1914* (Honolulu, 2010).

9 Totaram Sanadhya, *My Twenty One Years in the Fiji Islands* (Suva, 1991).

10 Lal, *Broken Waves*, for Manilal see 46–8.

11 Margaret Mead, *Coming of Age in Samoa: a Study of Adolescence and Sex in Primitive Societies*, various editions (Penguin, [1928], 1943); Derek Freeman, *Margaret Mead and Samoa: the Making and Unmaking of an Anthropological Myth* (Cambridge, MA, 1983).

12 Michael Field, *Mau: Samoa's Struggle Against New Zealand Oppression* (Auckland, 1991); David Chappell, "The Forgotten Mau: Anti-Navy Protest in American Samoa, 1920–1935," *Pacific Historical Review*, 29, 2 (2000), 217–60; Malama Meleisea and Penelope Schoeffel Meleisea, *Lagaga: A Short History of Western Samoa* (Suva, 1987); Albert Wendt, "Olaf Nelson," in *Guardians and Wards* (Wellington, 1965).

13 Cited in Michael Field, *Black Saturday: New Zealand's Tragic Blunders in Samoa* (Auckland, 2006).

14 Paul Cohen, *History in Three Keys: The Boxers as Event, Experience, and Myth* (New York, 1997); Jonathan Spence, *The Search for Modern China* (New York, 1990), 230–7; Robert Bickers and R. G. Tiedmann (eds.), *The Boxers, China, and the World* (Lanham, MD, 2007).

15 James Scott, *Weapons of the Weak* (New Haven, 1985).

16 For Kartini's role, see Benedict Anderson, *Imagined Communities: Reflections on the Origin and Spread of Nationalism* (London and New York, 1983); for

Kartini's life and Dutch Ethical Policy, see Frances Gouda, *Dutch Culture Overseas* (Amsterdam, 1995), 39, 53, 80, 268, quote, 87, modern form, 293; Joost Coté and Gunawan Mohamad (eds.), *On Feminism and Nationalism: Kartini's Letters to Stella Zeehandelaar, 1899–1903* (Monash, 2005); Ahmat Adam, *The Vernacular Press and the Emergence of Modern Indonesian Consciousness, 1855–1913* (Ithaca, 1995).

17 Kris Alexanderson, "Fluid Mobility: Global Maritime Networks and the Dutch Empire, 1918–1942," unpublished PhD dissertation, Rutgers University, 2011, 83–112; Michael B. Miller, "Pilgrim's Progress: The Business of the Hajj," *Past and Present*, 191 (May 2006), 189–228.

18 Michael Francis Laffan, *Islamic Nationhood and Colonial Indonesia: The Umma Below the Winds* (Abingdon, 2003); Huub de Jonge and Nico Kaptein, *Transcending Borders: Arabs, Politics, Trade and Islam in Southeast Asia* (Leiden, 2002); Alexanderson, *Fluid Mobility*, 167–205.

18 War stories from the Pacific theater

1 For Joyoboyo's prophecy, see Khoon Choy Lee, *A Fragile Nation: The Indonesian Crisis* (Singapore, 1999), 125–30.

2 Ramon Myers and Mark Peattie (eds.), *The Japanese Colonial Empire, 1895–1945* (Princeton, 1984); Sydney Giffard, *Japan Among the Powers, 1890–1990* (New Haven, 1997).

3 For the Yu Gwan Sun story, see Alexis Dudden, *Japan's Colonization of Korea: Discourse and Power* (Honolulu, 2007); for complex studies, see Gi-Wook Shin and Michael Edson Robinson, *Colonial Modernity in Korea* (Cambridge, MA, 1999).

4 Thomas Burkman, *Japan and the League of Nations: Empire and World Order: 1914–1938* (Honolulu, 2007); Joshua Fogel (ed.), *The Nanjing Massacre: History and Historiography* (Berkeley and Los Angeles, 2000); Iris Chang, *The Rape of Nanking: Forgotten Holocaust of World War II* (New York, 1998).

5 For George Maelalo, see Geoffrey M. White, David Gegeo, Karen Ann Watson-Gegeo, and David Akin (eds.), *The Big Death/Bikfala Faet Olketa Solomon Aelanda Rimembarem Wol Wo Tu/Solomon Islanders Remember World War II* (Suva, 1988), 176–8.

6 Harry Gailey, *The War in the Pacific: From Pearl Harbor to Tokyo Bay* (Presidio, 1996); John Dower, *War Without Mercy: Race and Power in the Pacific War* (New York, 1987); Ienaga Saburo, *The Pacific War 1931–1945* (New York, 1979).

7 John Mason, *The Pacific War Remembered: An Oral History* (Annapolis, 1986), 246; Louis Ortega, www.history.navy.mil/faqs/faq87-3c.htm; Genjirou Inoui, www.nettally.com/jrube/Genjirou/genjirou.htm; Haruko Taya Cook and Theodore Cook, *Japan at War: An Oral History* (New York, 1995).

8 For Elizabeth Van Kampen's recollections, see www.dutch-east-indies.com/story/index.htm. For analyses and critiques of camp diaries, see Mariska Heijmans-van Bruggen and Remco Raben, "Sources of Truth: Dutch Diaries from Japanese Internment Camps" and Remco Raben (ed.), *Representing the Japanese Occupation of Indonesia* (Amsterdam, 1999); for comparison, see Curtis Whitfield Tong, *Child of War: A Memoir of World War II Internment in the Philippines* (Honolulu, 2010).

9 Paul. H. Kratoska (ed.), *Asian Labor in the Wartime Japanese Empire* (Singapore, 2006).

10 For the Pak Kumjoo interview, see www.unc.edu/news/archives/feb97/comfort.htm as reported by Caroline Berndt; Maria Rosa Henson, *Comfort Woman: A Filipina's Story of Prostitution and Slavery under the Japanese Military* (Lanham, 1999).

11 "Korean Comfort Women: The Slaves' Revolt," *The Independent*, (April 24, 2008); Yoshiaki Yoshimi, *Comfort Women: Sexual Slavery In the Japanese Military During World War II* (New York, 1995); Chunghee Sarah Soh, *The Comfort Women: Sexual Violence and Postcolonial Memory in Korea and Japan* (Chicago, 2008); Margaret D. Stetz and Bonnie B. C. Oh (eds.), *Legacies of the Comfort Women of World War II* (Armonk, 2001).

12 Hank Nelson, "The Consolation Unit: Comfort Women at Rabaul," *The Journal of Pacific History*, 43 (2008), 1–22.

13 Chief Moll's story in Pamela J. Stewart and Andrew Strathern, *Identity Work: Constructing Pacific Lives* (Pittsburgh, 2000); Geoffrey White and Lamont Lindstrom (eds.), *The Pacific Theater: Island Representations of World War II* (Honolulu, 1989); Lamont Lindstrom and Geoffrey White, *Island Encounters: Black and White Memories of the Pacific War* (Washington and London, 1990).

14 For Alfred Duna, see John Waiko, "Damp Soil My Bed, Rotten Log My Pillow: A Villager's Experience of the Japanese Invasion," *'O 'O: A Journal of Solomon Island Studies*, 4 (1988), 45–59.

15 Lindstrom and White, *Island Encounters*, for the Laulasi incident, see 65; for the hand grenade story, see 69.

16 Testimony by "George" (1946), www.diggerhistory.info/pages-battles/ww2/kokoda.htm

17 Geoff White and Lamont Lindstrom, *The Pacific Theater: Island Representations of World War II* (Honolulu, 1989), 58; Don Richter, *Where the Sun Stood Still: the Untold Story of Sir Jacob Vouza and the Guadalcanal Campaign* (Agoura, 1992).

18 Sir Fredrick Osifelo, *Kanaka Boy: an Autobiography* (Suva, 1985) 20–3.

19 Fifi'i, *Pig-theft*, 55.

20 Akiyama (Vicky Vaughan), in Bruce M. Petty, *Saipan: Oral Histories* (Jefferson, NC, 2002), 19; also Suzanne Falgout, Lin Poyer, and Laurence M. Carucci, *Memories of War: Micronesians in the Pacific War* (Honolulu, 2008).

21 For kamikaze attacks, see archived testimonies at: http://wgordon.web.
wesleyan.edu/kamikaze/index.htm

22 As detailed in Geoffrey White, "War Remains: The Culture of Preservation
in the Southwest Pacific," *Cultural Resource Management* 24, 5, 9–13;
Tsuyoshi Hasegawa (ed.), *The End of the Pacific War: Reappraisals*
(Stanford, 1998).

23 Malealo in White et al., *The Big Death*, 176–8.

24 For Van Kampen's testimony, see www.dutch-east-indies.com/story/index.htm

19 Prophets and rebels of decolonization

1 For Angganita Menufleur and Stephen Simopyaref, see Chris Marjen, "Cargo
Cult Movement, Biak," *Journal of the Papua and New Guinea Society* 1–2
(1967), 62–5; G. W. Trompf, *Payback: The Logic of Retribution in Melanesian
Religions* (Cambridge, 1994), 197–200; also Howe et al., *Tides of History*,
52–3.

2 For John Frum and cargo cults, see Lamont Lindstrom, *Cargo Cult: Strange
Stories of Desire from Melanesia and Beyond* (Honolulu, 1993); Martha
Kaplan, *Neither Cargo nor Cult: Ritual Politics and the Colonial Imagination
in Fiji* (Durham, 1995); Roger Keesing, *Custom and Confrontation: The Kwaio
Struggle for Cultural Autonomy* (Chicago, 1992).

3 Jonathan Fifi'i, *From Pig-theft to Parliament: My Life Between Two Worlds*,
Roger Keesing (ed. and trans.) (Suva, 1989), 52–5, 68–9; also Hugh Laracy,
Pacific Protest: The Maasina Rule Movement (Suva, 1983), 99.

4 Haja Maideen, *The Nadra Tragedy, the Maria Hertogh Controversy* (Petaling
Jaya, 1989); Tom Eames Hughes, *Tangled Worlds: the Maria Hertogh Story*
(Singapore, 1982).

5 For Cold War upheavals in Asia, see Ronald Spector, *In the Ruins of Empire:
The Japanese Surrender and the Battle for Postwar Asia* (New York, 2007);
Roger Thompson, *The Pacific Basin Since 1945* (Harlow, 2001).

6 Benedict Anderson, *Java in a Time of Revolution: Occupation and Resistance,
1944–46* (Ithaca, 1972); Adam Schwartz, *A Nation in Waiting: Indonesia's
Search for Stability* (Boulder, 2000).

7 See Mary S. Zurbuchen (ed.), *Beginning to Remember: The Past in the
Indonesian Present* (Singapore, 2005); Taylor, *Indonesia*, 351; Nicholas Tarling
(ed.), *The Cambridge History of Southeast Asia*, vol. II, part 2 (London, 1999),
218; Peter King, "Morning Star Rising? Indonesia Raya and the New Papuan
Nationalism," *Indonesia*, 73 (2002), 89–127.

8 See Nic MacIlelan, Cairns Forum, "West Papua Off the Forum Agenda,"
(September 9, 2009), http://papuastory.wordpress.com; also E. P. Wolters,
*Beyond the Border: Indonesia and Papua New Guinea – Southeast Asia and
the South Pacific* (Suva, 1988).

9 Jack Alexander, *Bandung: An On-The-Spot Description of the Asian-African Conference, Bandung, Indonesia,1955* (Ann Arbor, 1955).

10 Robert Kiste, K. R. Howe, and Brij V. Lal (eds.), *Tides of History* (Honolulu, 1994), 147–280; Donald Denoon (ed.), *Emerging from Empire: Decolonization in the Pacific* (Canberra, 1997); also Peter Hempenstall and Noel Rutheford, *Protest and Dissent in the Colonial Pacific* (Suva, 1984).

11 H. Morton, "Remembering Freedom and the Freedom to Remember: Tongan Memories of Independence," in J. M. Mageo (ed.), *Cultural Memory: Reconfiguring History and Identity in thePostcolonial Pacific* (Honolulu, 2001), 37–57.

12 J. Kehaulani Kauanui, *Hawaiian Blood: Colonialism and the Politics of Sovereignty and Indigeneity* (Durham, 2008); Elinor Langer, "Famous Are the Flowers," *The Nation* (April 28, 2008), 23.

13 For Kahoʻolawe, Busby, and Helms, see Zohl dé Ishtar, *Daughters of the Pacific* (Melbourne, 1994), 110; also George Heʻeu Sanford Kanahele, *Ku Kanaka Stand Tall* (Honolulu, 1986); also Rodney Morales (ed.), *Hoʻihoʻi Hou: A Tribute to George Helm and Kimo Mitchell* (Honolulu, 1984).

14 For the *Hokuleʻa* narrative, see Finney, *Sea to Space*; also the Polynesian Voyaging Society website: http://pvs.kcc.hawaii.edu/

15 Albert Wendt (ed.), *Nuanua: Pacific Writing in English Since 1980* (Honolulu and Auckland, 1995); Vilsoni Hereniko and Rob Wilson (eds.), *Inside Out: Literature, Cultural Politics, and Identity in the New Pacific* (Oxford, 1994); Michelle Keown, *Pacific Islands Writing: The Postcolonial Literatures of Aotearoa/New Zealand and Oceania* (New York and London, 2007).

16 Ratu Sir Kamisese Mara, *The Pacific Way: A Memoir* (Honolulu, 1997).

17 David Robie, *Blood On Their Banner: Nationalist Struggles in the South Pacific* (London, 1989), 214–19; also Brij V. Lal, *Broken Waves: A History of the Fiji Islands in the Twentieth Century* (Honolulu, 1992); Victor Lal, *Fiji: Coups in Paradise: Race, Politics, and Military Intervention* (London, 1990).

18 Robie, *Blood on Their Banner*, 66–81; also Margaret Jolly, *Women of the Place: Kastom, Colonialism and Gender in Vanuatu* (Amsterdam, 1994); Grace Mera Molisa, "Colonised People," in *Colonised People: Poems by Grace Mera Molisa* (Port Vila, 1987).

19 Susanna Ounei and Free Kanaky in Zohl de Ishtar (ed.), *Pacific Women Speak Out for Independence and Denuclearisation* (Christchurch, 1998), 246.

20 Ton Otto and Nicholas Thomas (eds.), *Narratives of Nation in the South Pacific* (Amsterdam, 1997); Tjibaou in Robie, *Blood On Their Banner*, 82–141; also Herman Lebovics, *Bringing the Empire Back Home: France in the Global Age* (Durham, 2004), and Eric Waddell, *Jean-Marie Tjibaou, Kanak Witness to the World* (Honolulu, 2008).

21 France, Ministry of Overseas Departments and Territories, *From the Matignon Accords to the Noumea Accord* (Paris, 1998).

20 Critical mass for the earth and ocean

1 Toyofumi Ogura, *Letters from the End of the World: A Firsthand Account of the Bombing of Hiroshima* (New York, 1997); Andrew Jon Rotter, *Hiroshima: The World's Bomb* (Oxford, 2008); Richard Minear (ed.), *Hiroshima: Three Witnesses* (Princeton, 1990); Michael J. Hogan (ed.), *Hiroshima in History and Memory* (Cambridge, 1996).

2 Teresia Teaiwa, "Bikinis and other s/Pacific n/Oceans," *The Contemporary Pacific*, 6, 1 (Spring 1994), 87–109; Stewart Firth, *Nuclear Playground* (Sydney, 1987); Daniel Kelin and Nashton T. Naston, *Marshall Islands Legends and Stories* (Honolulu, 2003), 143; also see documentaries, including Robert Stone, *Radio Bikini* (1988) and Dennis O'Rourke, *Half Life: A Parable for the Nuclear Age* (1985).

3 Jane Dibblin, *Day of Two Suns: U.S. Nuclear Testing and the Pacific Islanders* (London, 1988); J. R. McNeill and Corinna Unger (eds.), *Environmental Histories of the Cold War* (Cambridge, 2010).

4 Nic Maclellan and Jean Chesneaux, *After Mururoa: France in the South Pacific* (Ann Arbor, 1998).

5 Roy Smith, *The Nuclear Free and Independent Pacific Movement: After Mururoa* (New York, 1997), see People's Charter 227–31; Robie, *Blood on Their Banner*, 147.

6 For Lijon Eknilang, see Anono Lieom Loeak, Veronica Kiluwe, and Linda Crowl (eds.), *Life in the Republic of the Marshall Islands* (Suva, 2004), 123–7; for Bridget Roberts, Lijon Eknilang, and Darlene Keju-Johnson, see Zohl de Ishtar (ed.), *Pacific Women Speak Out for Independence and Denuclearisation* (Christchurch, 1998).

7 For the Rarotonga Treaty, see Stewart Firth and Karin von Strokirch, "The Idea of a Nuclear-free Pacific," in Denoon (ed.), *The Cambridge History of the Pacific Islanders*, 355–6; Robie, *Blood on Their Banner*, 152–8.

8 Oscar Temaru as reported in *Green Left Weekly*, issue 195 (July 26, 1995); also Colin Newbury, *Tahiti Nui: Change and Survival in French Polynesia, 1767–1945* (Honolulu, 1980); McLennan and Chesneaux, *After Mururoa: France in the South Pacific*.

9 Lawrence Wittner, *Toward Nuclear Abolition: A History of the World Nuclear Disarmament Movement, 1971–Present* (Stanford, 2003), 464.

10 See Keith Camacho and Setsu Shigematsu, *Militarized Currents: Toward a Decolonized Future in Asia and the Pacific* (Minneapolis, 2010); also http://decolonizeguam.blogspot.com/2008/10/ testimony-harmful-effects-of-guams.

html by Craig Santos Perez; Catherine Lutz (ed.), *The Bases of Empire: The Global Struggle against U.S. Military Posts* (New York, 2009), chs. 5, 8, 10; Keith Camacho, *Cultures of Commemoration: The Politics of War, Memory, and History in the Mariana Islands* (Honolulu, 2011).

11 For sea prawn and Suliana Siwatibu, see "Women of Wisdom are Pillars of Nations," *Pan-Pacific and Southeast Asian Women's Association Meeting* (Nuku'alofa, 1994), 143.

12 Roniti Teiwaki, *Management of Marine Resources in Kiribati* (Suva, 1988), 35–7; Shankar Aswani, "Customary sea tenure in Oceania as a case of rights-based fishery management: Does it work?" *Reviews in Fish Biology and Fisheries* 15 (2002), 285–307; Edvard Hviding, *Guardians of Marovo Lagoon: Practice, Place, and Politics in Maritime Melanesia* (Honolulu, 1996), chs. 4–5.

13 Yang Aseng interviewed by Satiman Jamin, *New Straits Times* (November 17, 2008); Esteban Magannon, "Where the Spirits Roam," *UNESCO Courier* (August 1998). Cynthia Chou, *The Orang Suku Laut of Riau, Indonesia* (New York, 2010).

14 For industrial fishing, see D'Arcy, *People of the Sea*; also Chen Ta-Yuan, *Japan and the Birth of Takao's Fisheries in Nan'yo 1895–1945* (Perth, 2006); Micah Muscolino, *Fishing Wars and Environmental Change in Late Imperial and Modern China* (Cambridge, MA, 2009).

15 David Doulman, *Tuna Issues and Perspectives in the Pacific Islands Region* (Honolulu, 1987); also Sandra Tarte, *Diplomatic Strategies: the Pacific Islands and Japan* (Canberra, 1997); Sandra Tarte, *Japan's Aid Diplomacy and the Pacific Islands* (Canberra, 1998).

16 Atu Emberson Bain, "Fishy Business: Labour in a Fijian Tuna Cannery is Enough to Make YouWeep ... The Human and Environmental Cost of Working for World Markets," *New Internationalist Magazine* (June 1, 1997).

17 Paul Moon, *The Sealord Deal* (Auckland, 1999); Sidney Moko Mead, *Landmarks, Bridges, and Visions* (Wellington, 1997), ch. 10; Jocelyn Linnekin and Lin Poyer, *Cultural Identity and Ethnicity in the Pacific* (Honolulu, 1990).

18 Anthony Regan and Helga-Maria Griffin, *Bougainville before the Conflict* (Canberra, 2005); Rosmarie Gillespie, "Ecocide, Industrial Chemical Contamination, and the Corporate Profit Imperative: The Case of Bougainville," in Christopher Williams (ed.), *Environmental Victims: New Risks, New Injustice* (London, 1998), 97–113. On women and local authority, see Anna Lowenhaupt Tsing, *In the Realm of the Diamond Queen: Marginality in an Out-of-the-Way Place* (Princeton, 1993); on local understandings of "development," see David W. Gegeo, "Indigenous Knowledge and Empowerment: Rural Development Examined from Within," *The Contemporary Pacific*, 10, 2 (1998), 289–315.

19 Josephine Tankunani Sirivi and Marilyn Taleo Havini, *As Mothers of the Land: The Birth of the Bougainville Women for Peace and Freedom* (Canberra, 2004); Commonwealth of Australia, *Bougainville: The Peace Process and Beyond* (1999), 20–1; Moses Havini and Vikki John, "Mining, Self-Determination, and Bougainville," in Geoffrey Russell Evans, James Goodman, and Nina Lansbury, *Moving Mountains: Communities Confront Mining and Globalization* (Sydney, 2001), ch. 8.

20 United Nations speech: www.un.org/esa/gopher-data/conf/fwcw/conf/gov/ 950913183413.txt

21 For Helen Hakena and the Asia Pacific Forum on Women, Law, and Development, see: www.apwld.org/bougainville_why_was_magdalene.html; for Joan and Linet Ona's declaration, see: http://www.indigenouspeoplesissues. com (May 12, 2010).

21 Specters of memory, agents of development

1 Geoff Leane and Barbara Von Tigerstrom (eds.), *International Law Issues in the South Pacific* (Hampshire, 2005), 28.

2 Mark Atwood Lawrence, *The Vietnam War: A Concise International History* (New York, 2008); Marilyn B. Young, *The Vietnam Wars, 1945–1990* (New York, 1991); Jayne Werner and Luu Doan Huynh (eds.), *The Vietnam War: Vietnamese and American Perspectives* (Armonk, 1993).

3 Mary Terrell Cargill and Jade Ngoc Quang Huynh, *Voices of the Vietnamese Boat People: Nineteen Narratives of Escape and Survival* (Jefferson, 2000); www.boatpeople.org/a_true_story.htm

4 Cesar Adib Majul, "The Moro Struggle in the Philippines," *Third World Quarterly*, 10, 2 (April 1988), 897–922; Wan Kadir Che Man, *Muslim Separatism: The Moros of Southern Philippines and the Malays of Southern Thailand* (Oxford, 1990), ch. 3; Thomas McKenna, *Muslim Rulers and Rebels: Everyday Politics and Armed Separatism in the Southern Philippines* (Berkeley and Los Angeles, 1998).

5 McKenna, *Muslim Rulers and Rebels*; Eric Tagliacozzo (ed.), *Southeast Asia and the Middle East: Islam, Movement, and the Longue Durée* (Singapore, 2009).

6 Onoda Hiroo, *No Surrender: My Thirty Year War* (Tokyo, 1973); Beatrice Trefalt, *Japanese Army Stragglers and Memories of the War in Japan, 1950–1975* (London, 2003).

7 For Japan's history and memory wars, see Tak Fujitani, Geoff White, and Lisa Yoneyama (eds.), *Perilous Memories: The Asia-Pacific War(s)* (Durham, 2001).

8 For Onoda see Trefalt, *Japanese Army Stragglers*, 158.

9 Michael Barr and Lee Kuan Yew, *The Beliefs Behind the Man* (Georgetown, 2000); Yao Souchou, *Confucian Capitalism: Discourse, Practice, and Myth of Chinese Enterprise* (London, 2002).

10 James W. Morley (ed.), *Driven by Growth: Political Change in the Asia-Pacific Region* (Armonk, 1999); Arif Dirlik (ed.), *What Is In a Rim? Critical Perspectives on the Pacific Region Idea* (Lanham, 1998); Teik Soon Lau and Leo Suryadinata (eds.), *Moving into the Pacific Century: The Changing Regional Order in the Asia-Pacific* (Singapore, 1988); Frank Gibney, *The Pacific Century: America and Asia in a Changing World* (New York, 1992); also David Hanlon, *Remaking Micronesia: Discourses over Development in a Pacific Territory* (Honolulu, 1998), ch. 4.

11 Andrew Gordon (ed.), *Postwar Japan as History* (Berkeley and Los Angeles, 1993), 16, 230; Trefalt, *Japanese Army Stragglers*, 150; also Scott O'Bryan, *The Growth Idea: Purpose and Prosperity in Postwar Japan* (Honolulu, 2009).

12 Fikret Birkes, *Sacred Ecology: Traditional Ecological Knowledge and Resource Management* (Philadelphia, 1999), 69–72.

13 For the Tasaday controversy, see John Nance, *The Gentle Tasaday: A Stone Age People in the Philippine Rain Forest* (New York, 1975); Thomas Headland, *The Tasaday Controversy: Assessing the Evidence* (American Anthropological Association, 1992); Robin Hemley, *Invented Eden: The Elusive, Disputed History of the Tasaday* (Lincoln, 2006).

14 Max E. Stanton, "The Polynesian Cultural Center: A Multi-Ethnic Model of Seven Pacific Cultures," in Valerie L. Smith, *Hosts and Guests: The Anthropology of Tourism* (Philadelphia, 1989); Andrew Ross, "Cultural Preservation in the Polynesia of the Latter Day Saints," in *The Chicago Gangster Theory of Life* (New York, 1994).

15 Ross, "Cultural Preservation," 44–5; Christine Skwiot, *The Purposes of Paradise: U.S. Tourism and Empire in Cuba and Hawai'i* (Philadelphia, 2010); Haunani-Kay Trask, "Lovely Hula Hands: Corporate Tourism and the Prostitution of Hawaiian Culture," in *From a Native Daughter: Colonialism and Sovereignty in Hawaii* (Monroe, ME, 1993), 163; also Heather Diamond, *American Aloha: Cultural Tourism and the Negotiation of Tradition* (Honolulu, 2008); James Mak, *Developing a Dream Destination: Tourism and Tourism Policy Planning in Hawai'i* (Honolulu, 2008).

16 Haunani Kay Trask in Trask, *From a Native Daughter*, 17; John Connell and Barbara Rugendyke, *Tourism at the Grassroots* (New York, 2008), 65, 85; also Miriam Kahn, *Tahiti Beyond the Postcard: Power, Place, and Everyday Life* (Seattle, 2011), 75–180.

17 Cited in Deborah Gewertz and Fredrick Karl Errington, *Twisted Histories, Altered Contexts: Representing the Chambri in a World System* (Cambridge, 1991), 55–7; see documentary, Dennis O'Rourke, *Cannibal Tours* (1988).

18 Rommel C. Banlaoi, "The Abu Sayyaf Group: Threat of Maritime Piracy and Terrorism," in Peter Lehr (ed.), *Violence at Sea: Piracy in the Age of Global Terrorism* (New York, 2008) 121–38.

19 Peter M. Burns and Marina Novelli, *Tourism and Politics: Global Frameworks and Local Realities* (Amsterdam, 2007); Michael Hitchcock, Victor T. King, and Michael Parnwell, *Tourism in Southeast Asia: Challenges and New Directions* (Copenhagen, 2008); Arnaud de Borchgrave, Thomas Sanderson, and David Gordon (eds.), *Conflict, Community, and Criminality in Southeast Asia and Australia* (Washington, DC, 2009).

22 Repairing legacies, claiming histories

1 Yen Ching-hwang, *The Ethnic Chinese in East and Southeast Asia* (Singapore, 2002); Adam McKeown, *Chinese Migrant Networks and Cultural Change: Peru, Chicago, Hawaii, 1930–1936* (Chicago, 2001); Aihwa Ong, *Spirits of Resistance and Capitalist Discipline: Factory Women in Malaysia* (Albany, 1987).

2 See Catharina Purwani Williams, *Maiden Voyages: Eastern Indonesian Women on the Move* (Singapore, 2007), testimonies, 138, 147–50; Karen Beeks and Delila Amir (eds.), *Trafficking and the Global Sex Trade* (Lanham, 2006); "Feds Uncover American Samoa Sweatshop," *Honolulu Star-Bulletin* (March 24, 2001).

3 Toon van Meijl, "Beyond Economics: Transnational Labour Migration in Asia and the Pacific," *IIAS Newsletter*, 43 (Spring, 2007). Bernard Poirine, "Should We Hate or Love MIRAB?" *The Contemporary Pacific*, 10, 1 (1998).

4 Monina Allarey Mercado (ed.), *People Power: The Philippine Revolution of 1986, an Eyewitness History* (Manila, 1986).

5 New heroes in Vicente L. Rafael, *White Love and Other Events in Filipino History* (Durham, 2000), 210–11.

6 Rafael, *White Love*, 213.

7 For Mabo, see Nonie Sharp, *No Ordinary Judgment: Mabo, the Murray Islanders' Land Case* (Canberra, 1996), 4; J. Cordell, "Indigenous Peoples' Coastal–Marine Domains: Some Matters of Cultural Documentation," in *Turning the Tide: Conference on Indigenous Peoples and Sea Rights, 14 July–16 July 1993*, Faculty of Law, Northern Territory University, Darwin (NT, Australia, 1993), 159–74; Nonie Sharp, *Saltwater People: The Waves of Memory* (New South Wales, Australia, 2002).

8 Sharp, *No Ordinary Judgment*, 211–17; Peter Russell, *Recognizing Aboriginal Title: The Mabo Case and Indigenous Resistance to English Settler Colonialism* (Toronto, 2005).

9 For Hawaiian history and sovereignty, see Noenoe Silva, *Aloha Betrayed: Native Hawaiian Resistance to American Colonialism* (Durham, 2004); Jonathan K. Osorio, *Dismembering Lahui: A History of the Hawaiian Nation to 1887* (Honolulu, 2002); Jon M. Van Dyke, *Who Owns the Crown Lands of Hawai'i?* (Honolulu, 2007); Haunani Kay Trask, *From a Native Daughter* (Honolulu, 1999).

10 Gordon Y. K. Pang, "Hawaiian Independence Groups Send 'No' Message," *Honolulu Advertiser* (July 1, 2005); J. Kehaulani Kauanui, *Hawaiian Blood: Colonialism and the Politics of Sovereignty and Indigeneity* (Durham, 2008).

11 Thomas A. Tizon, "Rebuilding a Hawaiian Kingdom," *Los Angeles Times* (July 21, 2005); also http://bumpykanahele.com

12 See Jock Philipps, "A Nation of Two Halves," *New Zealand Listener*, 204, 3452 (July 8–14, 2006), www.listener.co.nz/issue/3452/features/6497/a_nation_of_two_halves.html

13 Sue Abel, *Shaping the News: Waitangi Day on Television* (Auckland, 1997), 151–4.

14 "Mataatua Declaration on Cultural and Intellectual Property Rights of Indigenous Peoples," First International Conference (Whakatane, June 12–18, 1993), 2–5; David W. Gegeo, "Indigenous Knowledge and Empowerment: Rural Development Examined from Within," *The Contemporary Pacific*, 10, 2 (1998), 289–315.

15 Peter G. Pan, "Bioprospecting: Issues and Policy Considerations," *Legislative Reference Bureau* (Honolulu, 2006), 79–84.

16 Kalinga Sevenirante, "South Pacific Region Moves to Protect Indigenous Wisdom," Interpress Service APC Networks (May 24, 1995); see http://forests.org/archived_site/today/recent/1995/spindkno.htm

17 Steve Yui-Sang Tsang, *A Modern History of Hong Kong* (London and New York, 2007); Suzanne Pepper, *Keeping Democracy at Bay: Hong Kong and the Challenge of Chinese Political Reform* (Lanham, MD, 2008).

18 Ron Crocombe, *Asia in the Pacific Islands: Replacing the West* (Suva, 2007); Barry Eichengreen, Yung Chul Park, and Charles Wyplosz, *China, Asia, and the New World Economy* (Oxford and New York, 2008).

19 T. J. Pempel (ed.), *The Politics of the Asian Economic Crisis* (Ithaca, 1999); Richard Carney (ed.), *Lessons from the Asian Financial Crisis* (New York, 2009).

20 Taylor, *Indonesia*, 340–86.

21 Testimonies, "Paramilitary Violence in East Timor," US House of Representatives, East Timor Action Network (May 4 and 7, 1999), 5; Joseph Nevins, *A Not-So-Distant-Horror: Mass Violence in East Timor* (Ithaca, 2005).

Afterword: World heritage

1 Kathy Marks, "Climate Change Forces South Sea Islanders to Seek Sanctuary Abroad," *The Independent* (June 6, 2008).

2 David Victor, *The Collapse of the Kyoto Protocol and the Struggle to Slow Global Warming* (Princeton, 2001); Joseph Aldy and Robert Stavins (eds.), *Architectures for Agreement: Addressing Global Climate Change in the Post-Kyoto World* (Cambridge, 2007); Elizabeth Economy, *The River Runs Black: The Environmental Challenge to China's Future* (Ithaca, 2004).

3 Tebaubwebwe Tiata, Kumon Uriam, Sister Alaima Talu, et al., *Kiribati: Aspects of History* (Kiribati, 1998).

4 David Fogarty, "Kiribati Creates World's Largest Marine Reserve," Reuters News Service (February 14, 2008).

INDEX

9 780521 715669